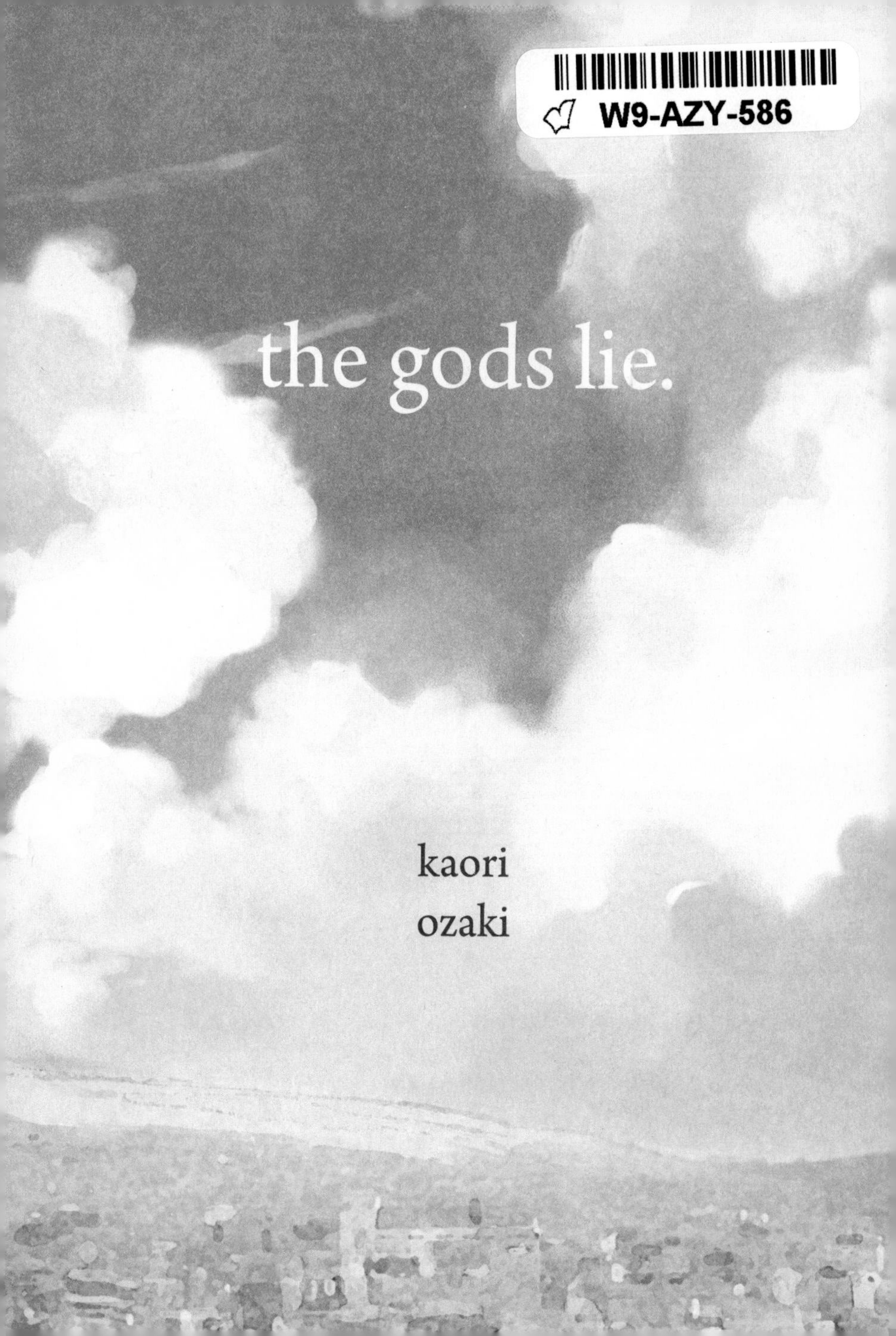

the gods lie.

kaori
ozaki

contents

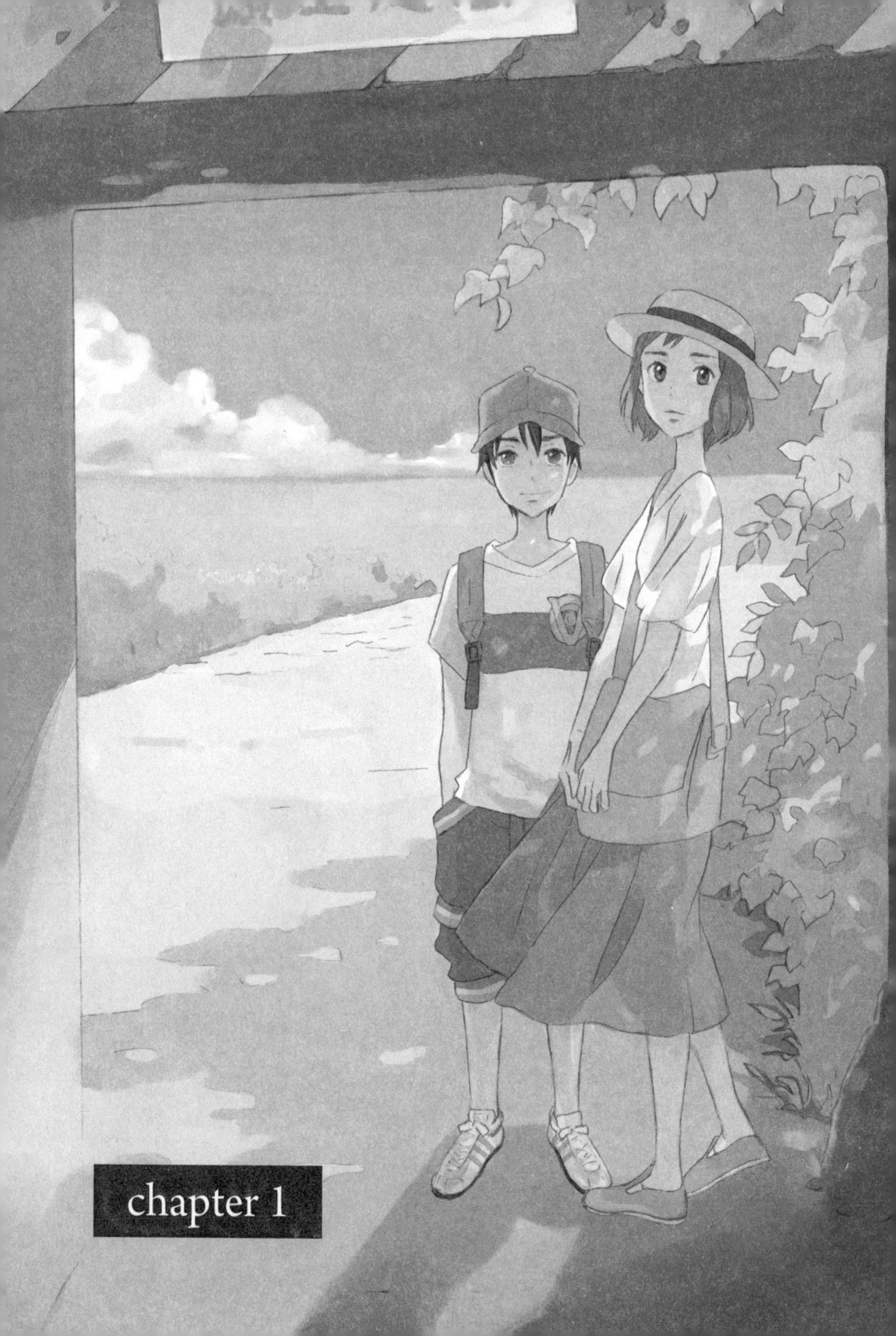

chapter 1

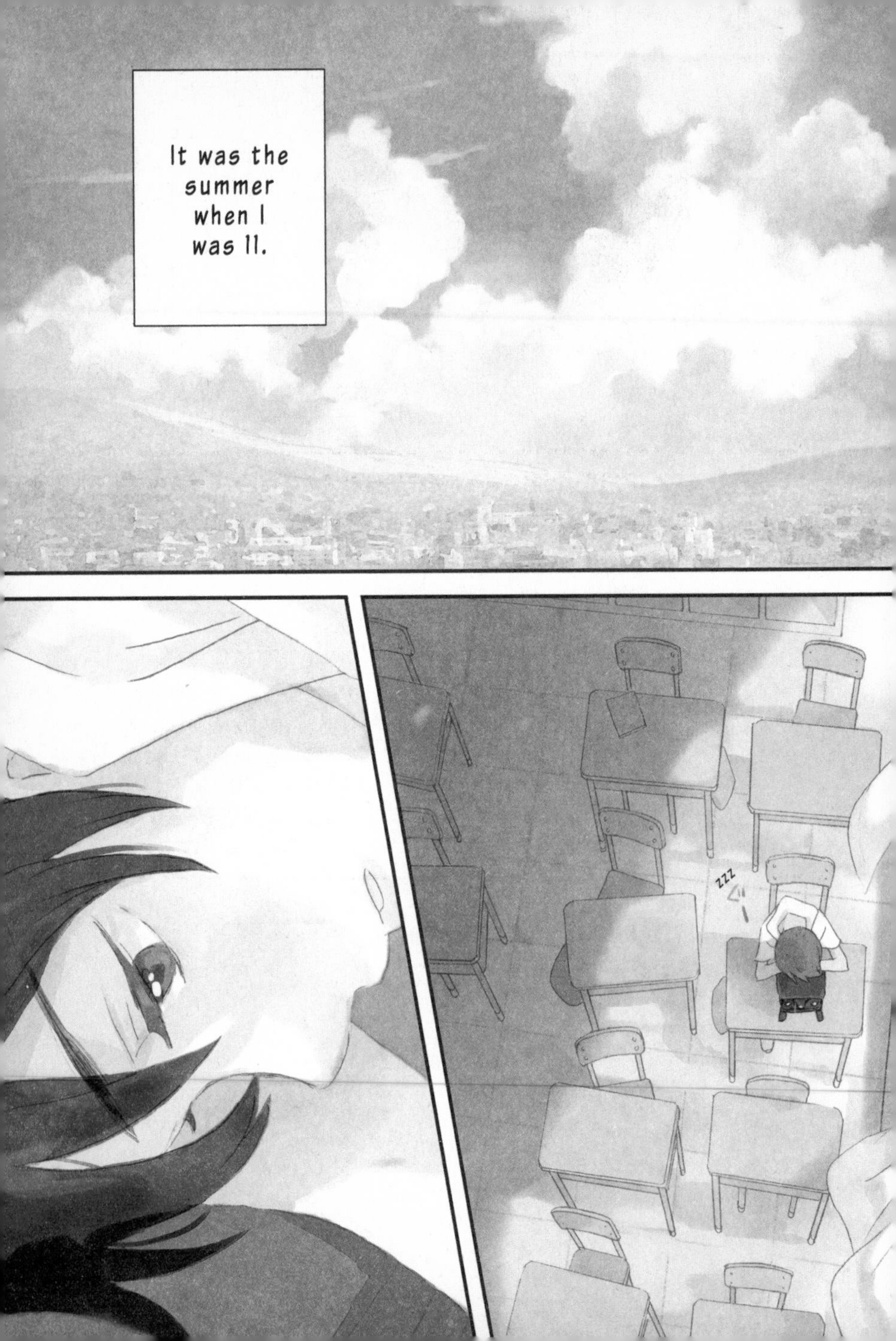
It was the summer when I was 11.
zzz

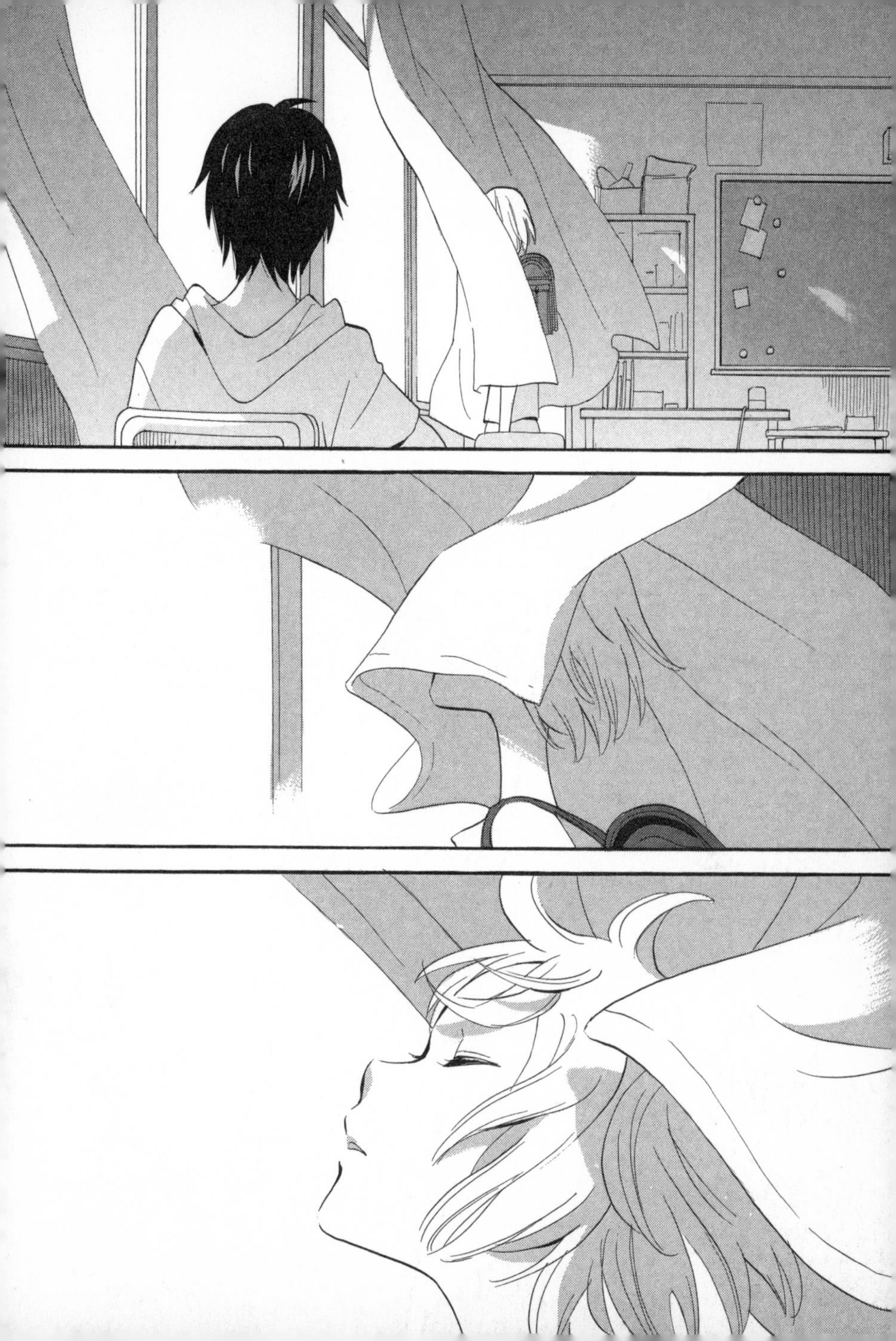

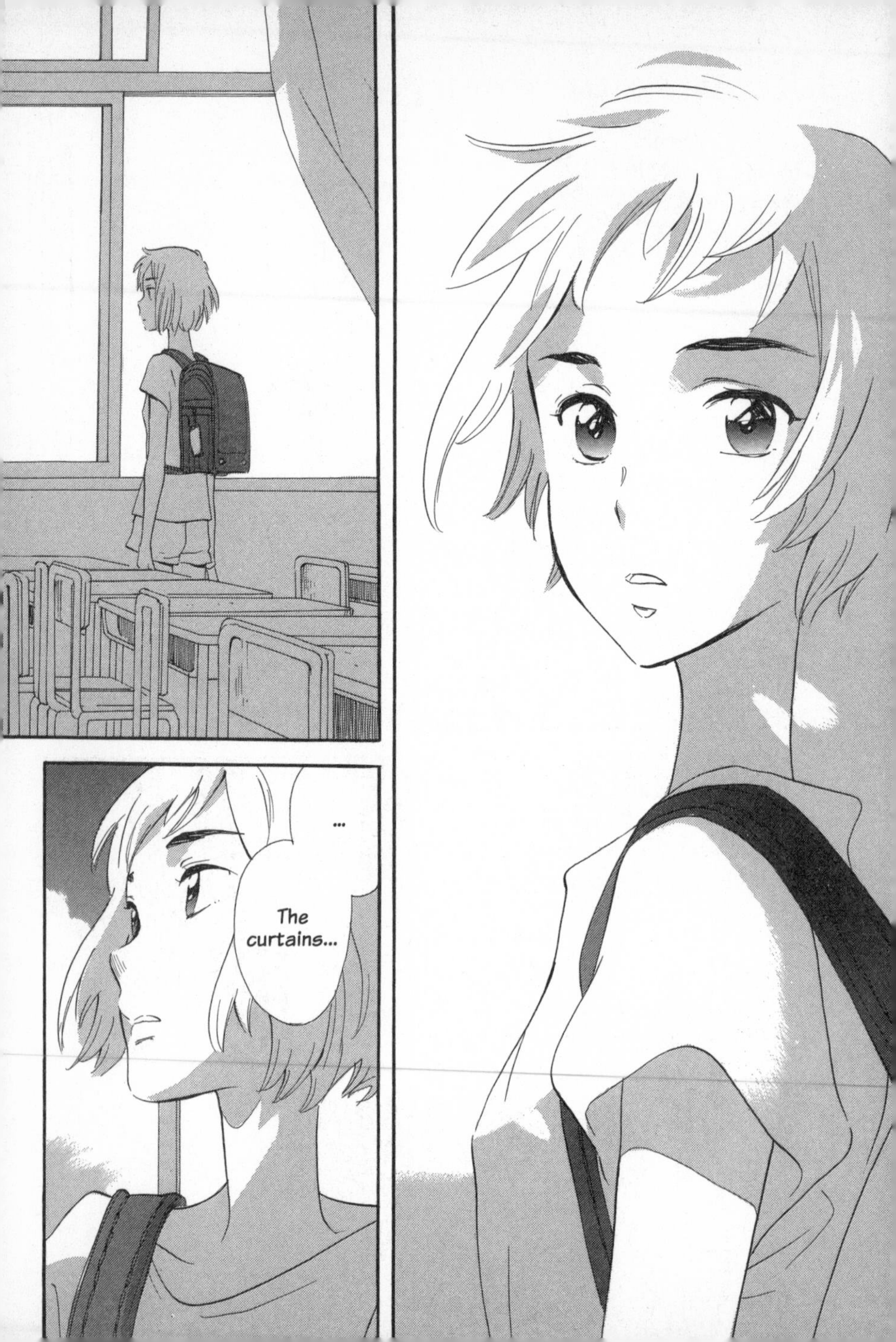
...
The curtains...

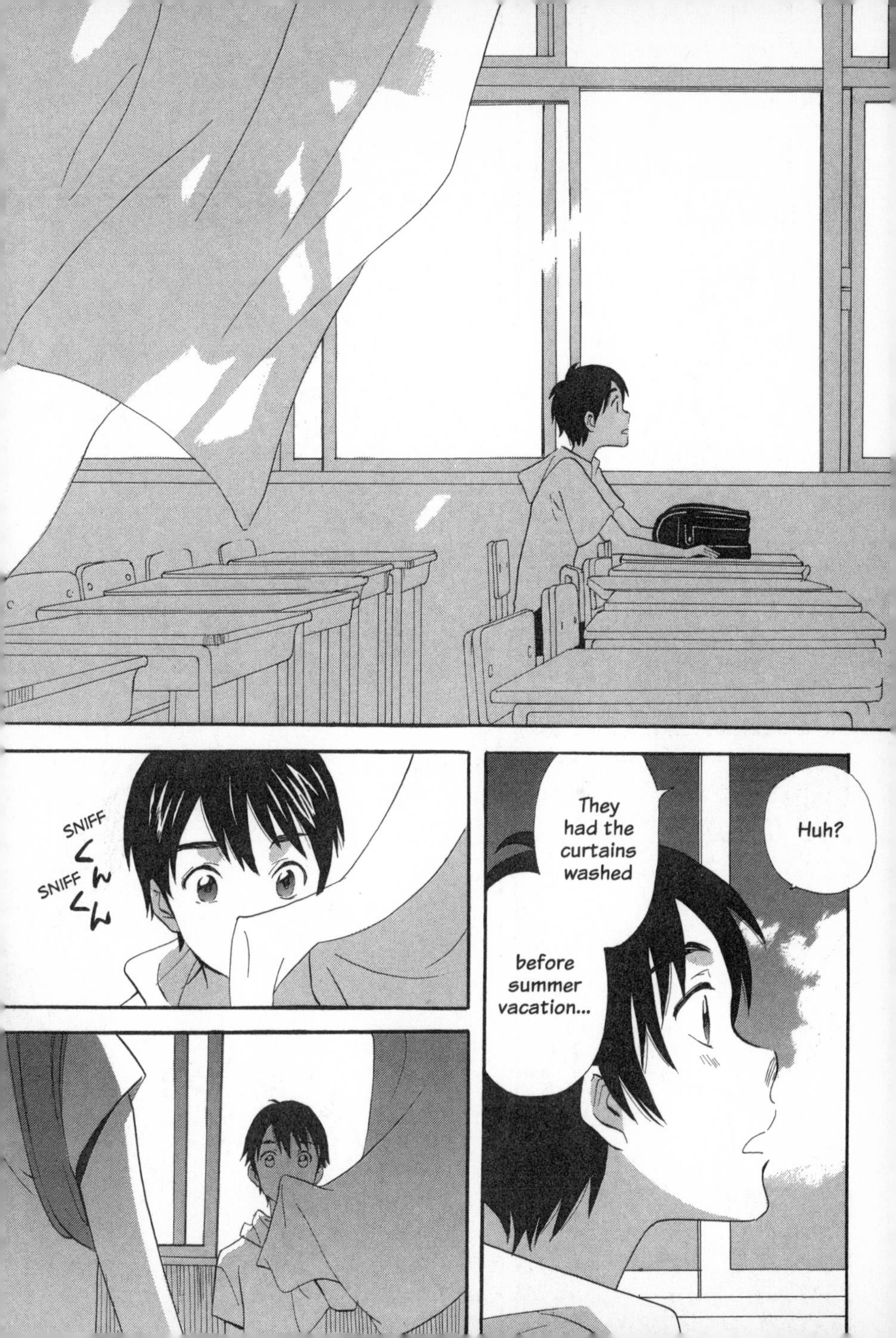
Huh?
They had the curtains washed
before summer vacation...
SNIFF くん
SNIFF くん

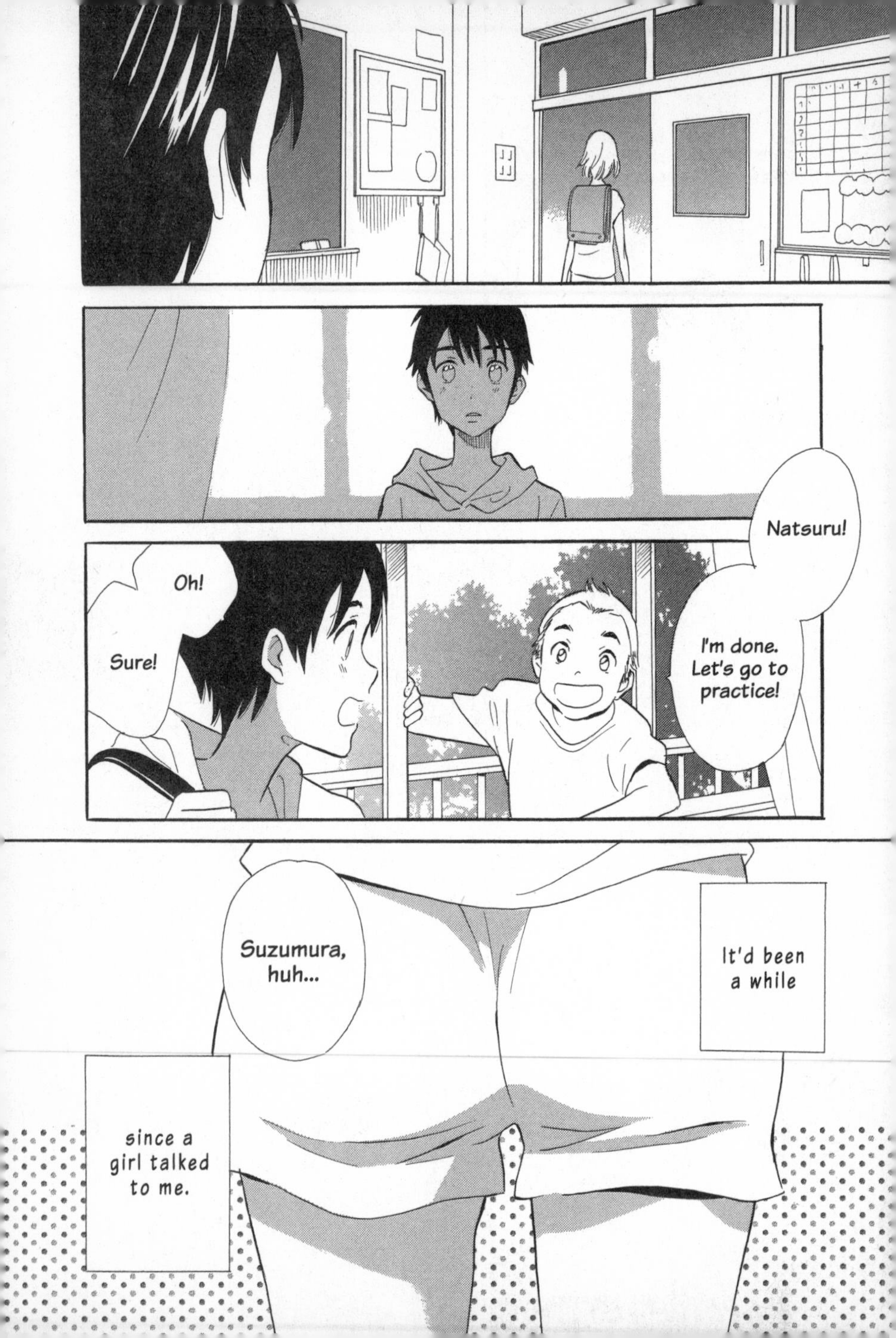

Natsuru!
I'm done. Let's go to practice!
Oh!
Sure!
It'd been a while
Suzumura, huh...
since a girl talked to me.

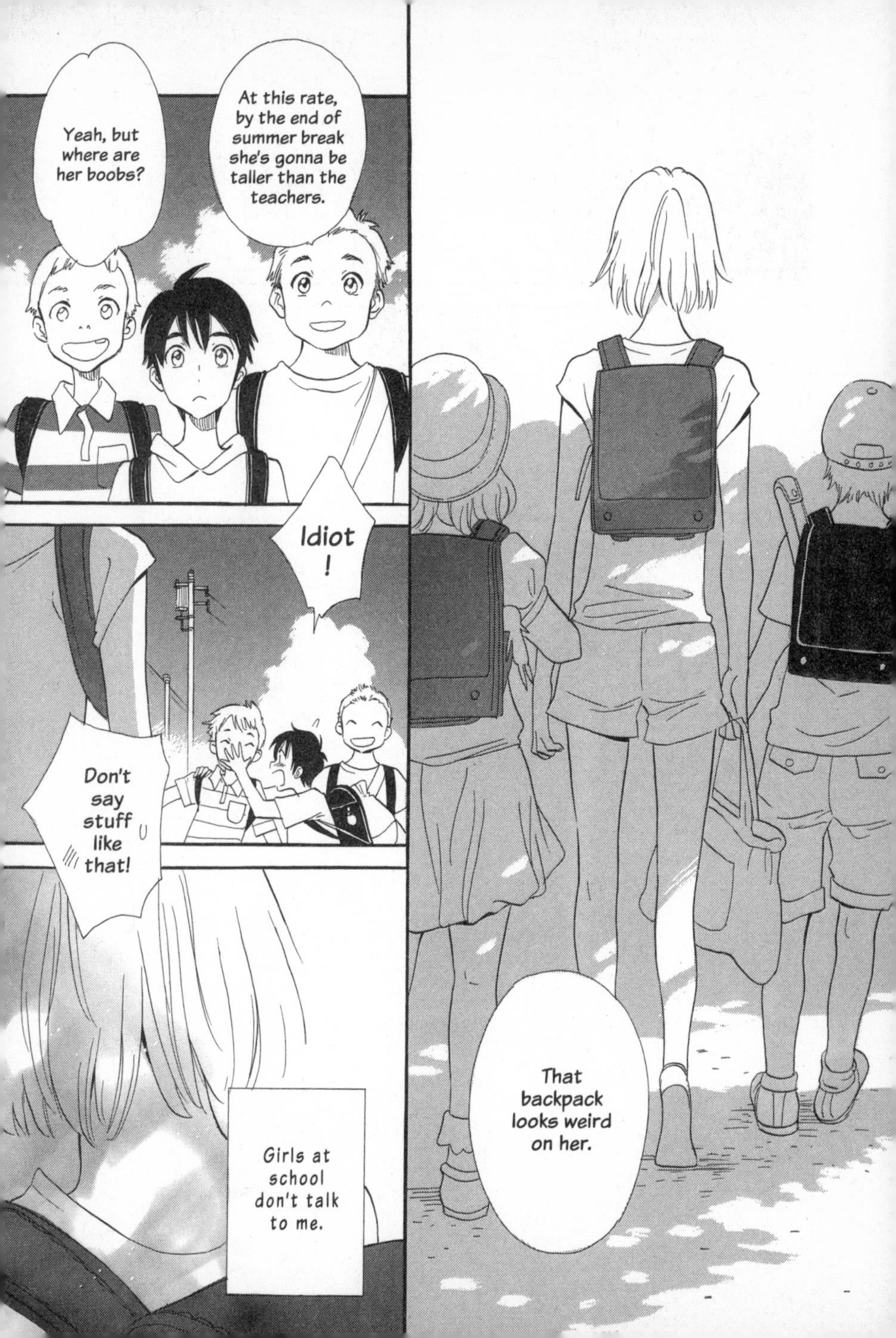
That backpack looks weird on her.
At this rate, by the end of summer break she's gonna be taller than the teachers.
Yeah, but where are her boobs?
Idiot!
Don't say stuff like that!
Girls at school don't talk to me.

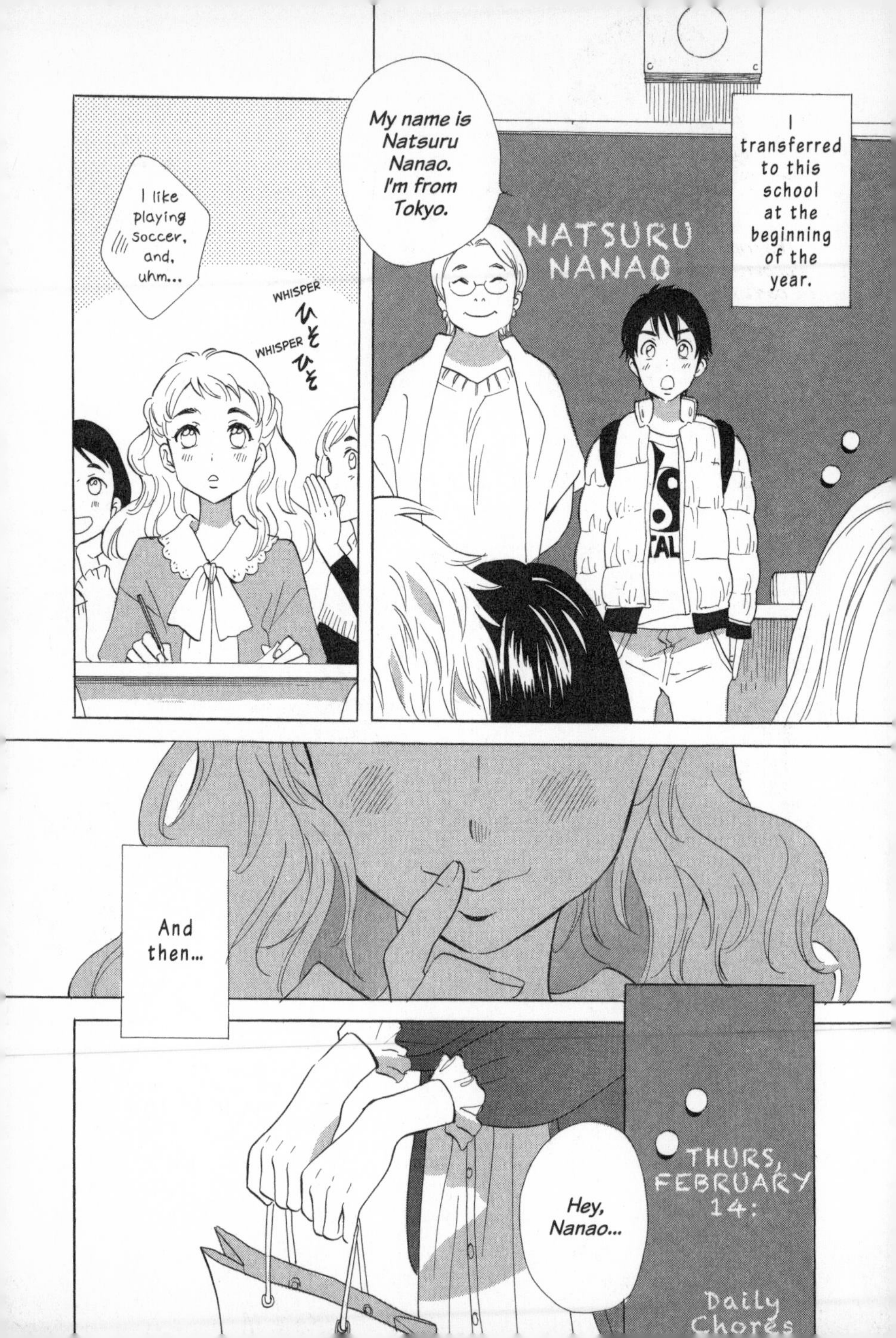
I transferred to this school at the beginning of the year.
My name is Natsuru Nanao. I'm from Tokyo.
NATSURU NANAO
I like playing soccer, and, uhm...
WHISPER ひそ
WHISPER ひそ
And then...
THURS, FEBRUARY 14:
Daily Chores
Hey, Nanao...

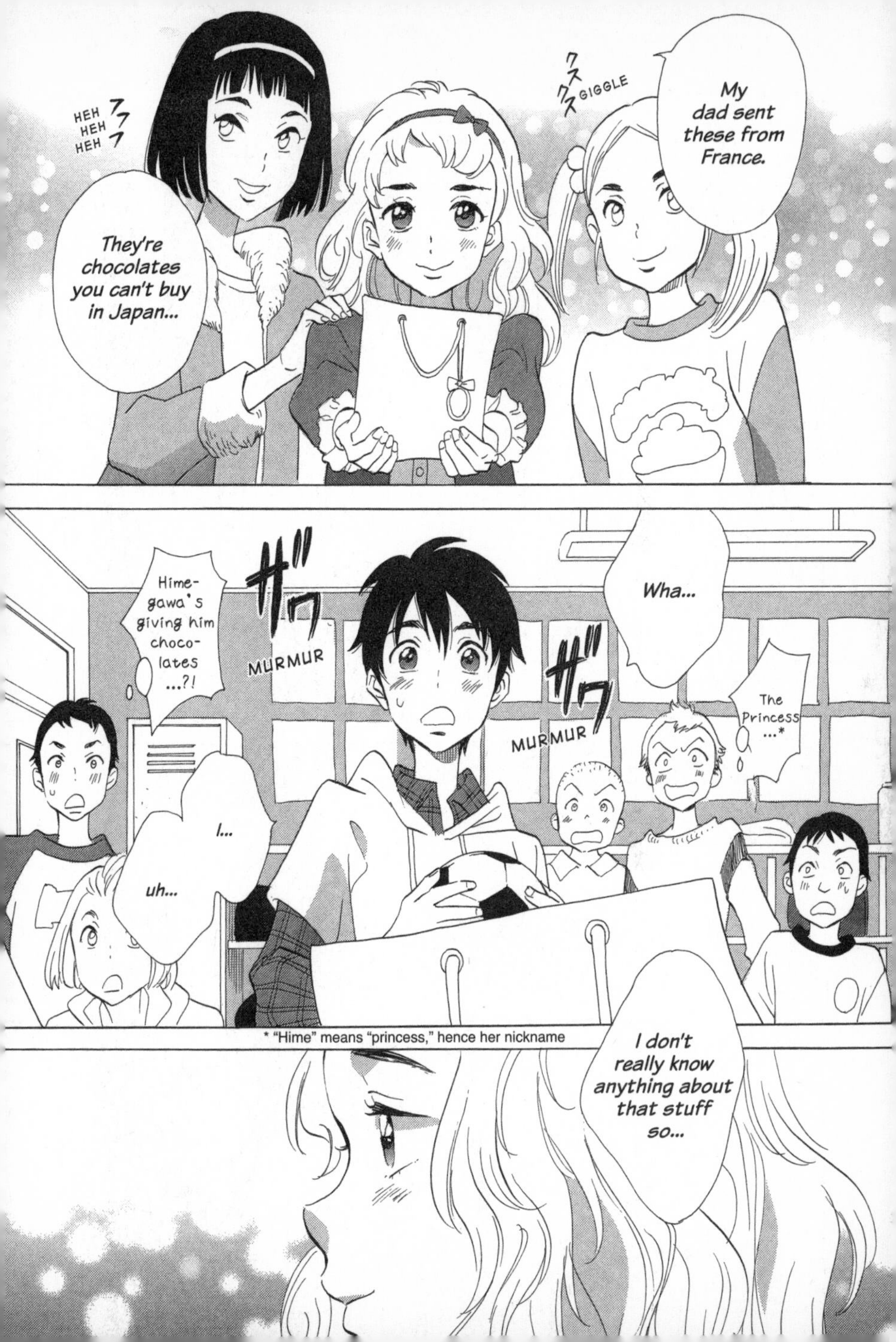
My dad sent these from France.
クスクス GIGGLE
HEH HEH HEH フフフ
They're chocolates you can't buy in Japan...
Wha...
The Princess ...*
ザワ MURMUR
ザワ MURMUR
Hime-gawa's giving him choco-lates ...?!
I...
uh...
I don't really know anything about that stuff so...
* "Hime" means "princess," hence her nickname

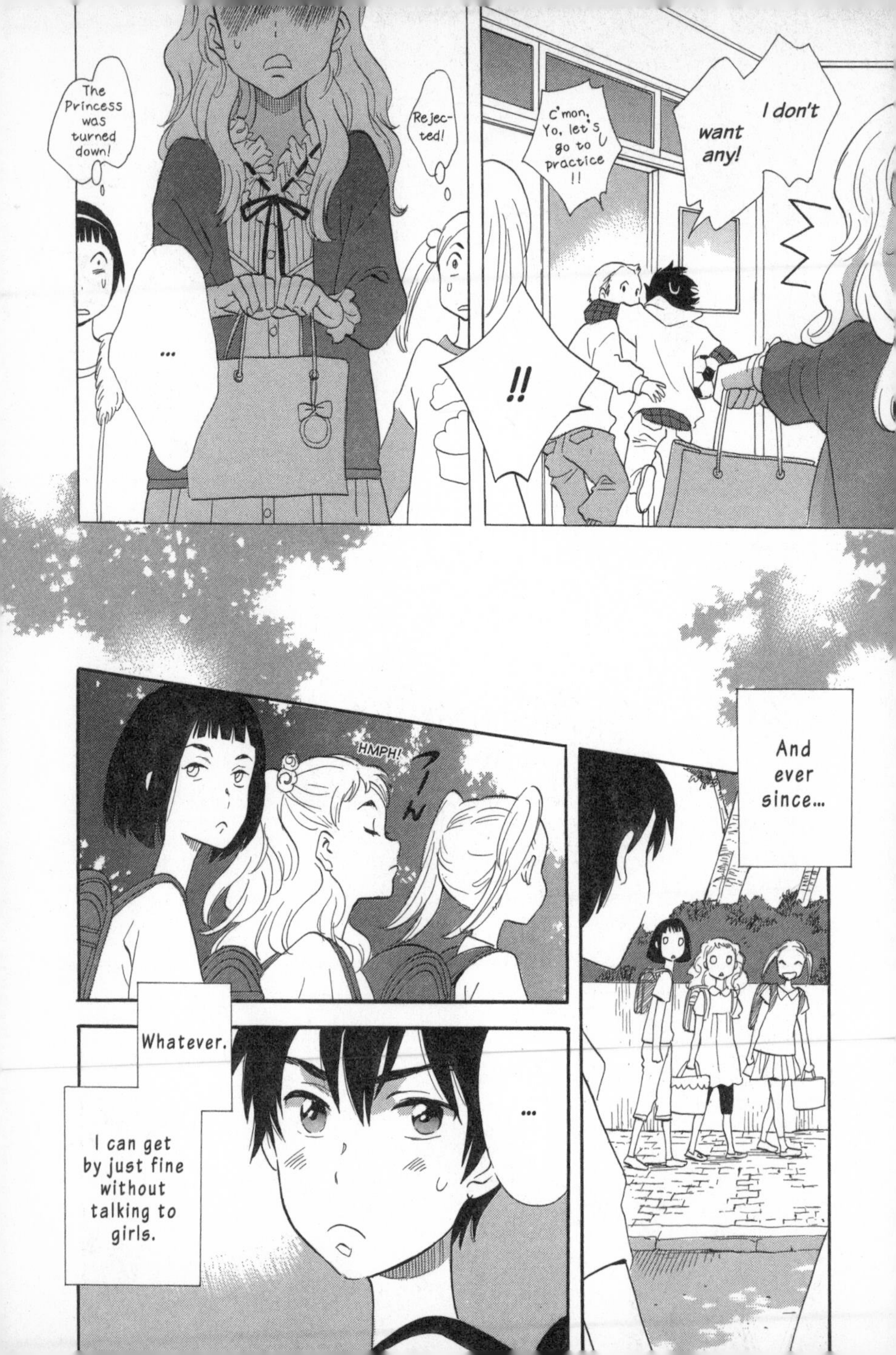
I don't want any!
C'mon, Yo, let's go to practice!!
!!
Rejected!
The Princess was turned down!
...
And ever since...
HMPH!
Whatever.
...
I can get by just fine without talking to girls.

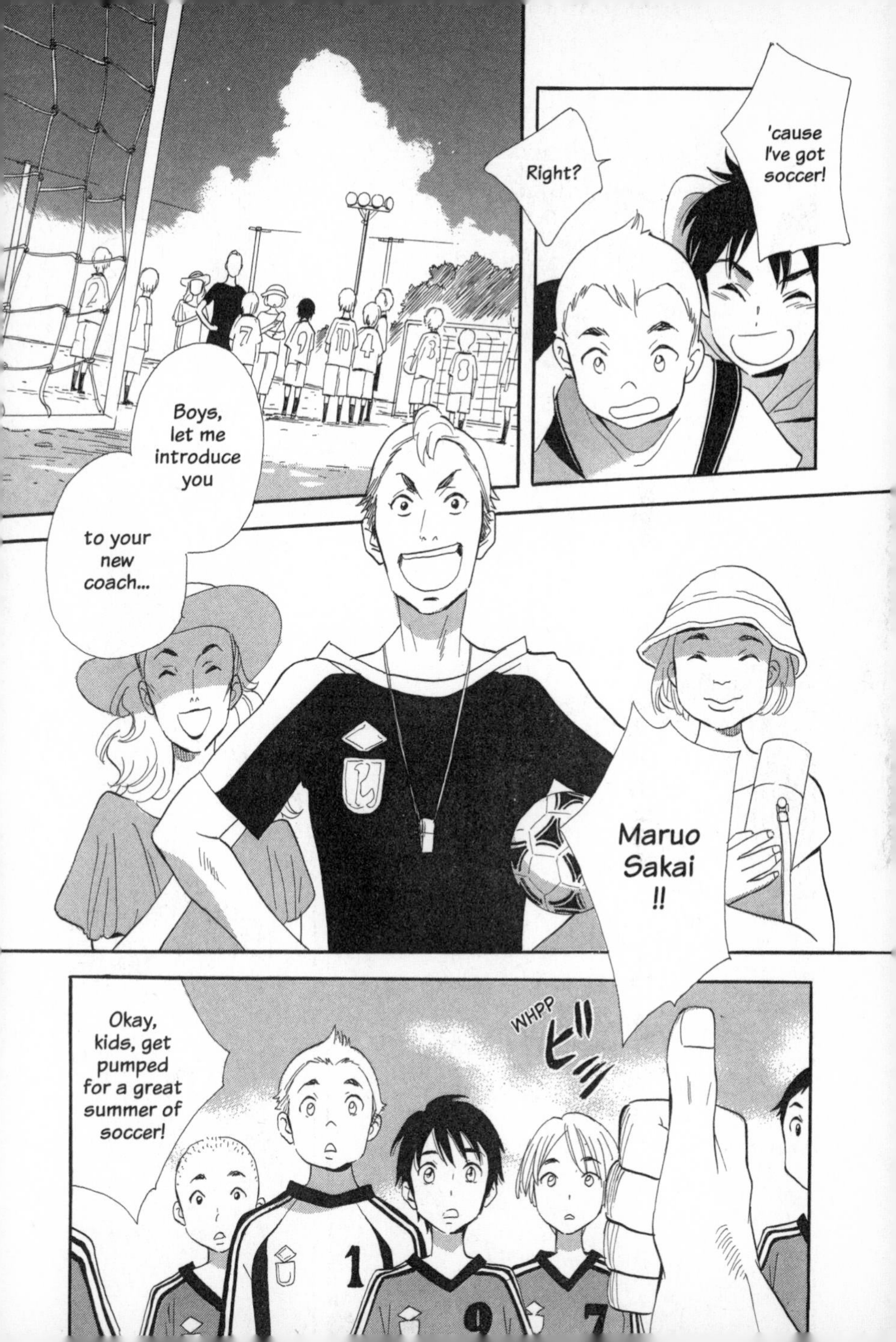
'cause I've got soccer!
Right?
Boys, let me introduce you
to your new coach...
Maruo Sakai !!
WHPP
Okay, kids, get pumped for a great summer of soccer!

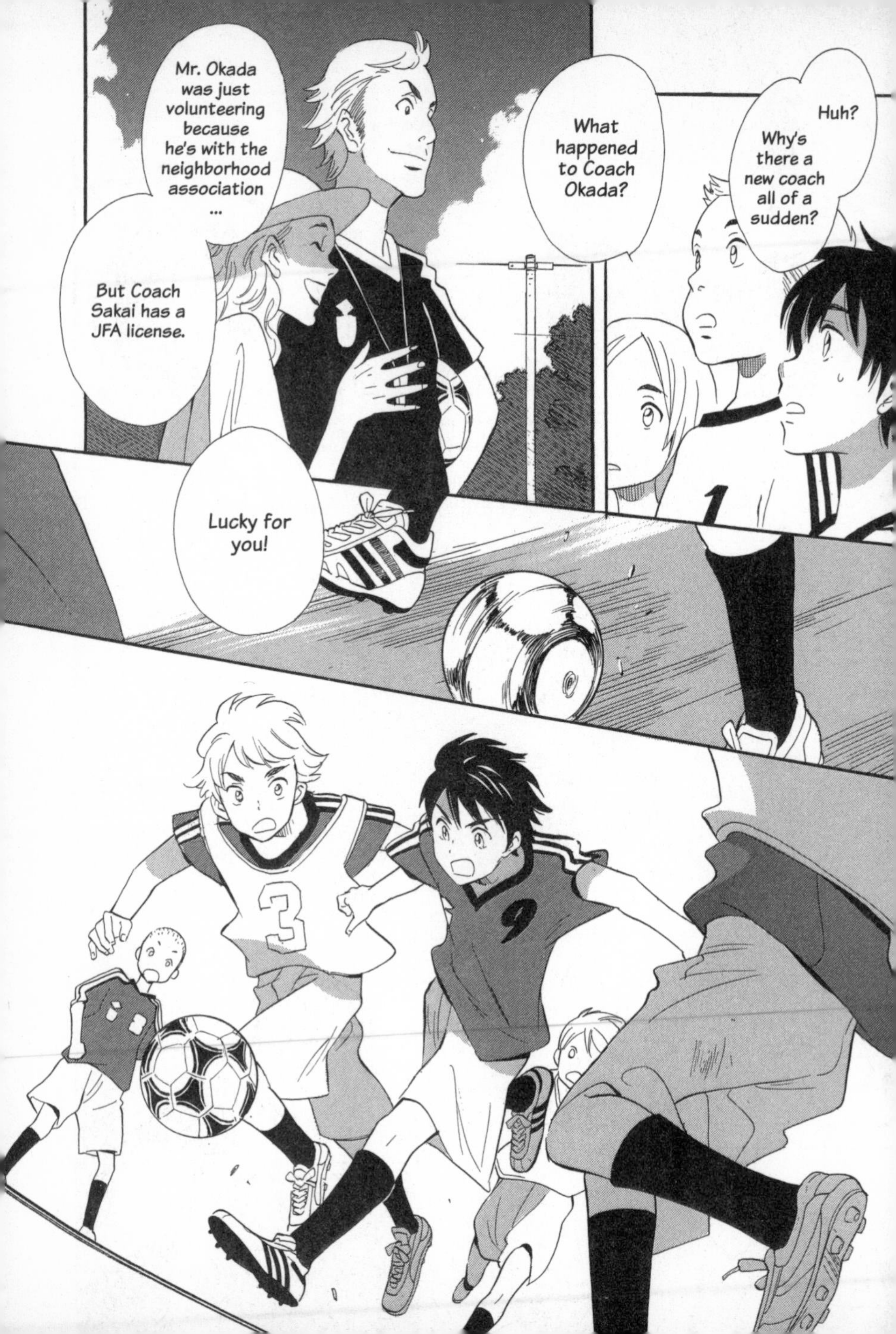
Huh? Why's there a new coach all of a sudden?
What happened to Coach Okada?
Mr. Okada was just volunteering because he's with the neighborhood association ...
But Coach Sakai has a JFA license.
Lucky for you!

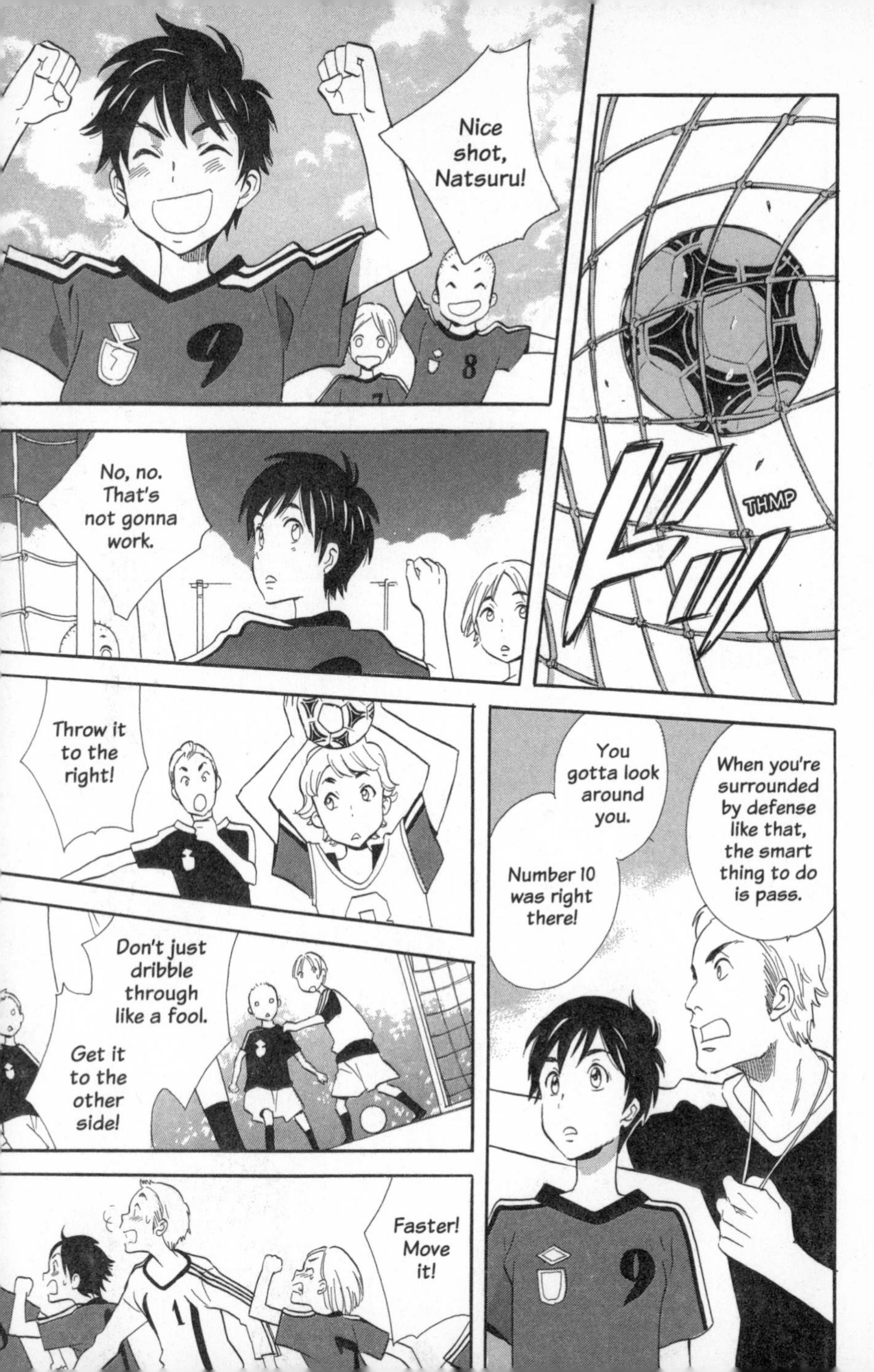
THMP
Nice shot, Natsuru!
No, no. That's not gonna work.
When you're surrounded by defense like that, the smart thing to do is pass.
You gotta look around you.
Number 10 was right there!
Throw it to the right!
Don't just dribble through like a fool.
Get it to the other side!
Faster! Move it!

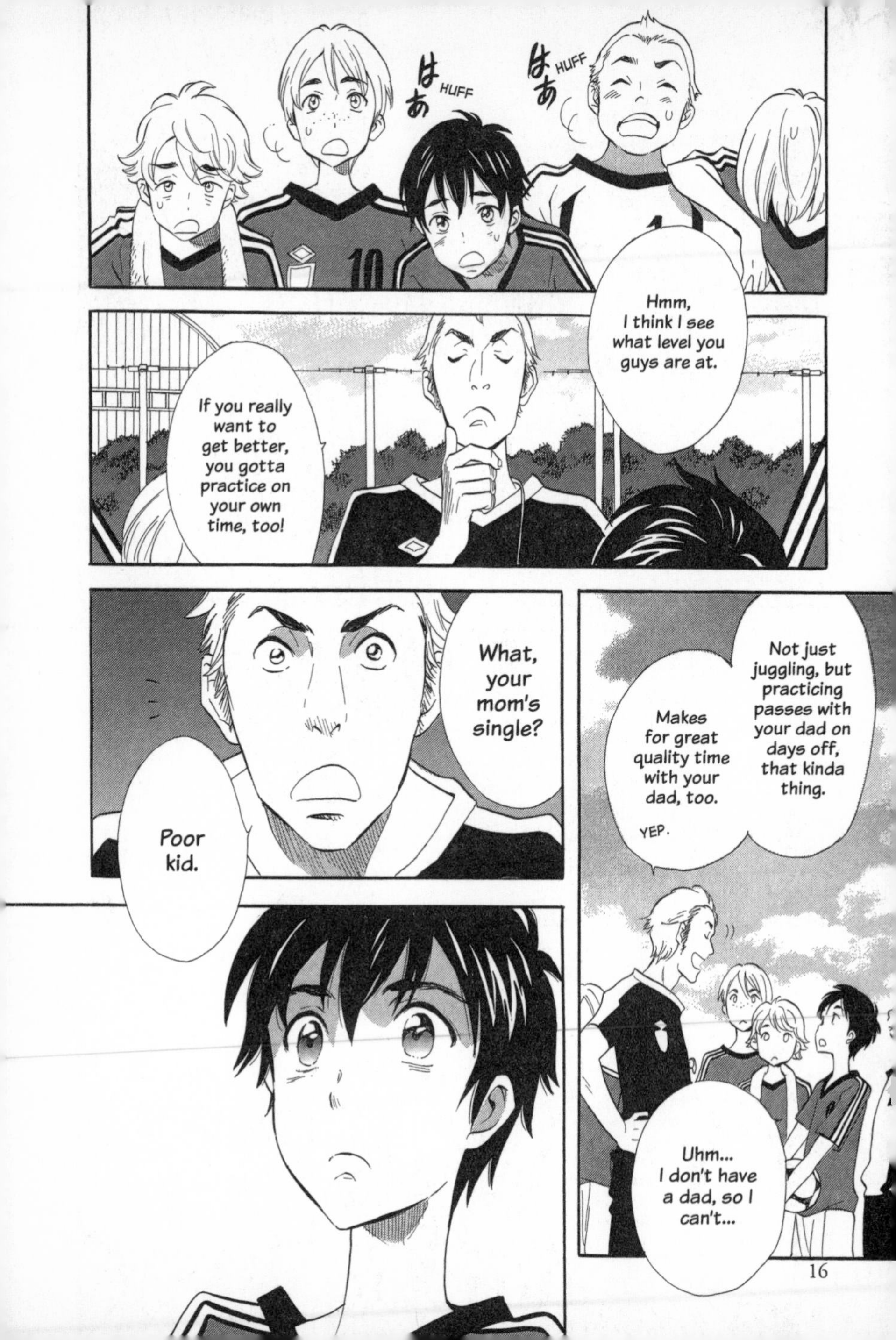

はあ HUFF
はあ HUFF
Hmm, I think I see what level you guys are at.
If you really want to get better, you gotta practice on your own time, too!
Not just juggling, but practicing passes with your dad on days off, that kinda thing.
Makes for great quality time with your dad, too.
YEP.
Uhm... I don't have a dad, so I can't...
What, your mom's single?
Poor kid.

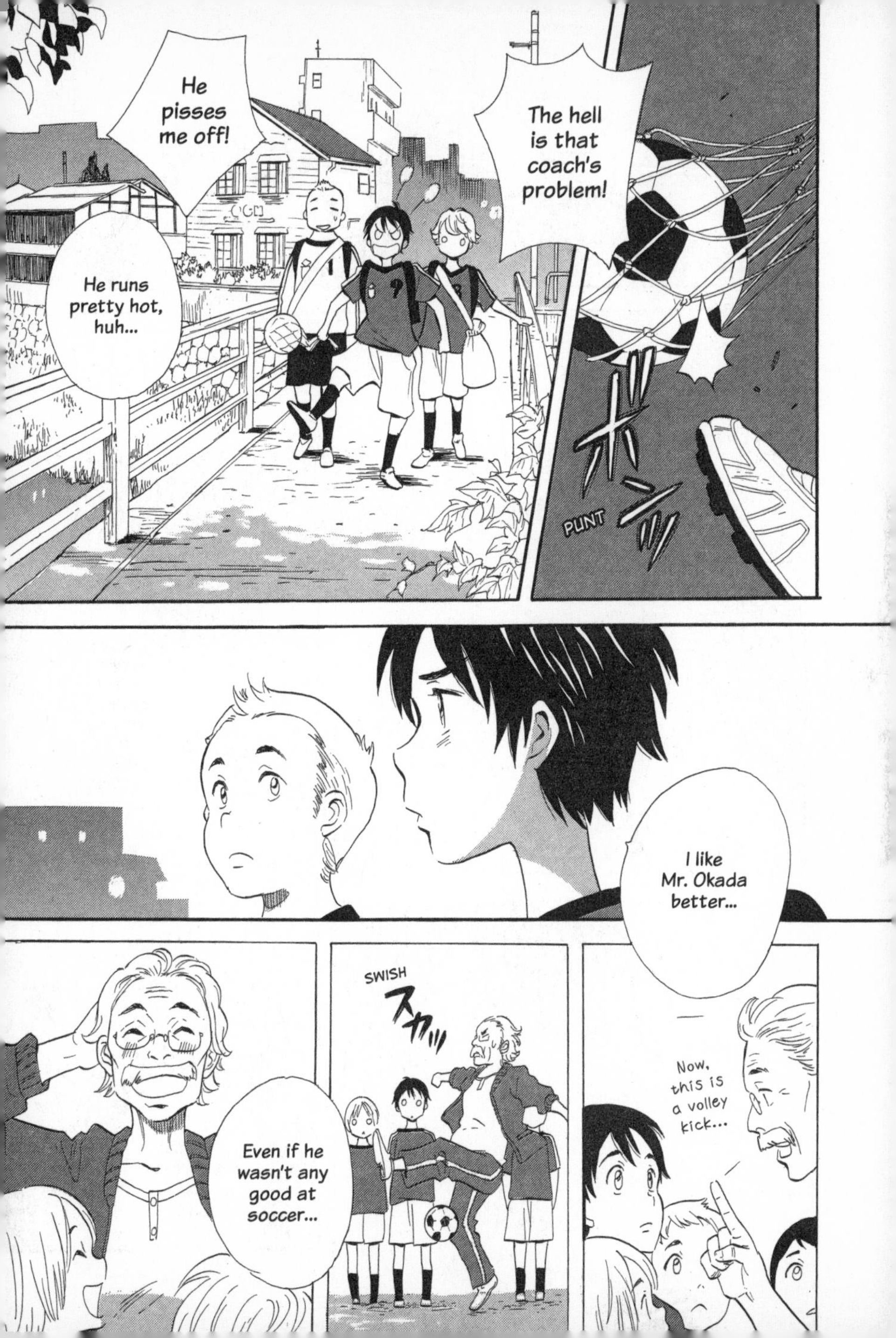
PUNT
The hell is that coach's problem!
He pisses me off!
He runs pretty hot, huh...
I like Mr. Okada better...
Now, this is a volley kick...
SWISH
Even if he wasn't any good at soccer...

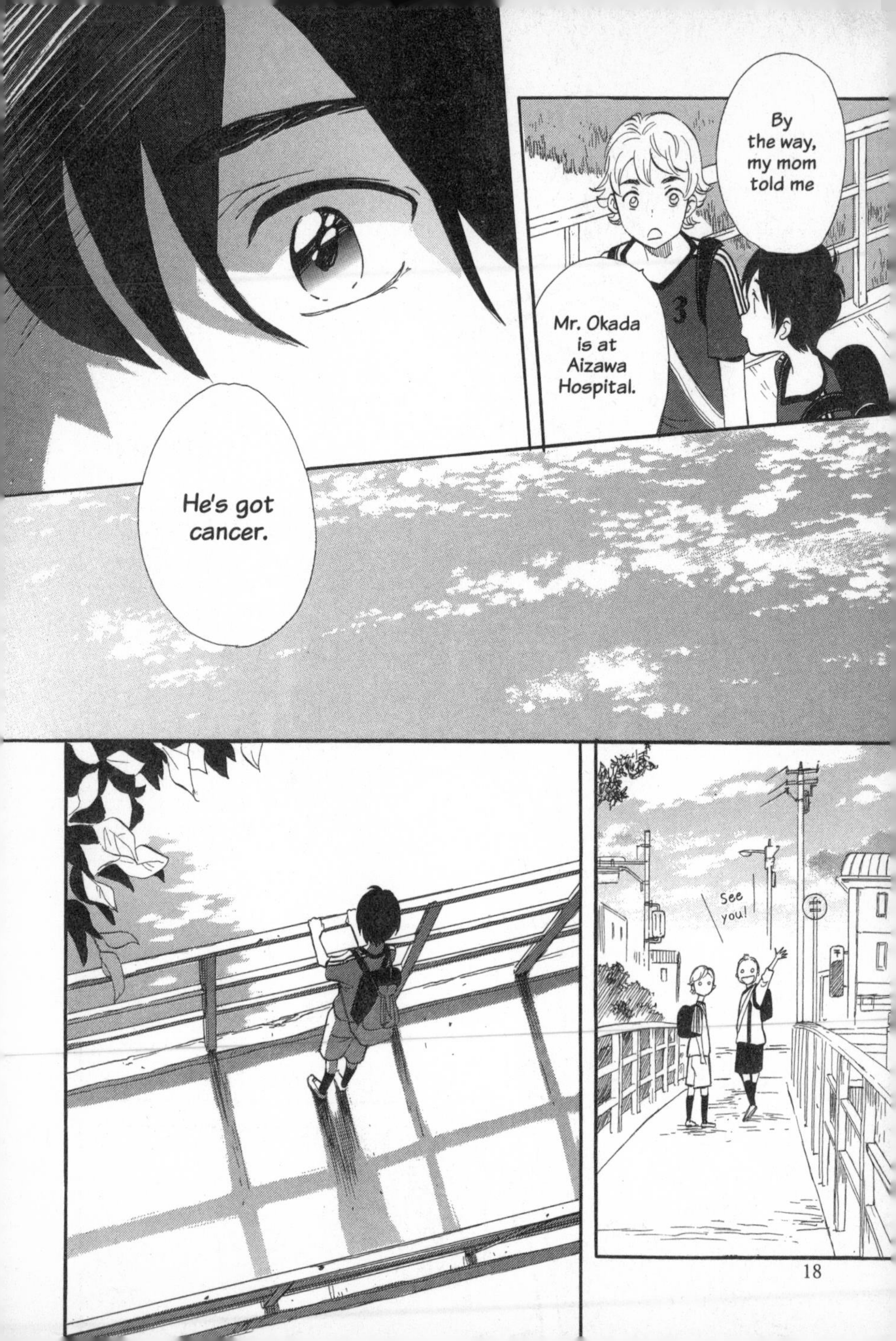
By the way, my mom told me
Mr. Okada is at Aizawa Hospital.
He's got cancer.
See you!

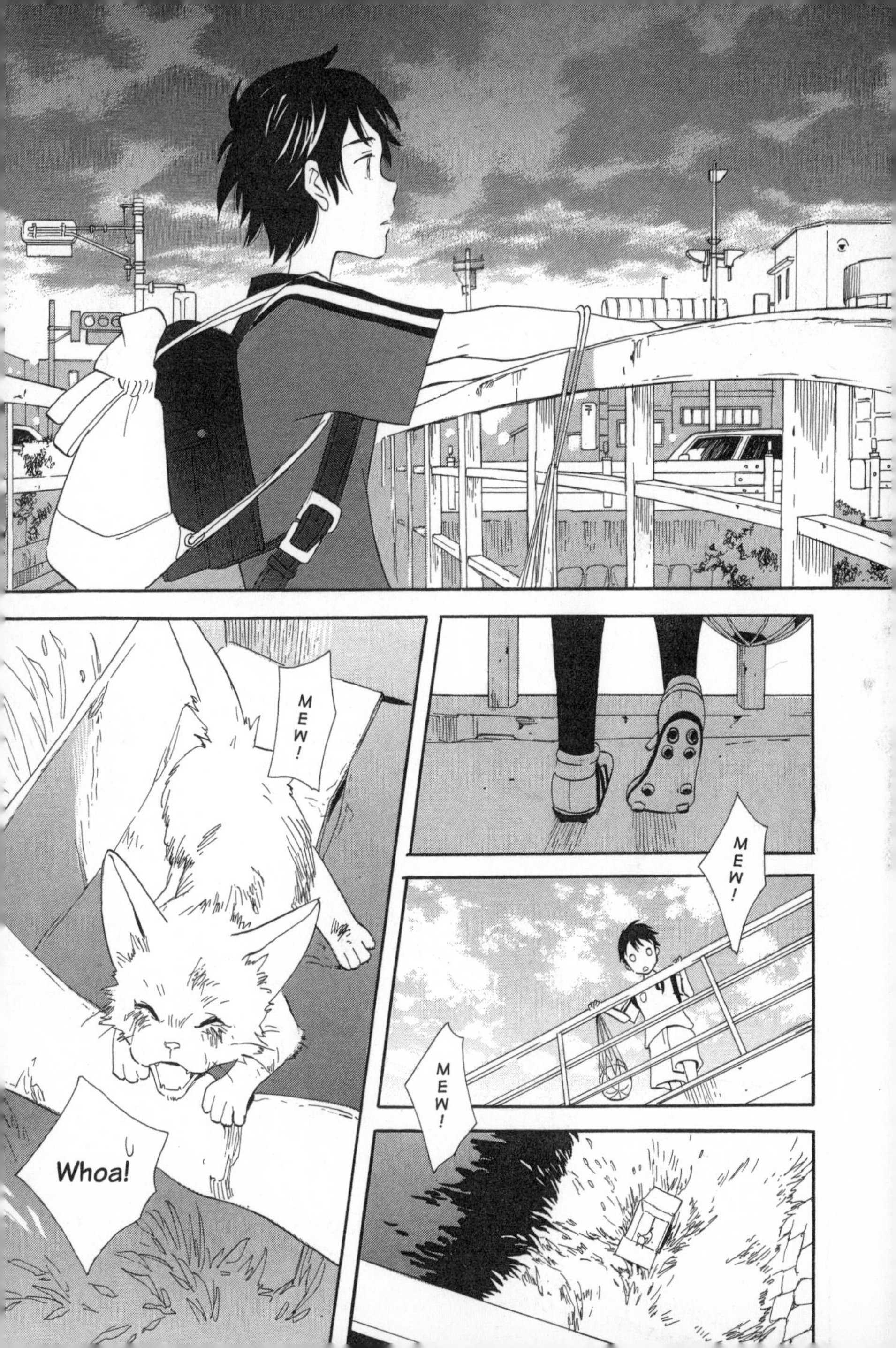
MEW!
MEW!
MEW!
Whoa!

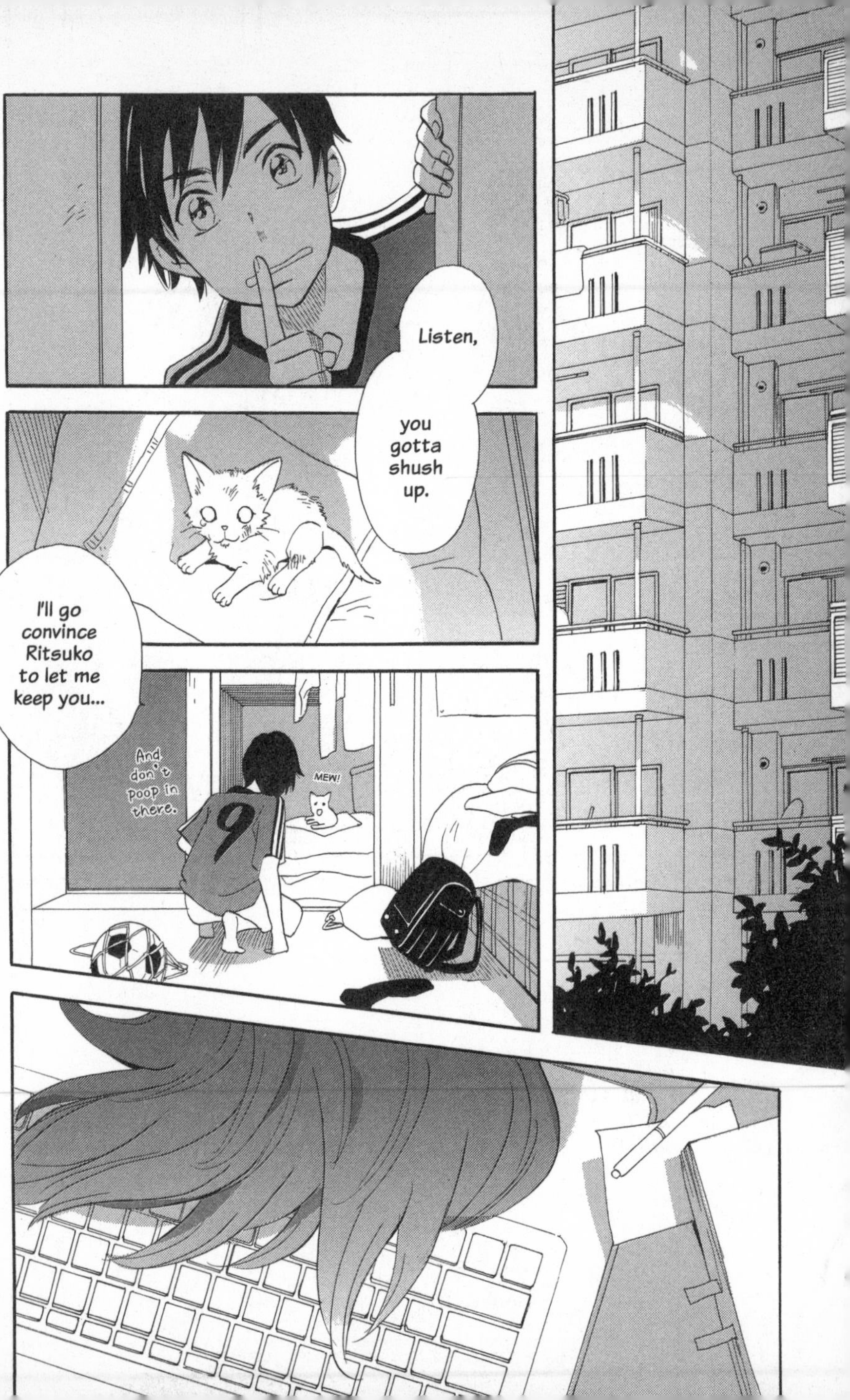
Listen,
you gotta shush up.
I'll go convince Ritsuko to let me keep you...
MEW!
And don't poop in there.

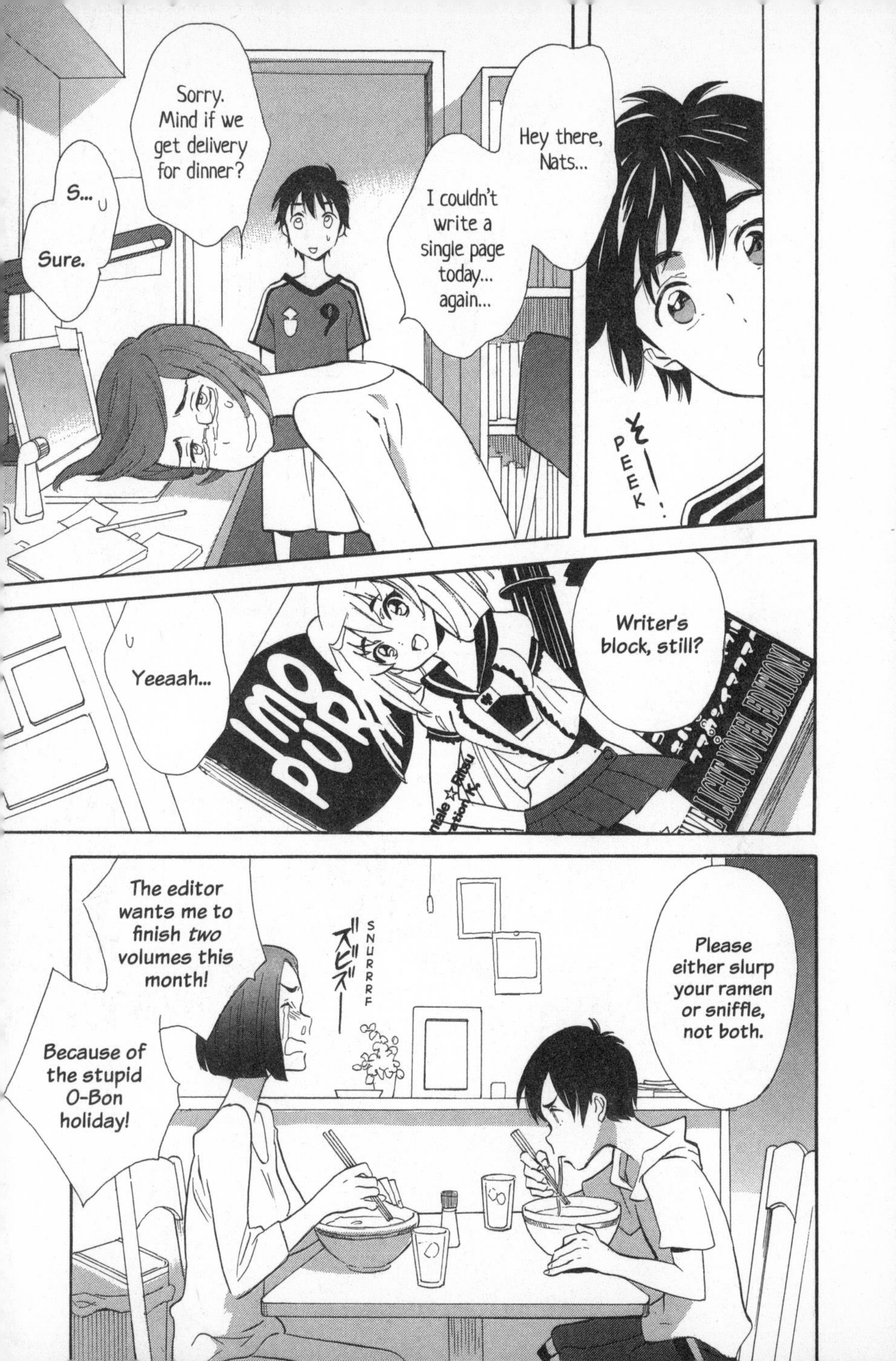
PEEK
Hey there, Nats...
I couldn't write a single page today... again...
Sorry. Mind if we get delivery for dinner?
S... Sure.
Writer's block, still?
Yeeaah...
SNURRRF
The editor wants me to finish *two* volumes this month!
Because of the stupid O-Bon holiday!
Please either slurp your ramen or sniffle, not both.

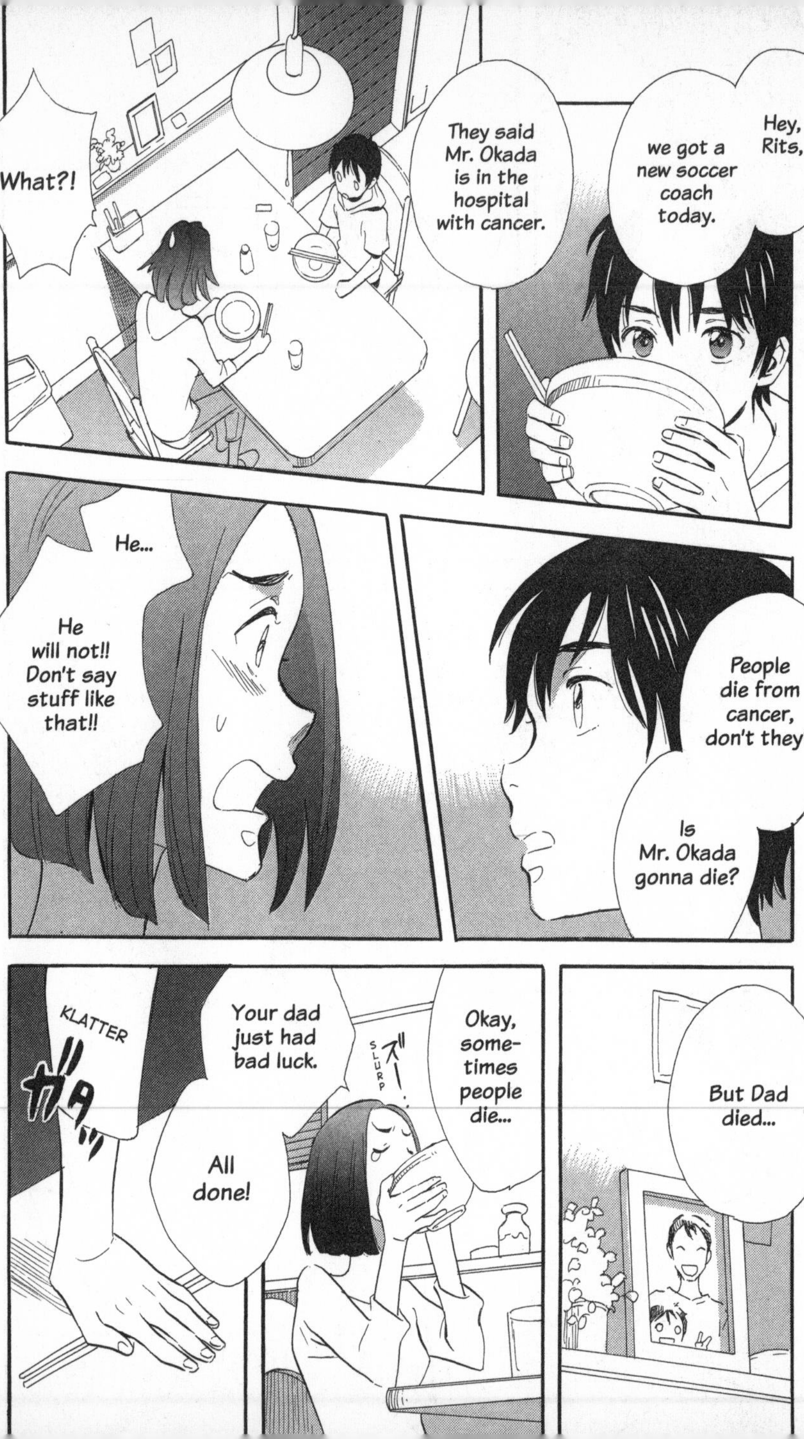
Hey, Rits,
we got a new soccer coach today.
They said Mr. Okada is in the hospital with cancer.
What?!
People die from cancer, don't they?
Is Mr. Okada gonna die?
He...
He will not!! Don't say stuff like that!!
But Dad died...
Okay, sometimes people die...
SLURP
Your dad just had bad luck.
All done!
KLATTER

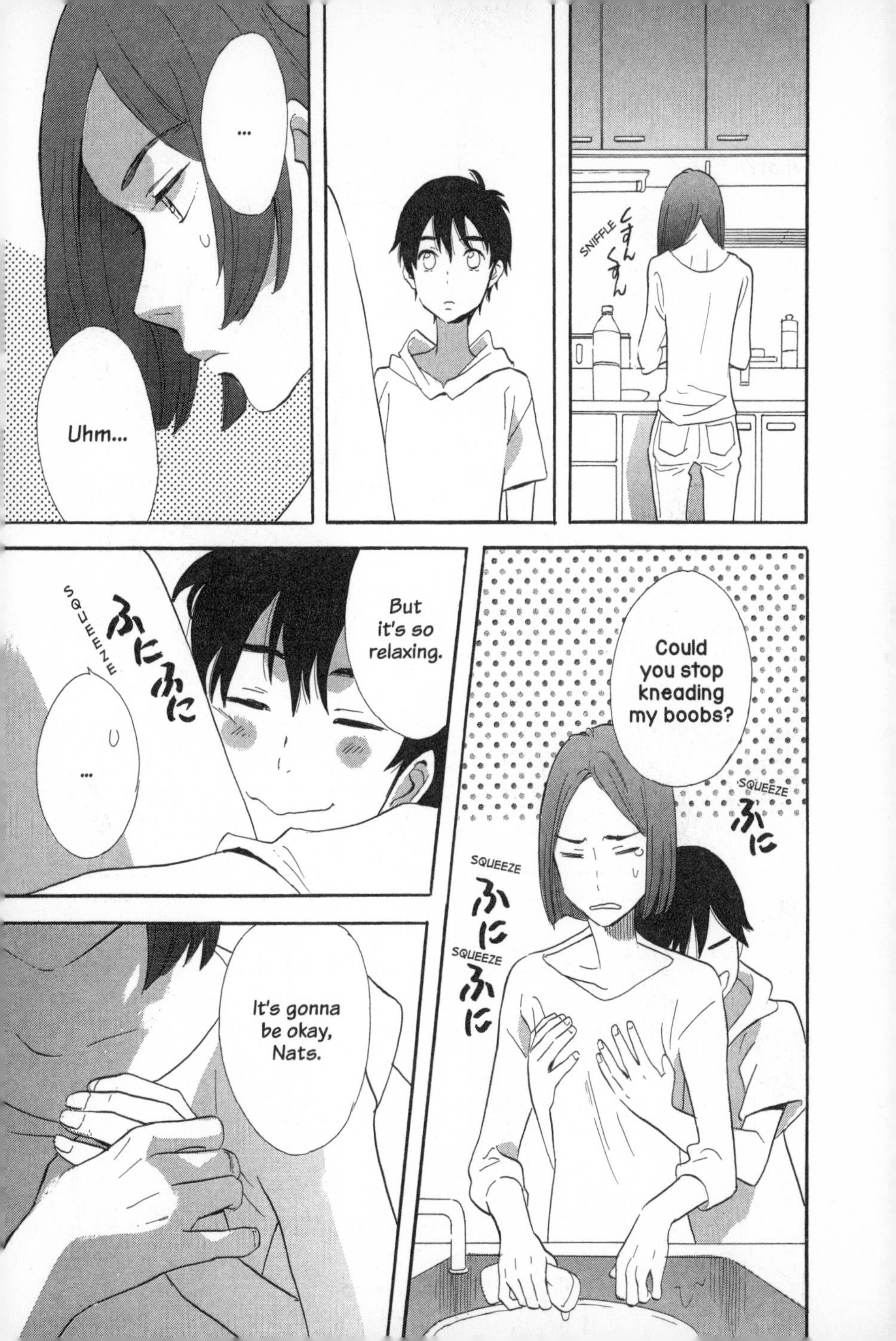
SNIFFLE
くすんくすん
...
Uhm...
Could you stop kneading my boobs?
SQUEEZE
ふに
SQUEEZE
ふに
SQUEEZE
ふに
But it's so relaxing.
SQUEEEZE
ふにふに
...
It's gonna be okay, Nats.

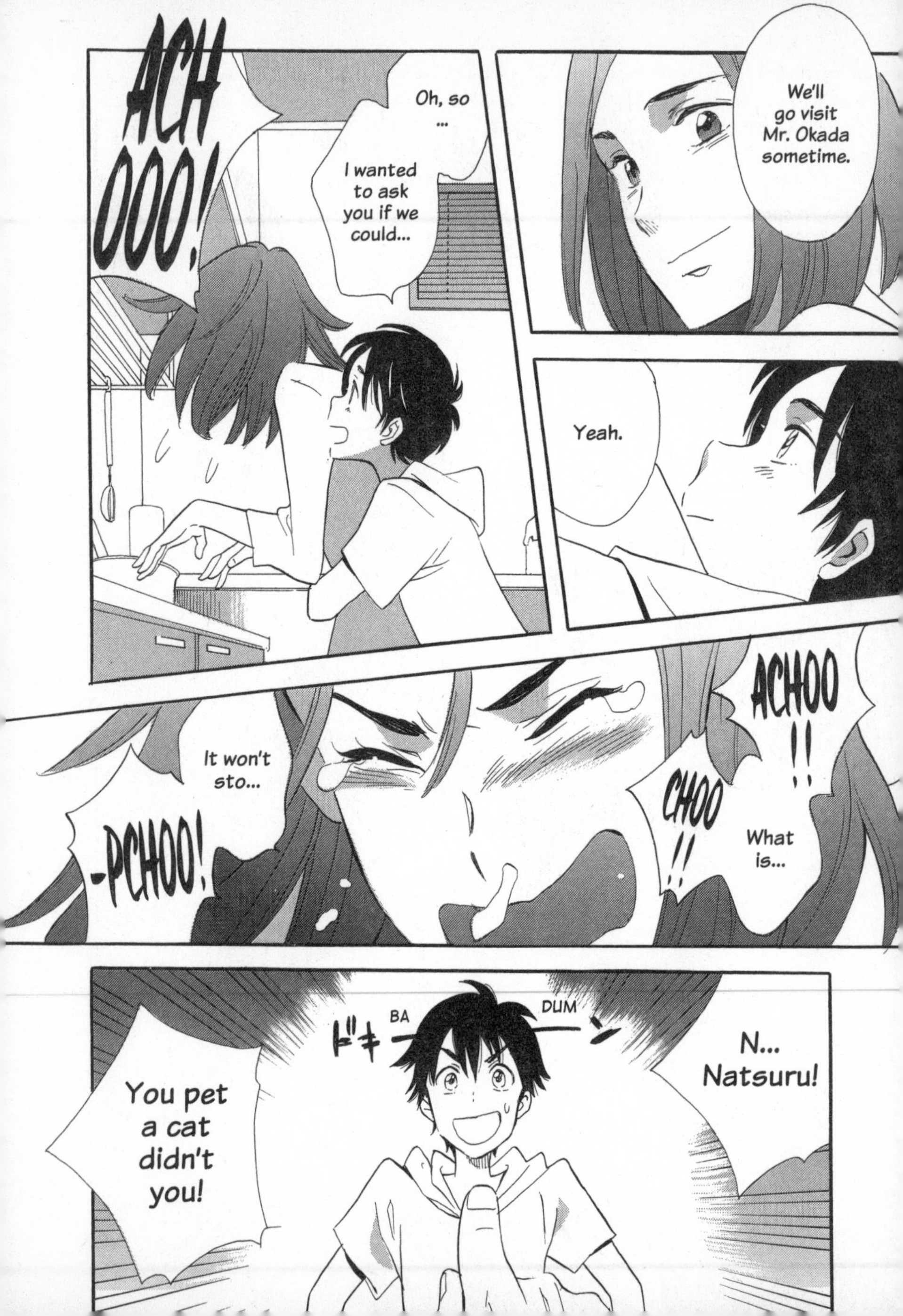
We'll go visit Mr. Okada sometime.
Yeah.
Oh, so ...
I wanted to ask you if we could...
ACHOOO!
ACHOO!!
What is...
CHOO!!
It won't sto...
-PCHOO!
N... Natsuru!
BA DUM
ドキ
You pet a cat didn't you!

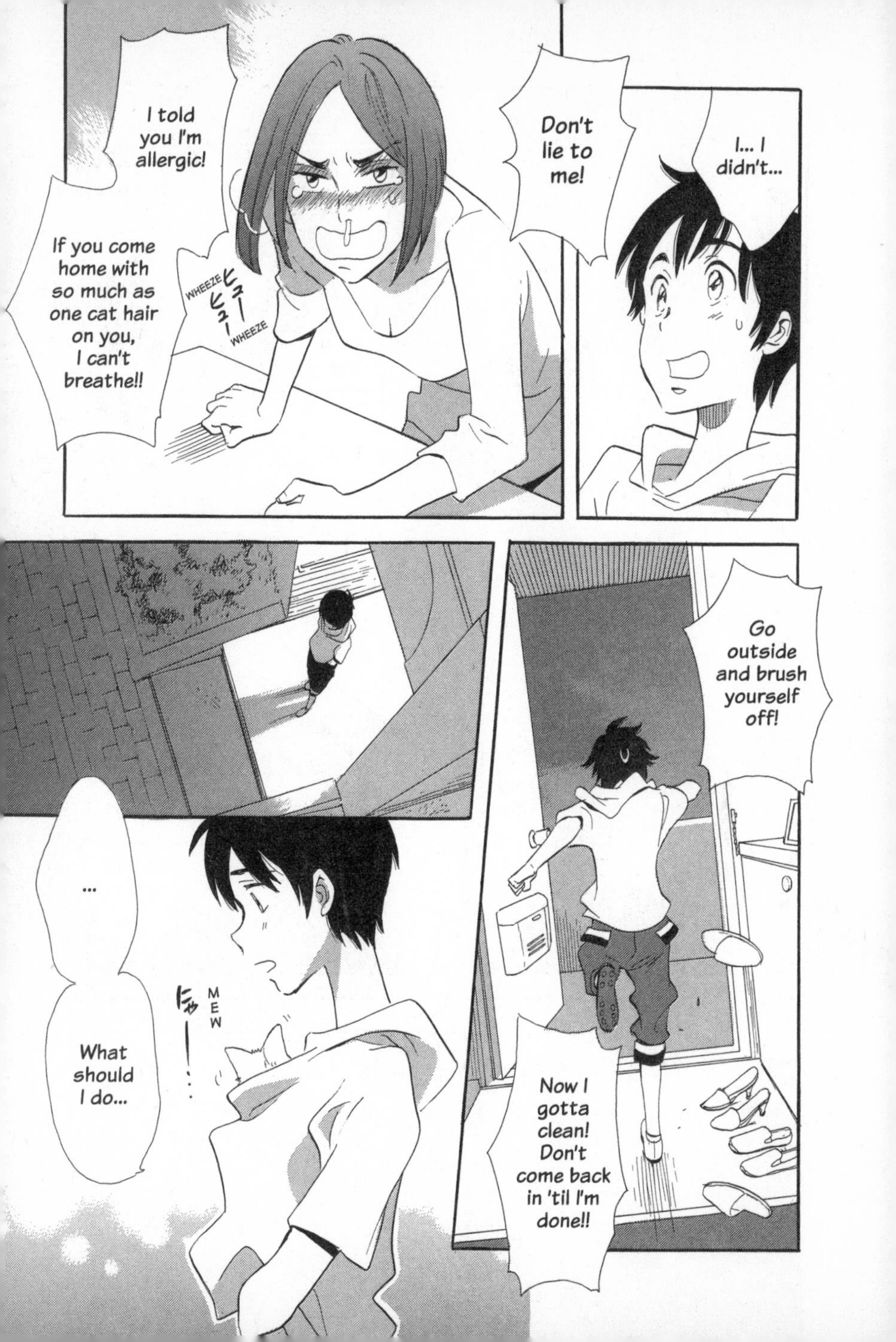
I... I didn't...
Don't lie to me!
I told you I'm allergic!
If you come home with so much as one cat hair on you, I can't breathe!!
ヒュー ヒュー WHEEZE WHEEZE
Go outside and brush yourself off!
Now I gotta clean! Don't come back in 'til I'm done!!
...
What should I do...
ニャー… MEW

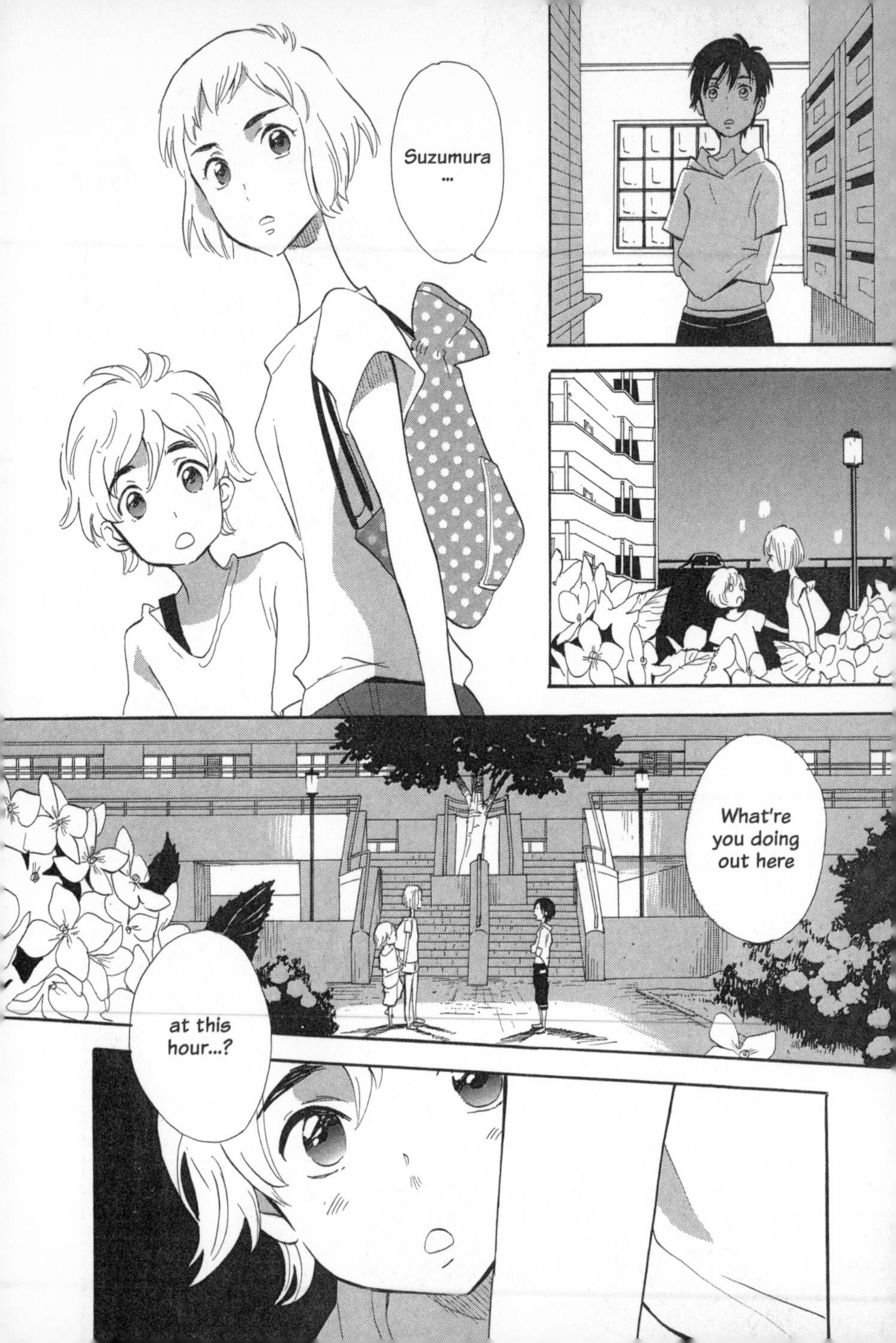
Suzumura ...
What're you doing out here
at this hour...?

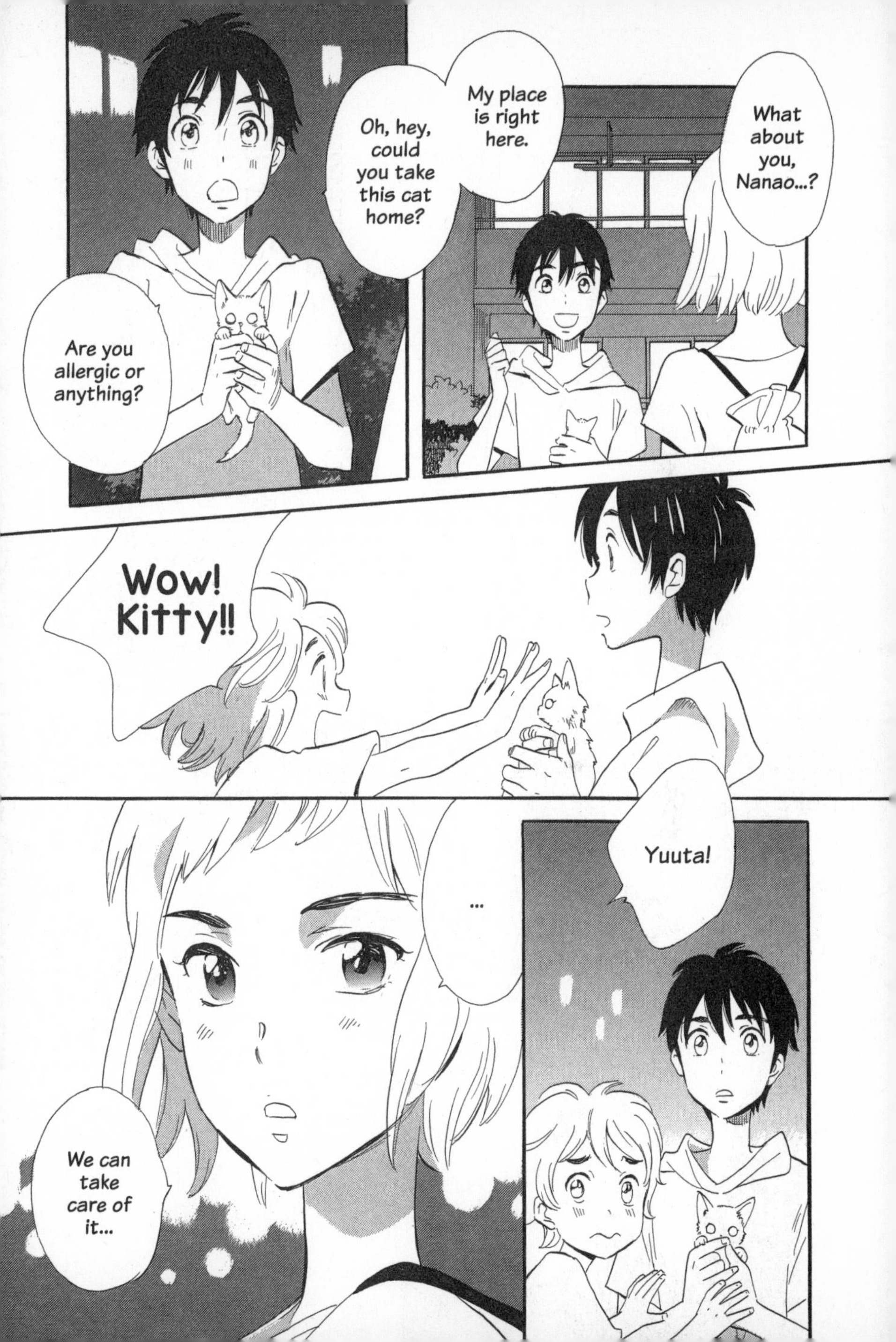
What about you, Nanao...?
My place is right here.
Oh, hey, could you take this cat home?
Are you allergic or anything?
Wow! Kitty!!
Yuuta!
...
We can take care of it...

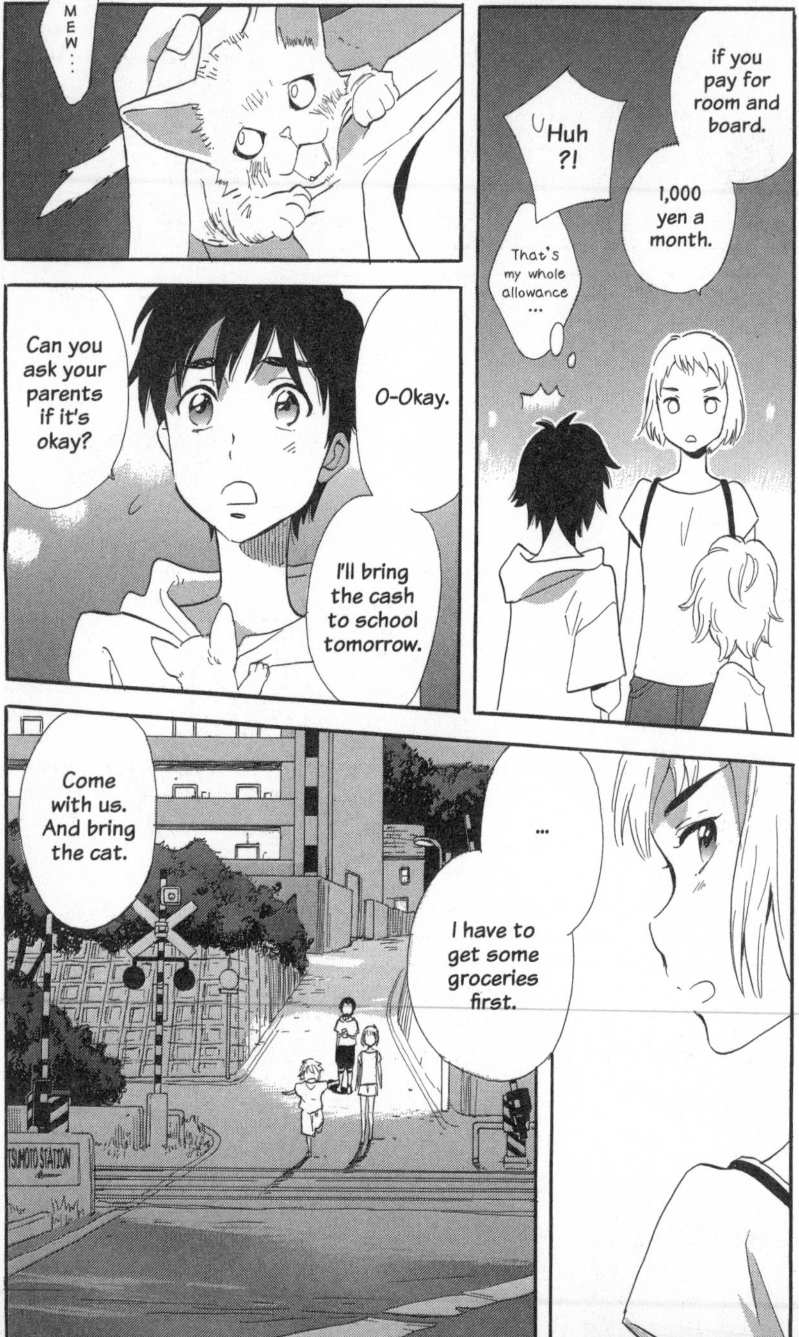
if you pay for room and board.
1,000 yen a month.
Huh ?!
That's my whole allowance ...
MEW...
Can you ask your parents if it's okay?
O-Okay.
I'll bring the cash to school tomorrow.
...
I have to get some groceries first.
Come with us. And bring the cat.
TSUMOTO STATION

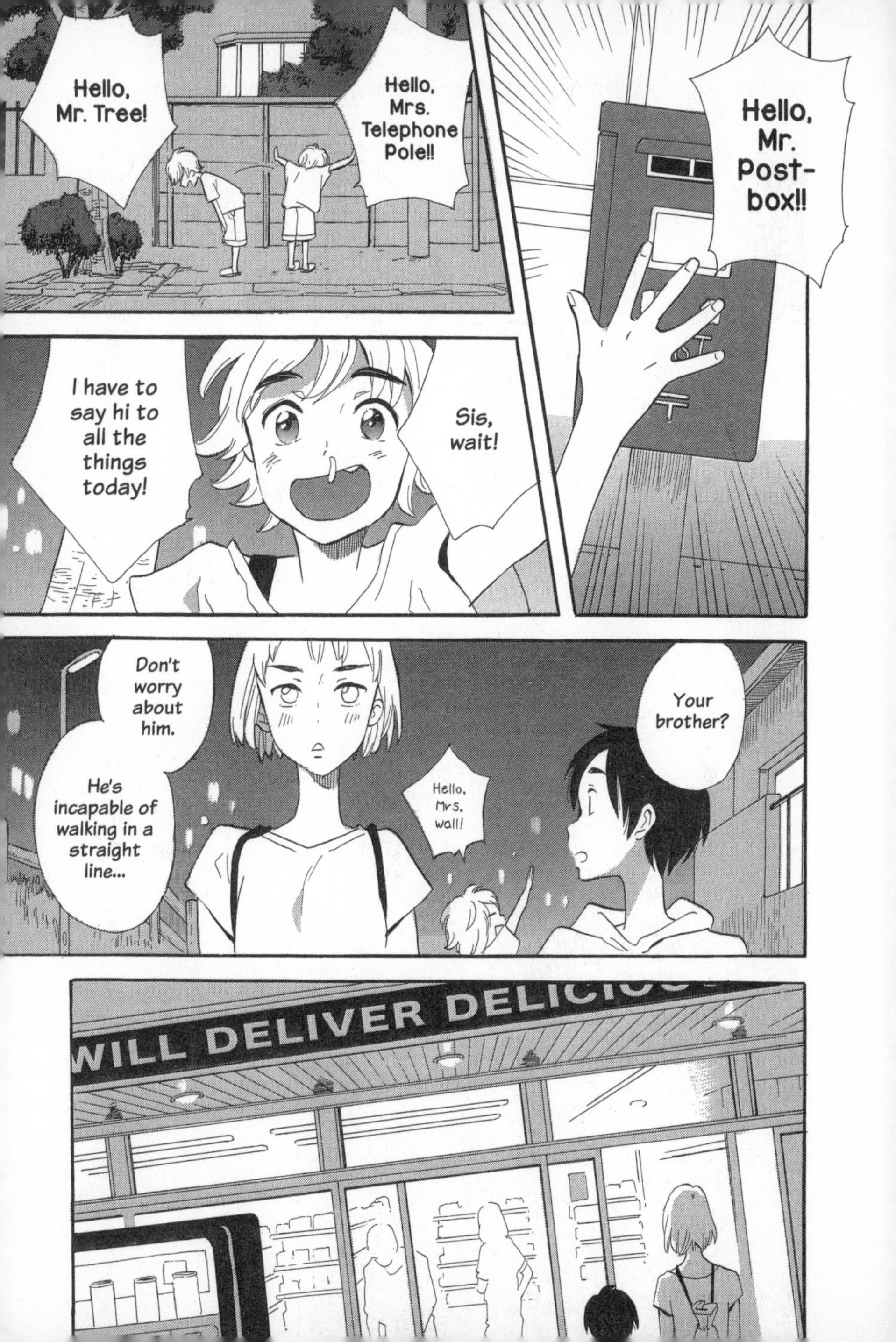
Hello, Mr. Post-box!!
Hello, Mrs. Telephone Pole!!
Hello, Mr. Tree!
Sis, wait!
I have to say hi to all the things today!
Your brother?
Hello, Mrs. wall!
Don't worry about him.
He's incapable of walking in a straight line...
WILL DELIVER DELICIO

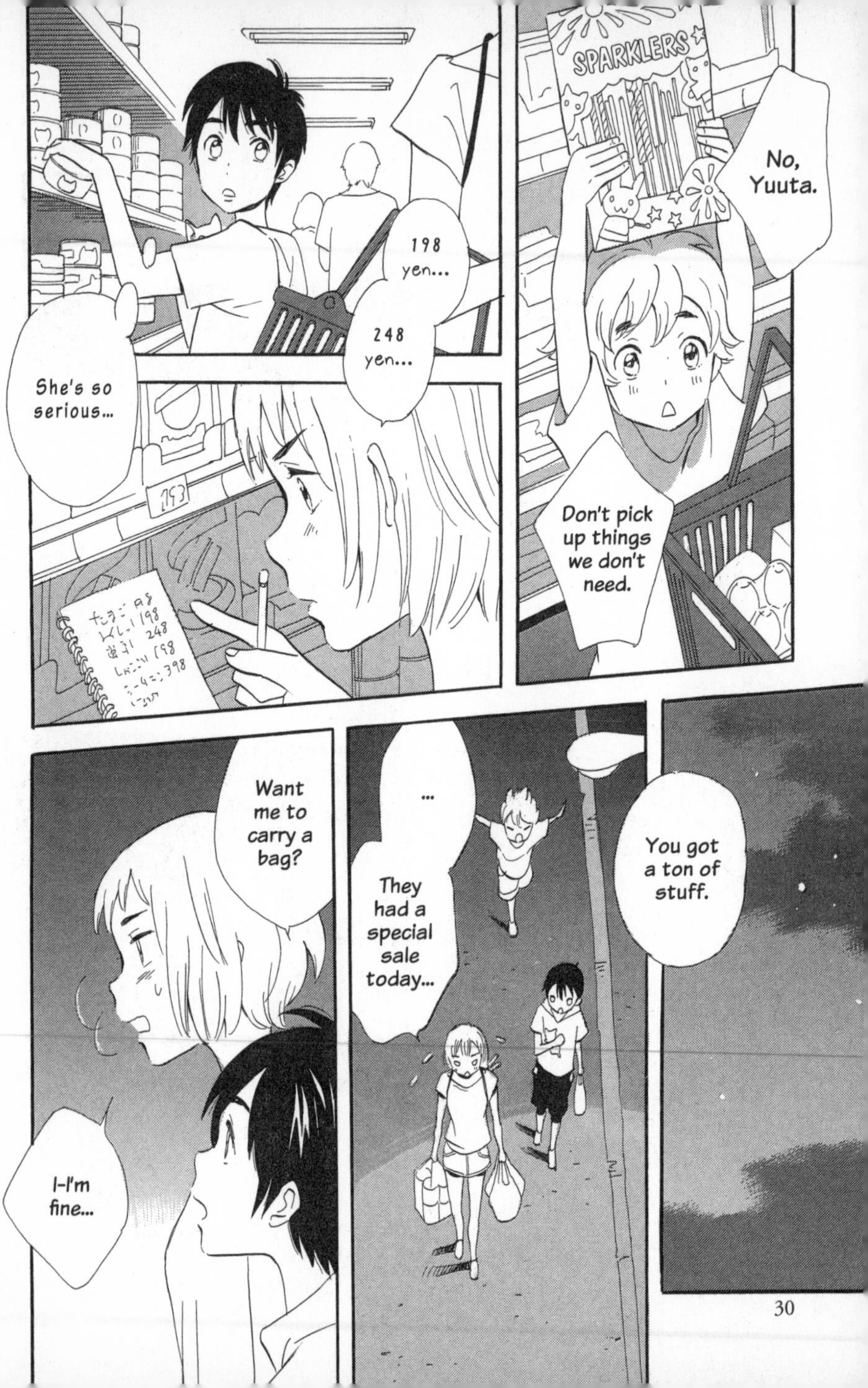
No, Yuuta.
Don't pick up things we don't need.
198 yen...
248 yen...
She's so serious...
You got a ton of stuff.
...
They had a special sale today...
Want me to carry a bag?
I-I'm fine...

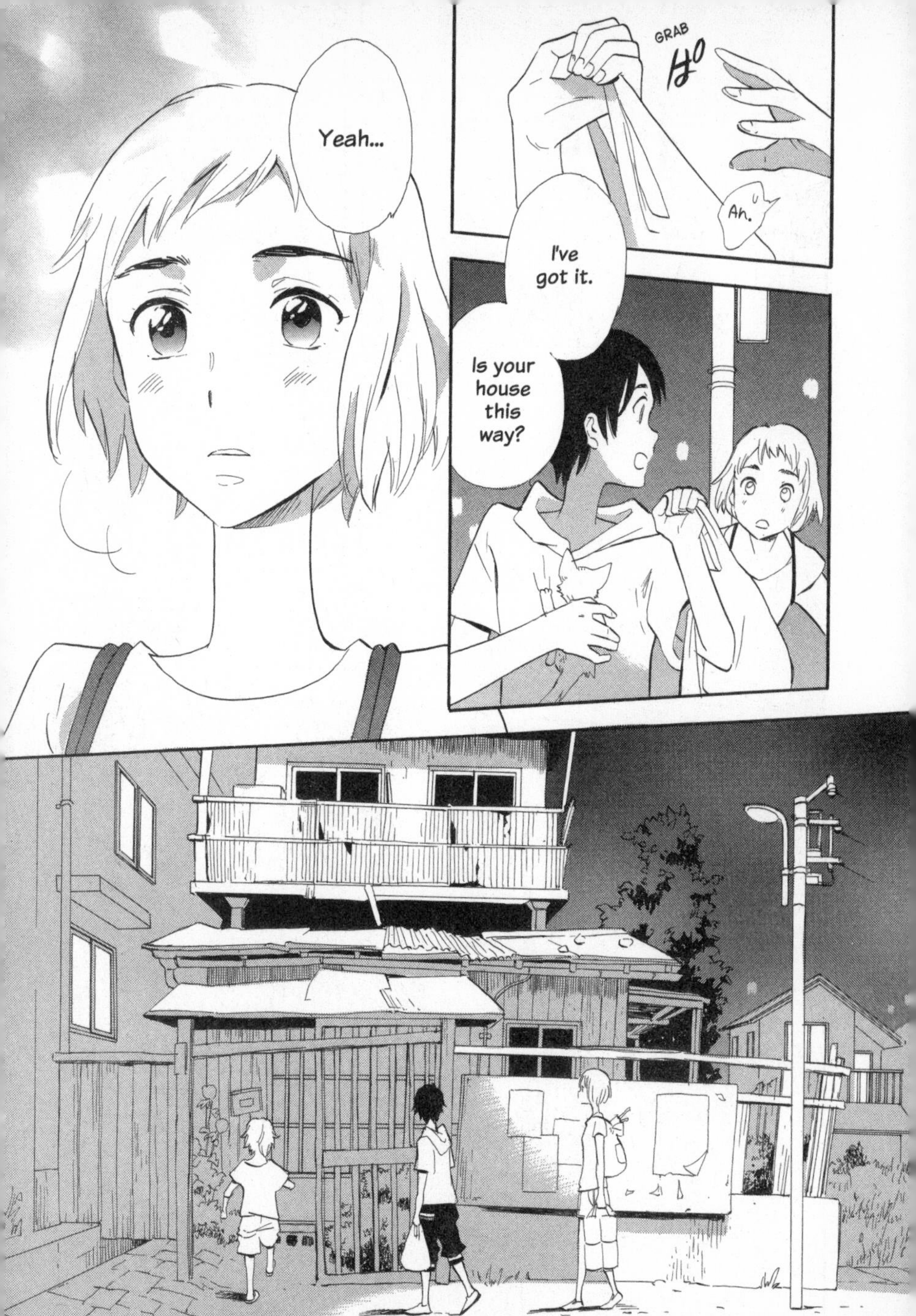
GRAB
Ah.
I've got it.
Is your house this way?
Yeah...

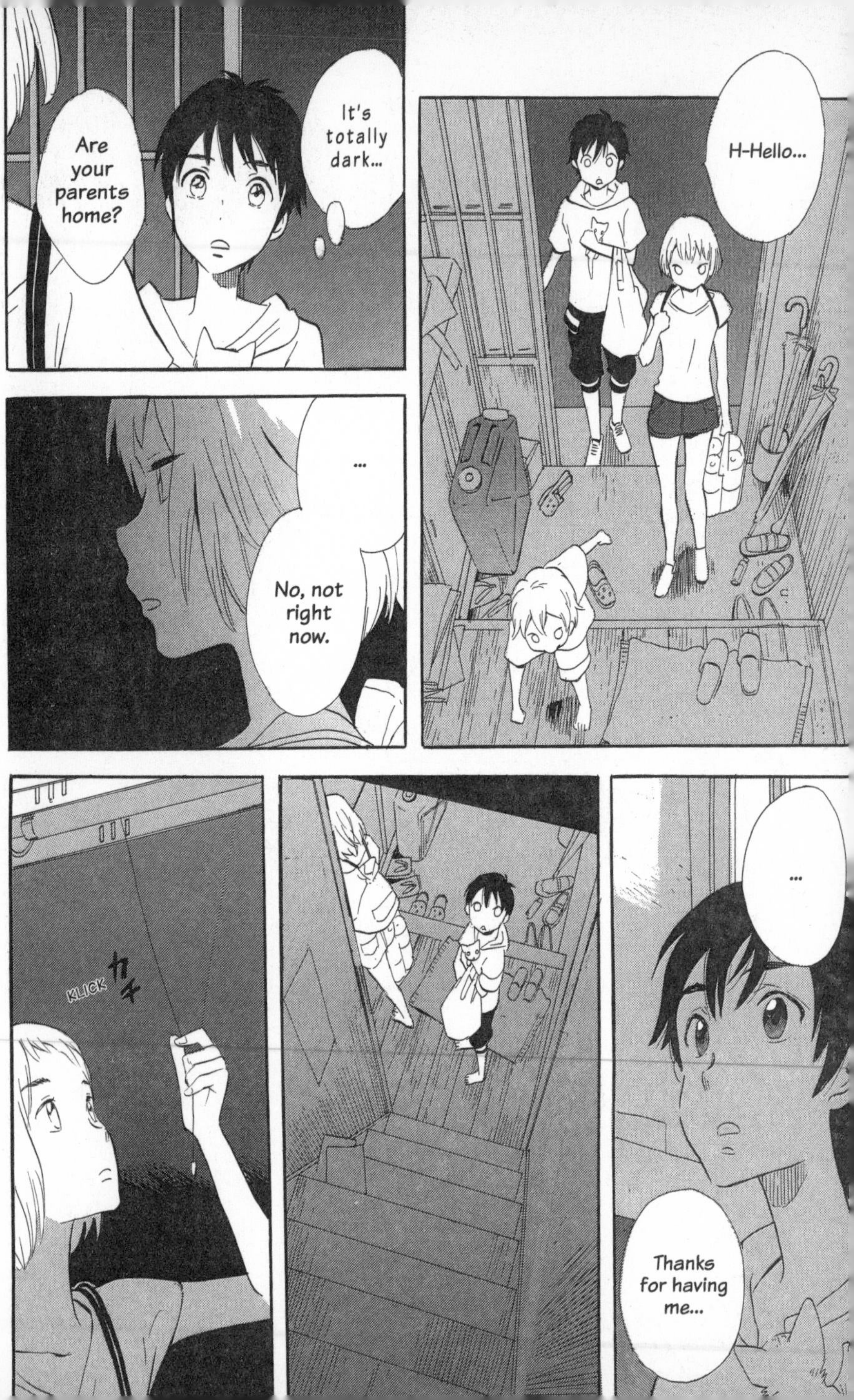
H-Hello...
It's totally dark...
Are your parents home?
...
No, not right now.
...
Thanks for having me...
カチ
KLICK

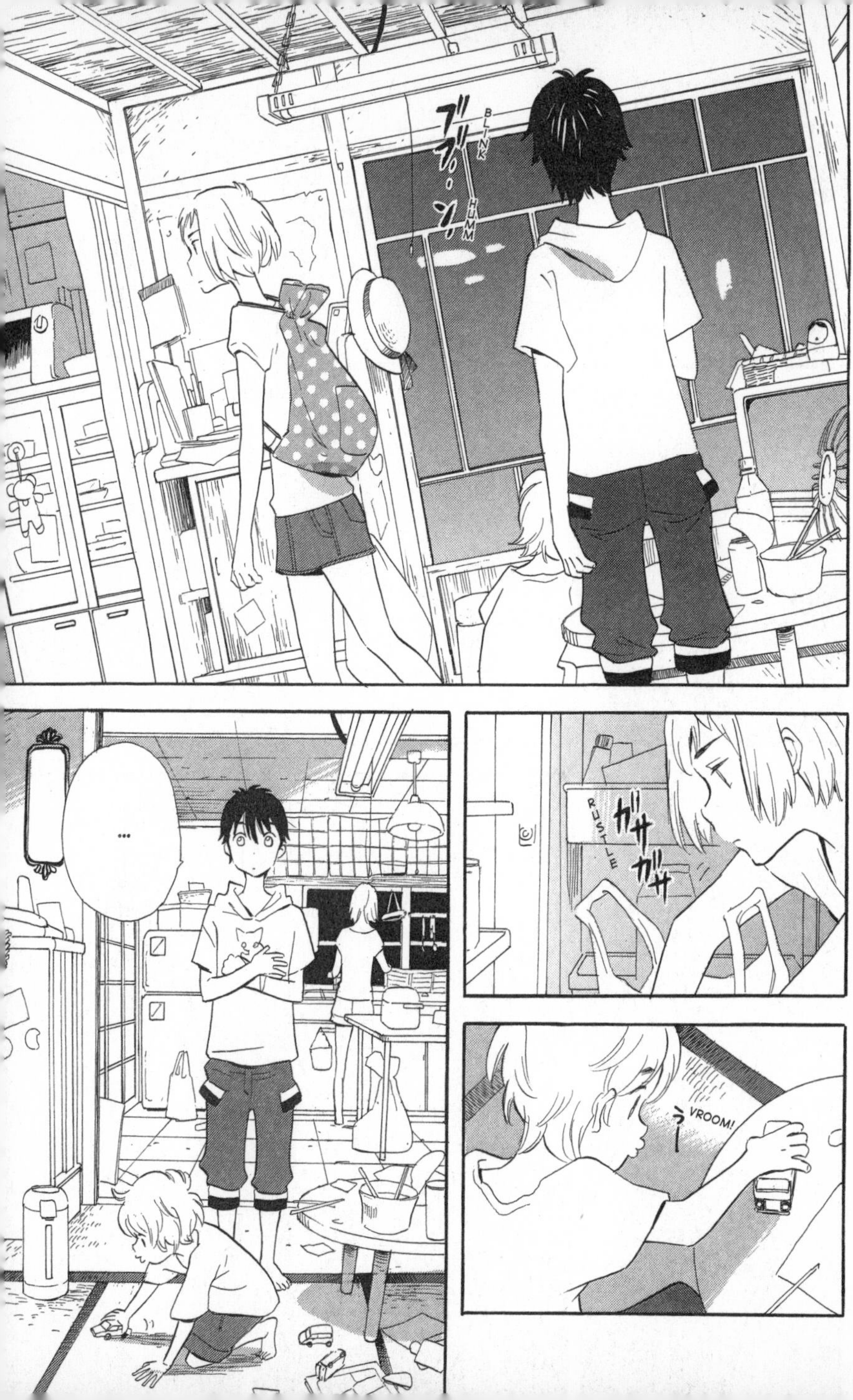

ブゥ…ン
BLINK
HUMM
ガサガサ
RUSTLE
…
ブー
VROOM!

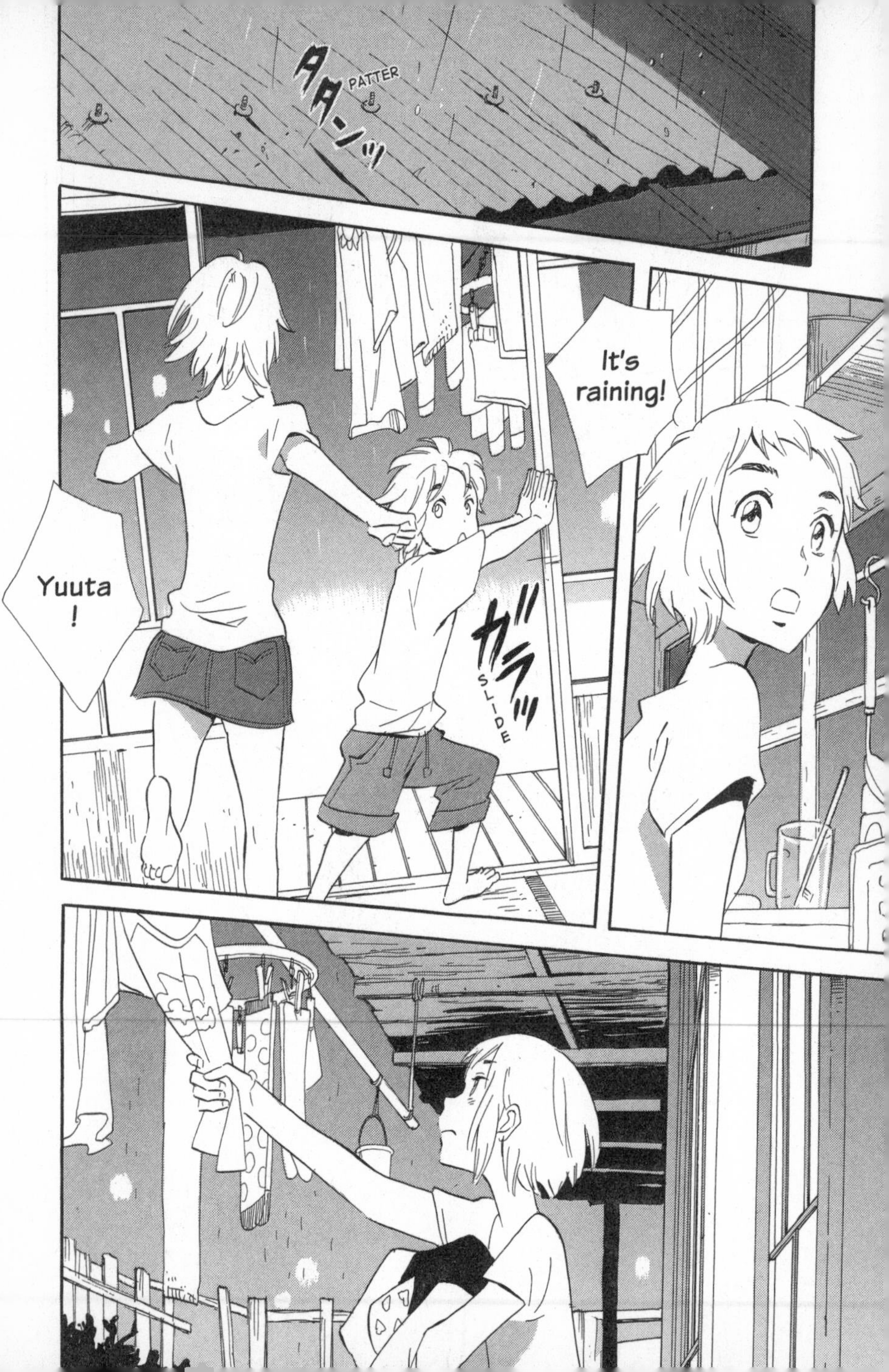
タタンッ
PATTER
It's raining!
Yuuta !
ガラッ
SLIDE

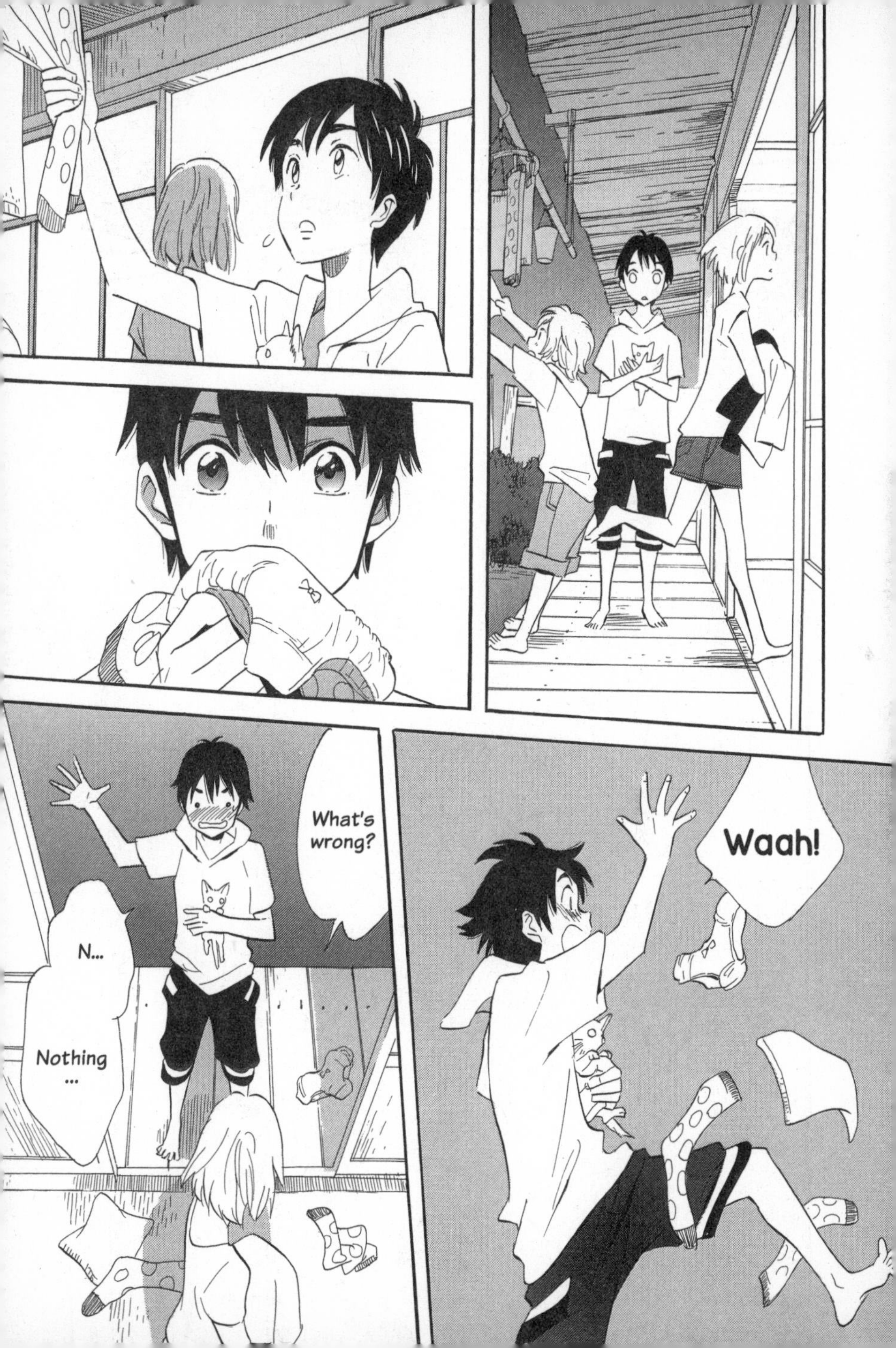
Waah!
What's wrong?
N... Nothing ...

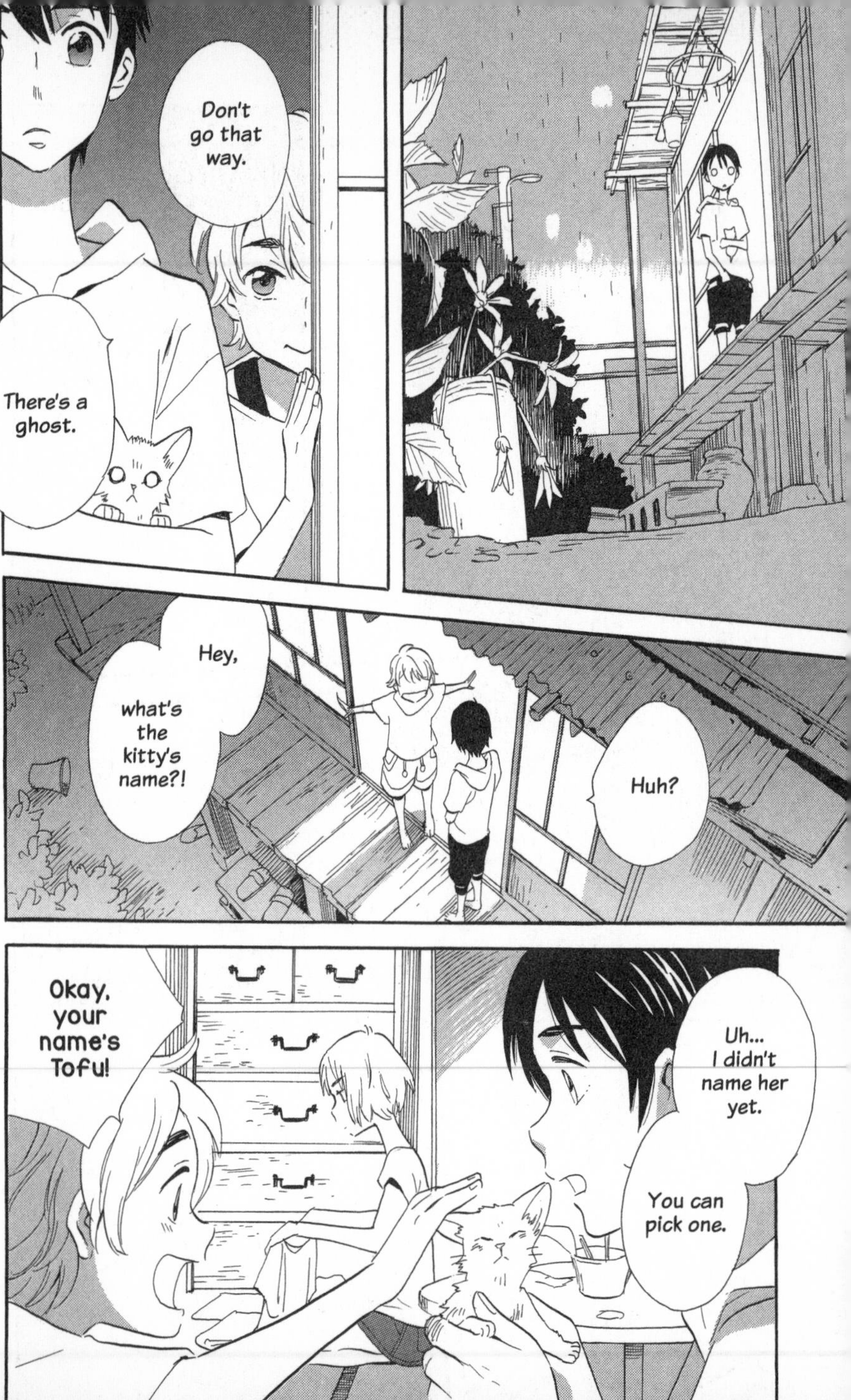
Don't go that way.
There's a ghost.
Hey, what's the kitty's name?!
Huh?
Uh... I didn't name her yet.
You can pick one.
Okay, your name's Tofu!

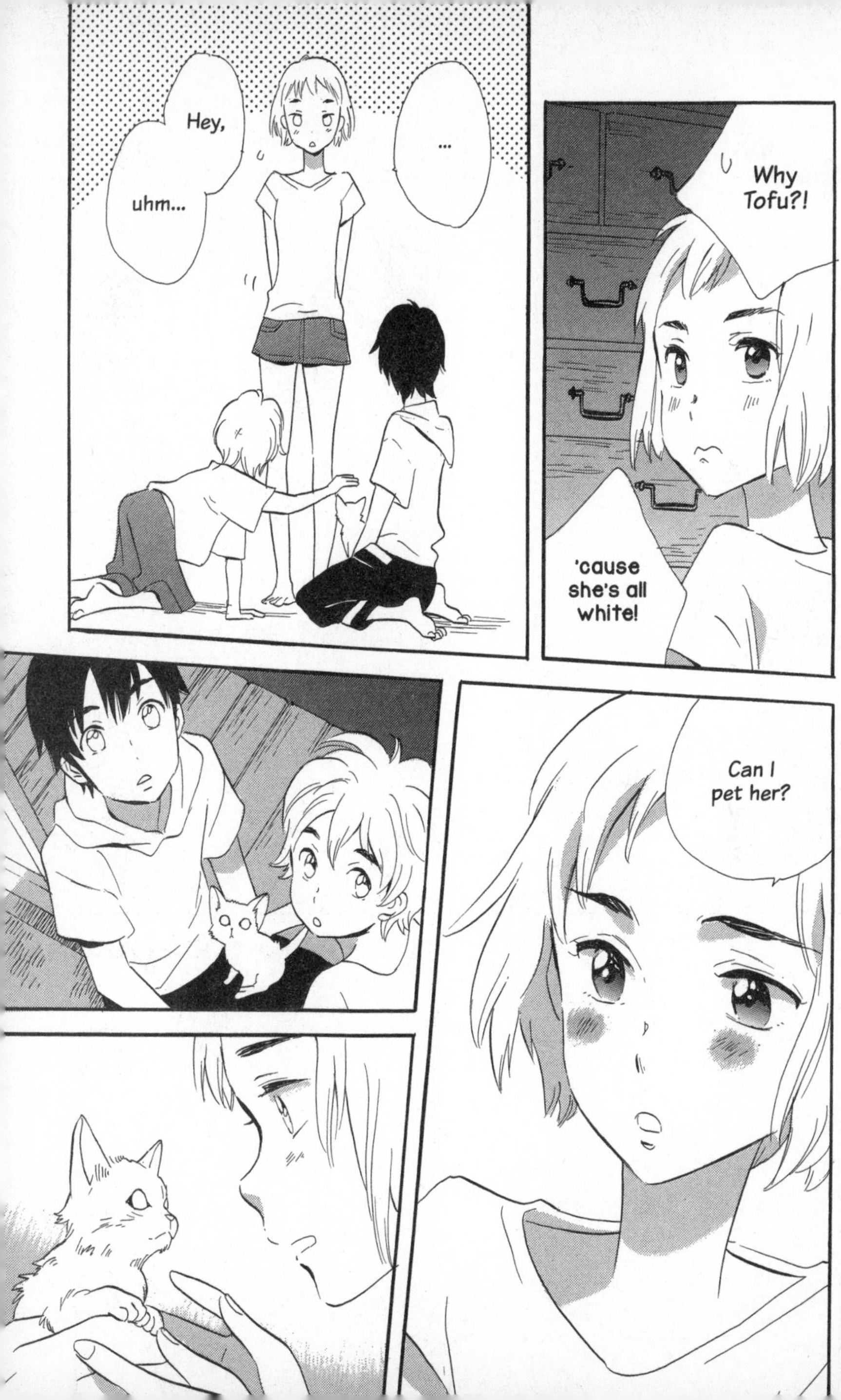
Why Tofu?!
'cause she's all white!
...
Hey,
uhm...
Can I pet her?

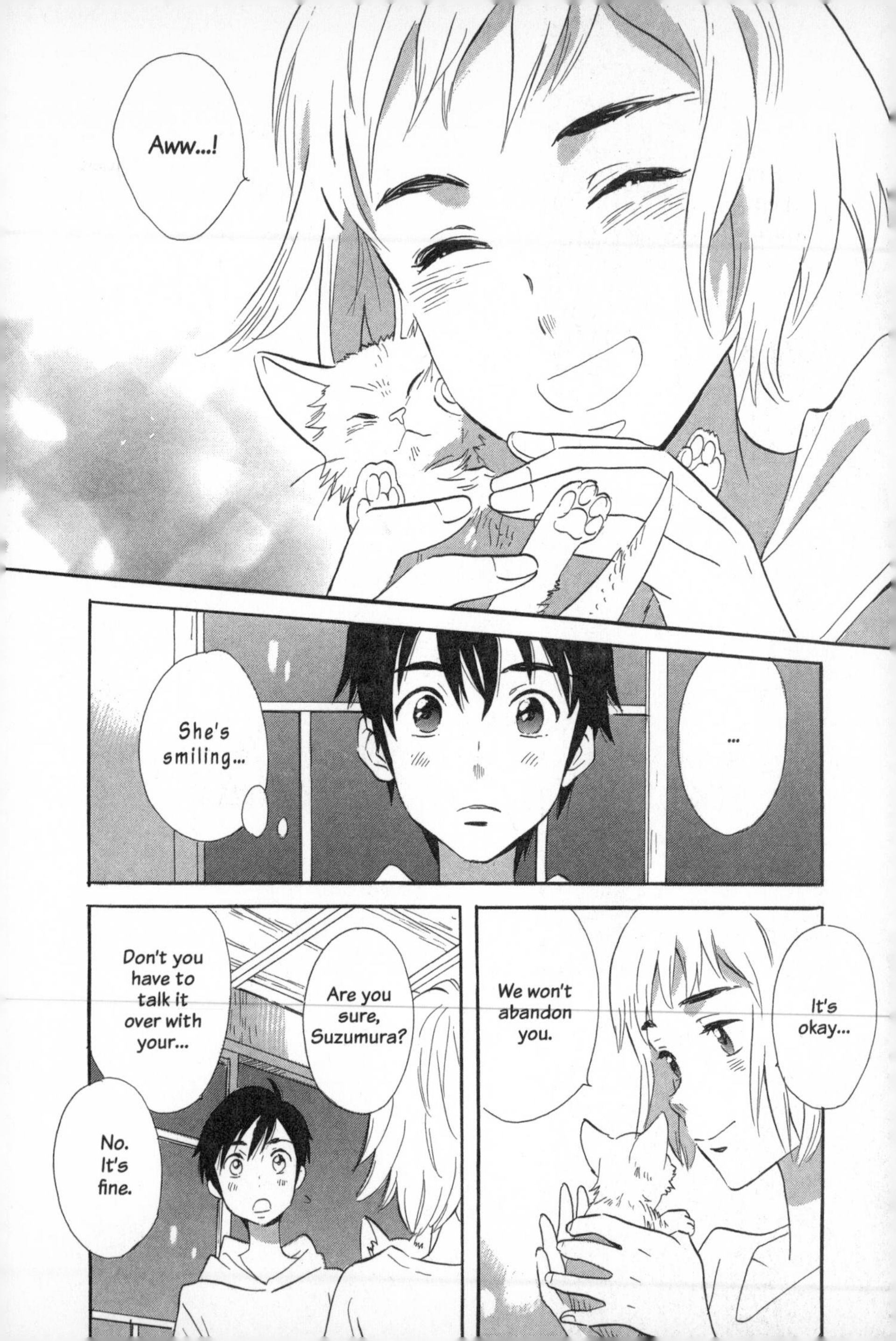
Aww...!
...
She's smiling...
It's okay...
We won't abandon you.
Are you sure, Suzumura?
Don't you have to talk it over with your...
No. It's fine.

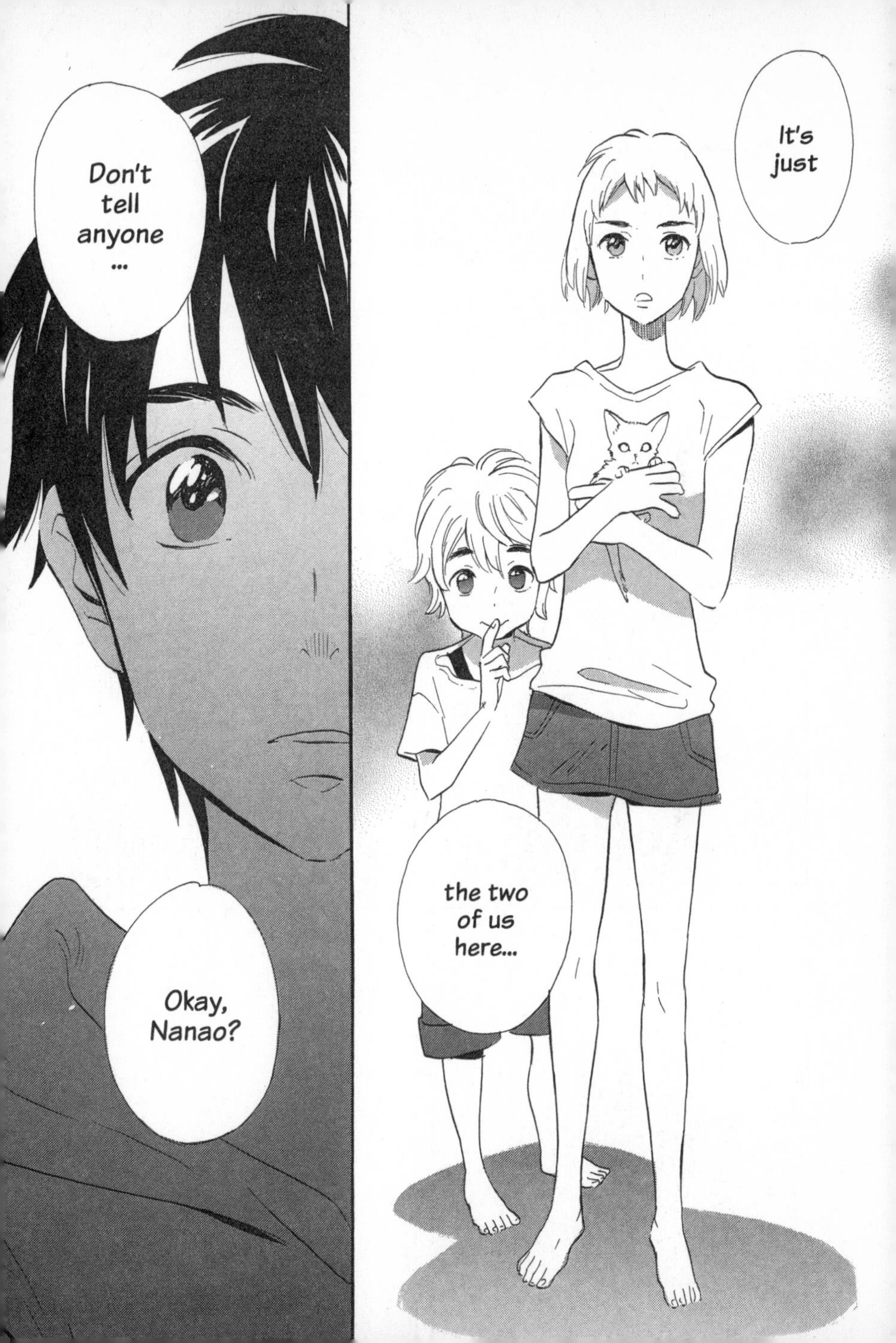
It's just
the two of us here...
Don't tell anyone ...
Okay, Nanao?

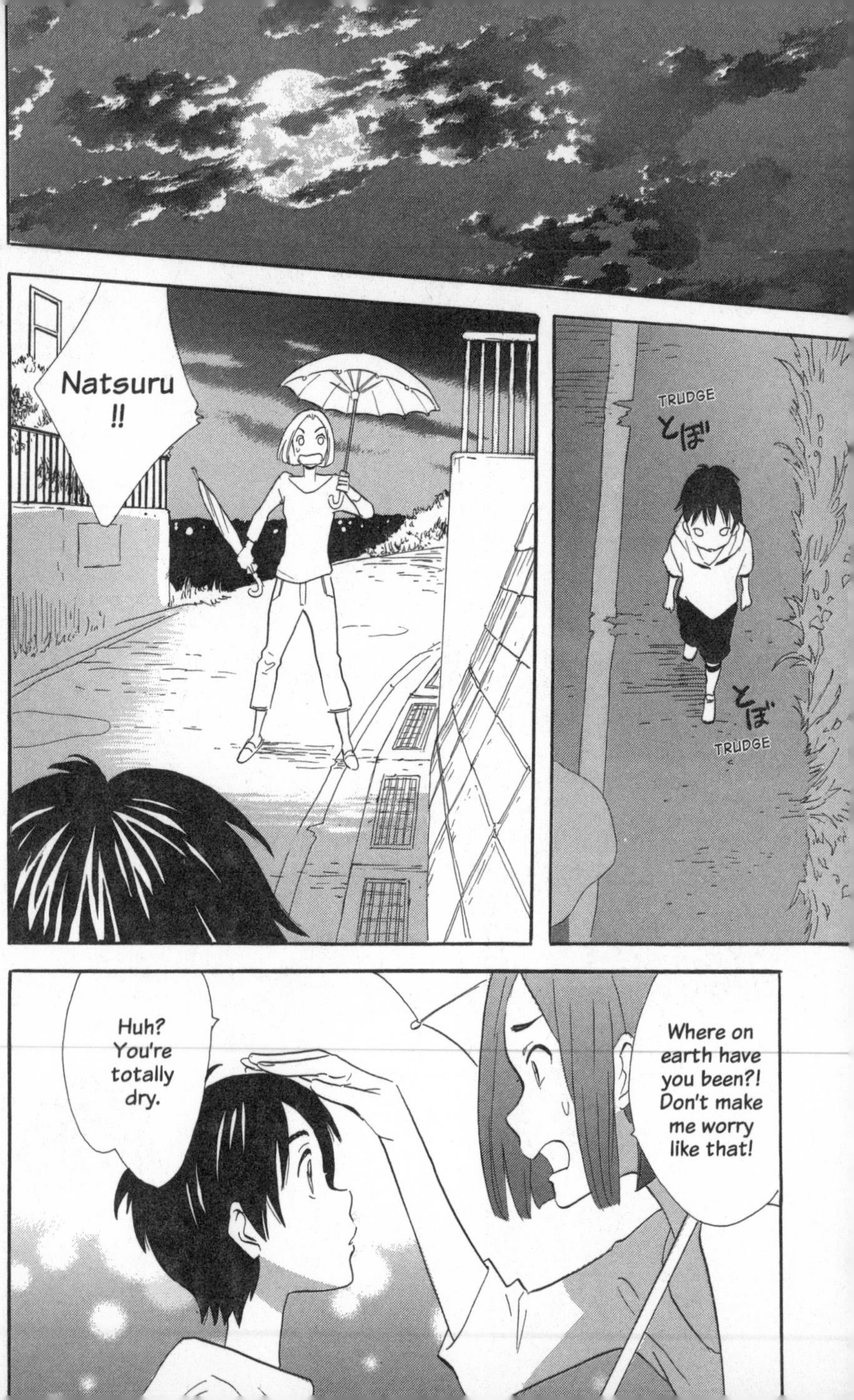
TRUDGE
とぼ
とぼ
TRUDGE
Natsuru
!!
Where on earth have you been?! Don't make me worry like that!
Huh? You're totally dry.

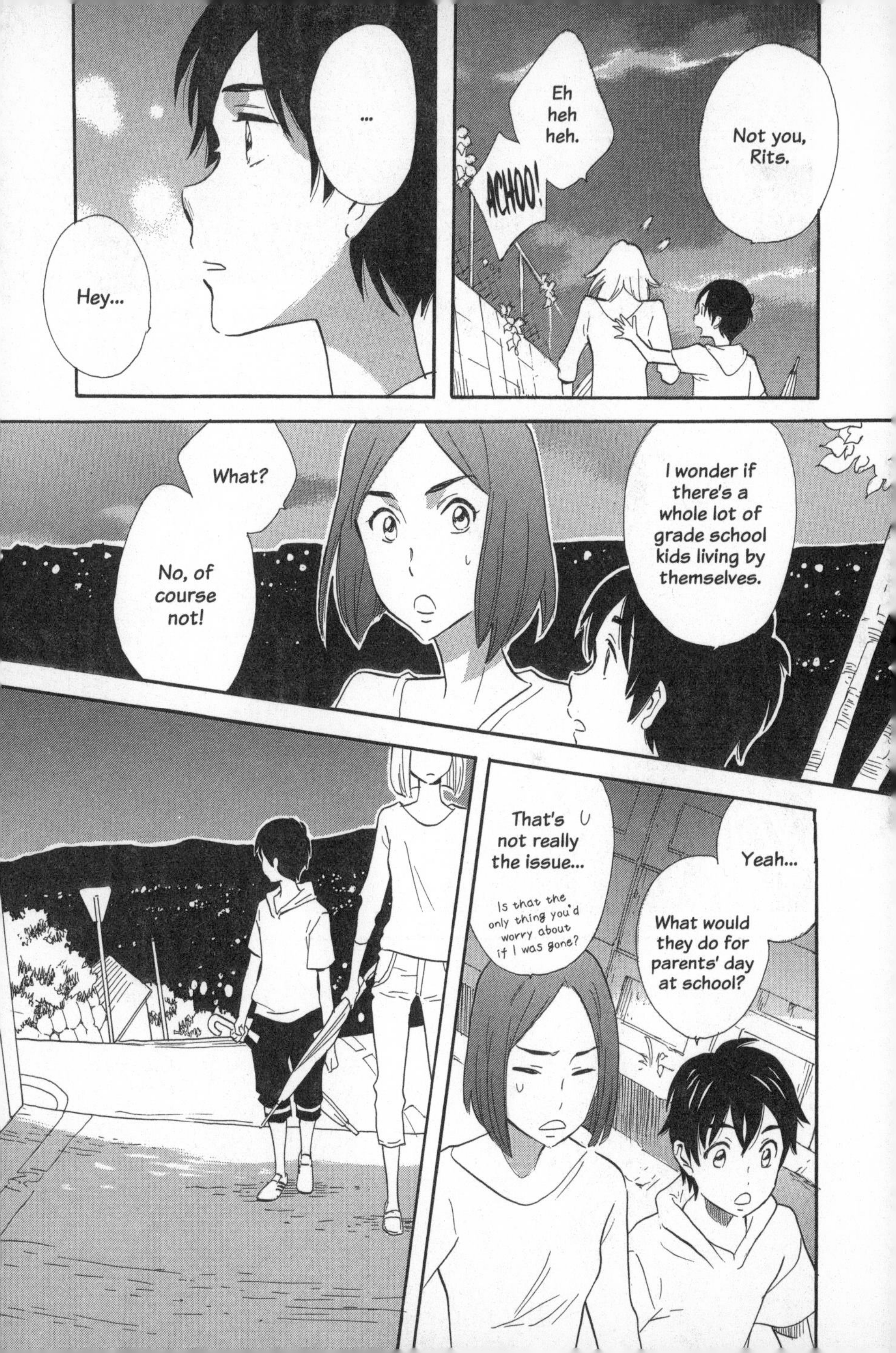

Not you, Rits.
Eh heh heh.
ACHOO!
...
Hey...
I wonder if there's a whole lot of grade school kids living by themselves.
What?
No, of course not!
Yeah...
What would they do for parents' day at school?
That's not really the issue...
Is that the only thing you'd worry about if I was gone?

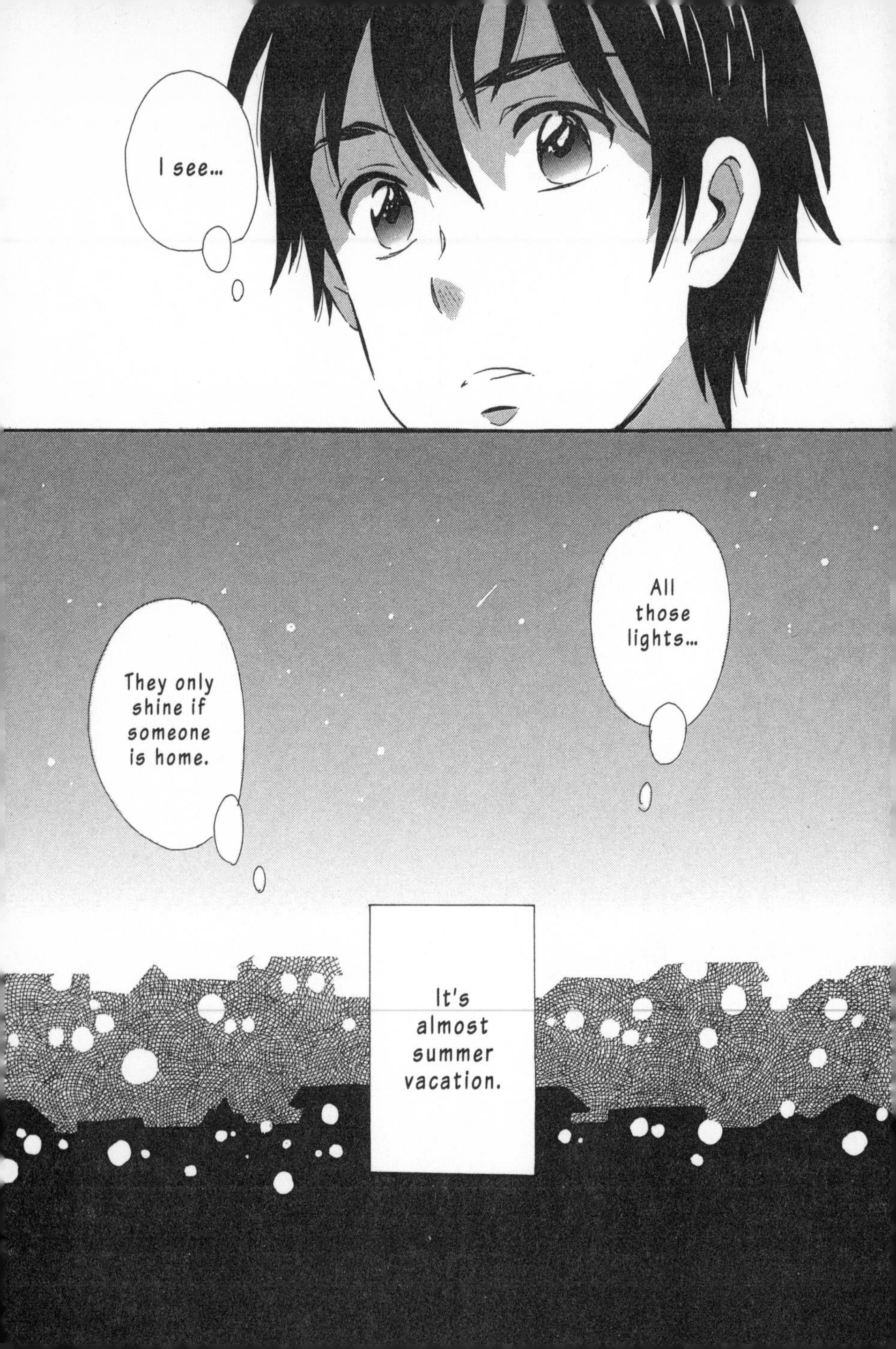
I see...
All those lights...
They only shine if someone is home.
It's almost summer vacation.

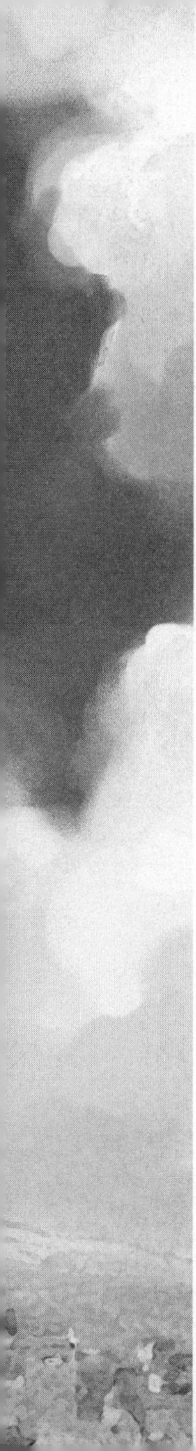

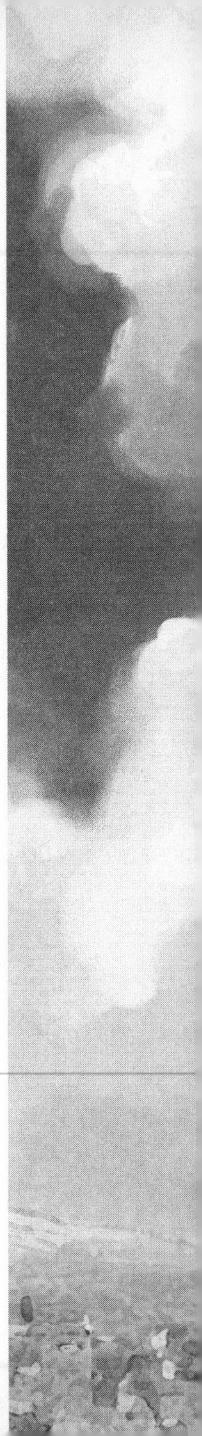

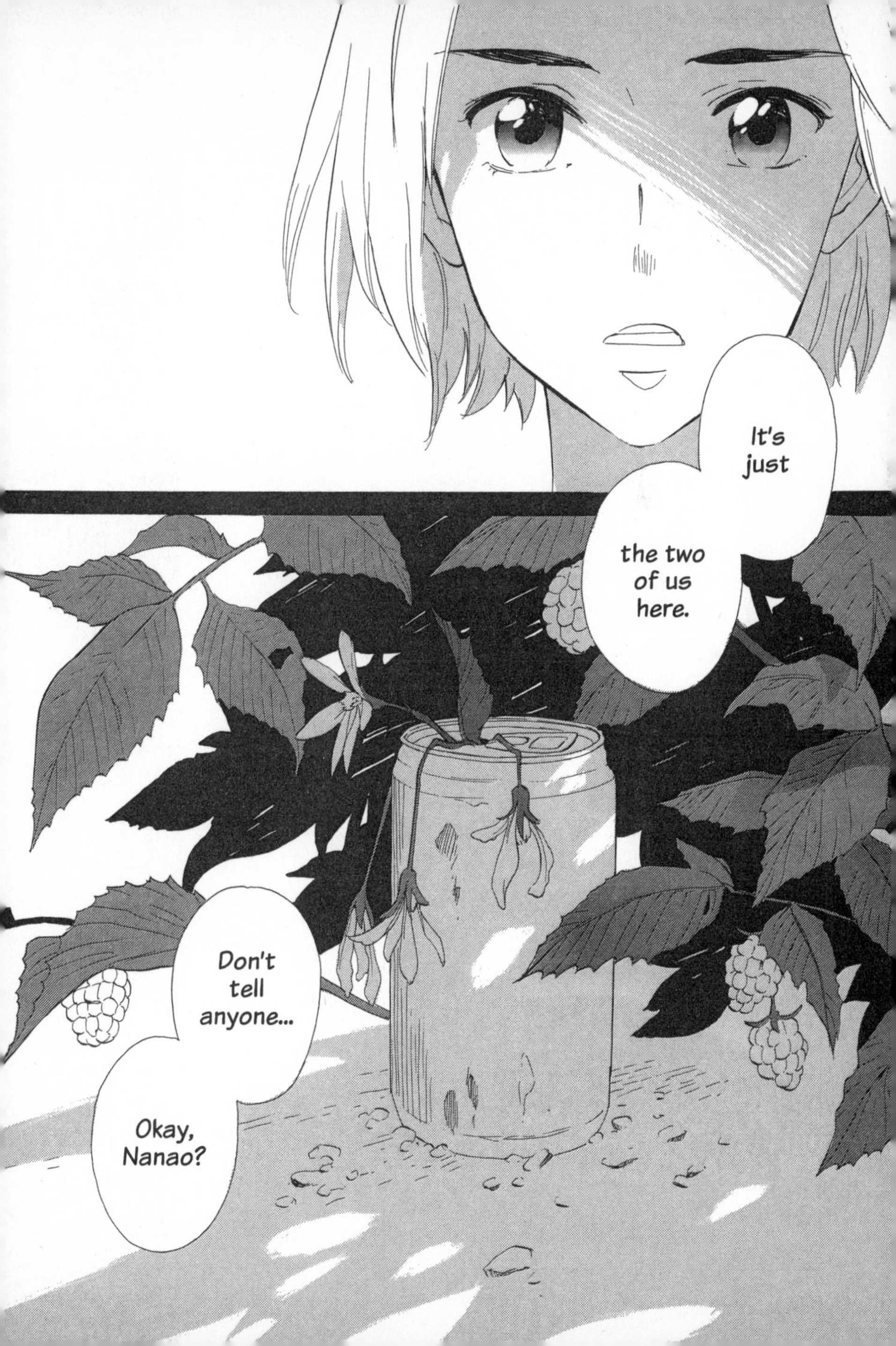
It's just
the two of us here.
Don't tell anyone...
Okay, Nanao?

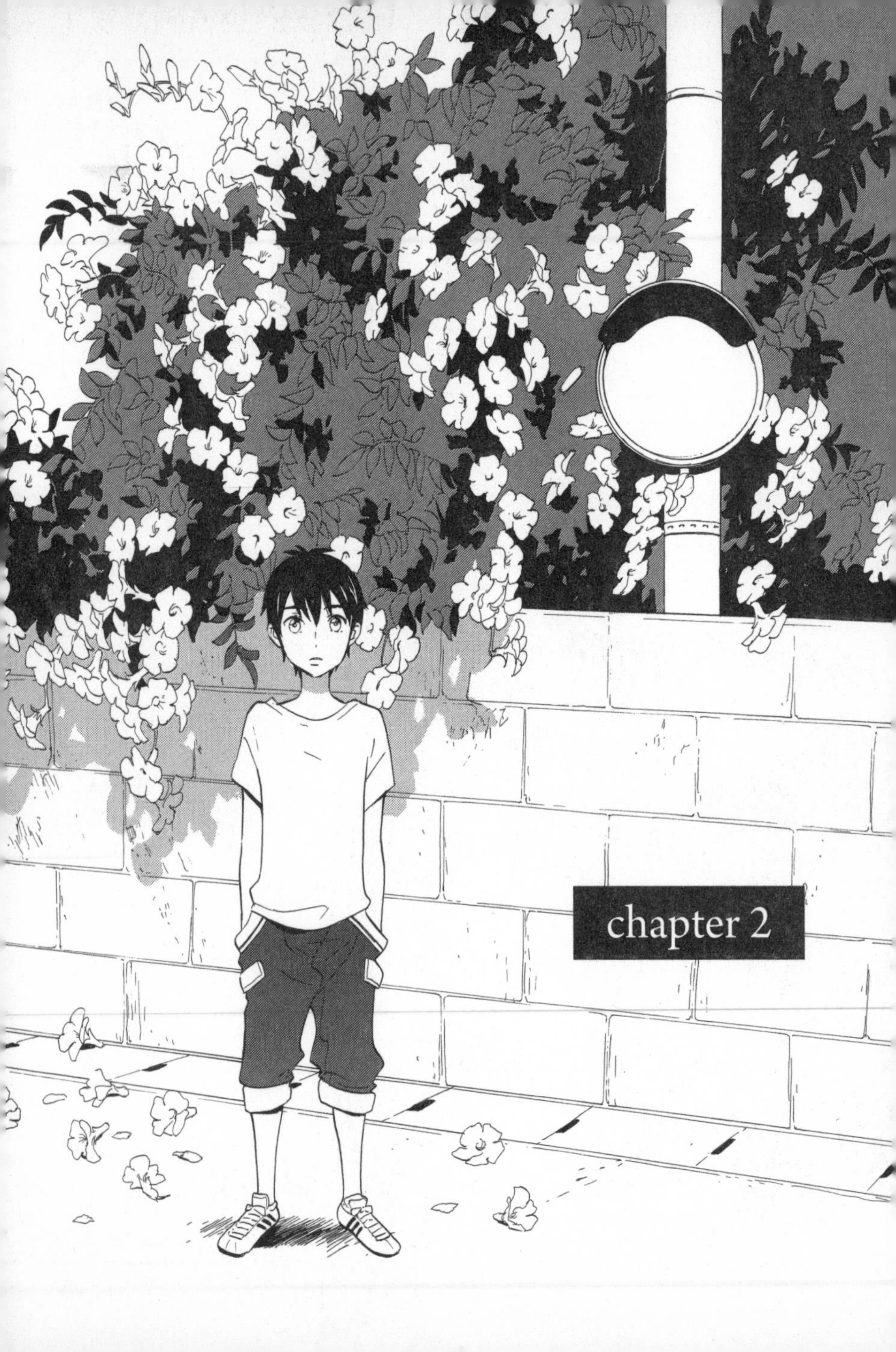
chapter 2

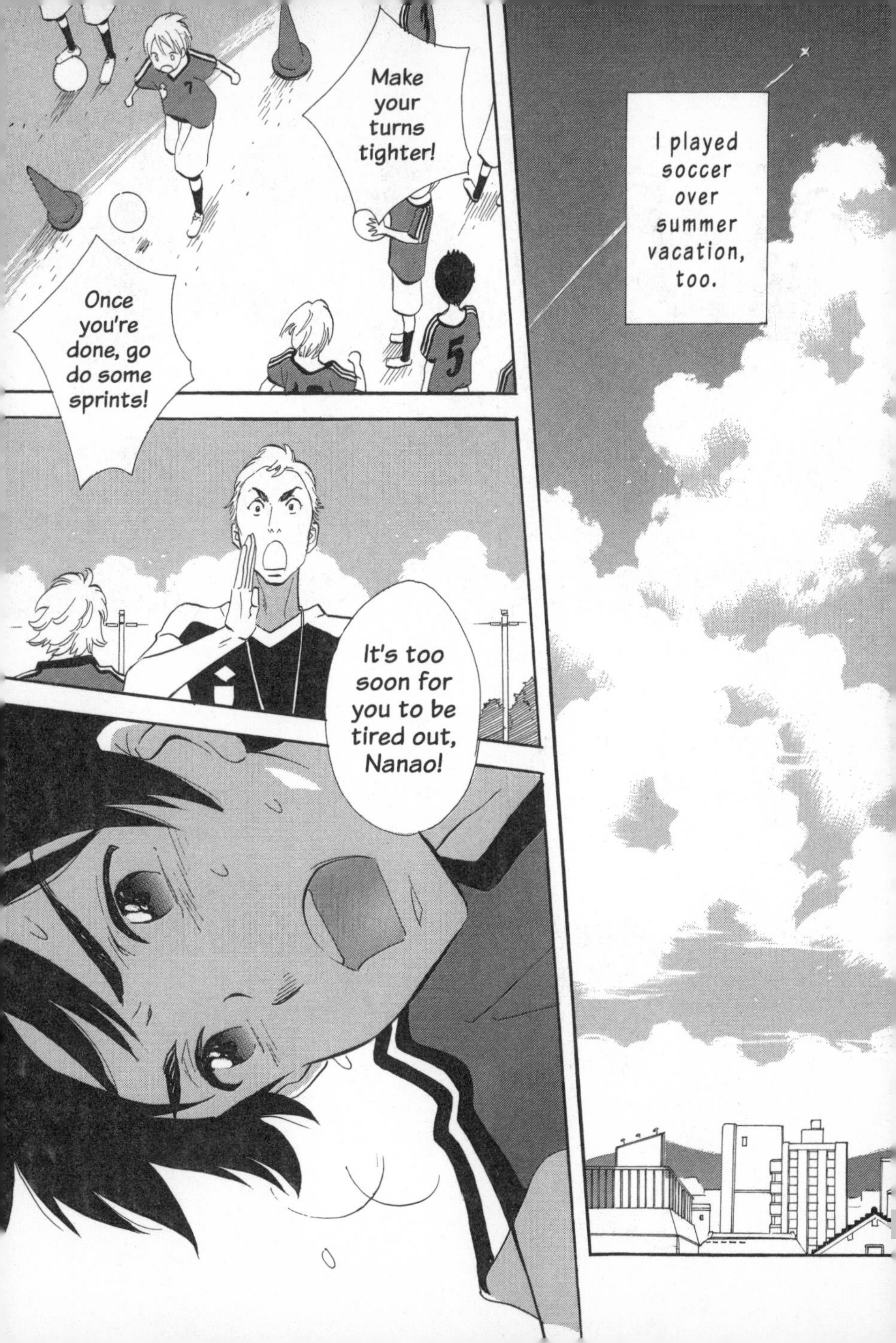
I played soccer over summer vacation, too.
Make your turns tighter!
Once you're done, go do some sprints!
It's too soon for you to be tired out, Nanao!

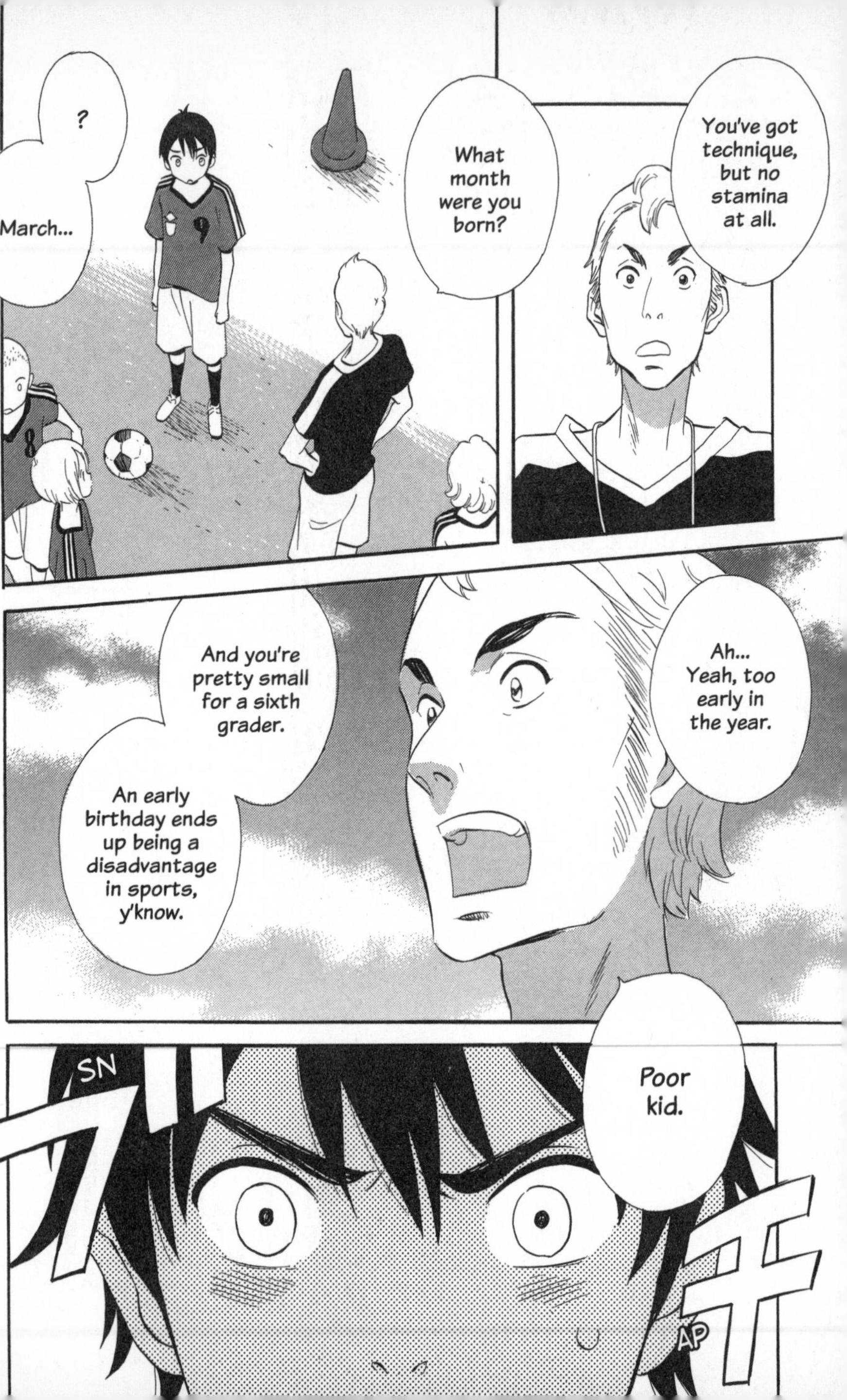
You've got technique, but no stamina at all.
What month were you born?
?
March...
Ah... Yeah, too early in the year.
And you're pretty small for a sixth grader.
An early birthday ends up being a disadvantage in sports, y'know.
Poor kid.
SN
AP

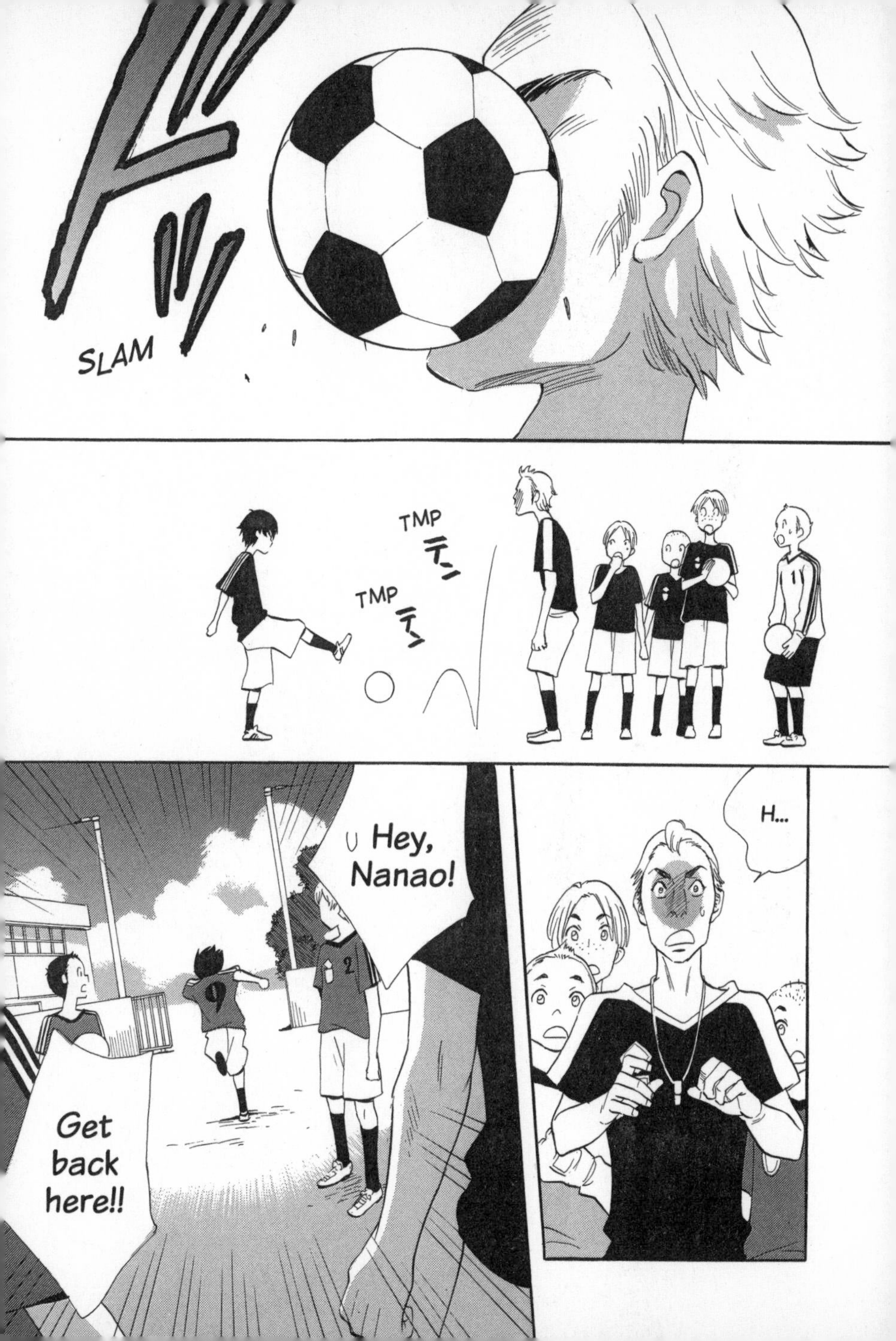
SLAM
TMP テン
TMP テン
H...
Hey, Nanao!
Get back here!!

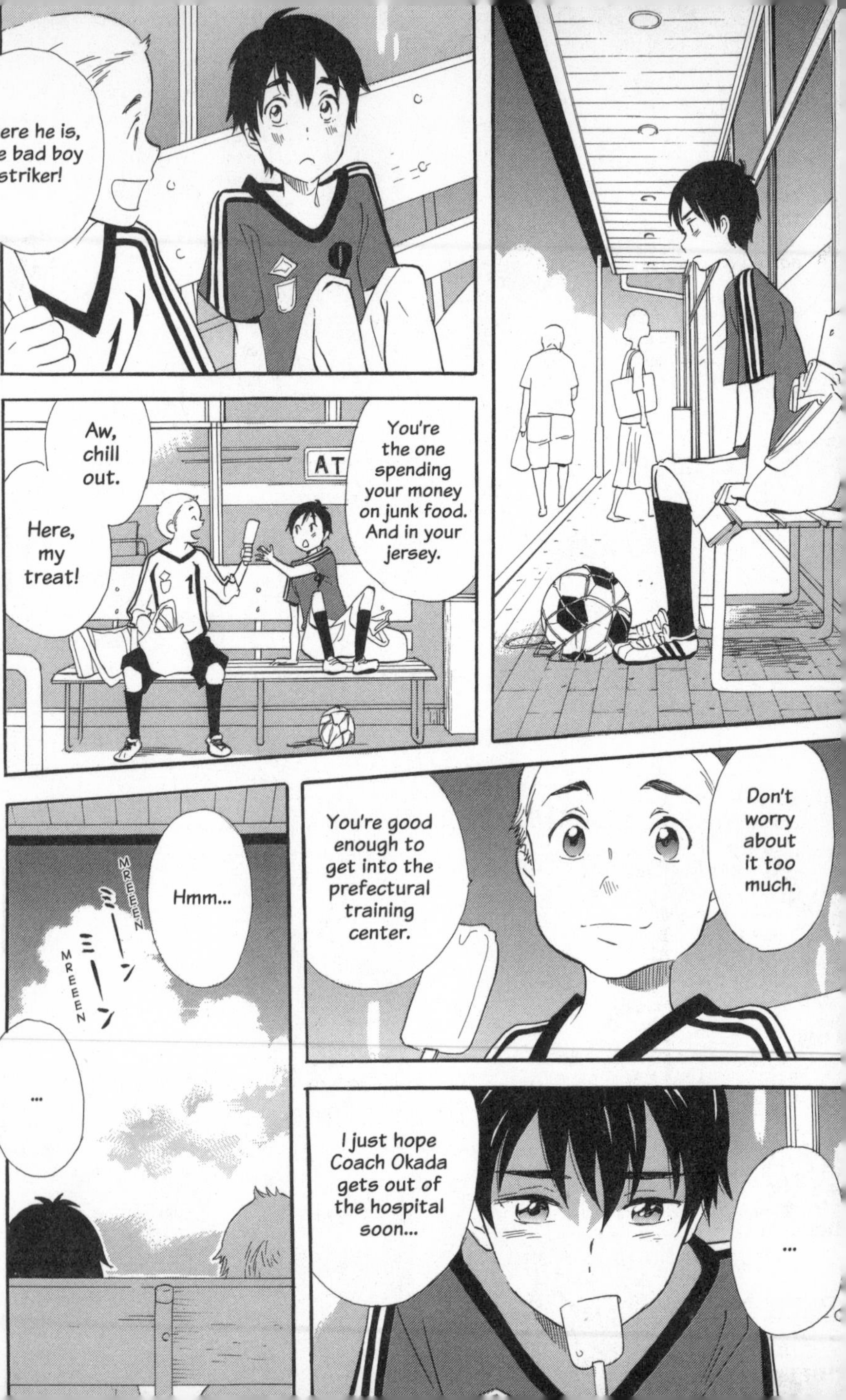
There he is, the bad boy striker!
You're the one spending your money on junk food. And in your jersey.
Aw, chill out.
Here, my treat!
Don't worry about it too much.
You're good enough to get into the prefectural training center.
I just hope Coach Okada gets out of the hospital soon...
...
Hmm...
MREEEN
MREEEN
...

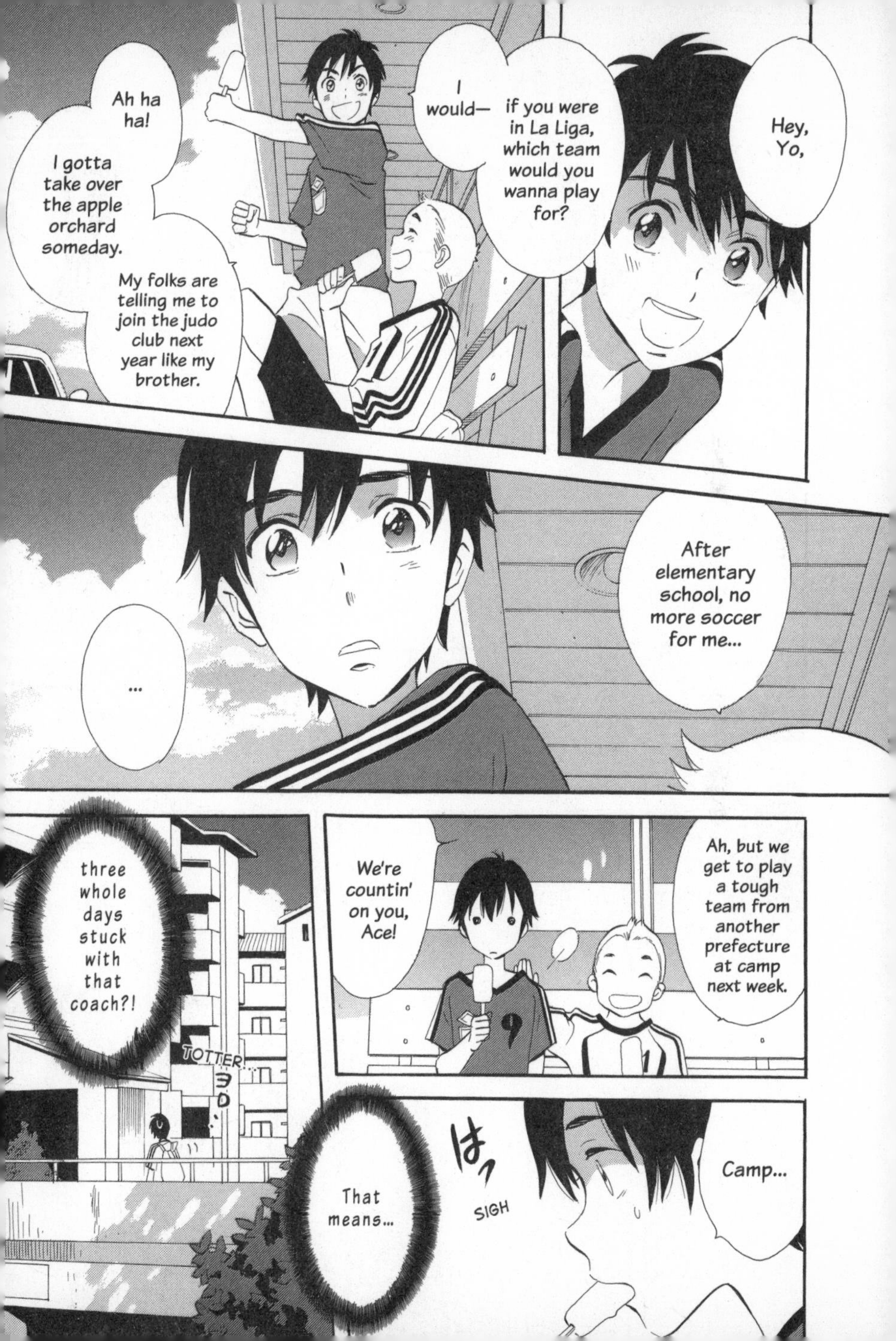
Hey, Yo,
if you were in La Liga, which team would you wanna play for?
I would—
Ah ha ha!
I gotta take over the apple orchard someday.
My folks are telling me to join the judo club next year like my brother.
After elementary school, no more soccer for me...
...
Ah, but we get to play a tough team from another prefecture at camp next week.
We're countin' on you, Ace!
Camp...
はっ
SIGH
That means...
three whole days stuck with that coach?!
TOTTER...

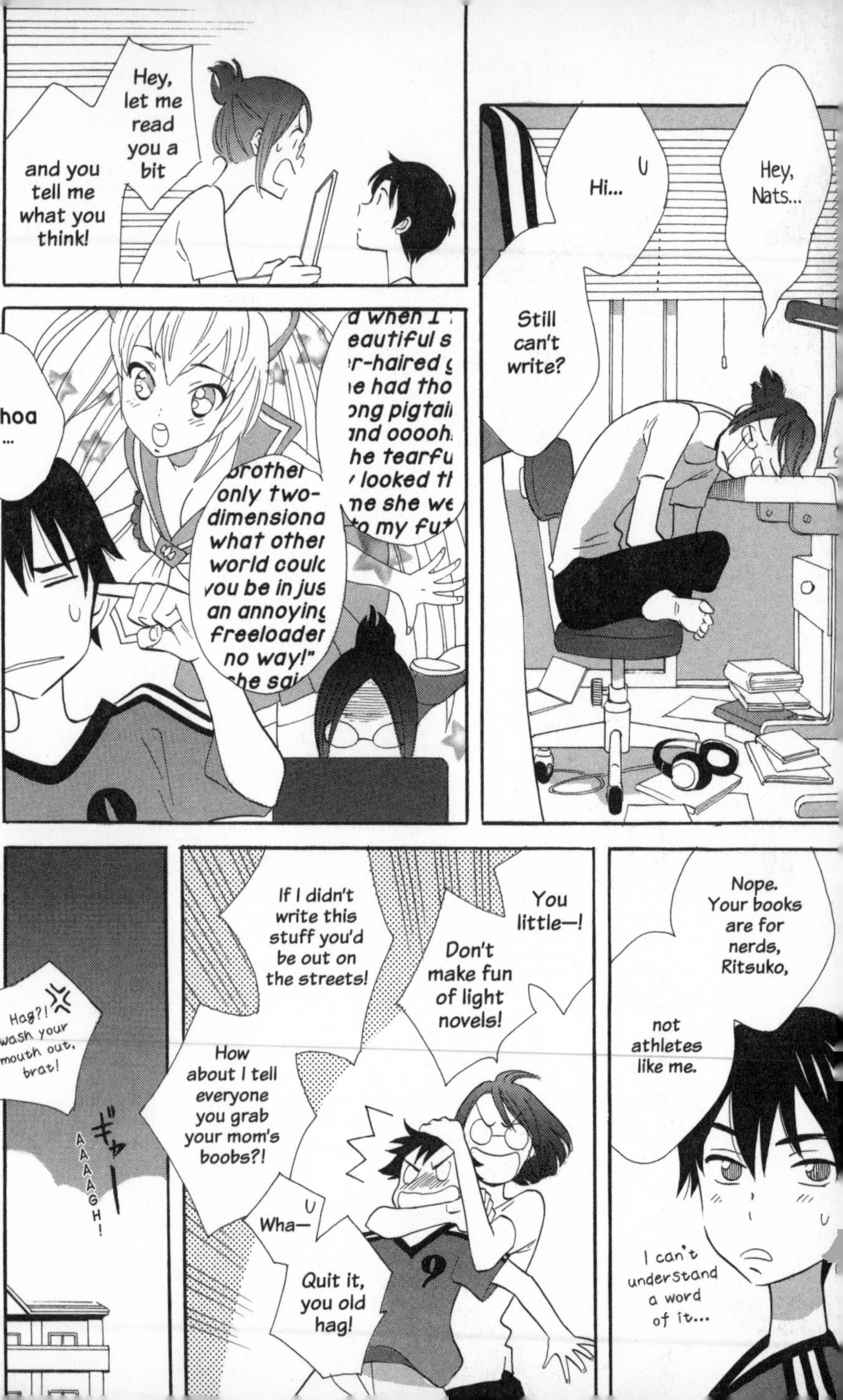
Hey, Nats...
Hi...
Still can't write?
Hey, let me read you a bit
and you tell me what you think!
d when I beautiful s r-haired g e had tho ong pigtai and ooooh. he tearfu looked th me she we to my fut
brother only two-dimensiona what other world coulc you be in jus an annoying freeloader no way!" she sai
Whoa...
Nope. Your books are for nerds, Ritsuko,
not athletes like me.
I can't understand a word of it...
You little—!
Don't make fun of light novels!
If I didn't write this stuff you'd be out on the streets!
How about I tell everyone you grab your mom's boobs?!
Wha—
Quit it, you old hag!
Hag?! wash your mouth out, brat!
ギャー
AAAAGH!

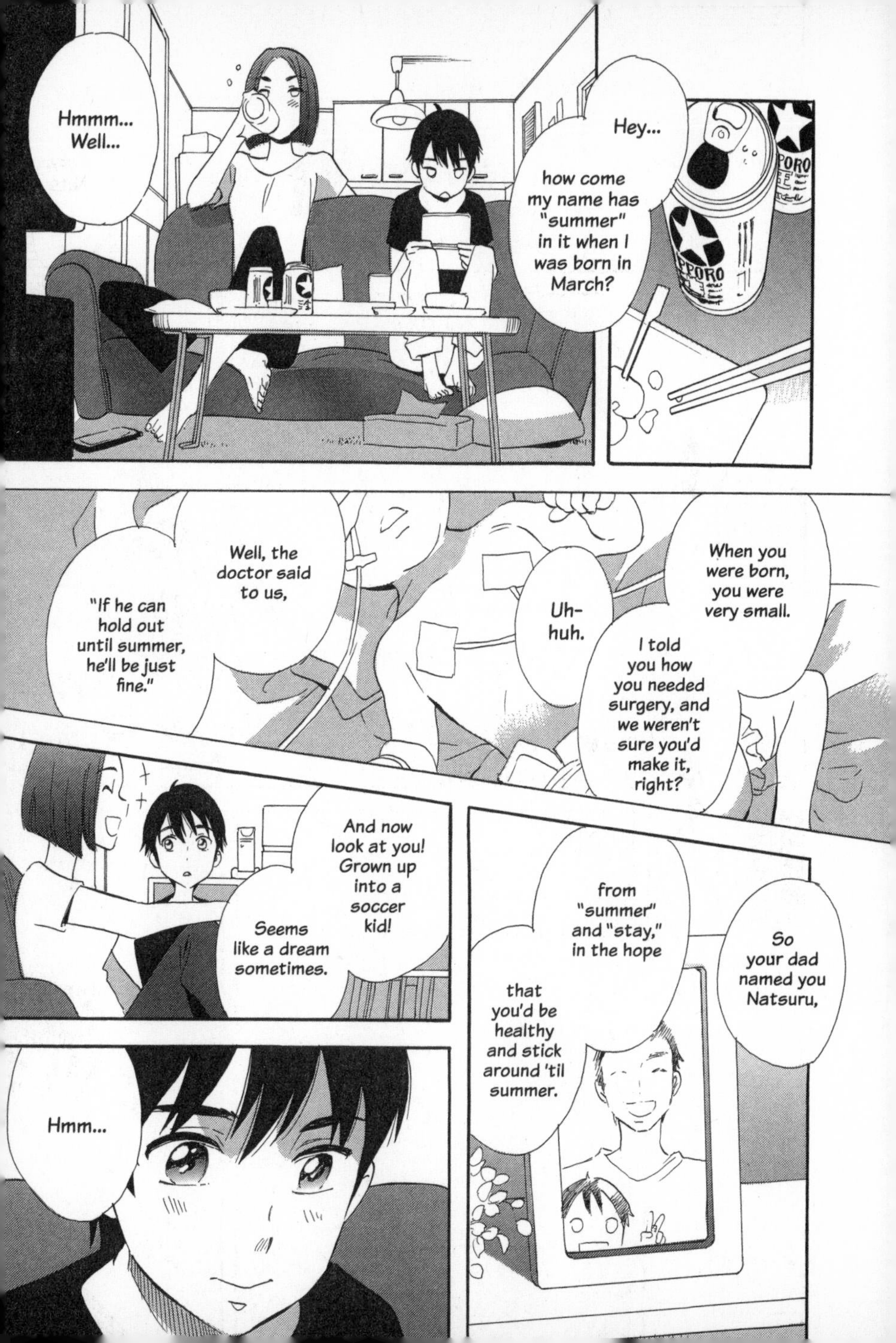
Hey...
how come my name has "summer" in it when I was born in March?
Hmmm... Well...
When you were born, you were very small.
I told you how you needed surgery, and we weren't sure you'd make it, right?
Uh-huh.
Well, the doctor said to us,
"If he can hold out until summer, he'll be just fine."
So your dad named you Natsuru,
from "summer" and "stay," in the hope
that you'd be healthy and stick around 'til summer.
And now look at you! Grown up into a soccer kid!
Seems like a dream sometimes.
Hmm...

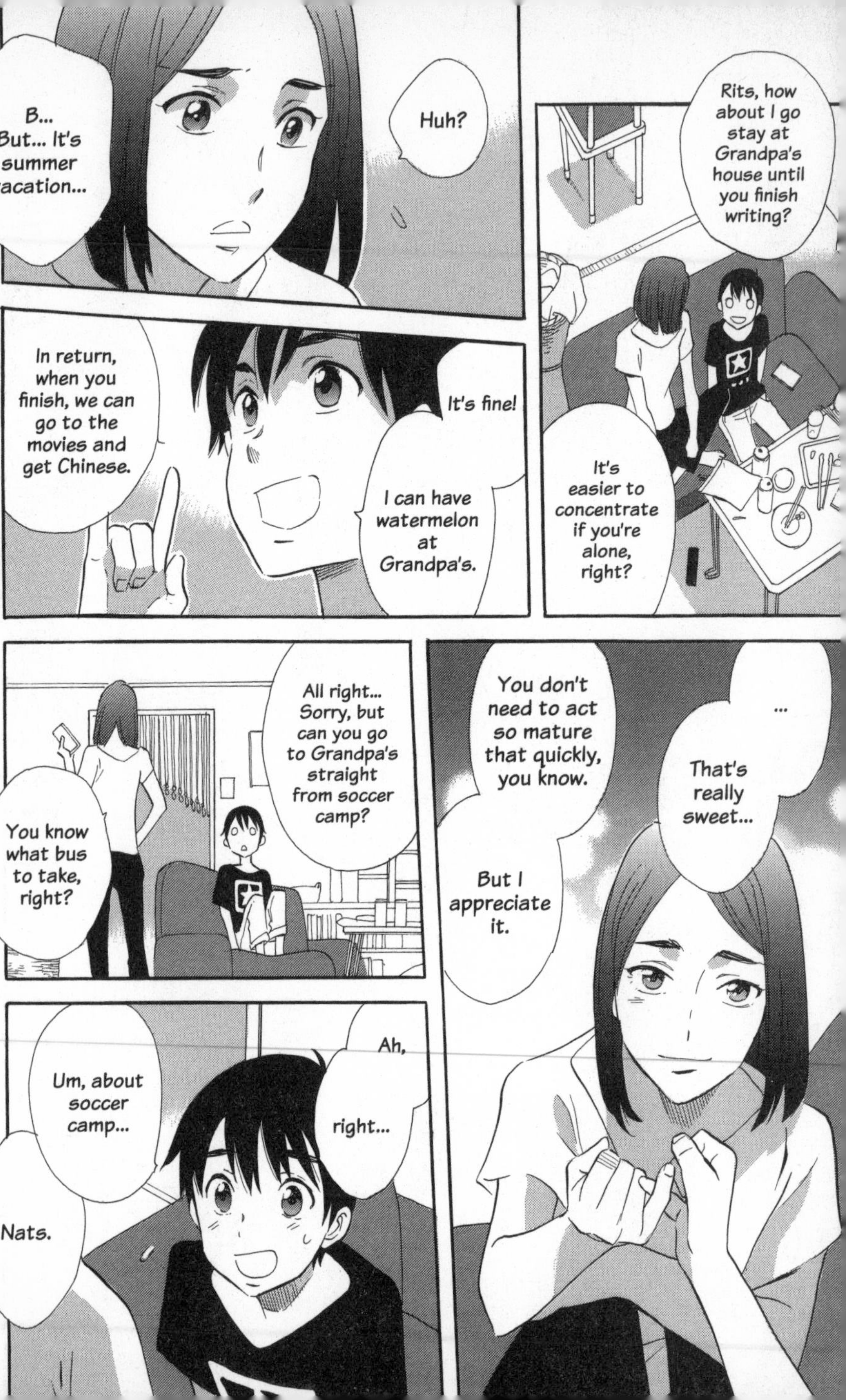
Rits, how about I go stay at Grandpa's house until you finish writing?
It's easier to concentrate if you're alone, right?
Huh?
B... But... It's summer vacation...
It's fine!
I can have watermelon at Grandpa's.
In return, when you finish, we can go to the movies and get Chinese.
...
That's really sweet...
You don't need to act so mature that quickly, you know.
But I appreciate it.
All right... Sorry, but can you go to Grandpa's straight from soccer camp?
You know what bus to take, right?
Ah,
right...
Um, about soccer camp...
Nats.

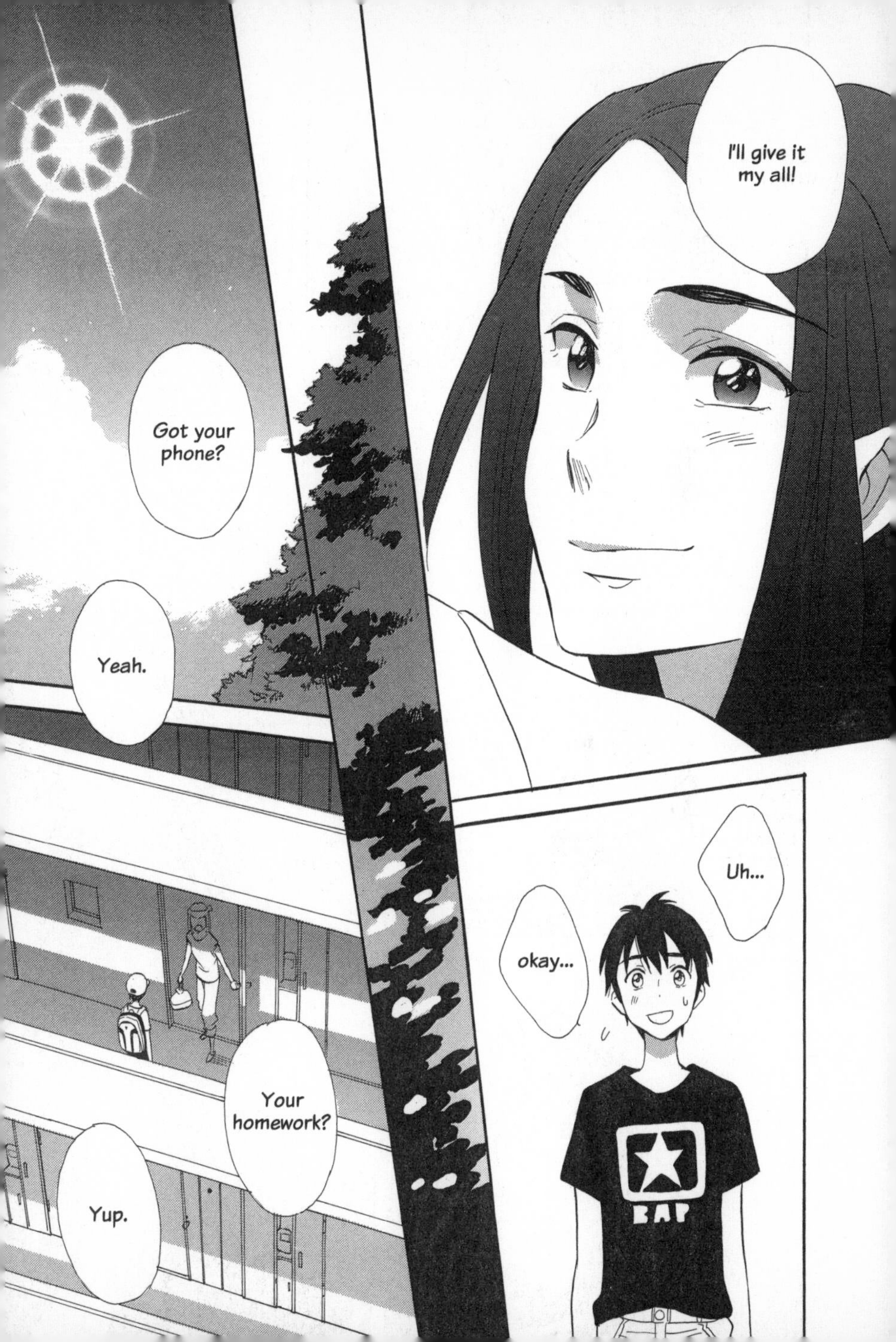
I'll give it my all!
Uh...
okay...
Got your phone?
Yeah.
Your homework?
Yup.

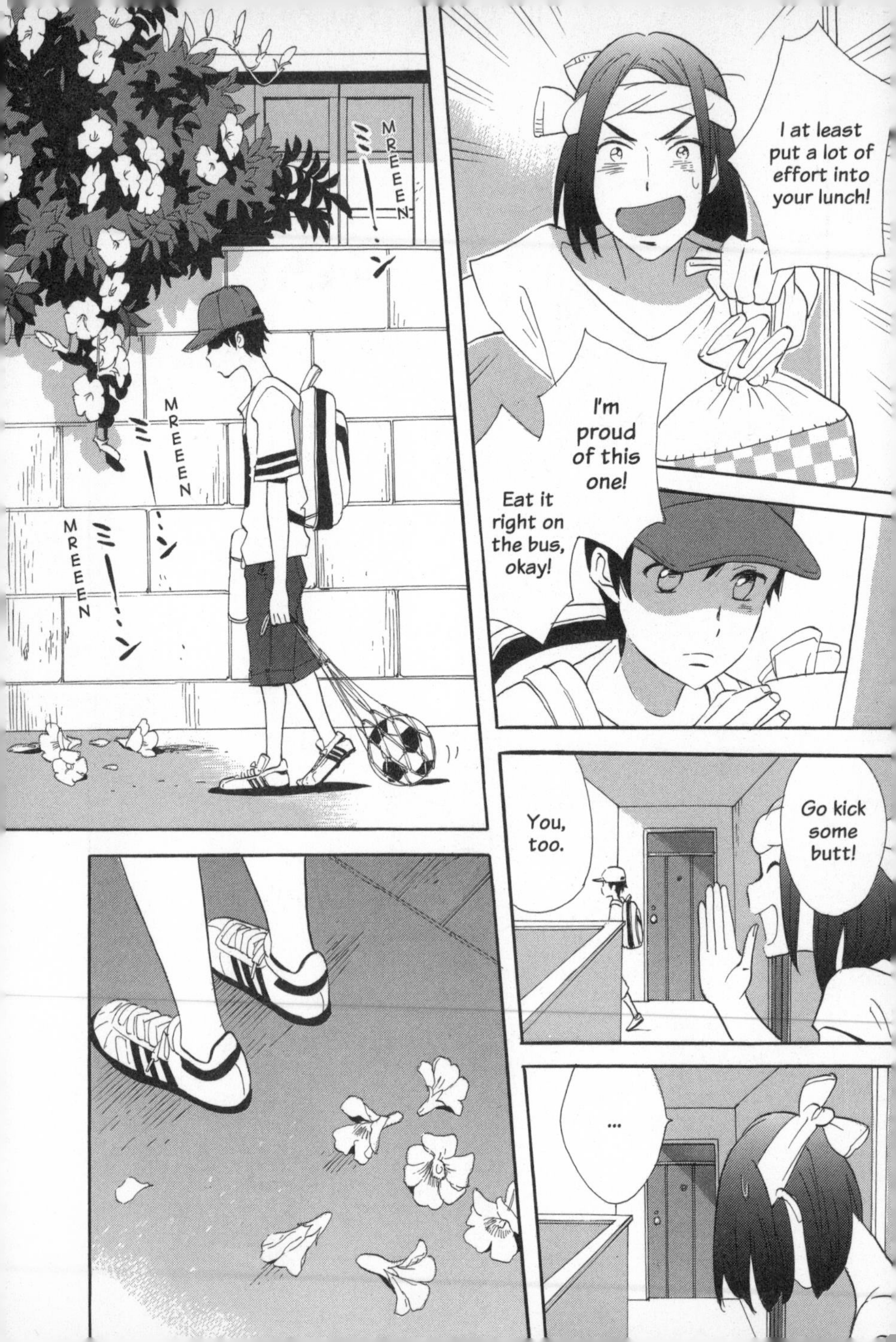
I at least put a lot of effort into your lunch!
I'm proud of this one!
Eat it right on the bus, okay!
Go kick some butt!
You, too.
...
MREEEN
MREEEN
MREEEN

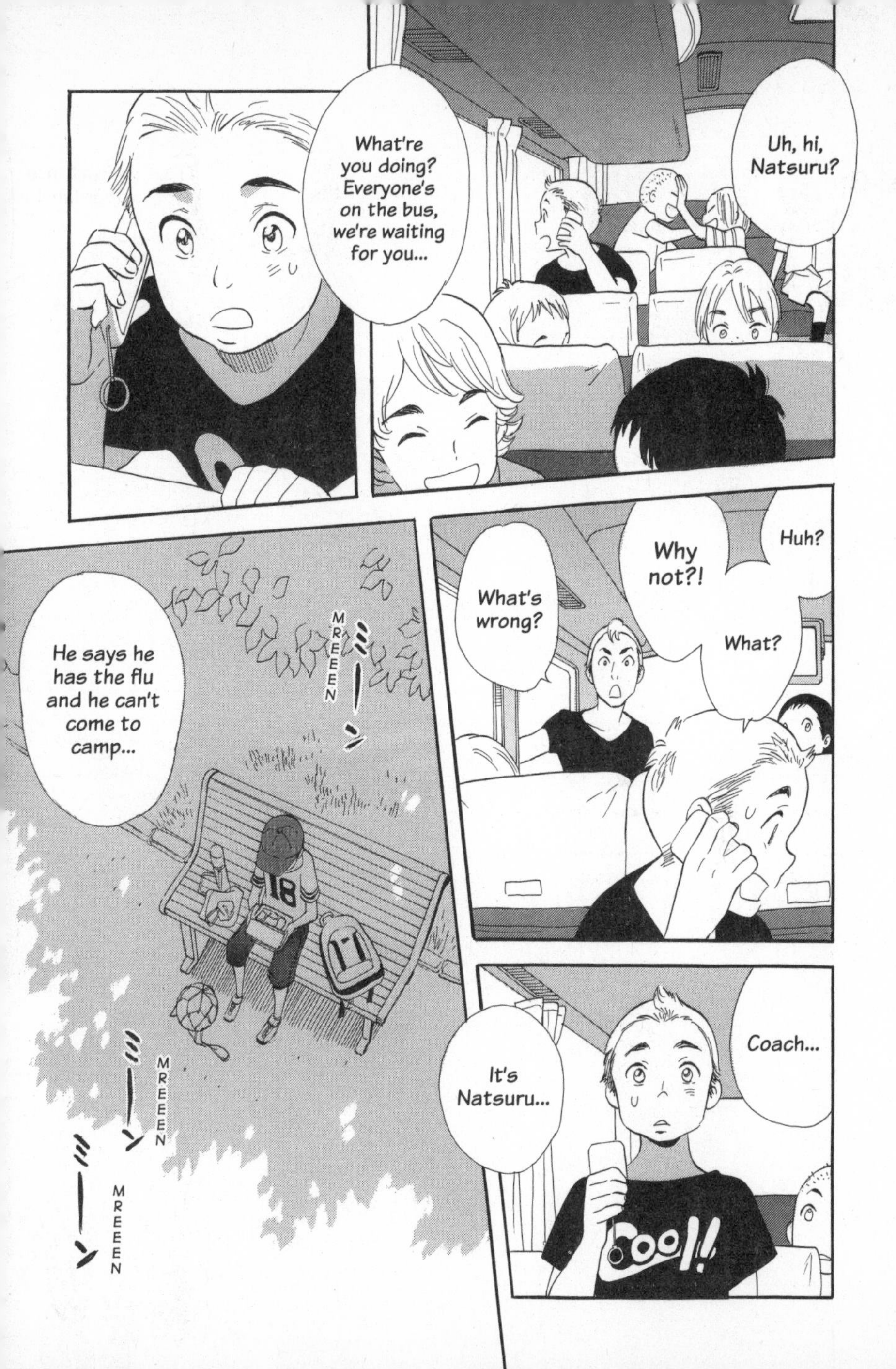
Uh, hi, Natsuru?
What're you doing? Everyone's on the bus, we're waiting for you...
Huh?
Why not?!
What?
What's wrong?
Coach...
It's Natsuru...
He says he has the flu and he can't come to camp...
MREEEN
MREEEN
MREEEN

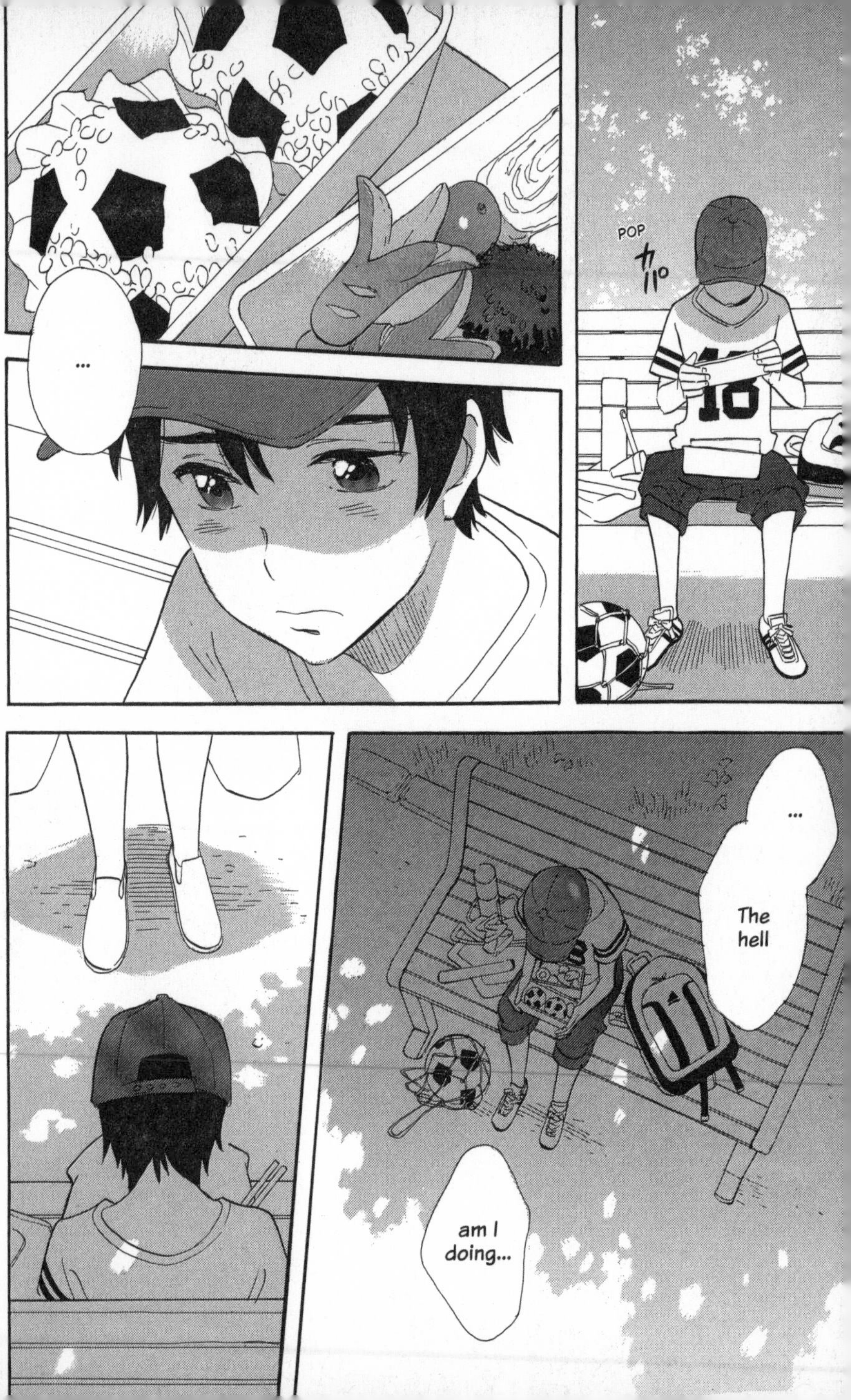
POP
...
...
The hell
am I doing...

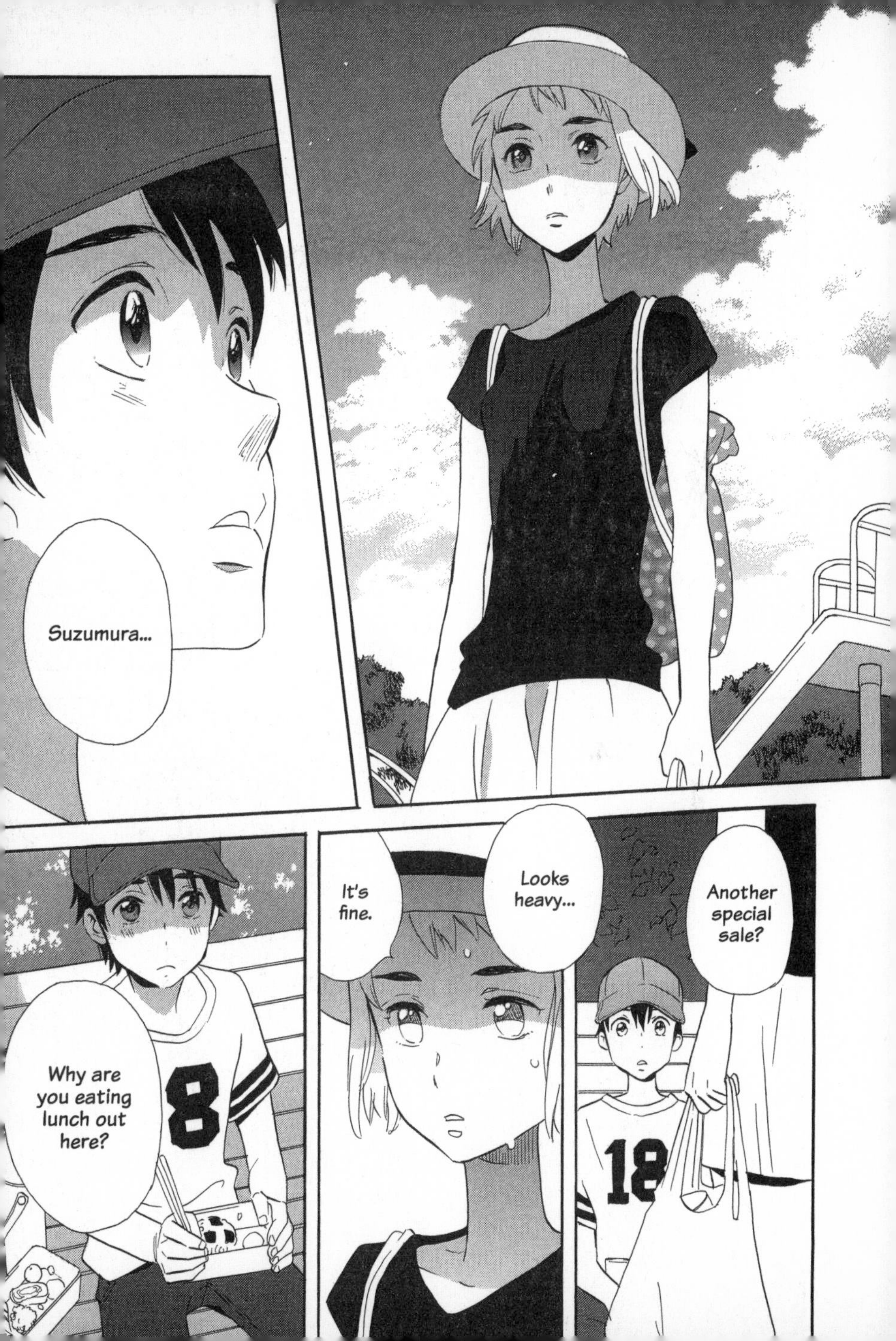
Suzumura...
Another special sale?
Looks heavy...
It's fine.
Why are you eating lunch out here?

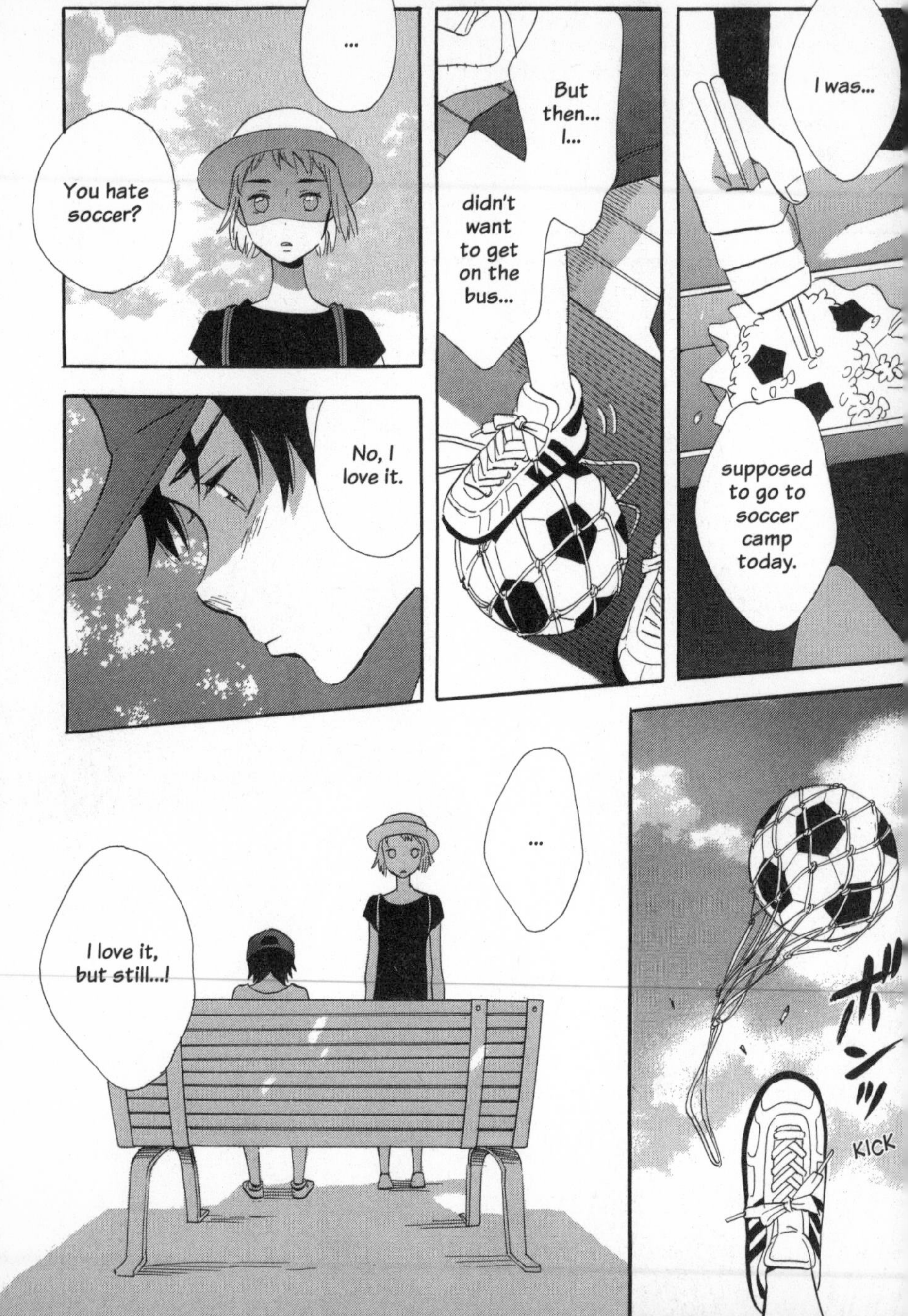

I was...
supposed to go to soccer camp today.
But then... I...
didn't want to get on the bus...
...
You hate soccer?
No, I love it.
ボンッ
KICK
...
I love it, but still...!

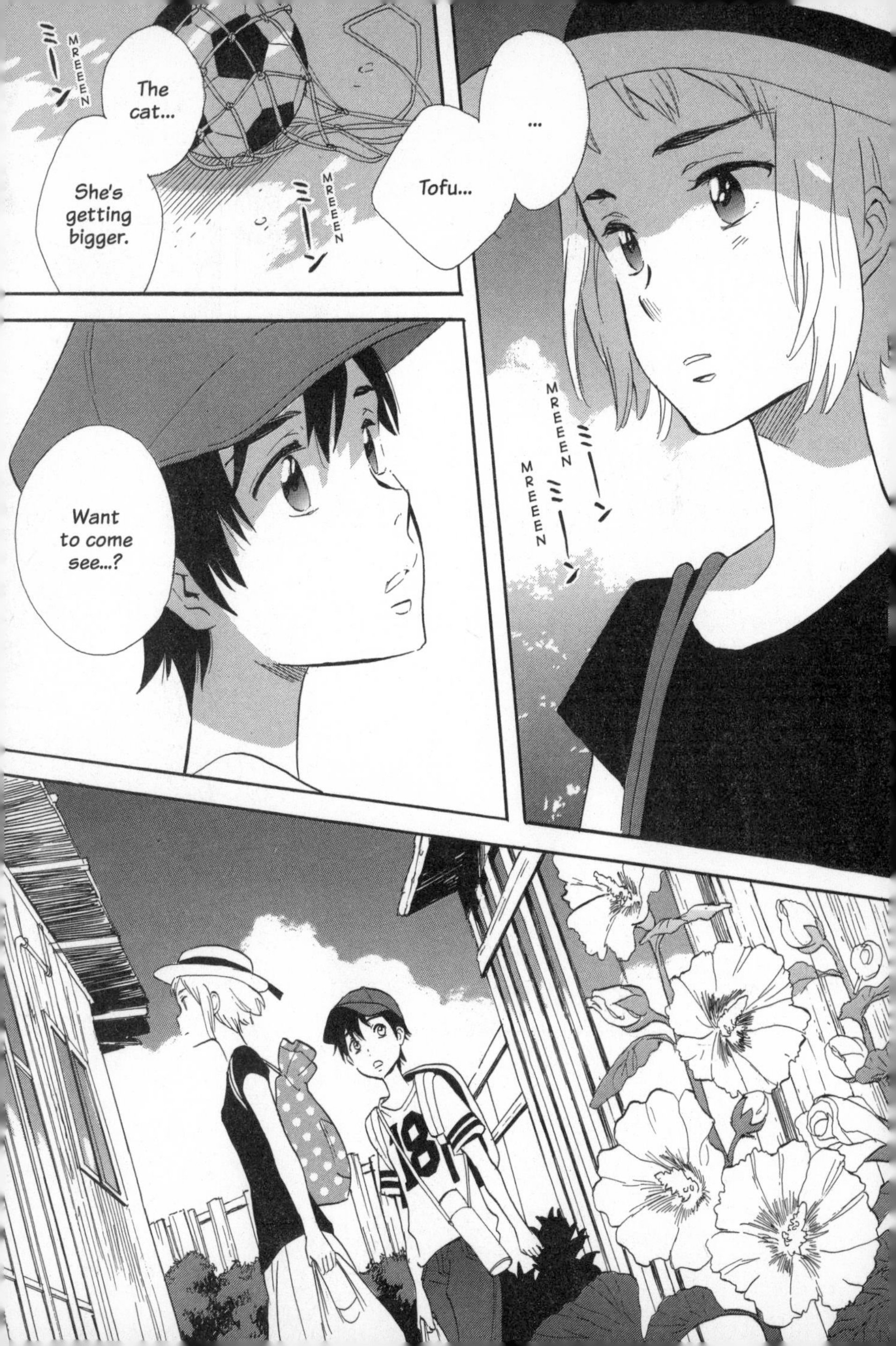
...
Tofu...
MREEEN
MREEEN
The cat...
MREEEN
She's getting bigger.
MREEEN
Want to come see...?

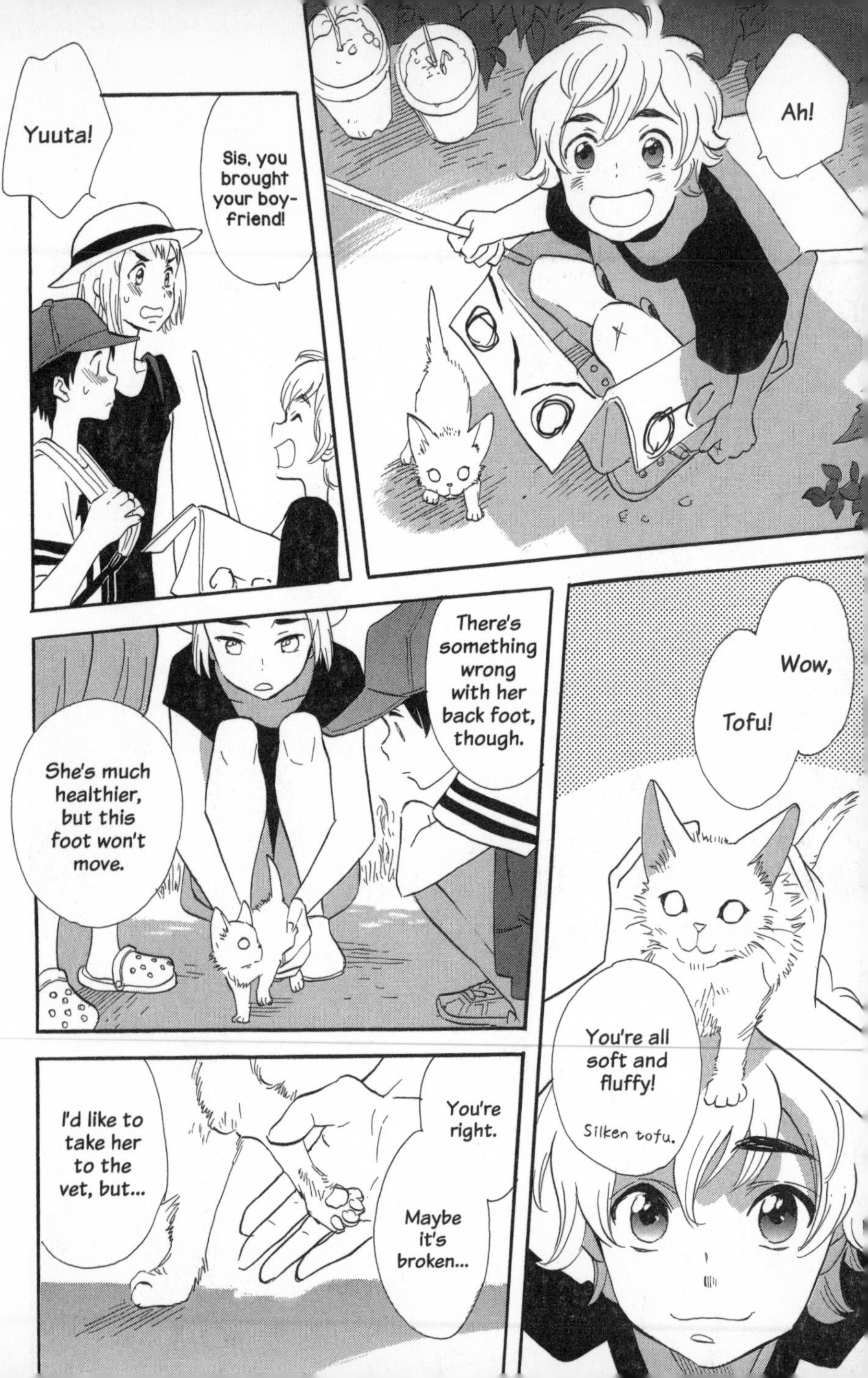
Ah!
Sis, you brought your boy-friend!
Yuuta!
Wow, Tofu!
You're all soft and fluffy!
Silken tofu.
There's something wrong with her back foot, though.
She's much healthier, but this foot won't move.
You're right.
Maybe it's broken...
I'd like to take her to the vet, but...

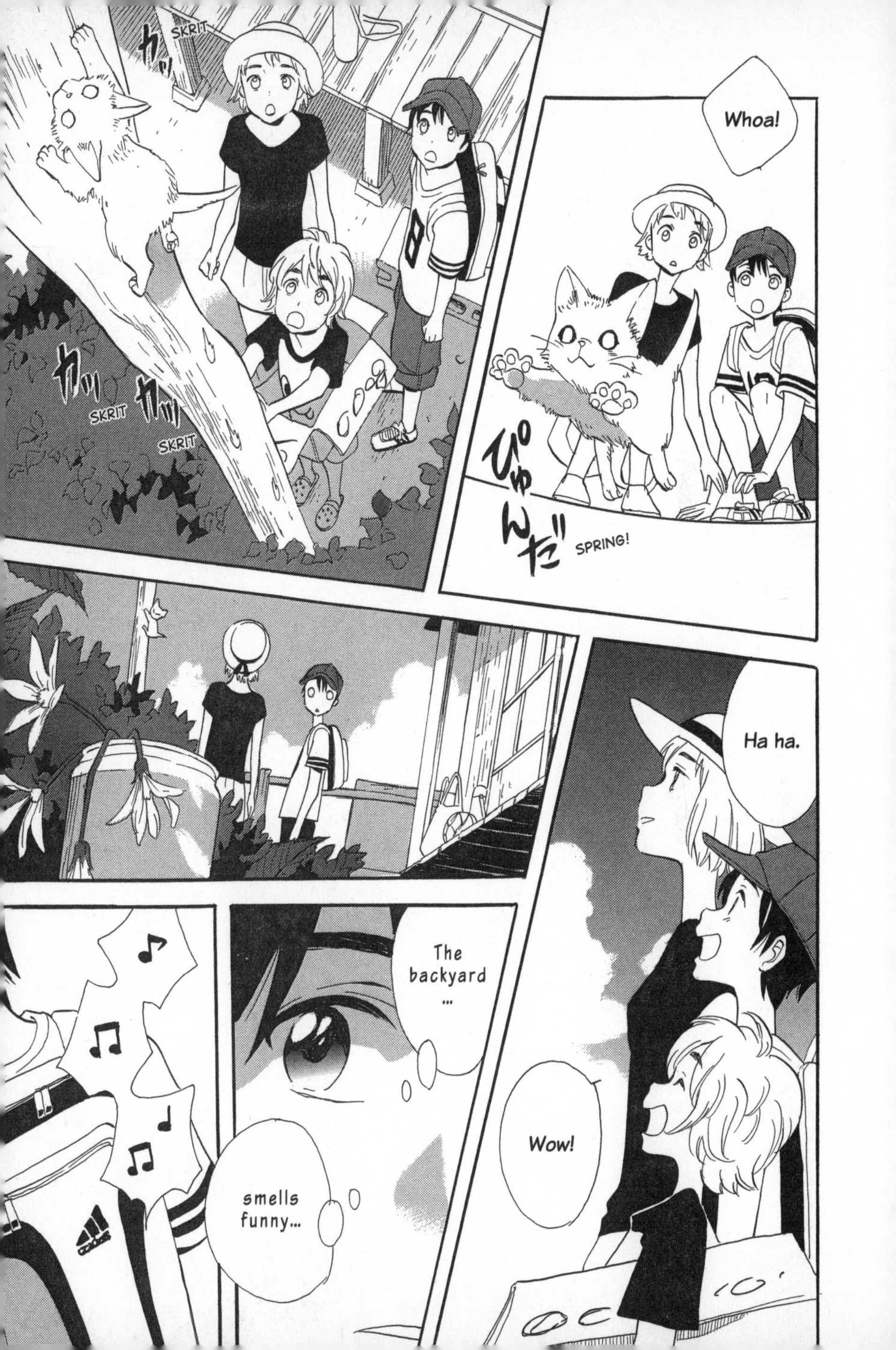

Whoa!
ぴゅんだ
SPRING!
カッ
SKRIT
カッ
SKRIT
カッ
SKRIT
Ha ha.
Wow!
The backyard ...
smells funny...

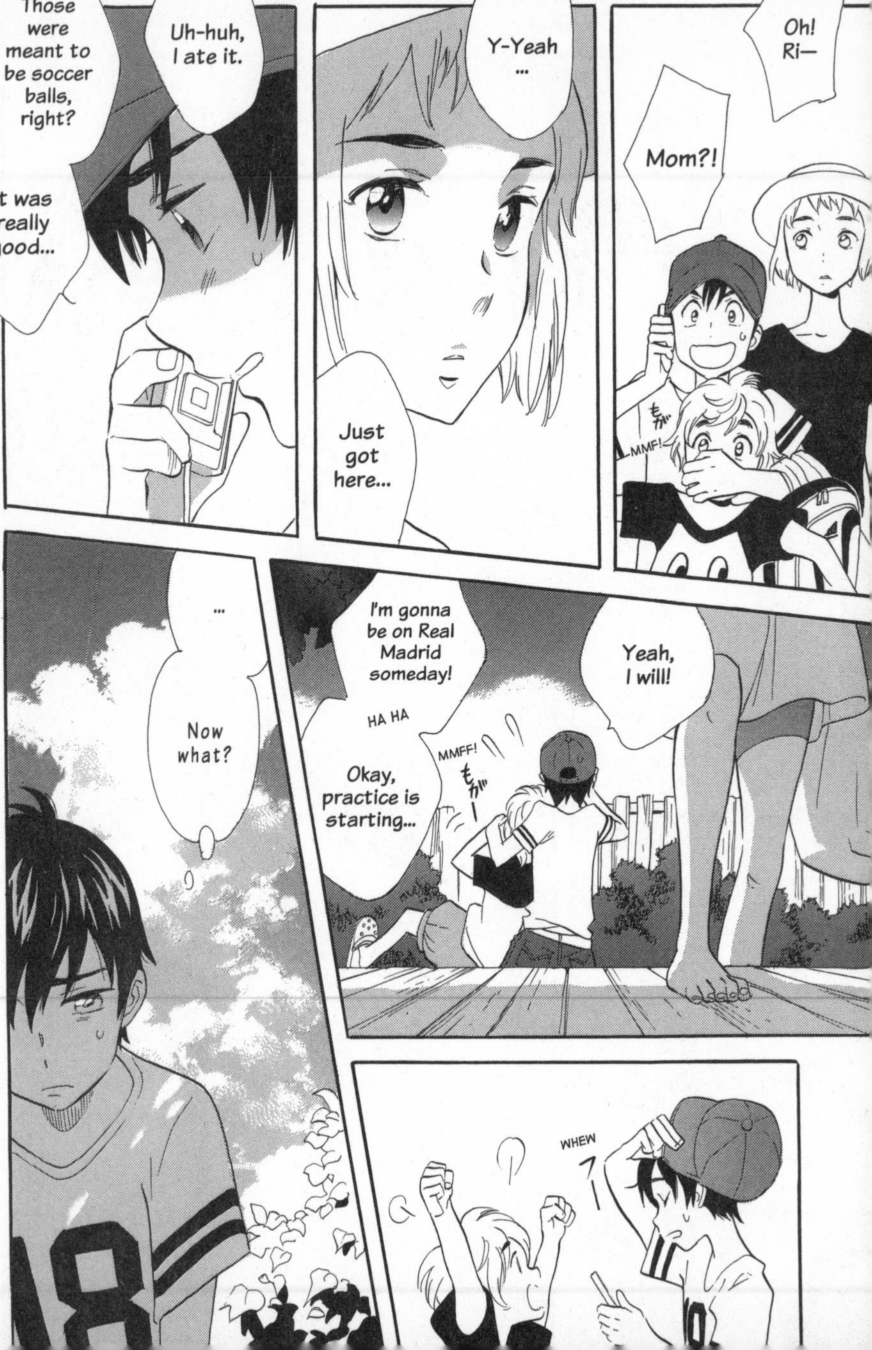

Oh! Ri—
Mom?!
MMF!
Y-Yeah ...
Just got here...
Uh-huh, I ate it.
Those were meant to be soccer balls, right?
It was really good...
Yeah, I will!
I'm gonna be on Real Madrid someday!
HA HA
MMFF!
Okay, practice is starting...
WHEW
...
Now what?

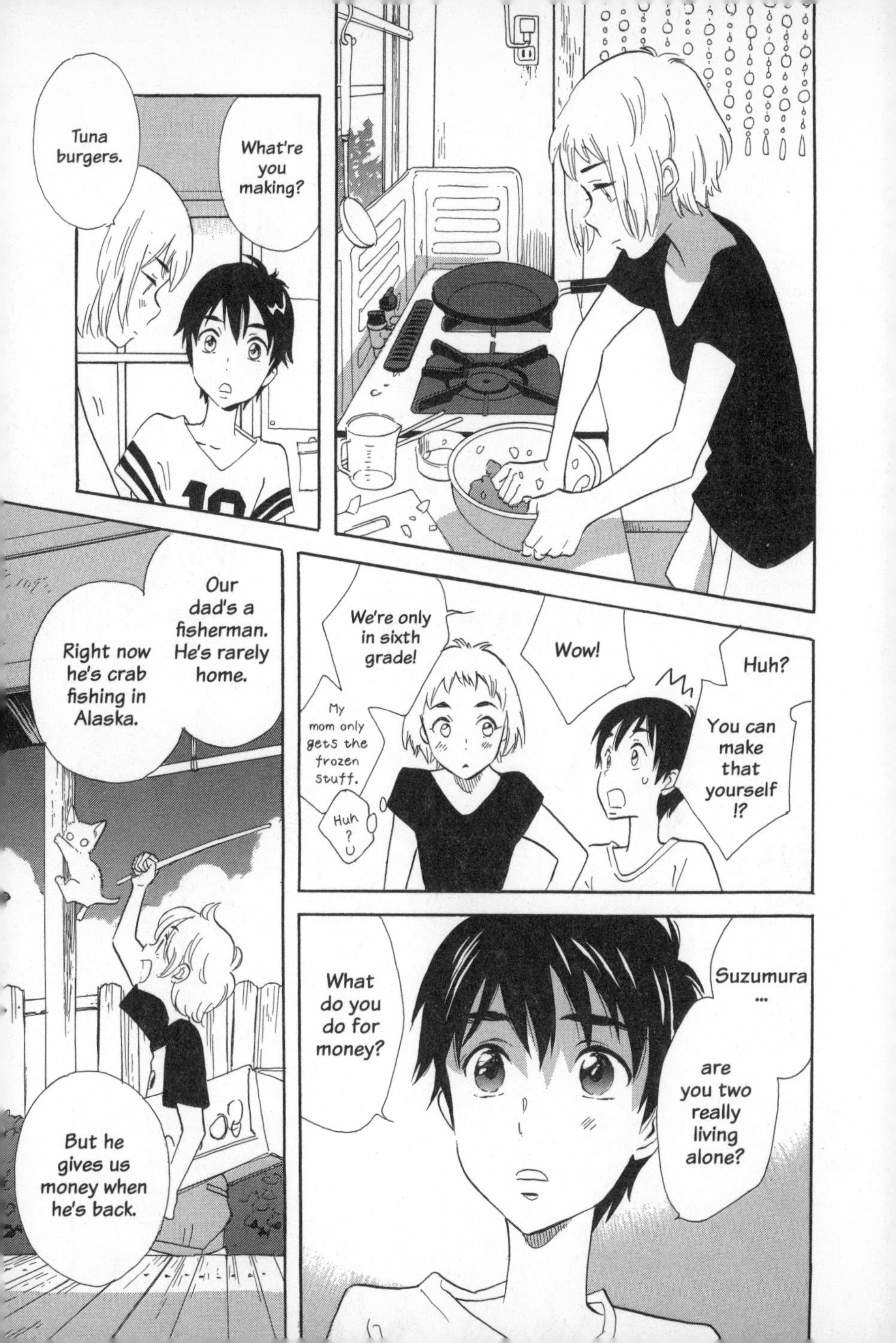

What're you making?
Tuna burgers.
Huh?
You can make that yourself!?
Wow!
We're only in sixth grade!
My mom only gets the frozen stuff.
Huh?
Suzumura...
are you two really living alone?
What do you do for money?
Our dad's a fisherman. He's rarely home.
Right now he's crab fishing in Alaska.
But he gives us money when he's back.

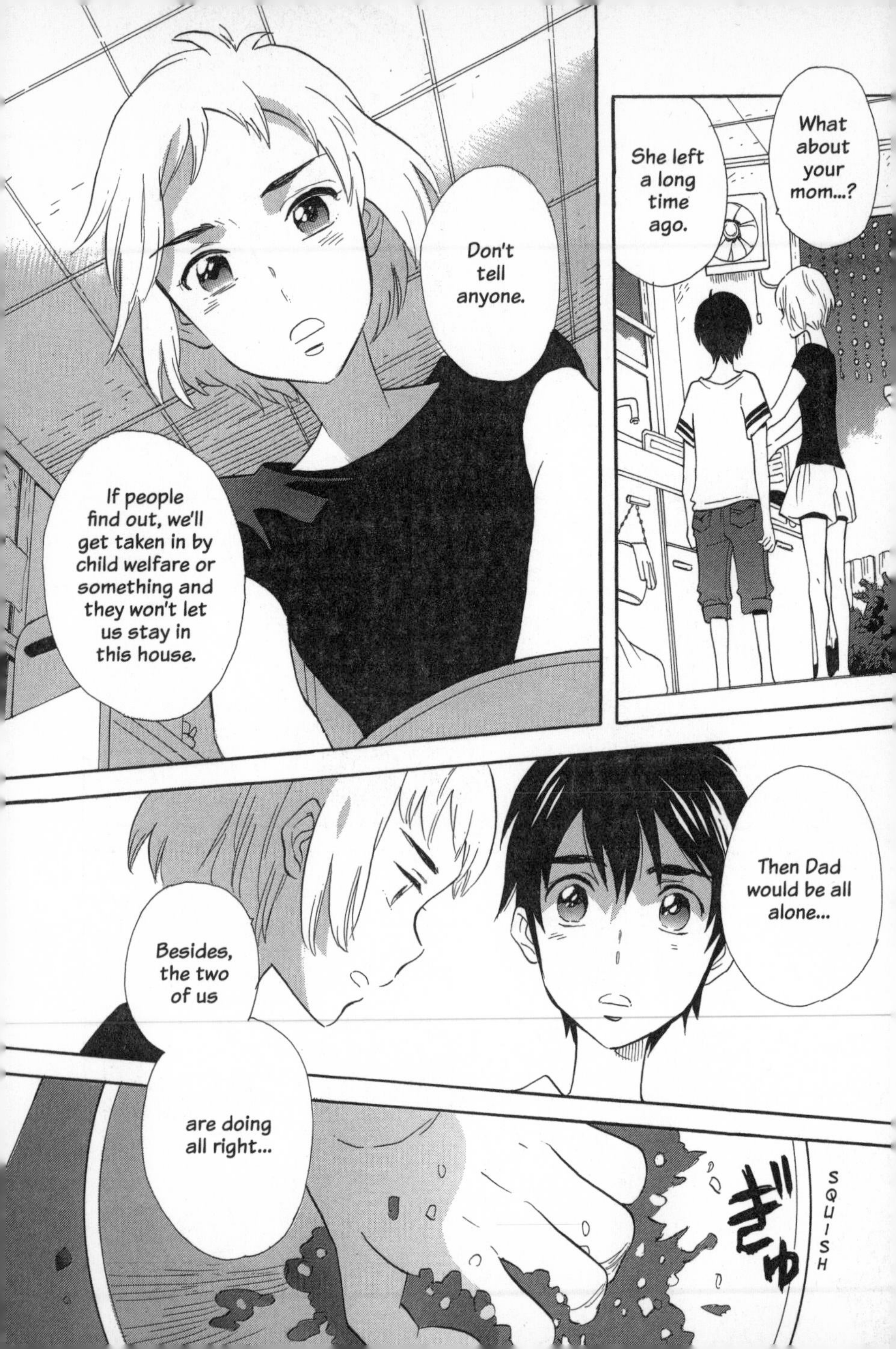
What about your mom...?
She left a long time ago.
Don't tell anyone.
If people find out, we'll get taken in by child welfare or something and they won't let us stay in this house.
Then Dad would be all alone...
Besides, the two of us
are doing all right...
ぎゅ
SQUISH

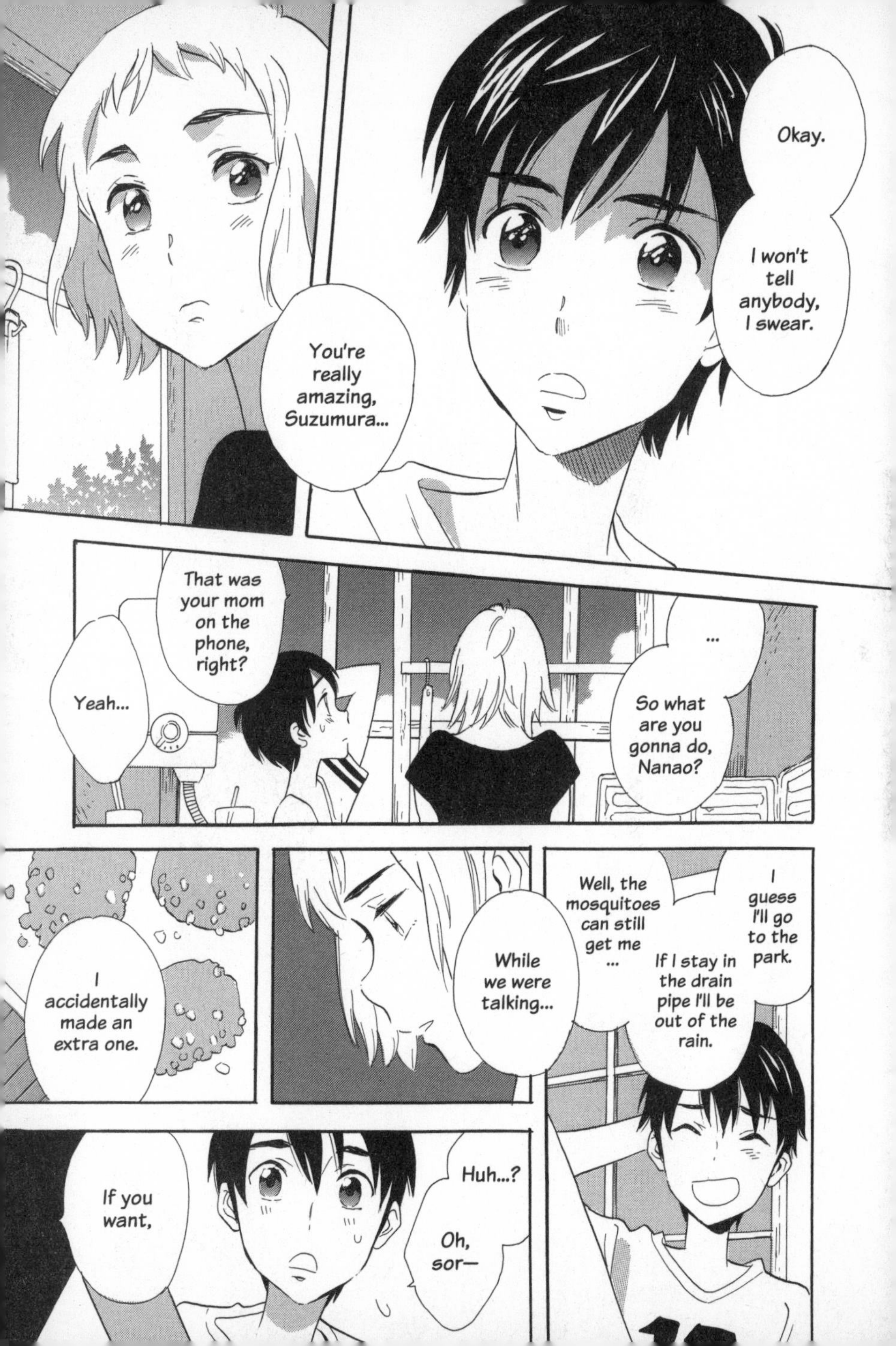

Okay.
I won't tell anybody, I swear.
You're really amazing, Suzumura...
That was your mom on the phone, right?
Yeah...
...
So what are you gonna do, Nanao?
I guess I'll go to the park.
If I stay in the drain pipe I'll be out of the rain.
Well, the mosquitoes can still get me ...
While we were talking...
I accidentally made an extra one.
Huh...?
Oh, sor—
If you want,

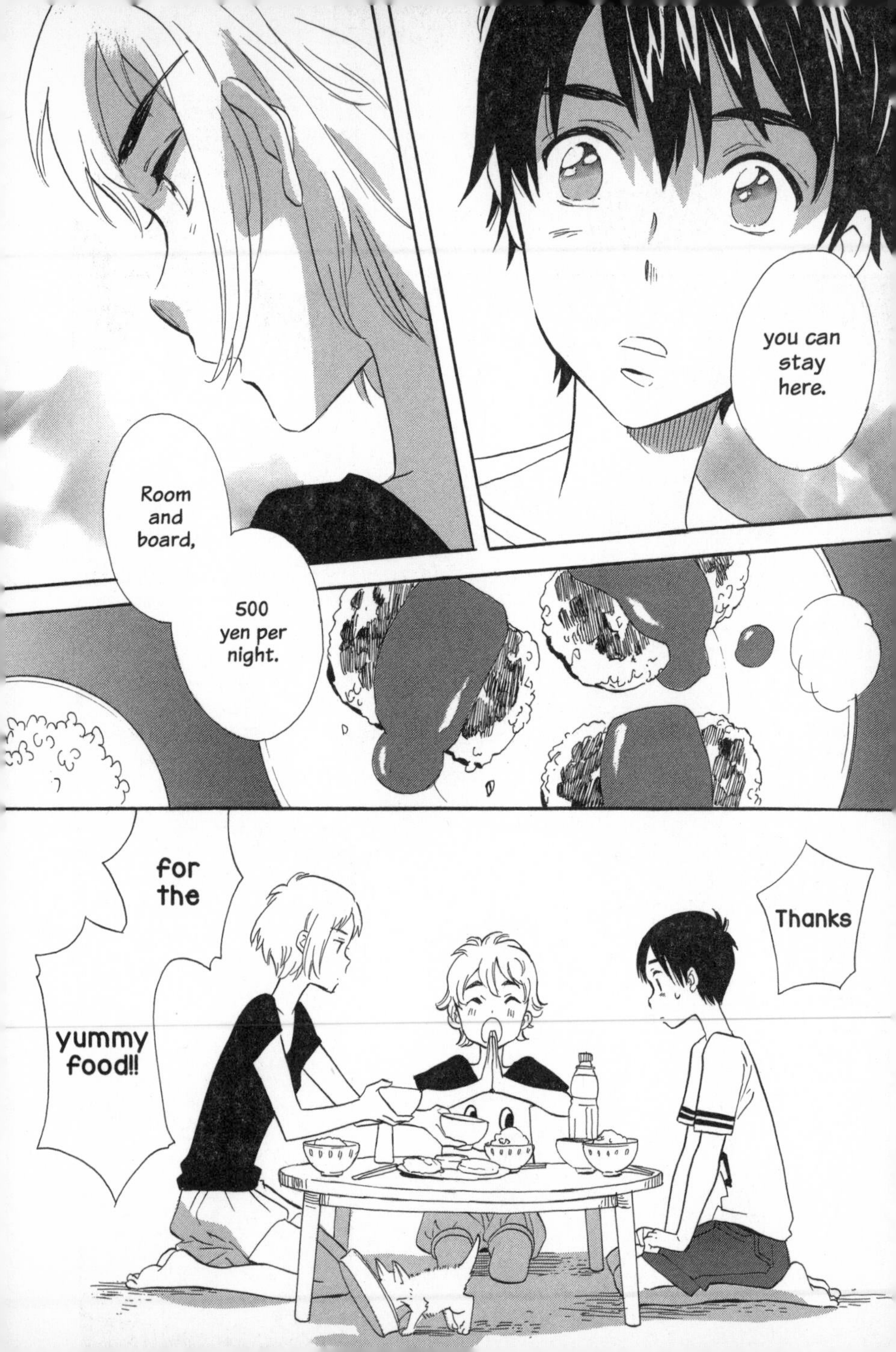
you can stay here.
Room and board,
500 yen per night.
Thanks
for the yummy food!!

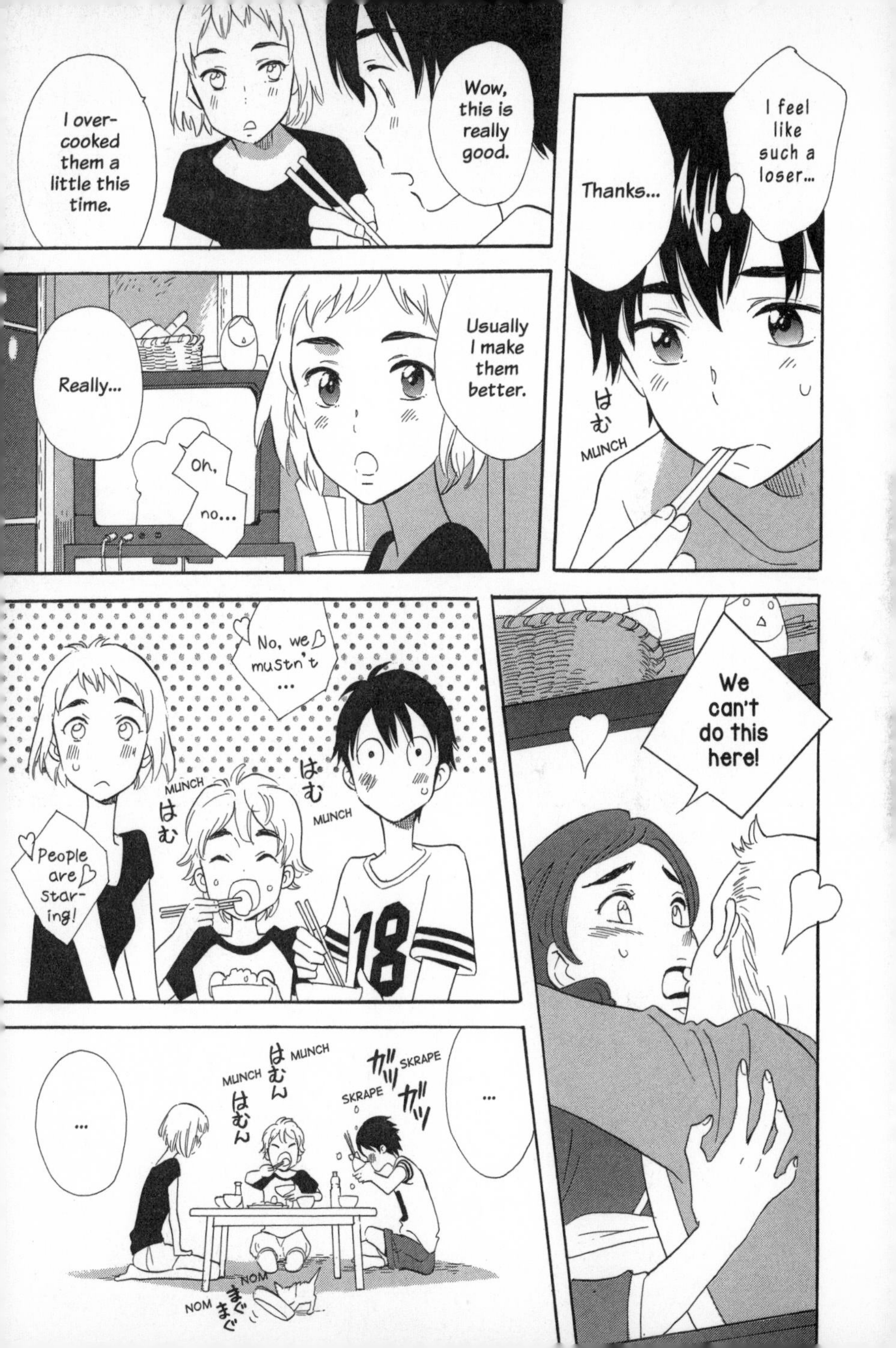

Wow, this is really good.
I over-cooked them a little this time.
Thanks...
I feel like such a loser...
はむ MUNCH
Usually I make them better.
Really...
Oh, no...
We can't do this here!
No, we mustn't ...
はむ MUNCH
はむ MUNCH
People are staring!
...
はむん MUNCH
はむん MUNCH
ガツ SKRAPE
ガツ SKRAPE
まぐ NOM
まぐ NOM
...

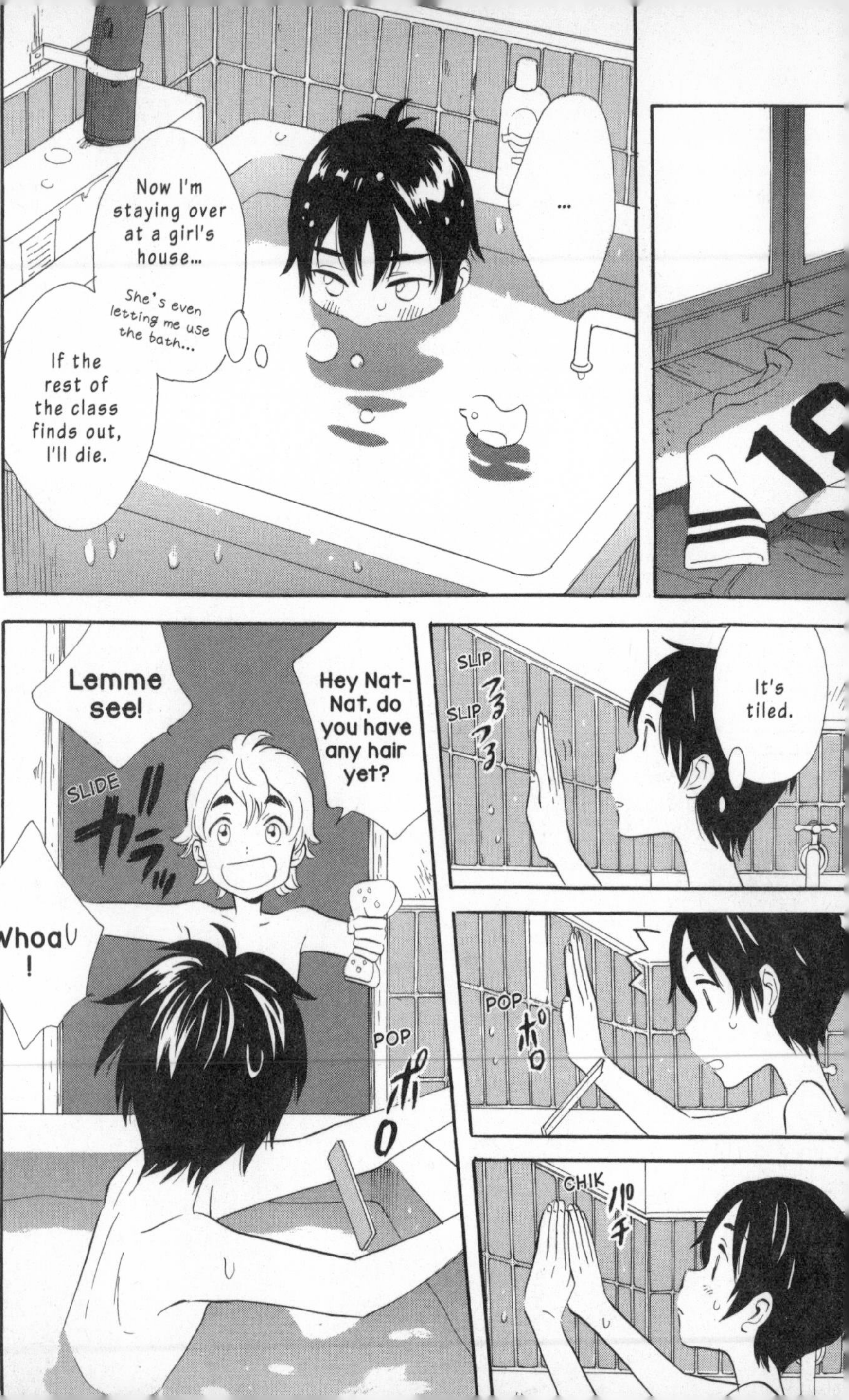
...
Now I'm staying over at a girl's house...
She's even letting me use the bath...
If the rest of the class finds out, I'll die.
It's tiled.
SLIP
SLIP
POP
CHIK
Hey Nat-Nat, do you have any hair yet?
Lemme see!
SLIDE
Whoa!
POP

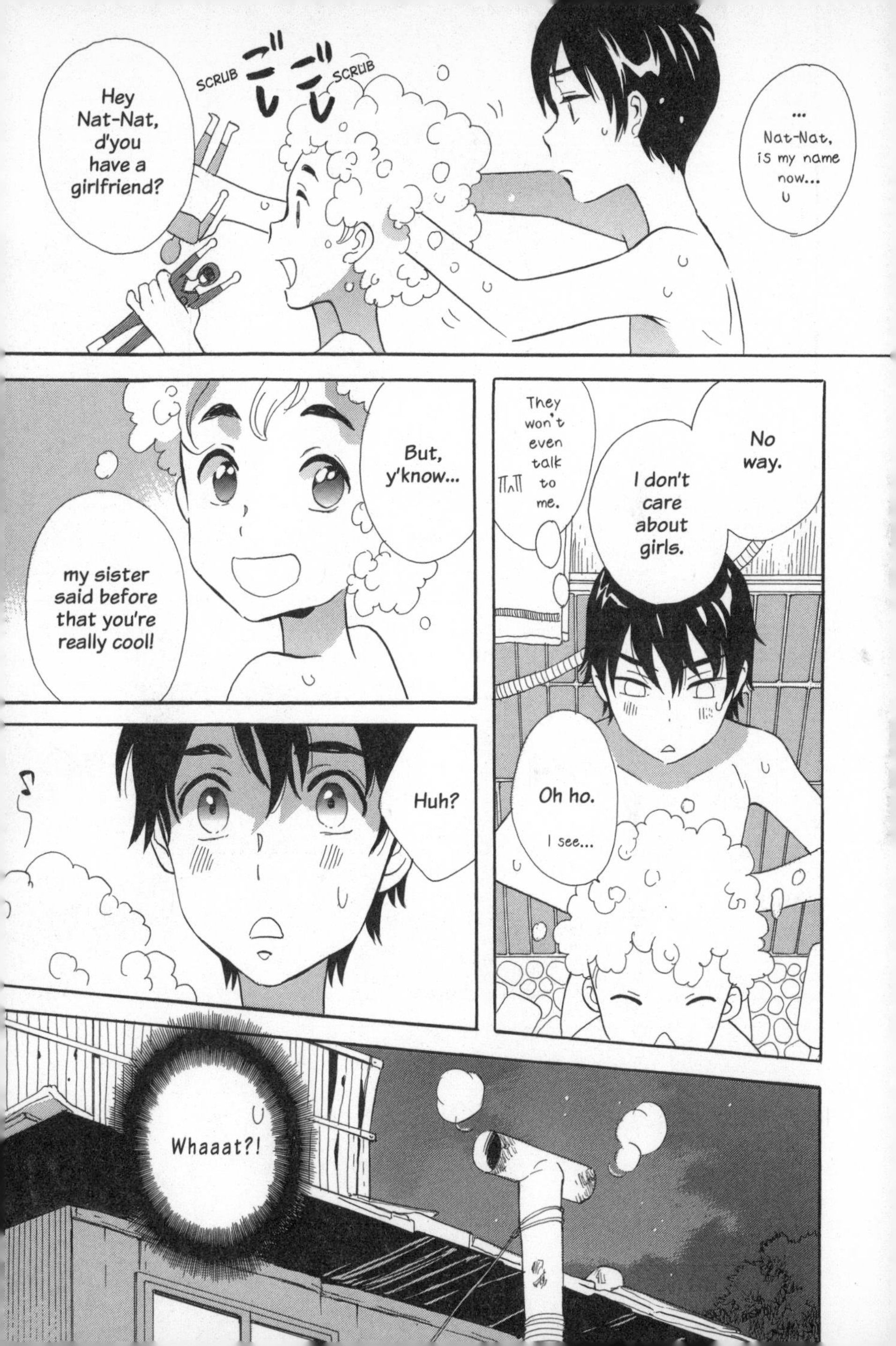

Hey Nat-Nat, d'you have a girlfriend?
SCRUB ごしごし SCRUB
... Nat-Nat, is my name now...
No way.
I don't care about girls.
They won't even talk to me.
Oh ho.
I see...
But, y'know...
my sister said before that you're really cool!
Huh?
Whaaat?!

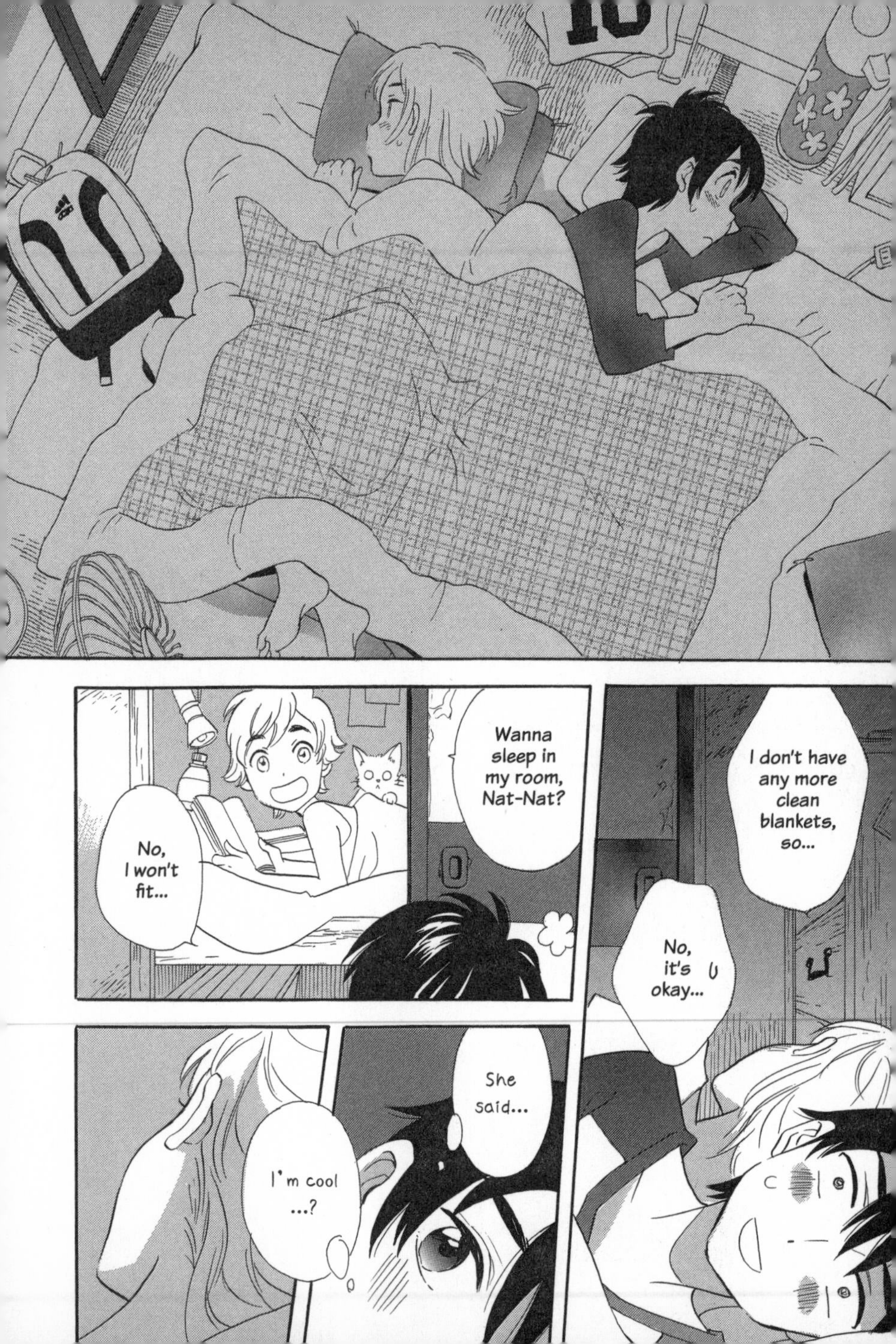
I don't have any more clean blankets, so...
No, it's okay...
Wanna sleep in my room, Nat-Nat?
No, I won't fit...
She said...
I'm cool ...?

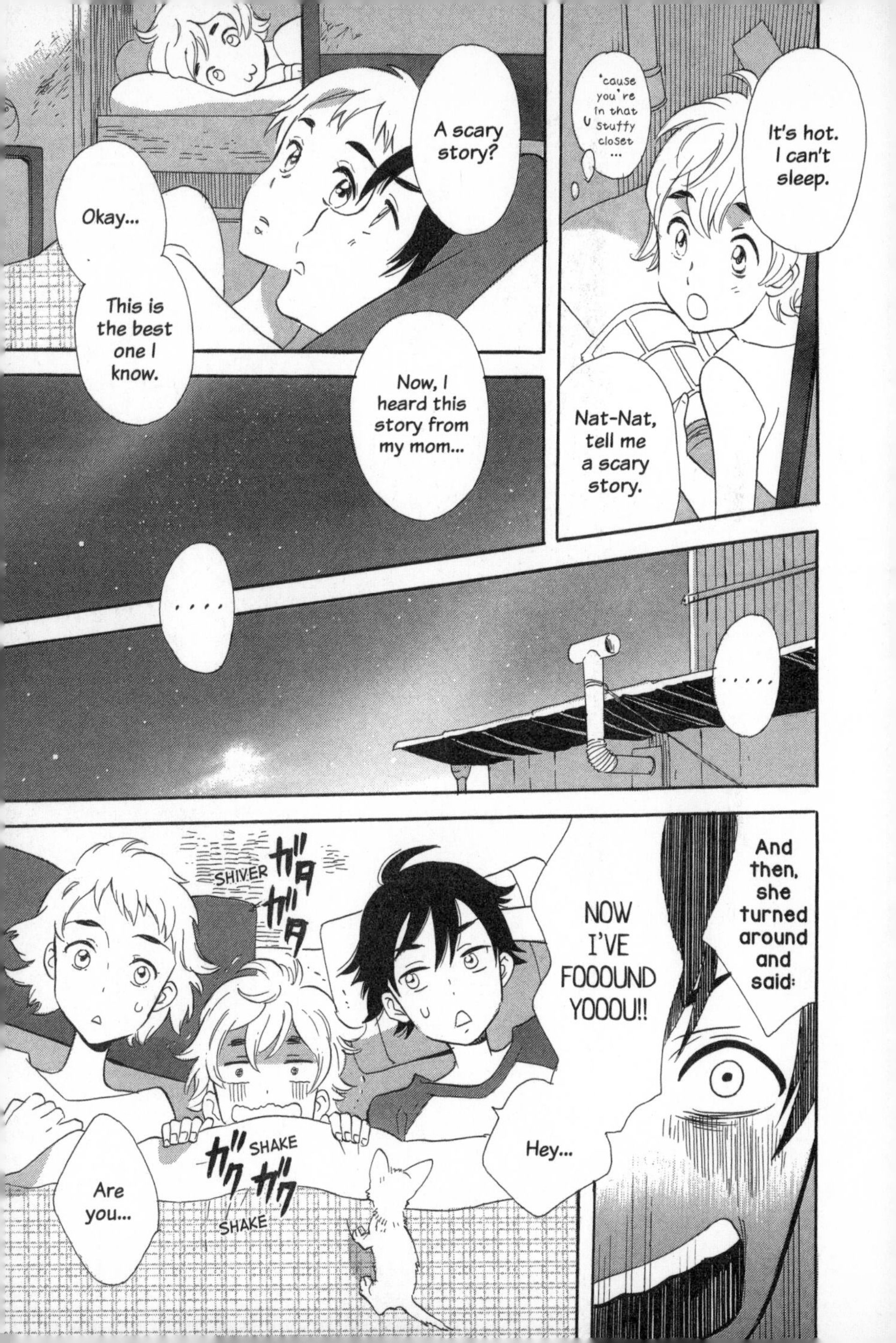
It's hot. I can't sleep.
'cause you're in that stuffy closet ...
Nat-Nat, tell me a scary story.
A scary story?
Okay...
This is the best one I know.
Now, I heard this story from my mom...
......
.....
And then, she turned around and said:
NOW I'VE FOOOUND YOOOU!!
SHIVER
Hey...
Are you...
SHAKE
SHAKE

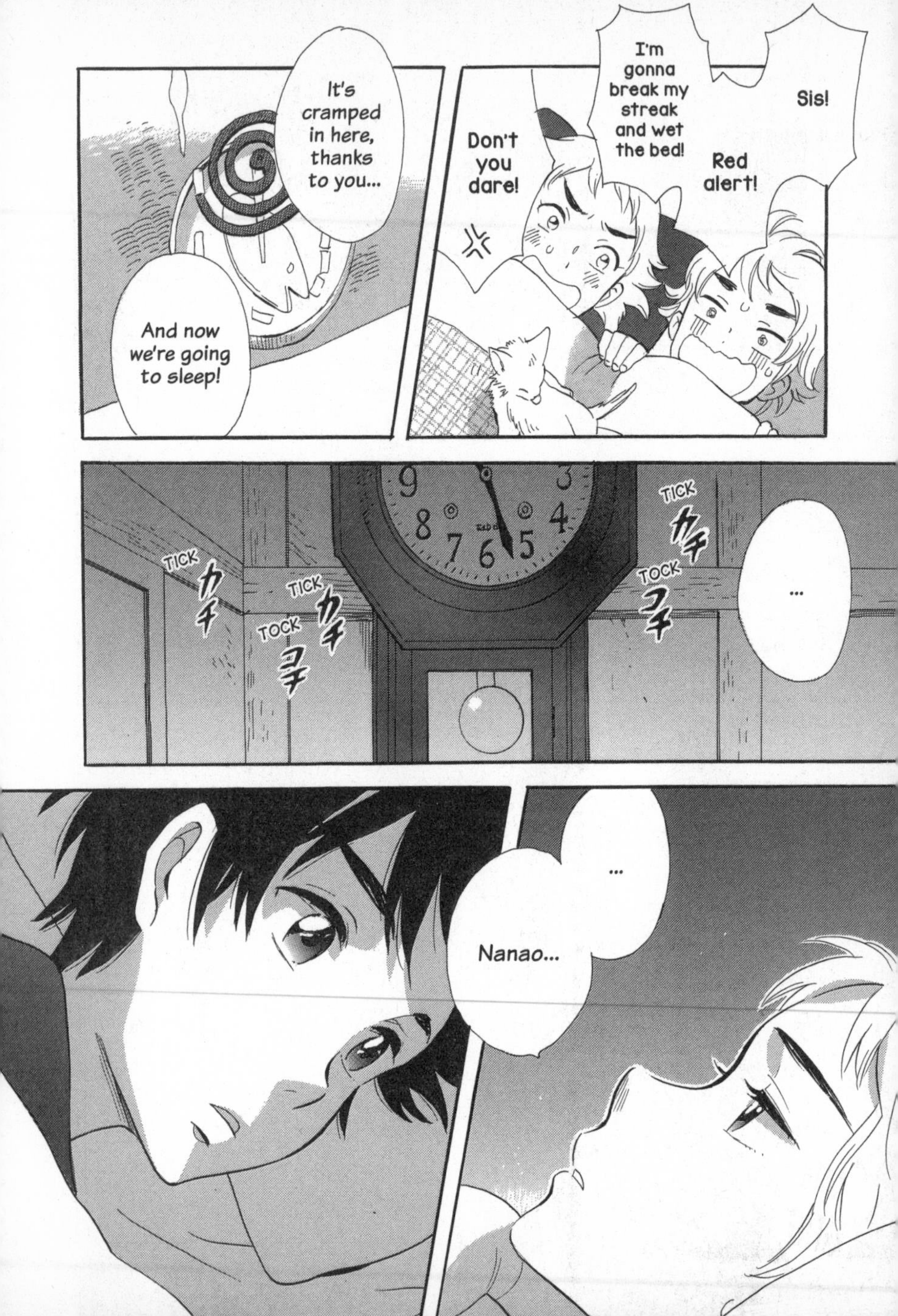
Sis!
I'm gonna break my streak and wet the bed!
Red alert!
Don't you dare!
It's cramped in here, thanks to you...
And now we're going to sleep!
...
TICK
カチ
TOCK
コチ
TICK
カチ
TOCK
コチ
TICK
カチ
...
Nanao...

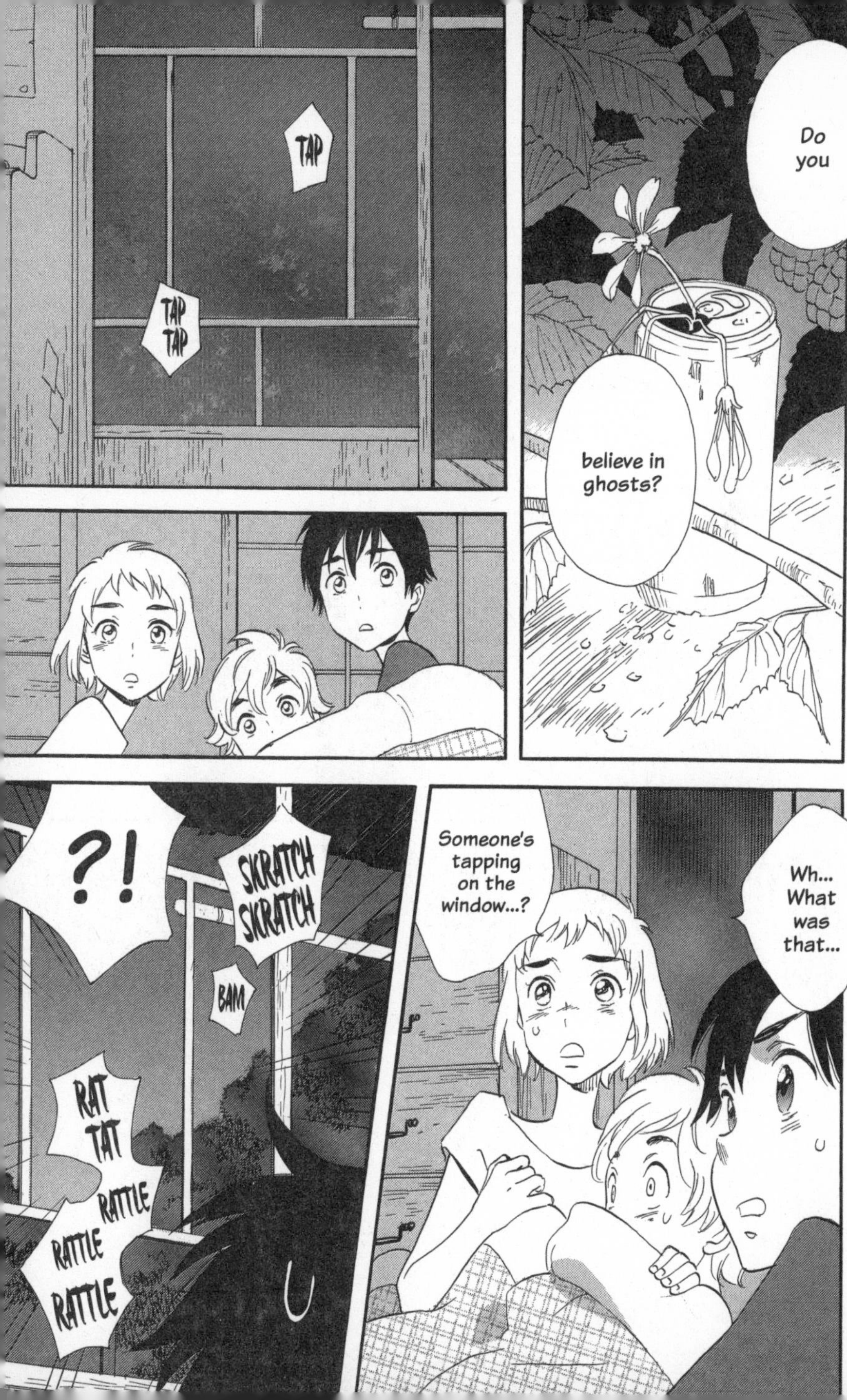
Do you
believe in ghosts?
TAP
TAP TAP
Wh... What was that...
Someone's tapping on the window...?
?!
SKRATCH SKRATCH
BAM
RAT TAT
RATTLE
RATTLE RATTLE

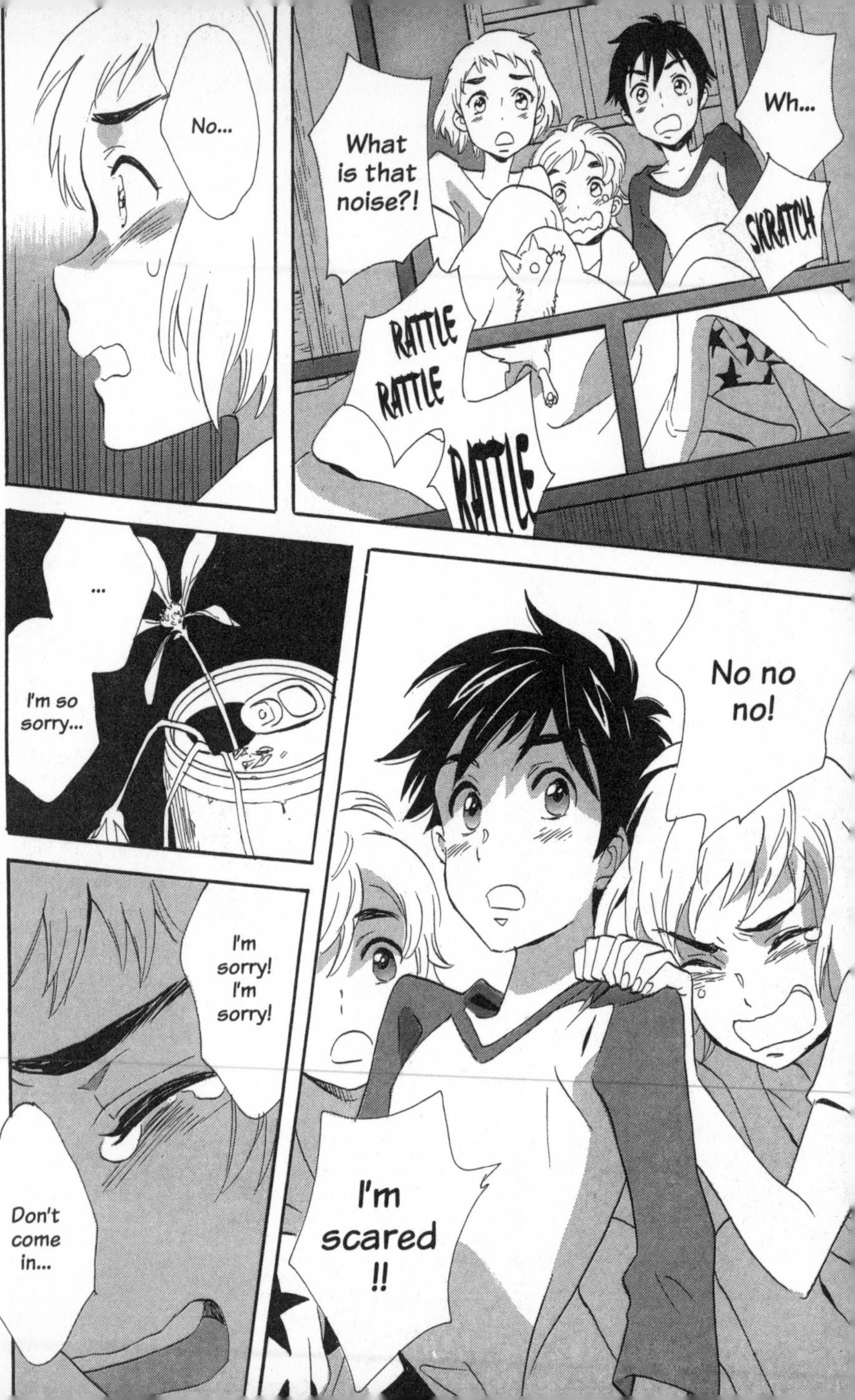
Wh...
What is that noise?!
SKRATCH
RATTLE
RATTLE
RATTLE
No...
No no no!
I'm scared !!
...
I'm so sorry...
I'm sorry! I'm sorry!
Don't come in...

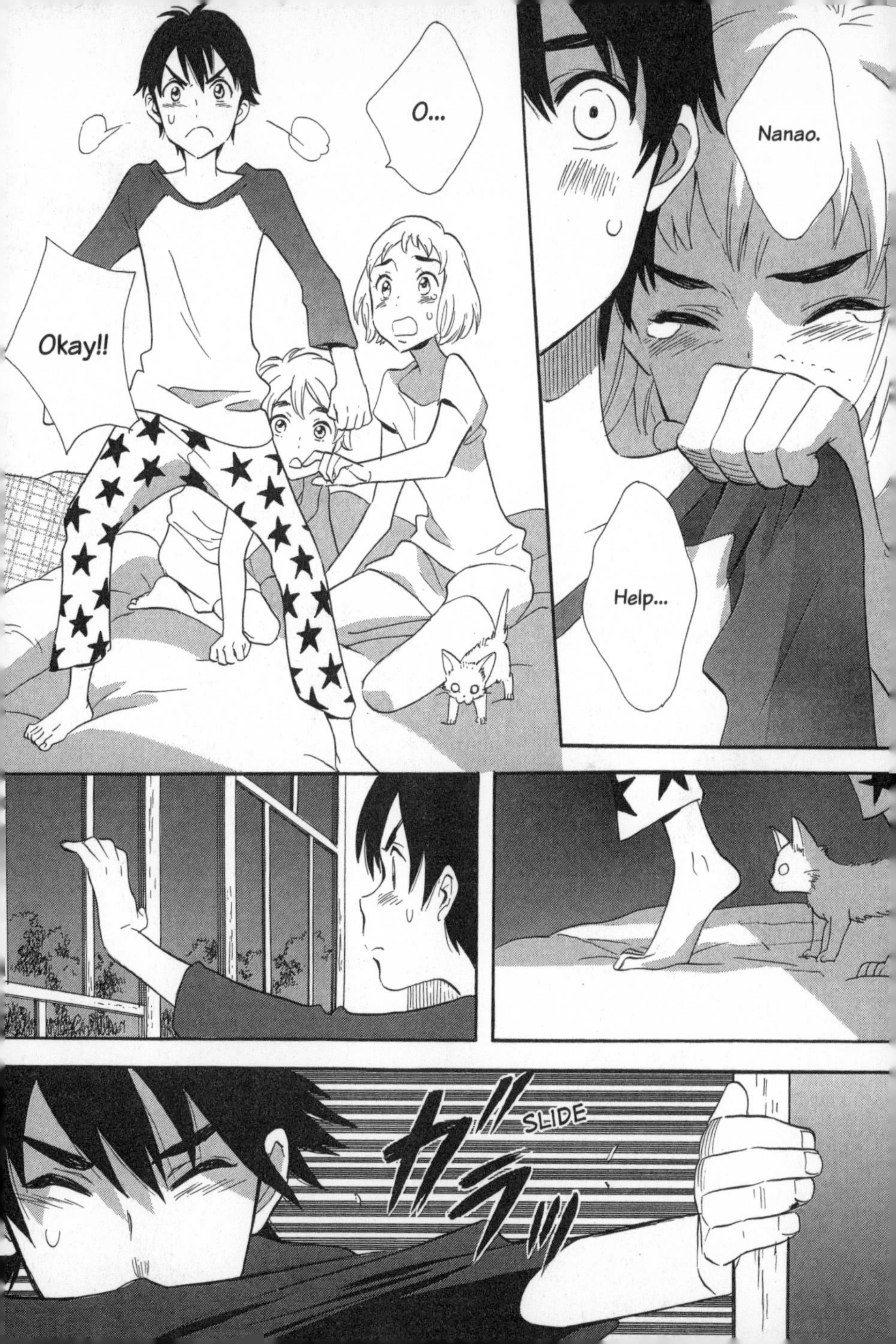
Nanao.
Help...
O...
Okay!!
SLIDE

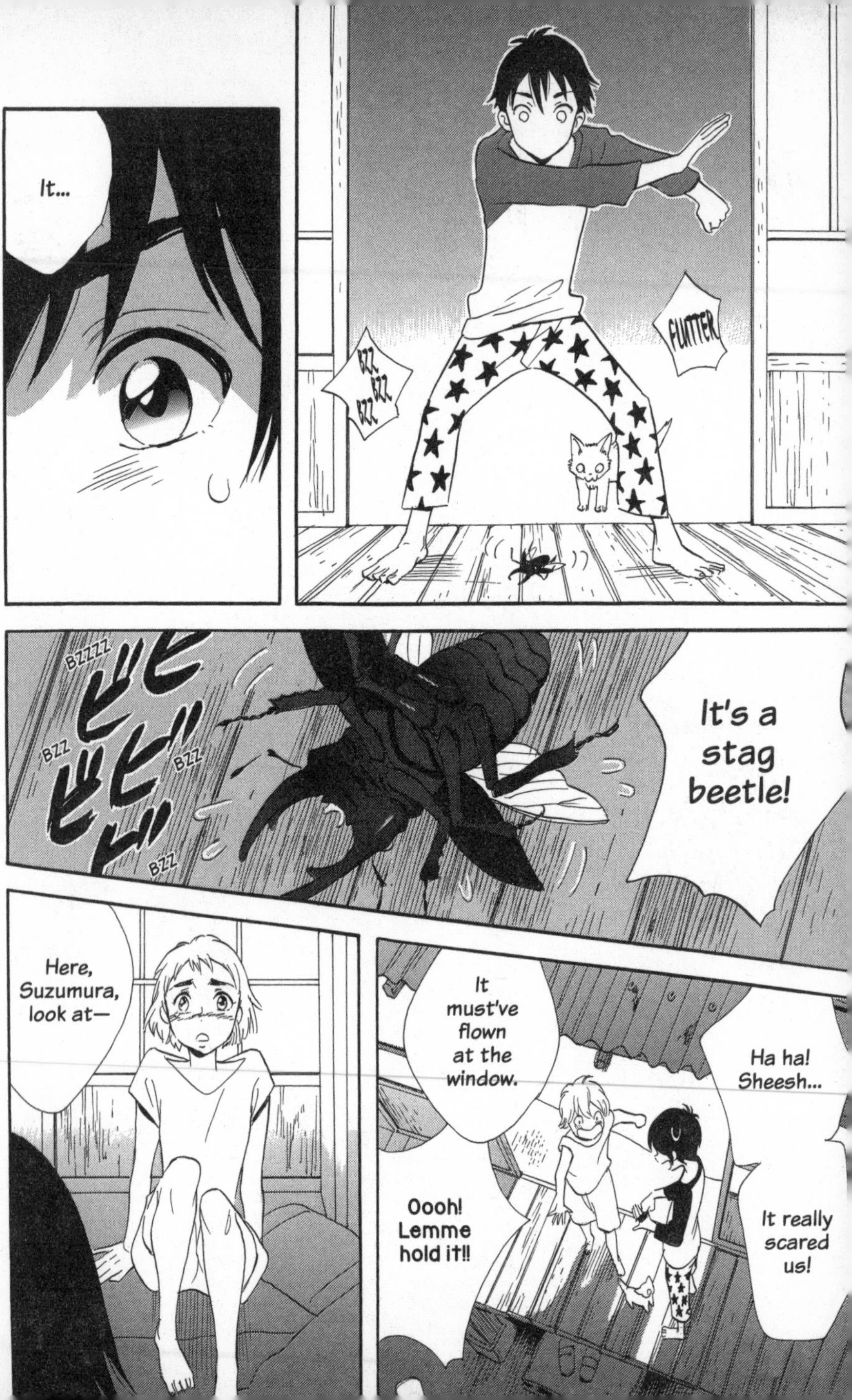
FLUTTER
BZZ BZZ BZZ
It...
BZZZZ
BZZ
BZZ
BZZ
It's a stag beetle!
Ha ha! Sheesh...
It must've flown at the window.
It really scared us!
Oooh! Lemme hold it!!
Here, Suzumura, look at—

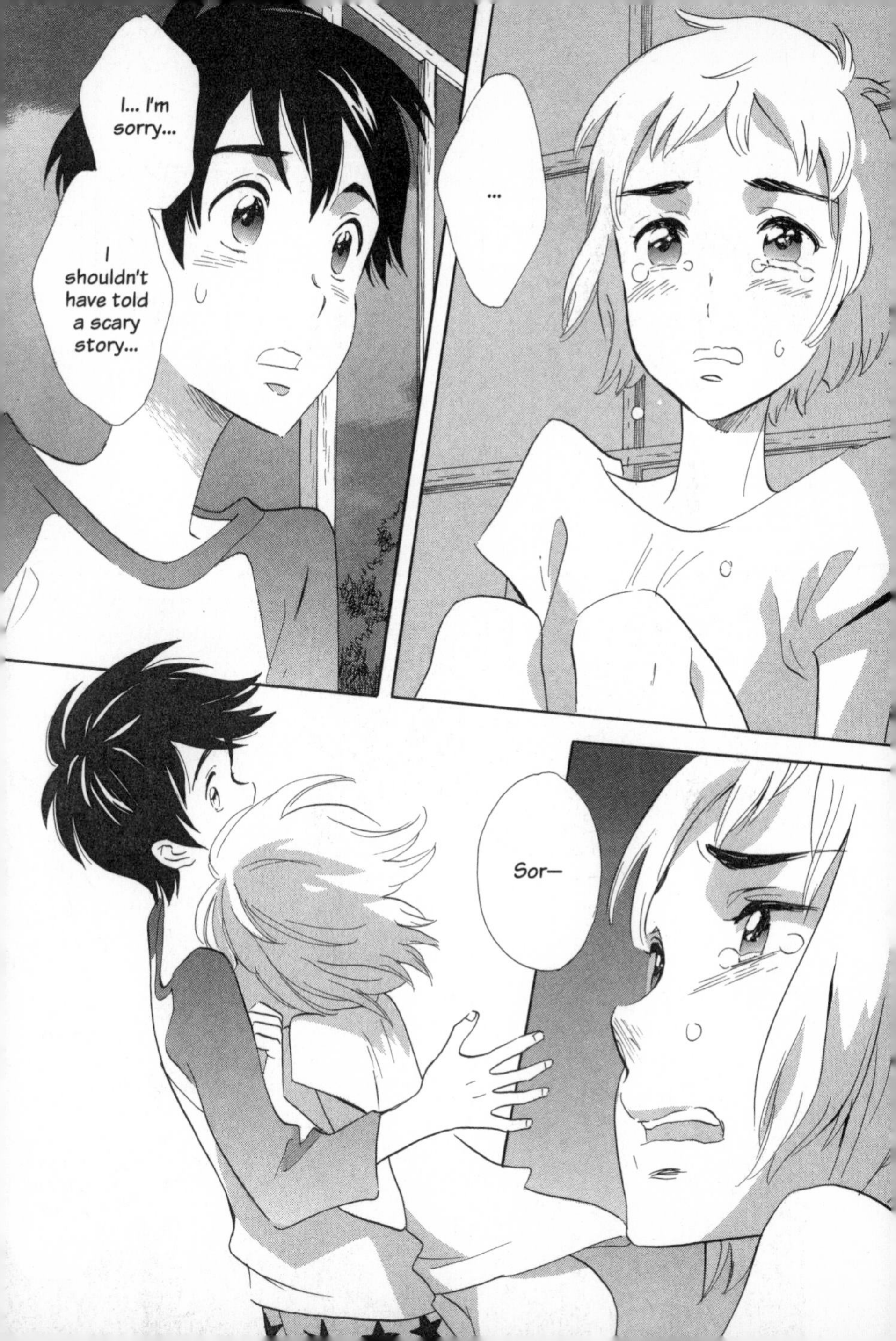
...
I... I'm sorry...
I shouldn't have told a scary story...
Sor—

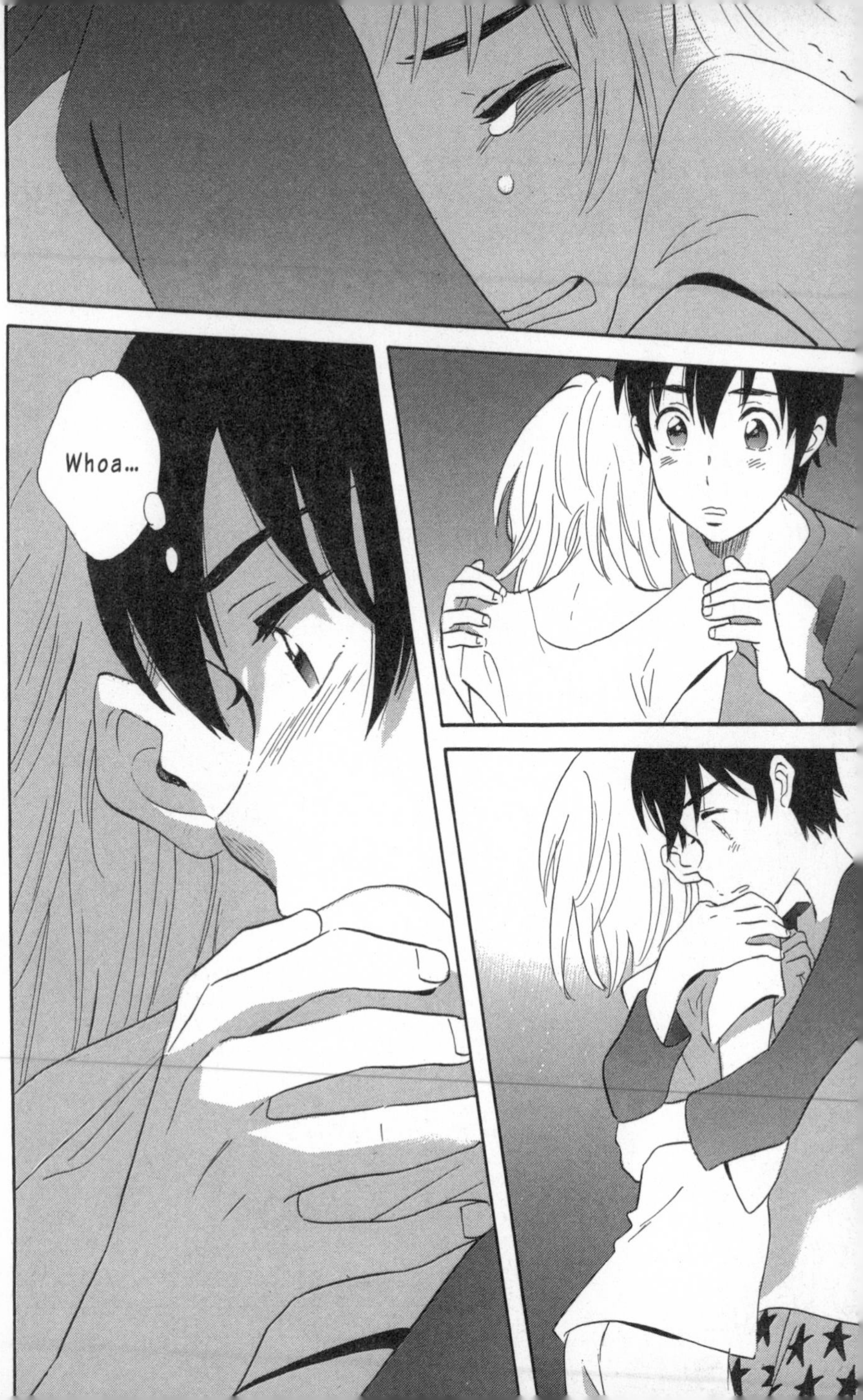
Whoa...

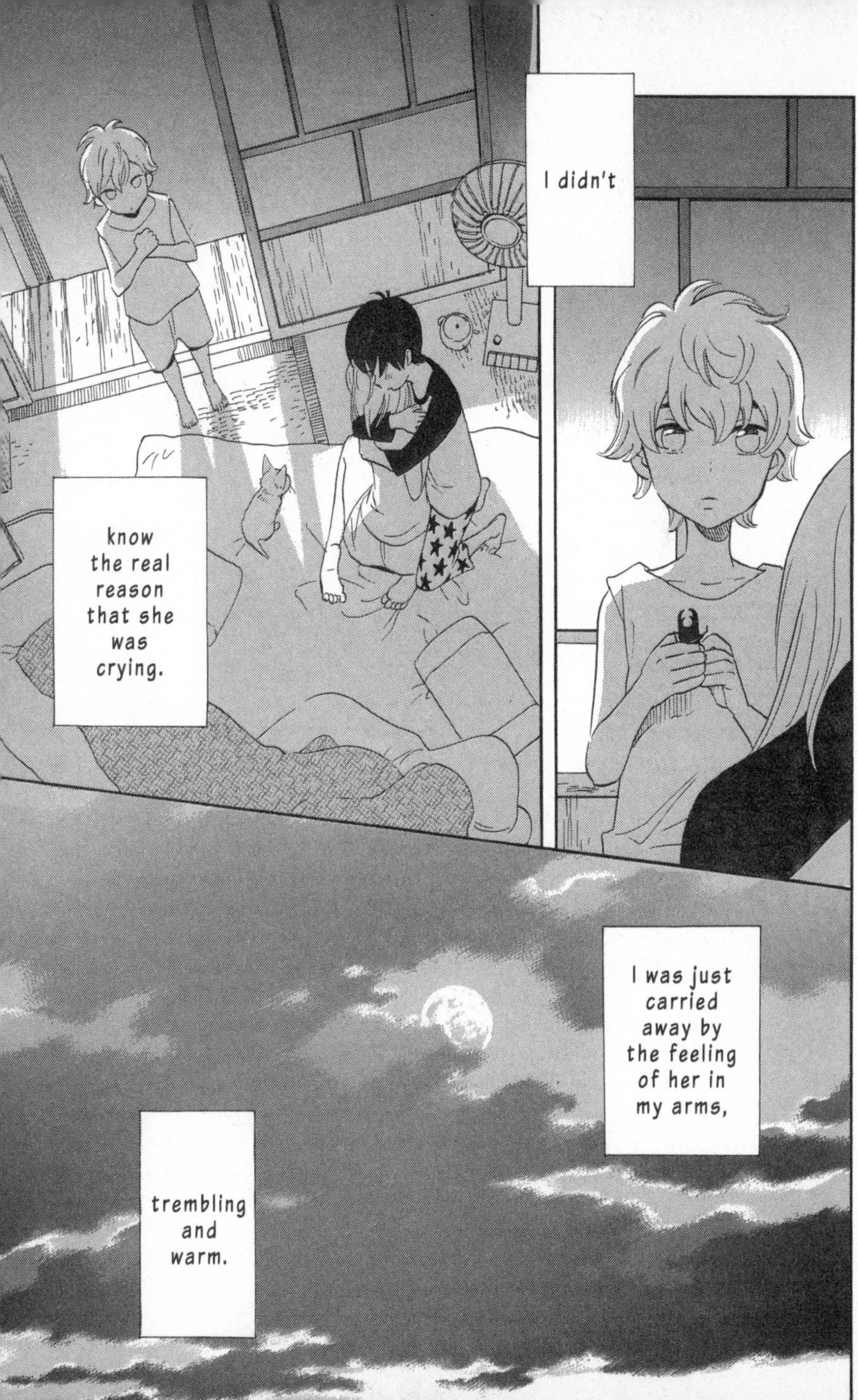
I didn't
know the real reason that she was crying.
I was just carried away by the feeling of her in my arms,
trembling and warm.

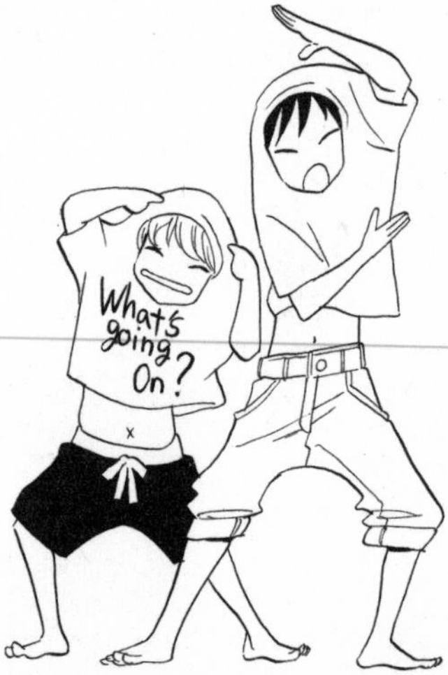
What's going On?

chapter 3

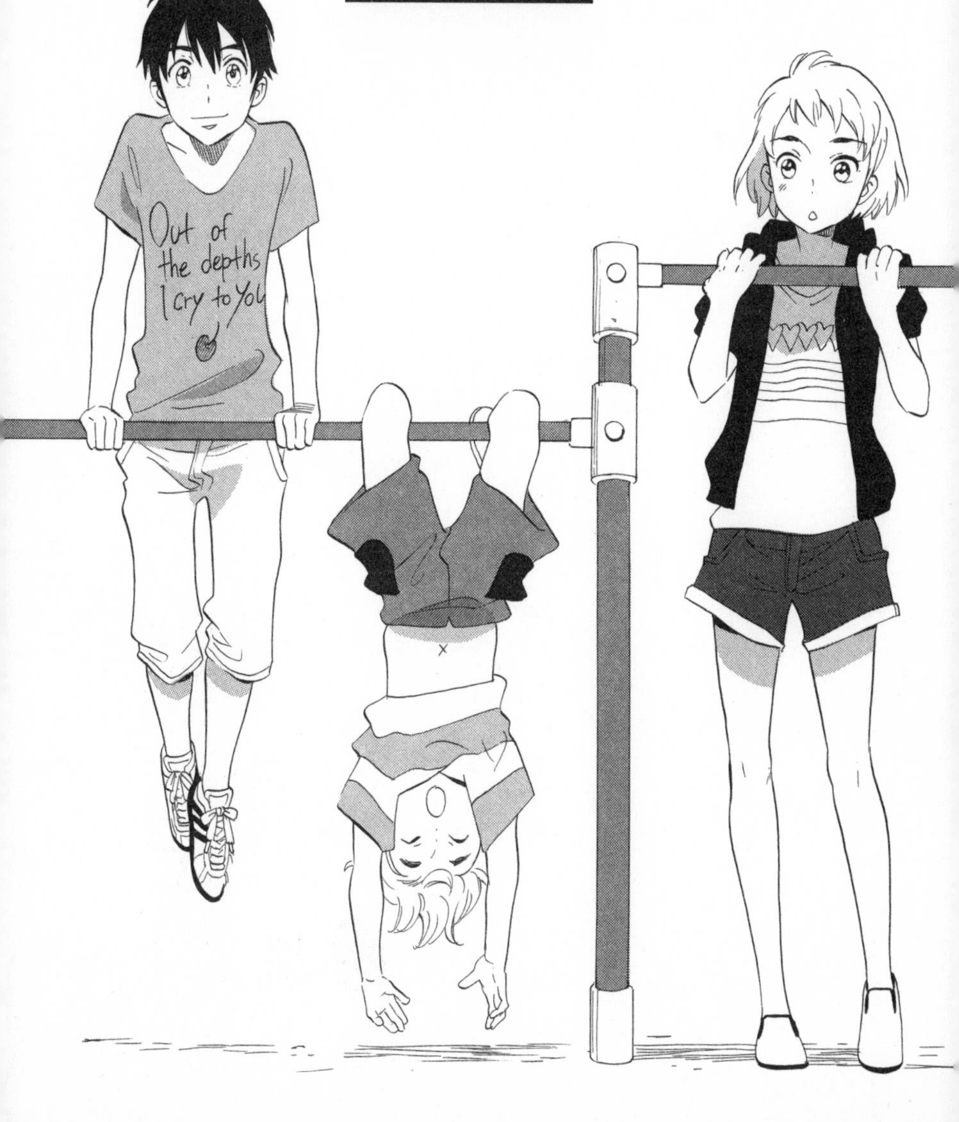
Out of the depths I cry to You

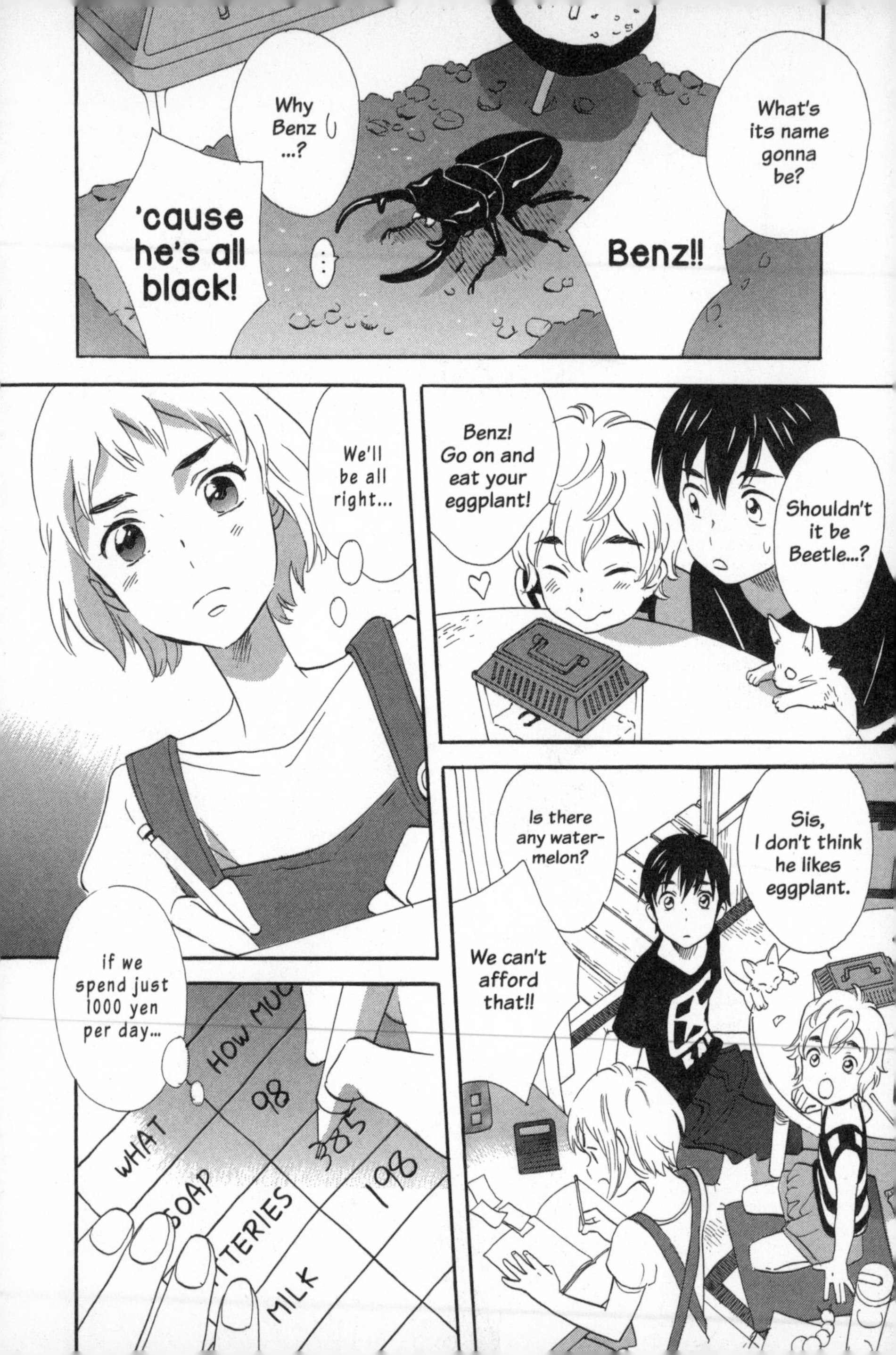

What's its name gonna be?
Benz!!
Why Benz ...?
...
'cause he's all black!
Benz! Go on and eat your eggplant!
Shouldn't it be Beetle...?
Sis, I don't think he likes eggplant.
Is there any water-melon?
We can't afford that!!
We'll be all right...
if we spend just 1000 yen per day...
HOW MUC
WHAT
98
SOAP
385
TTERIES
198
MILK

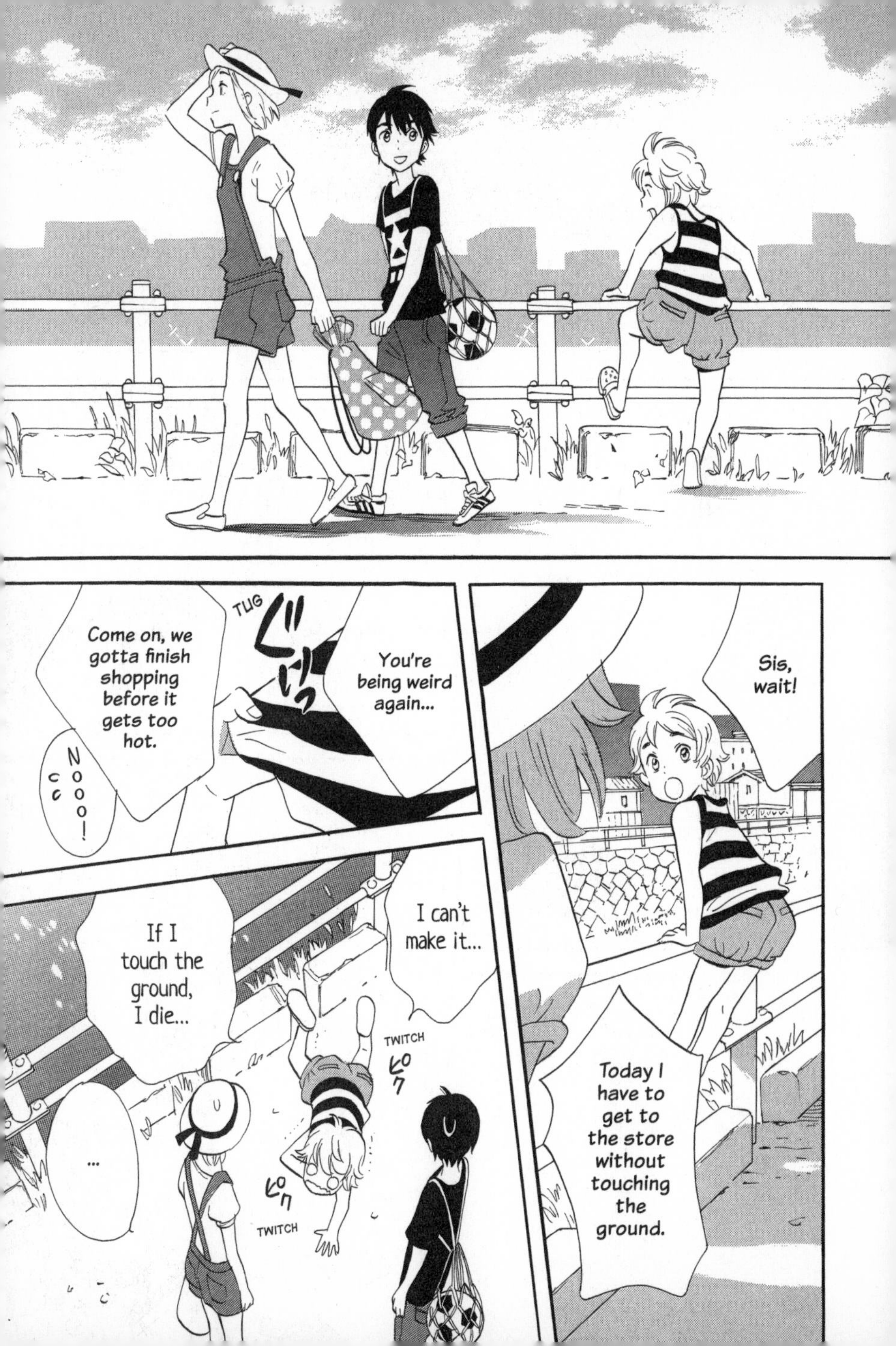

Sis, wait!
Today I have to get to the store without touching the ground.
You're being weird again...
TUG
Come on, we gotta finish shopping before it gets too hot.
Noooo!
I can't make it...
If I touch the ground, I die...
TWITCH
...
TWITCH

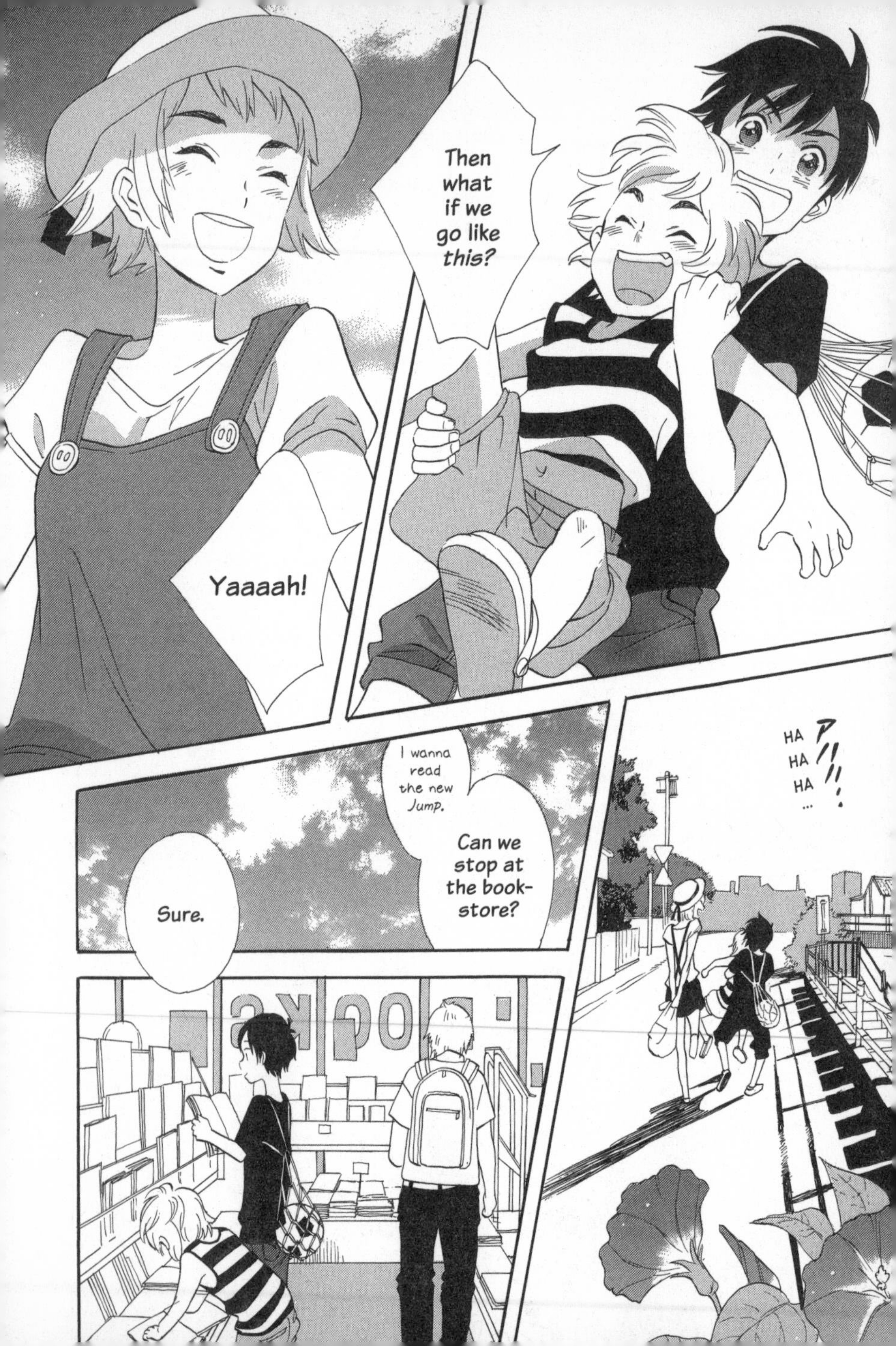
Then what if we go like this?
Yaaaah!
HA HA HA ...
I wanna read the new Jump.
Can we stop at the bookstore?
Sure.

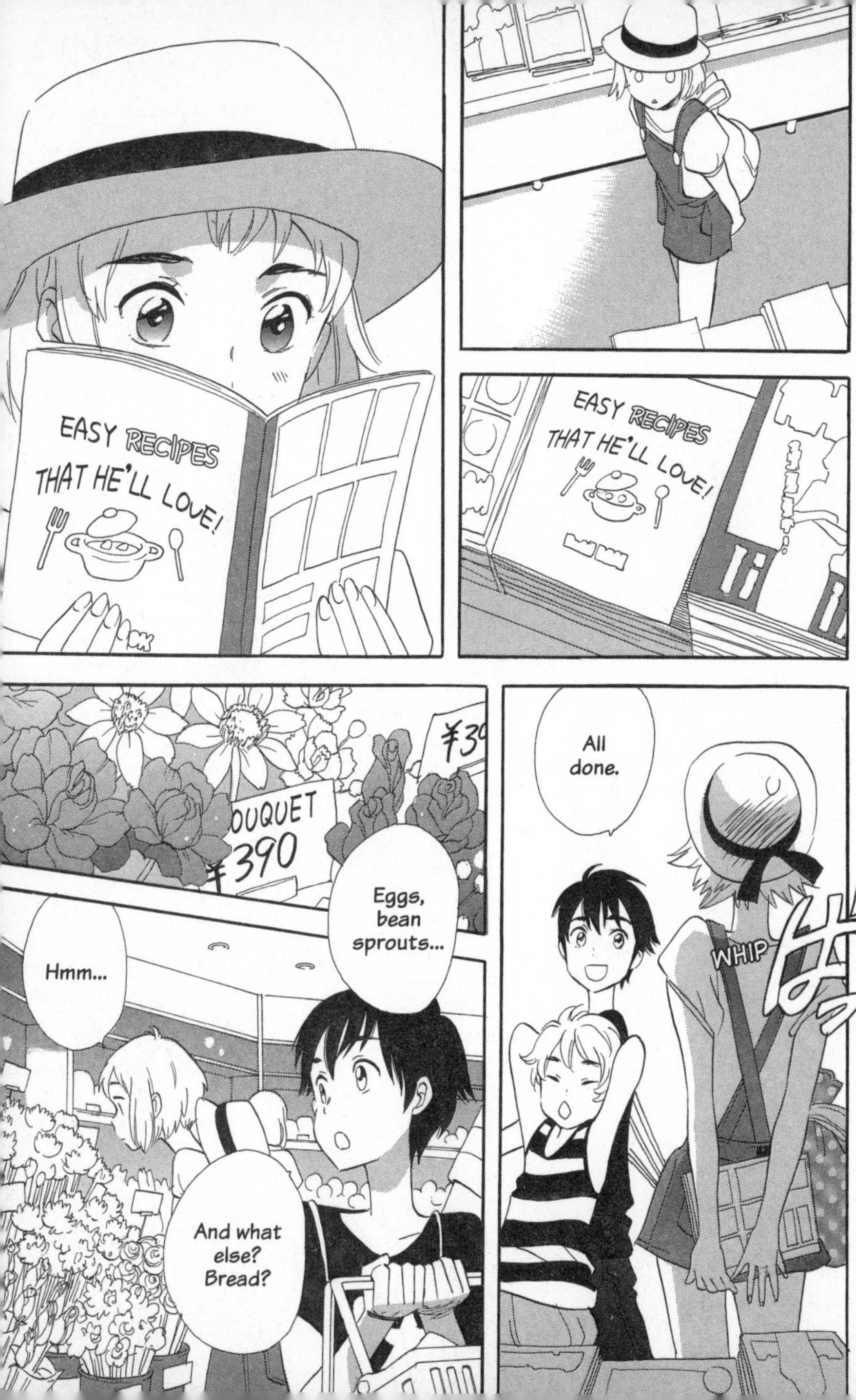
EASY RECIPES
THAT HE'LL LOVE!
EASY RECIPES
THAT HE'LL LOVE!
All done.
WHIP
ばっ
¥39
OUQUET
¥390
Eggs, bean sprouts...
Hmm...
And what else? Bread?

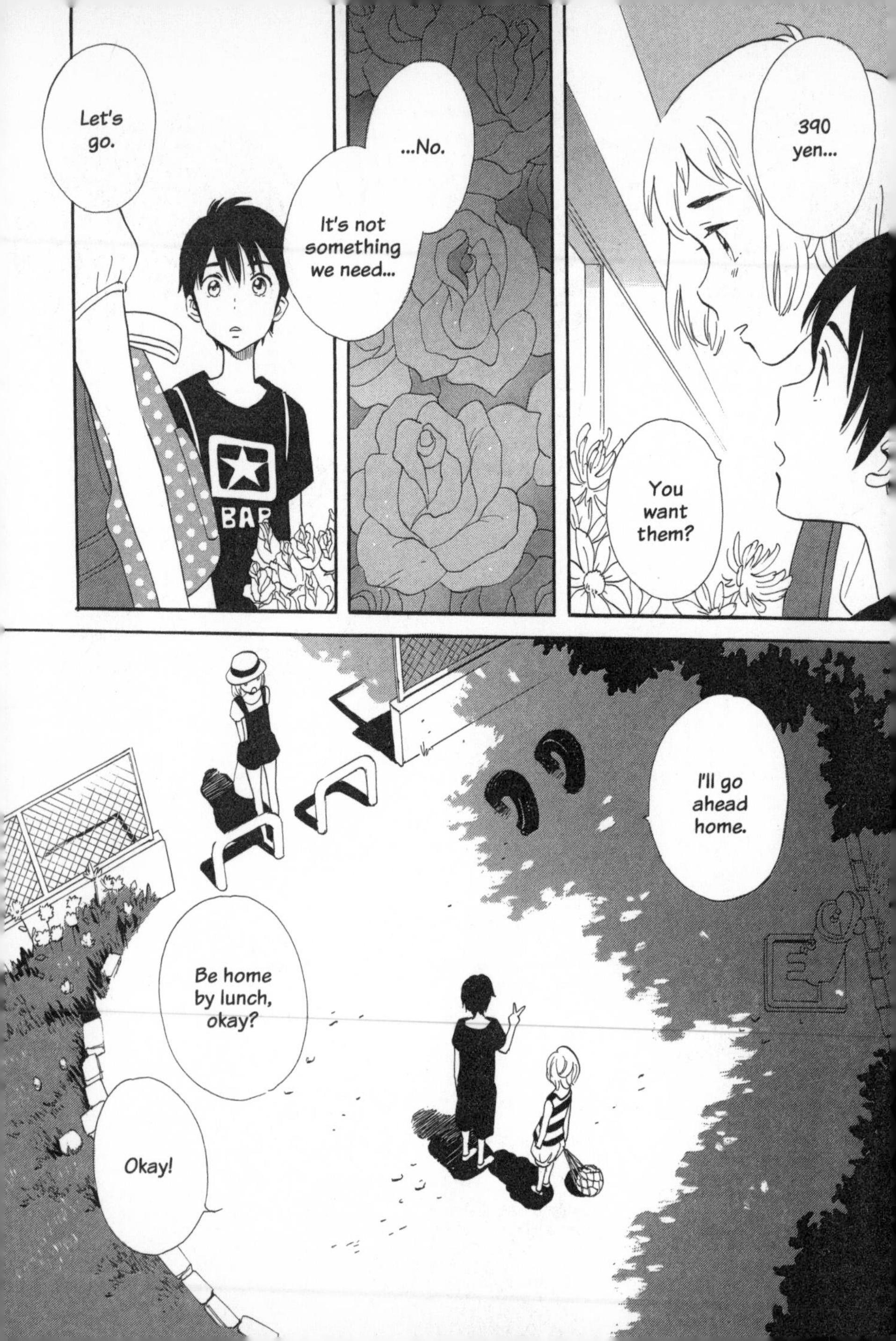
390 yen...
You want them?
...No.
It's not something we need...
Let's go.
I'll go ahead home.
Be home by lunch, okay?
Okay!

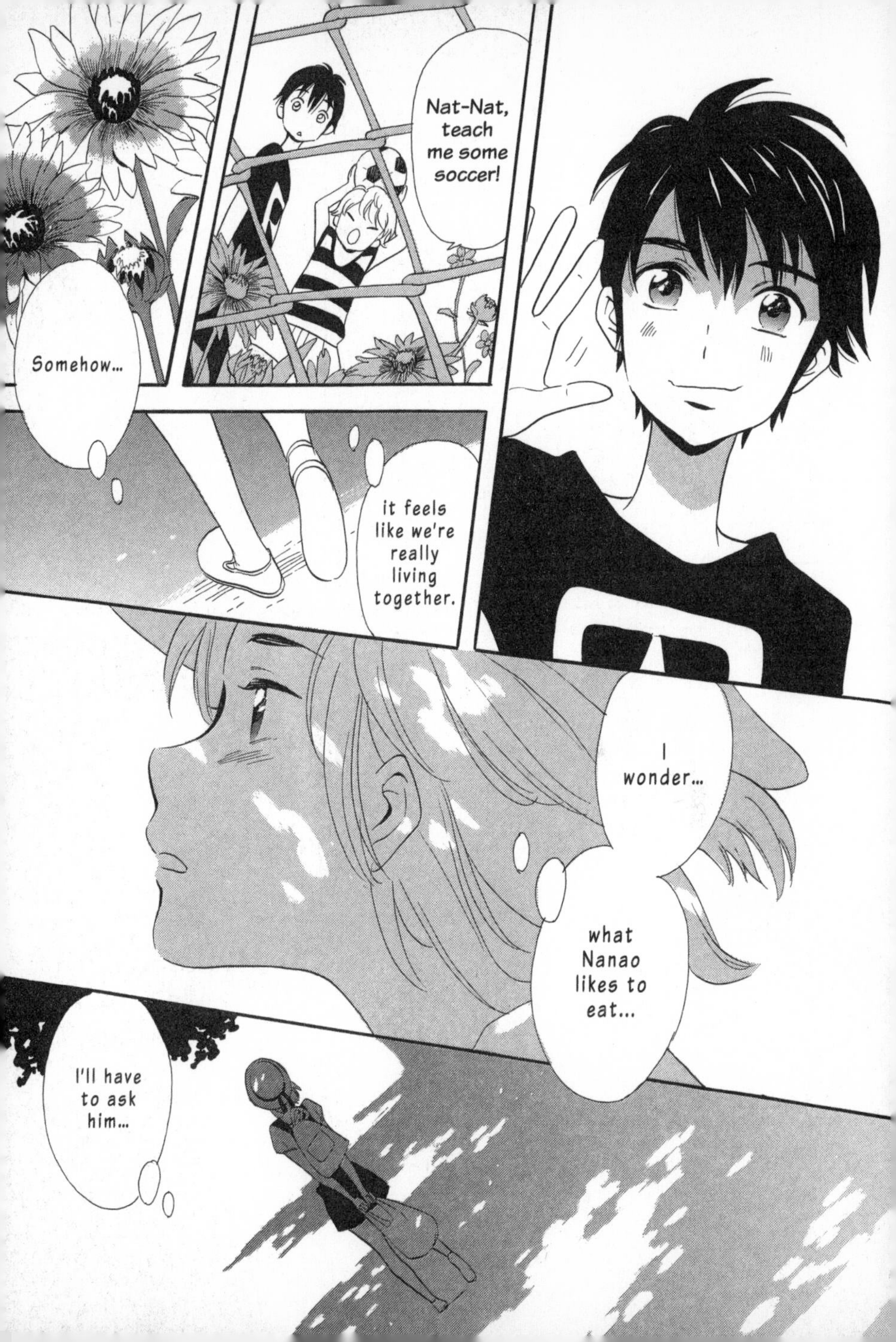
Nat-Nat, teach me some soccer!
Somehow...
it feels like we're really living together.
I wonder...
what Nanao likes to eat...
I'll have to ask him...

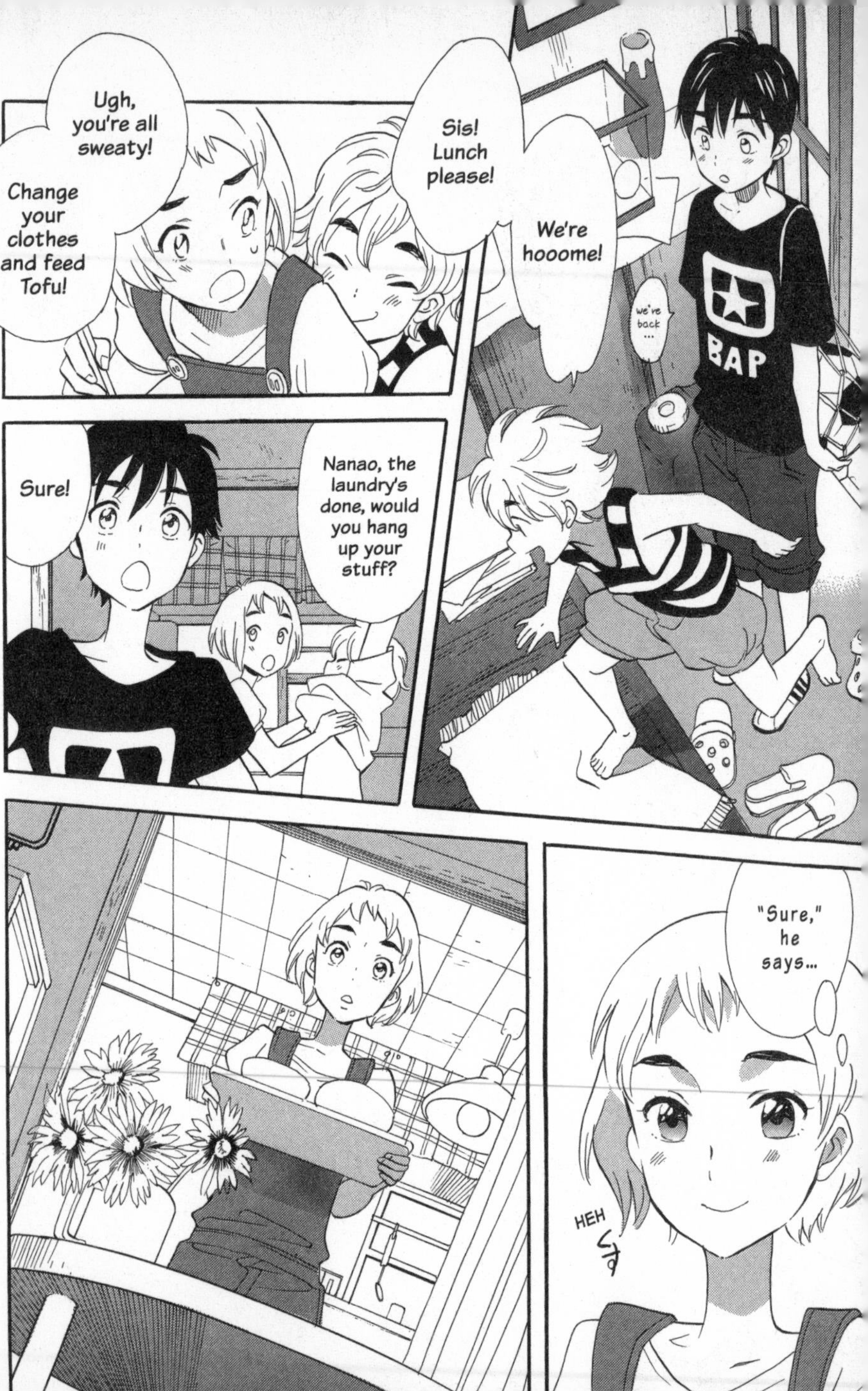
Sis! Lunch please!
We're hooome!
we're back...
Ugh, you're all sweaty!
Change your clothes and feed Tofu!
Nanao, the laundry's done, would you hang up your stuff?
Sure!
"Sure," he says...
HEH
くす

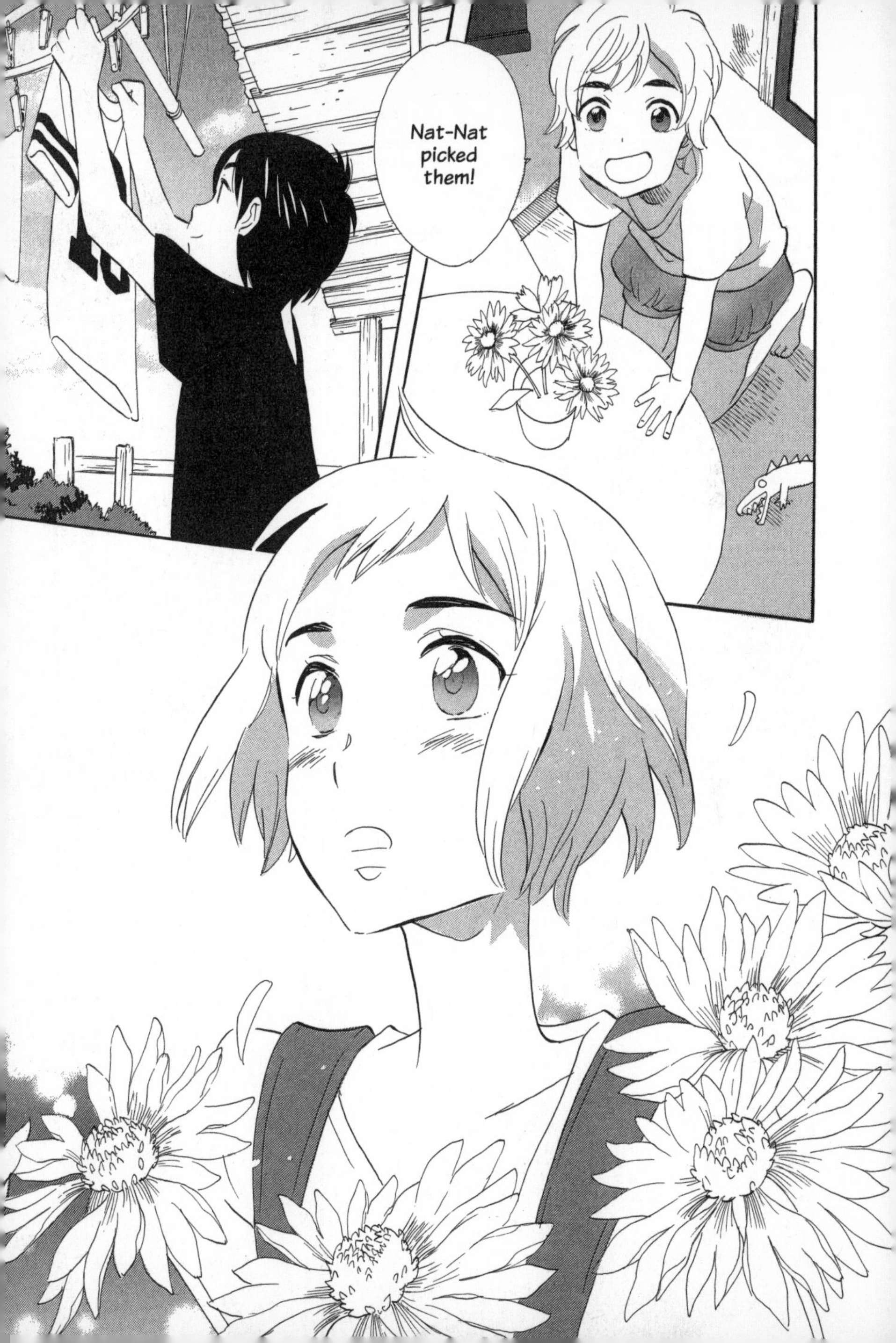
Nat-Nat picked them!

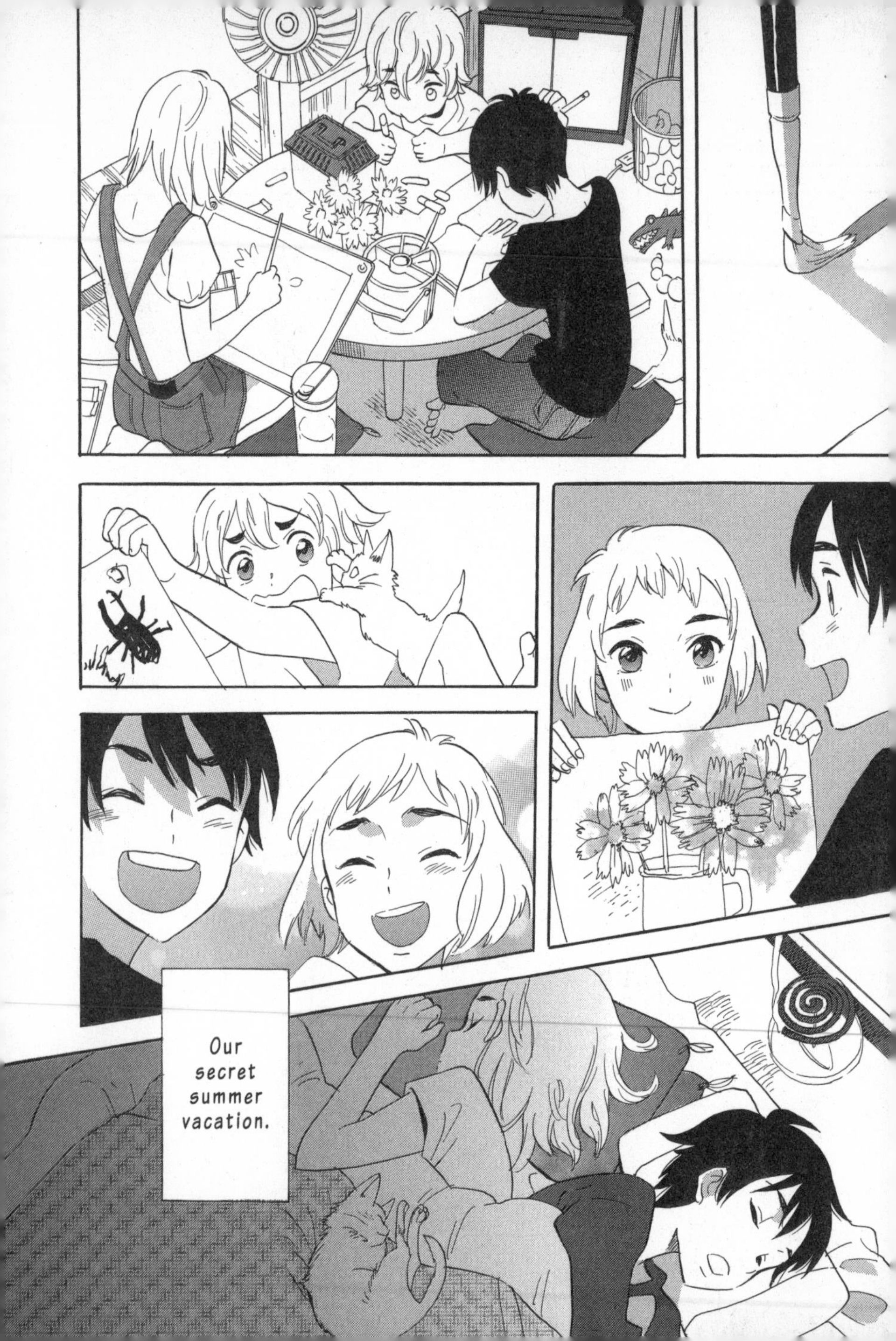
Our secret summer vacation.

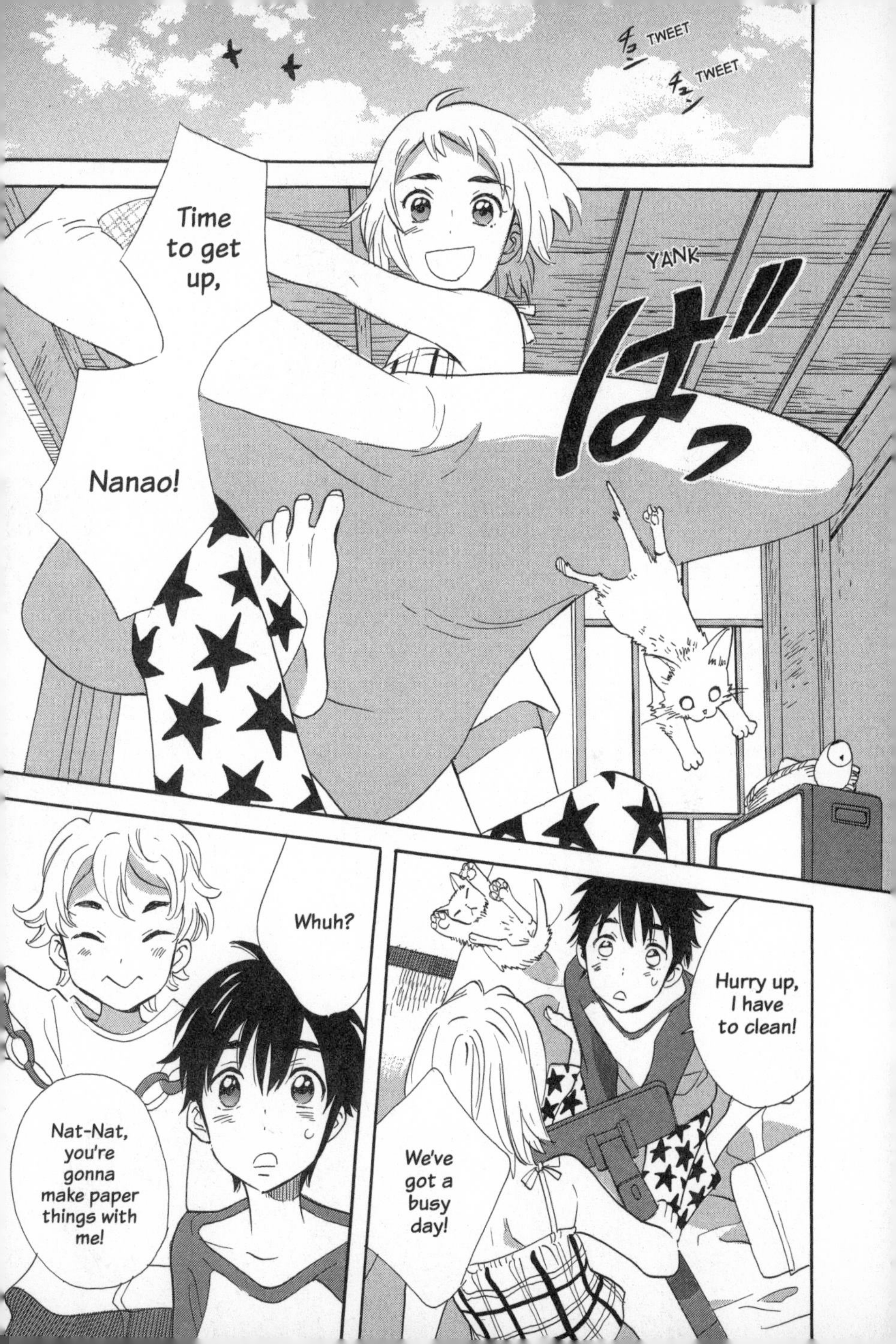
TWEET
TWEET
Time to get up, Nanao!
YANK
ばっ
Hurry up, I have to clean!
We've got a busy day!
Whuh?
Nat-Nat, you're gonna make paper things with me!

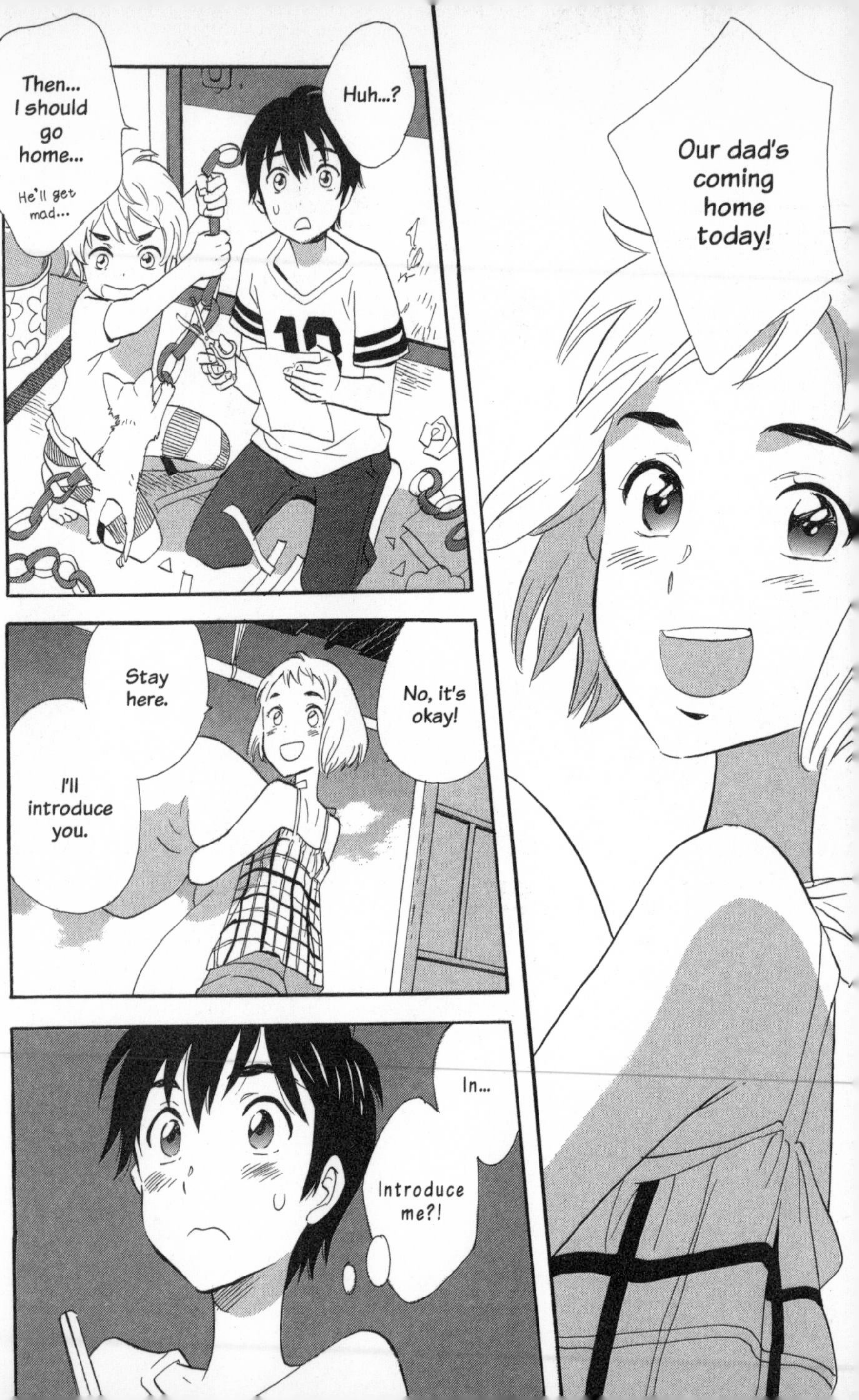
Our dad's coming home today!
Huh...?
Then... I should go home...
He'll get mad...
No, it's okay!
Stay here.
I'll introduce you.
In...
Introduce me?!

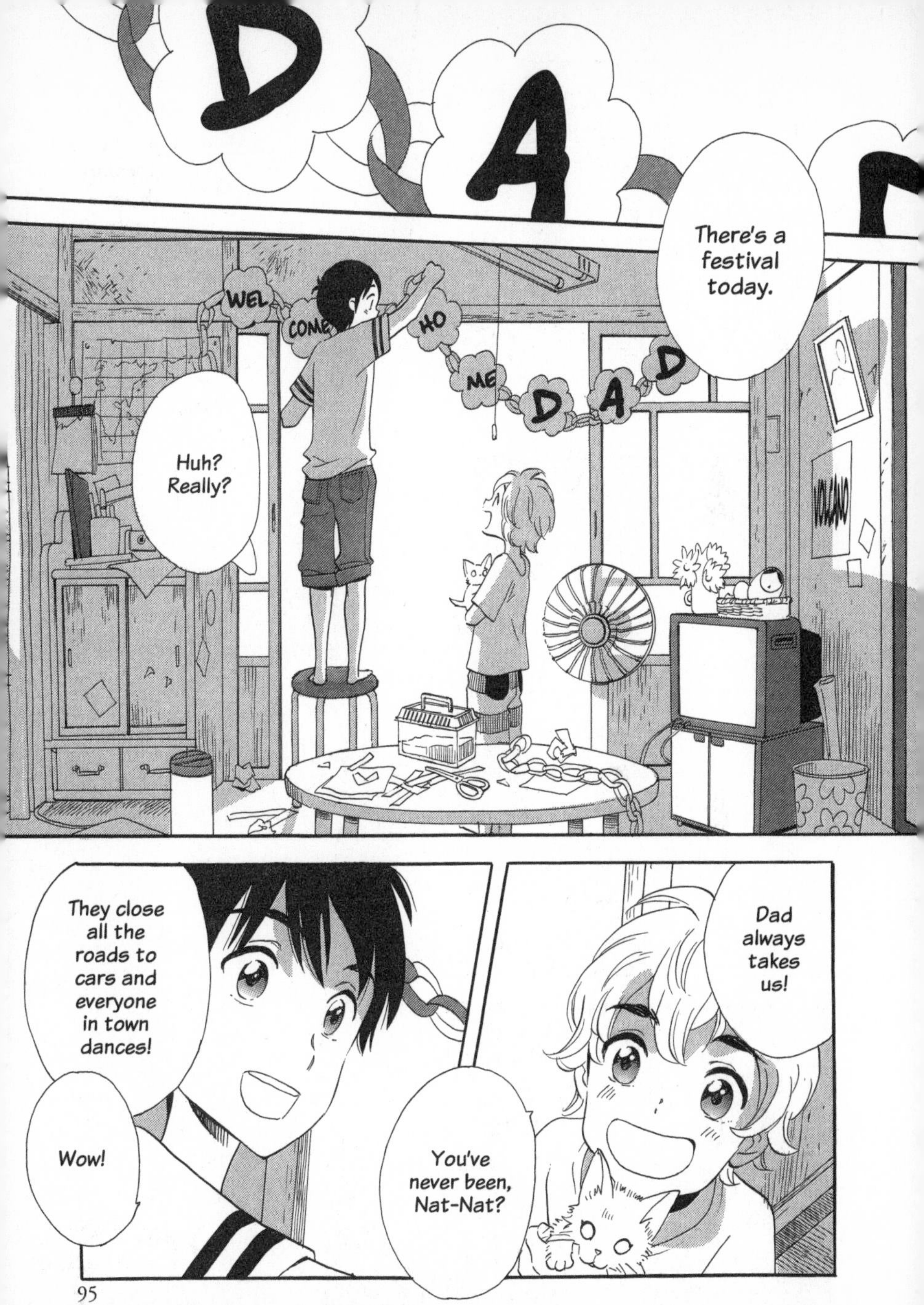
DAD
WEL COME HO ME DAD
There's a festival today.
Huh? Really?
Dad always takes us!
You've never been, Nat-Nat?
They close all the roads to cars and everyone in town dances!
Wow!

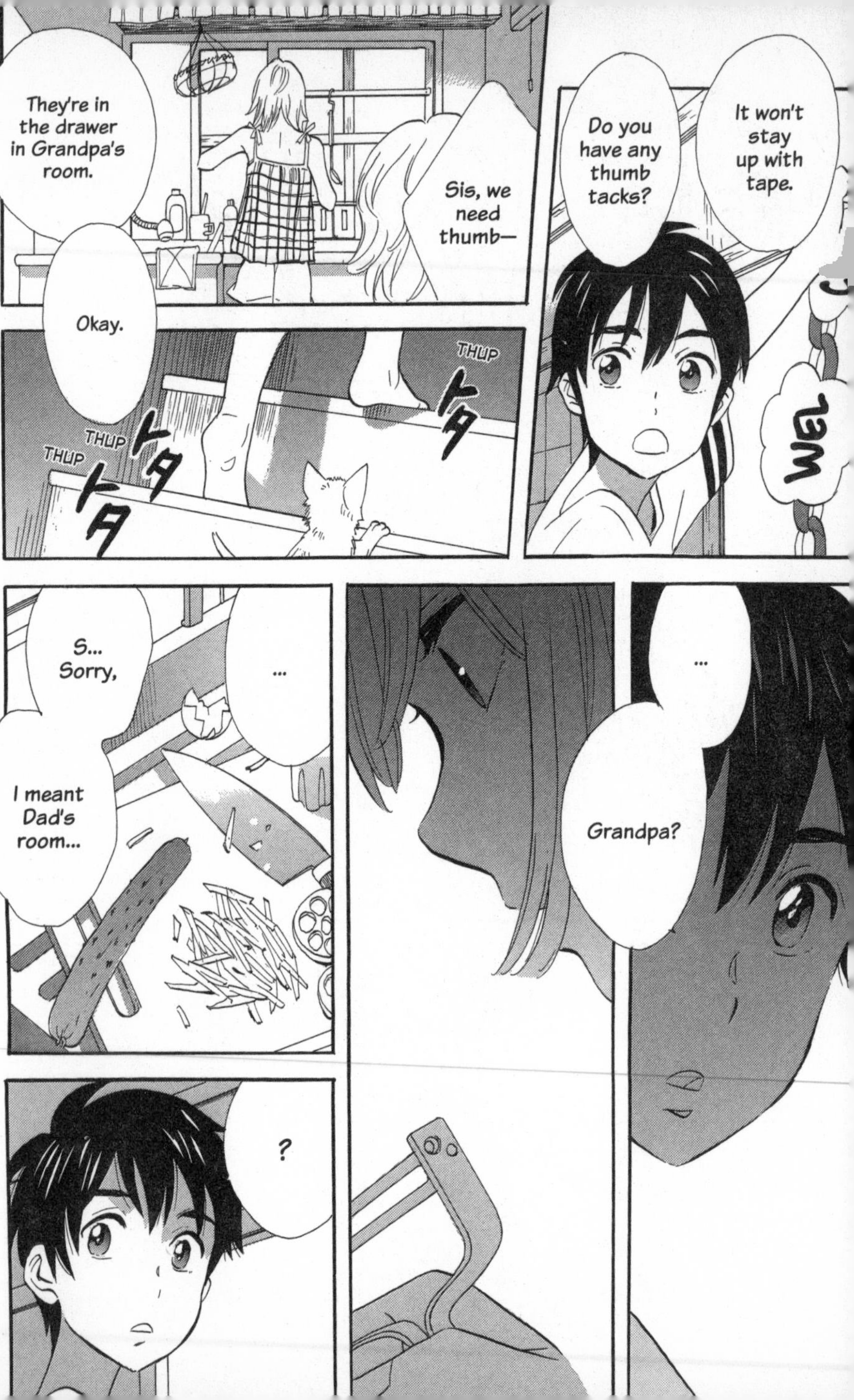
It won't stay up with tape.
Do you have any thumb tacks?
WEL
Sis, we need thumb—
They're in the drawer in Grandpa's room.
Okay.
THUP
トタ
THUP
トタ
THUP
トタ
...
Grandpa?
...
S... Sorry,
I meant Dad's room...
?

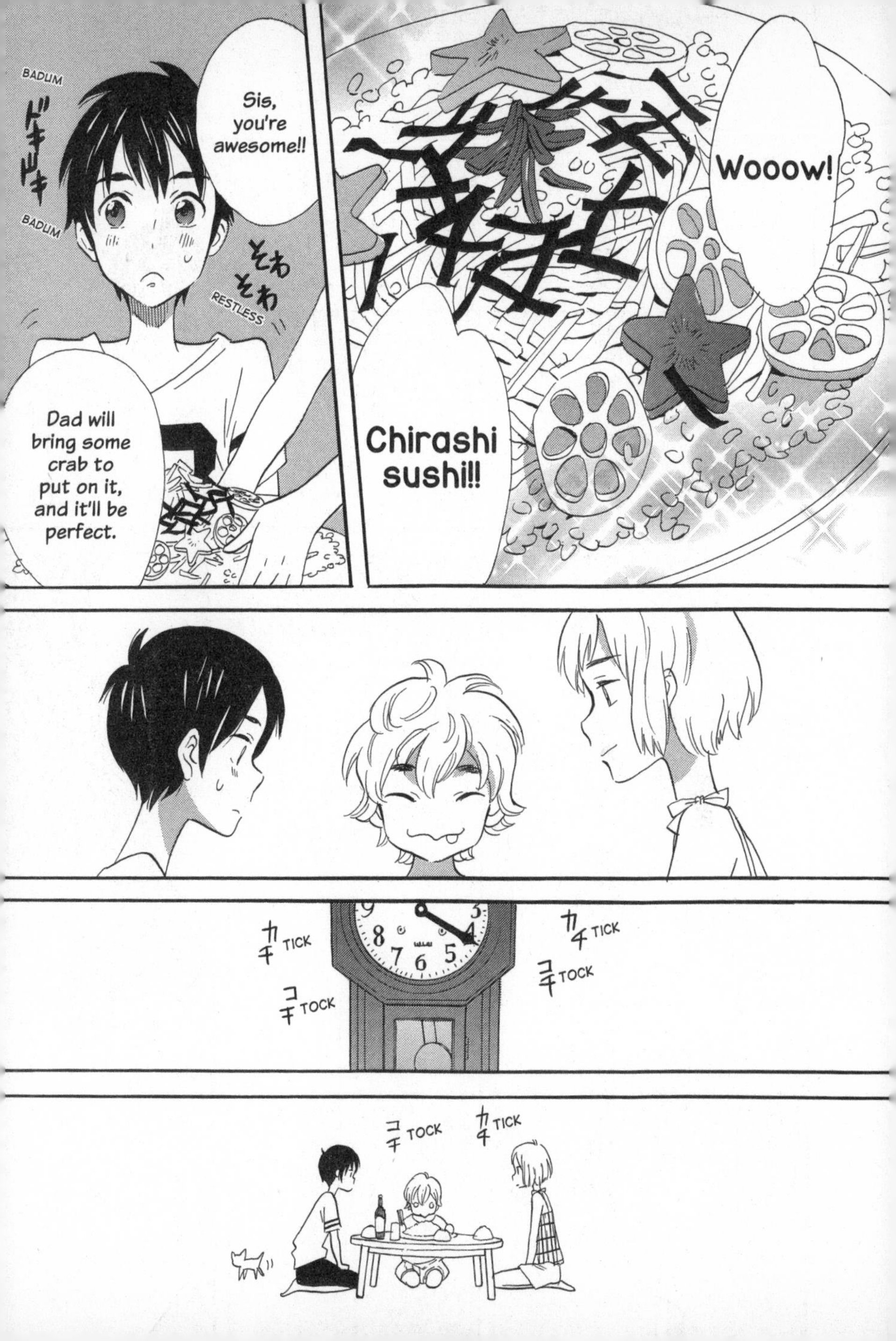
Wooow!
Chirashi sushi!!
Sis, you're awesome!!
ドキドキ
BADUM
BADUM
そわそわ
RESTLESS
Dad will bring some crab to put on it, and it'll be perfect.
カチ TICK
コチ TOCK
カチ TICK
コチ TOCK
カチ TICK
コチ TOCK

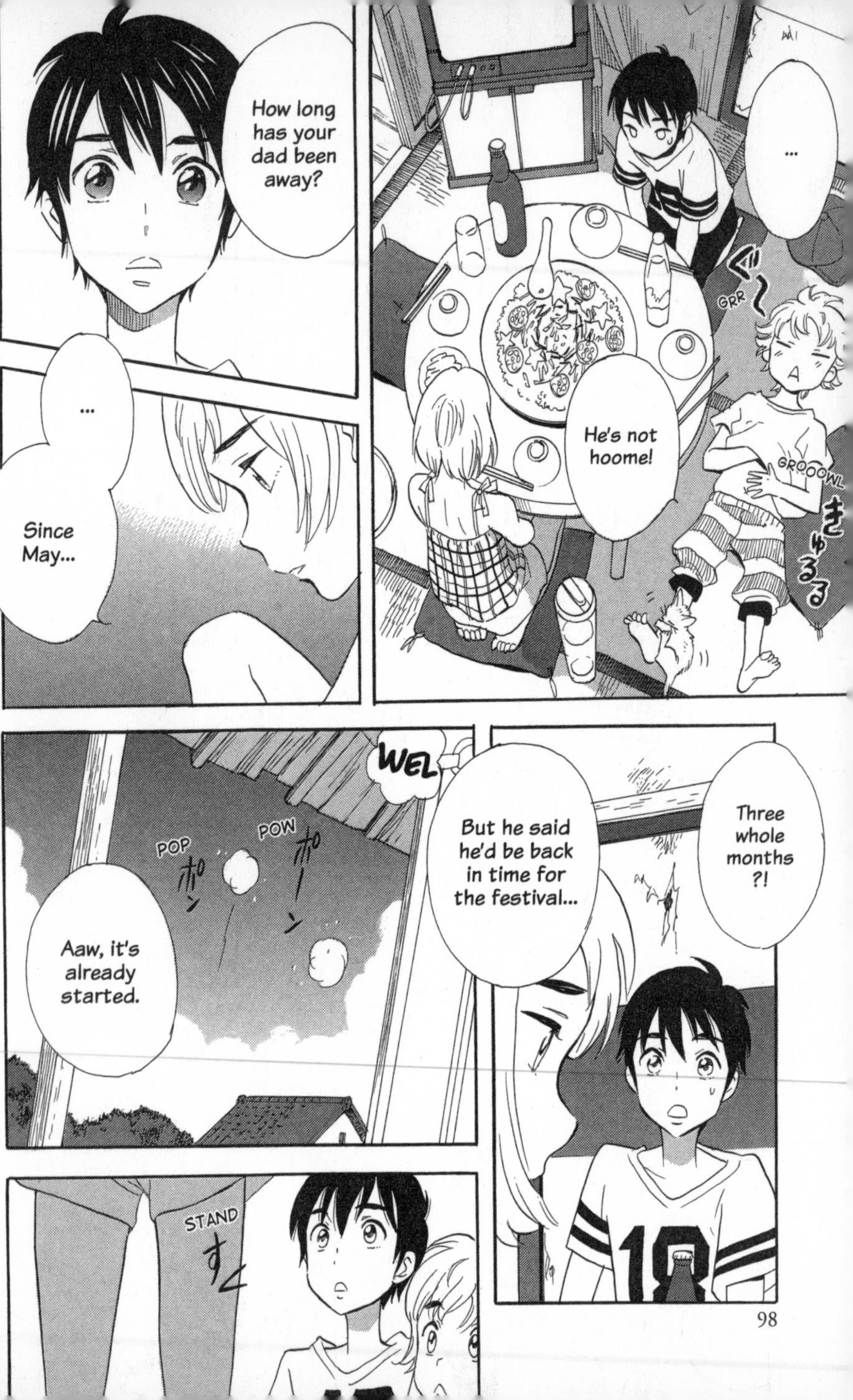
...
GRR
ぐ〜
He's not hoome!
GROOOWL
きゅるる
How long has your dad been away?
...
Since May...
Three whole months ?!
But he said he'd be back in time for the festival...
WEL
POW
ポーン
POP
ポン
Aaw, it's already started.
STAND
すく

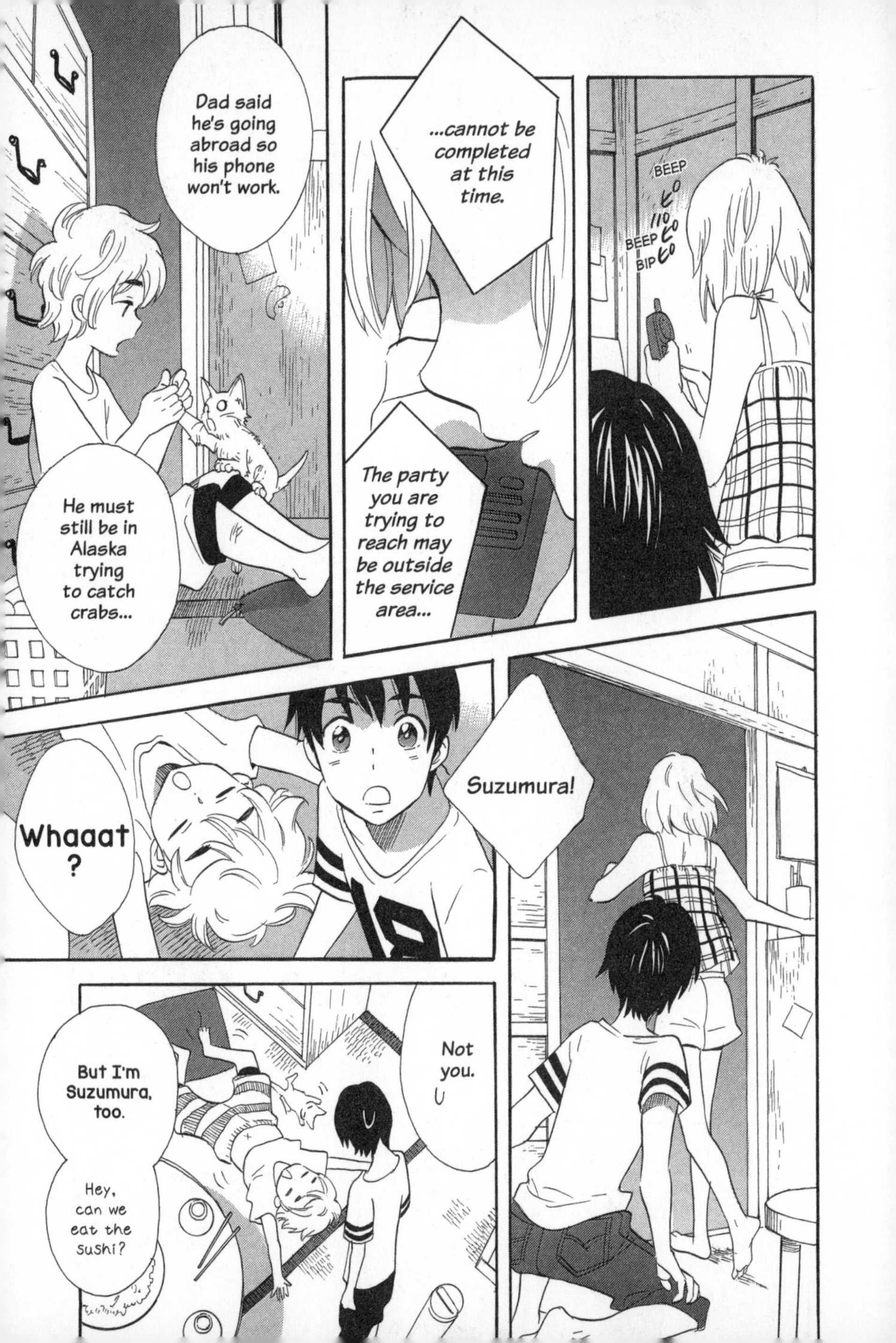
BEEP
BEEP
BIP
...cannot be completed at this time.
The party you are trying to reach may be outside the service area...
Dad said he's going abroad so his phone won't work.
He must still be in Alaska trying to catch crabs...
Suzumura!
Whaaat?
Not you.
But I'm Suzumura, too.
Hey, can we eat the sushi?

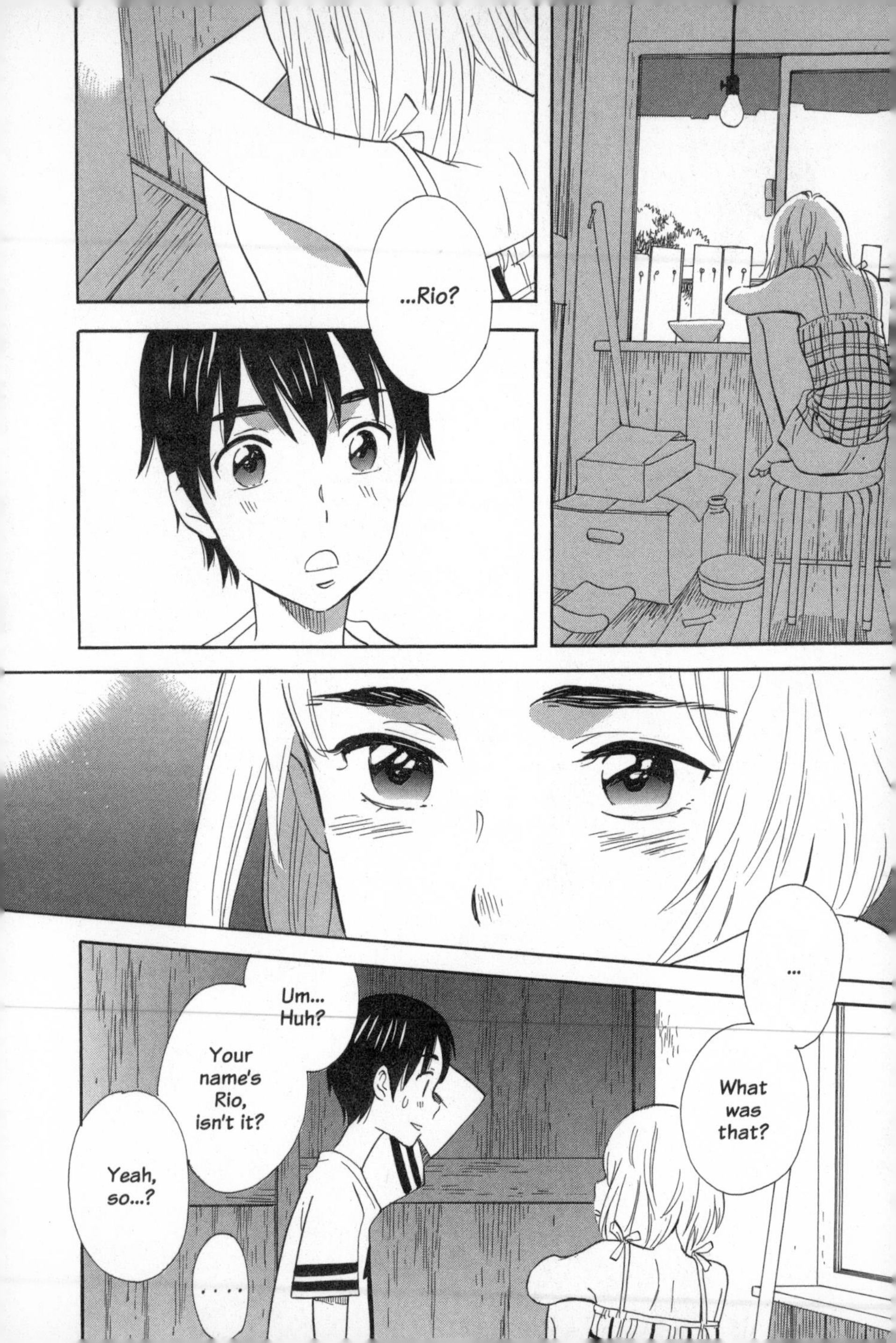
...Rio?
...
What was that?
Um... Huh?
Your name's Rio, isn't it?
Yeah, so...?
....

Rio...

I'll go to the festival with you.

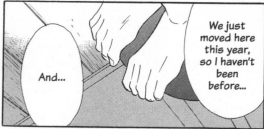

We just moved here this year, so I haven't been before...

And...

I don't have a dad, either...

...

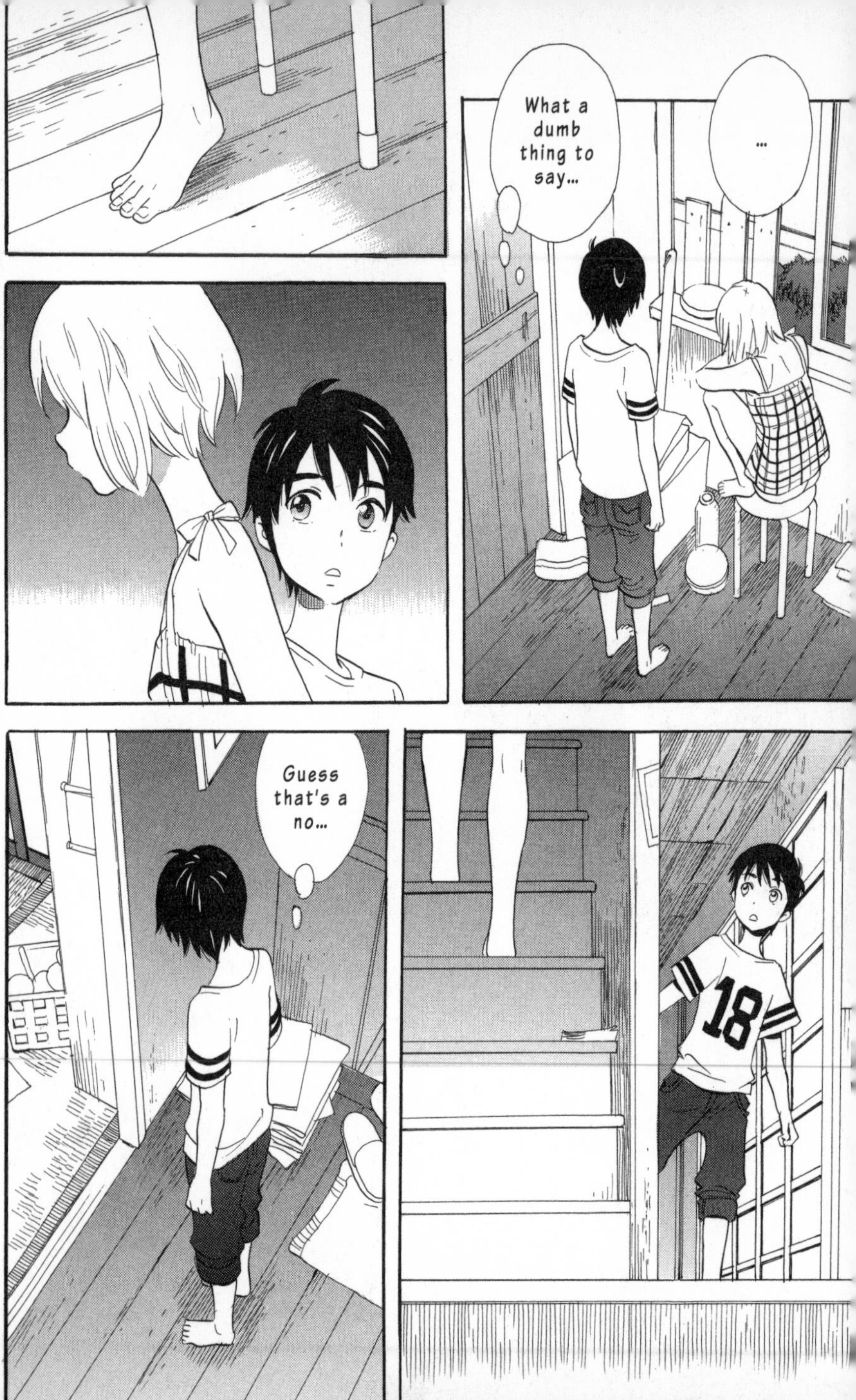
...
What a dumb thing to say...
Guess that's a no...

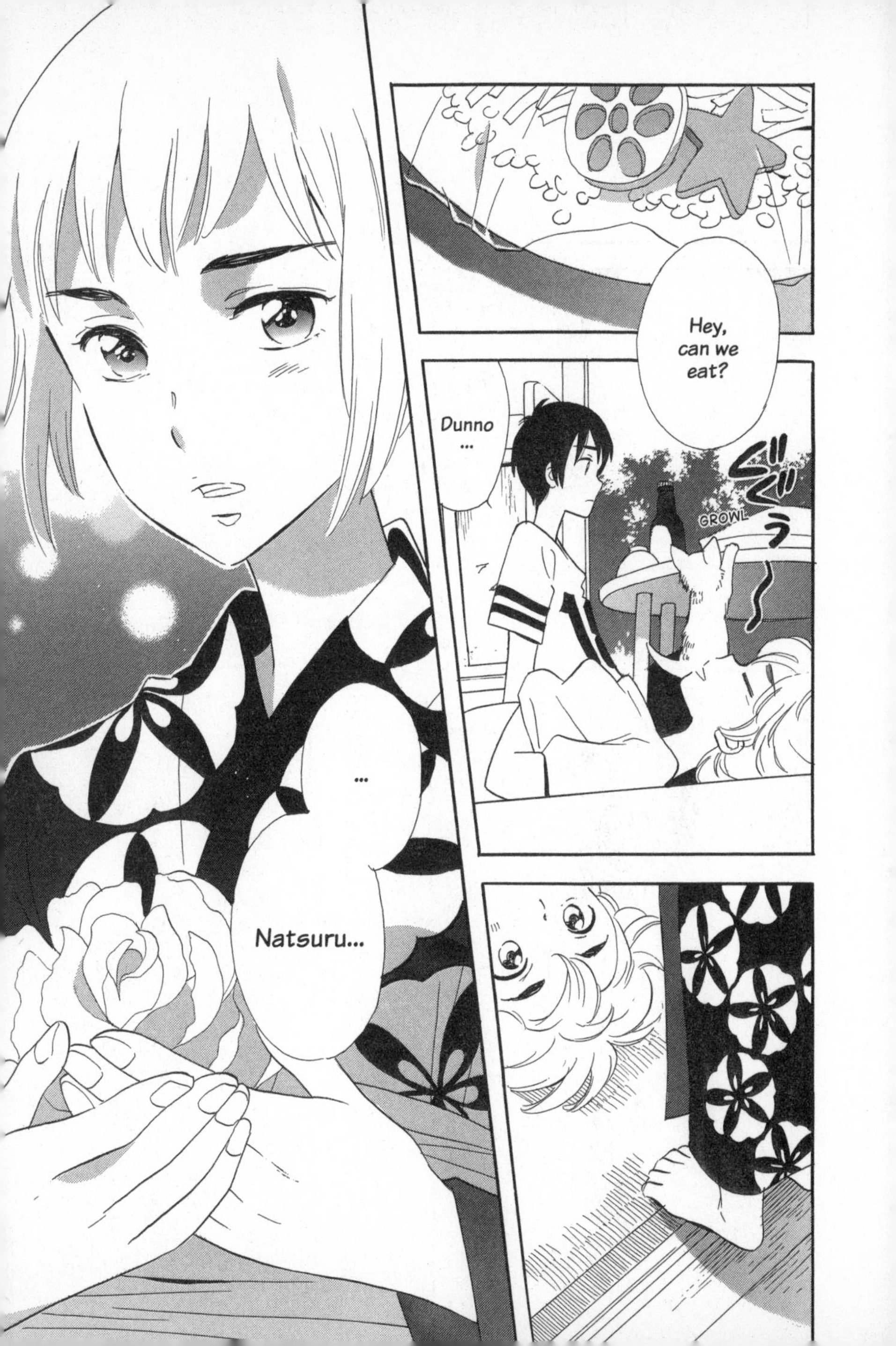
Hey, can we eat?
Dunno...
GROWL
...
Natsuru...

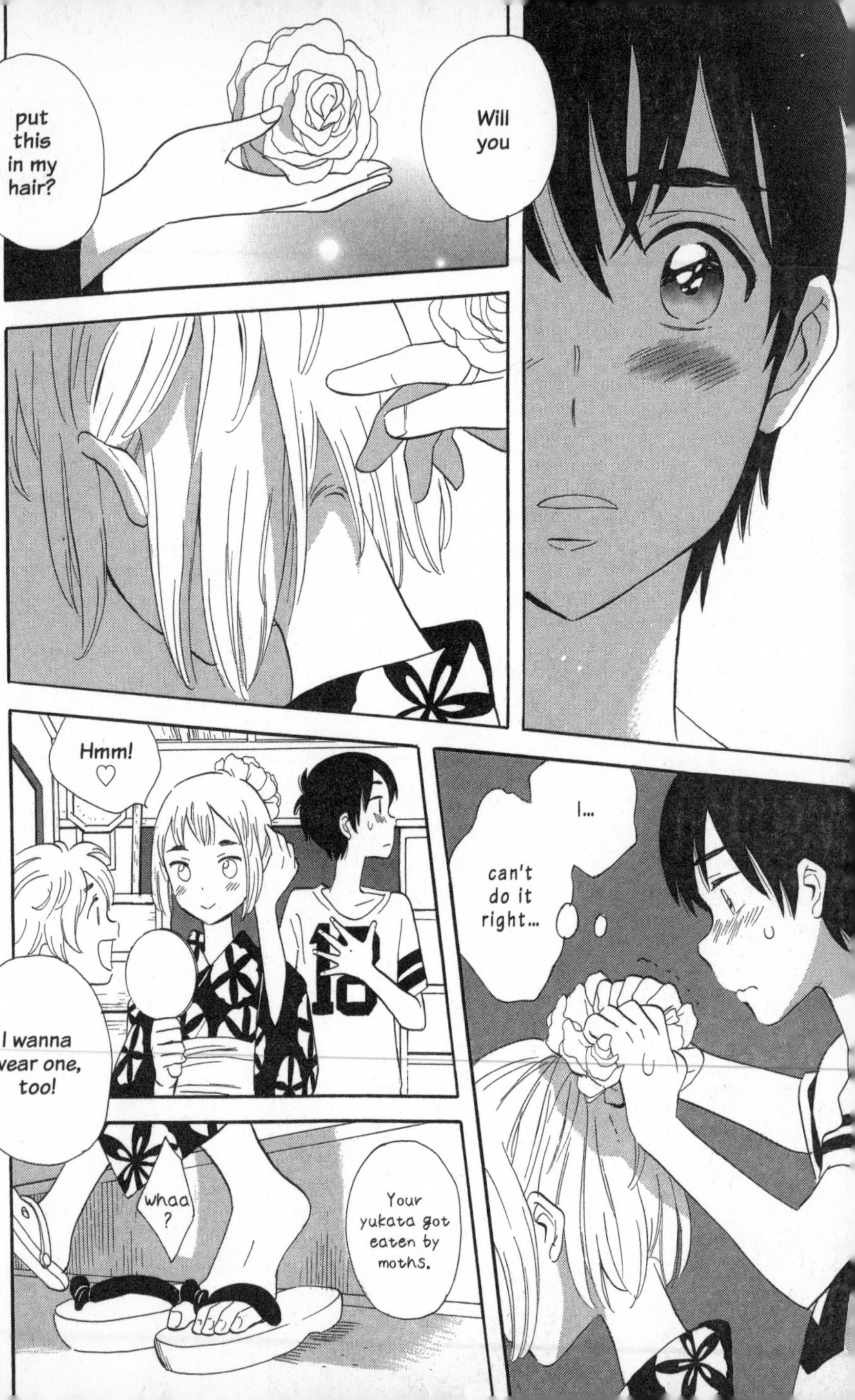
Will you
put this in my hair?
I...
can't do it right...
Hmm! ♡
I wanna wear one, too!
Your yukata got eaten by moths.
whaa ?

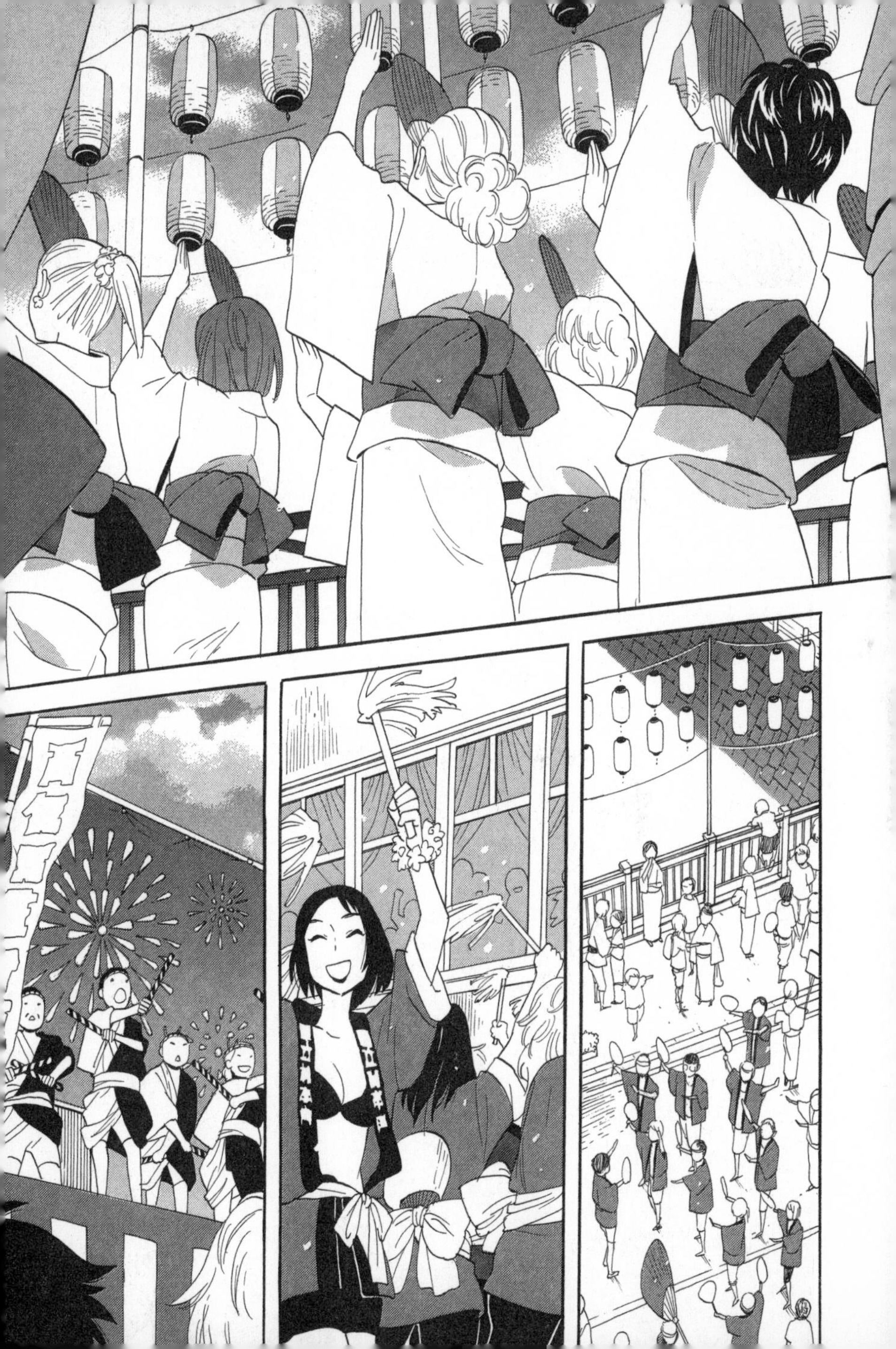

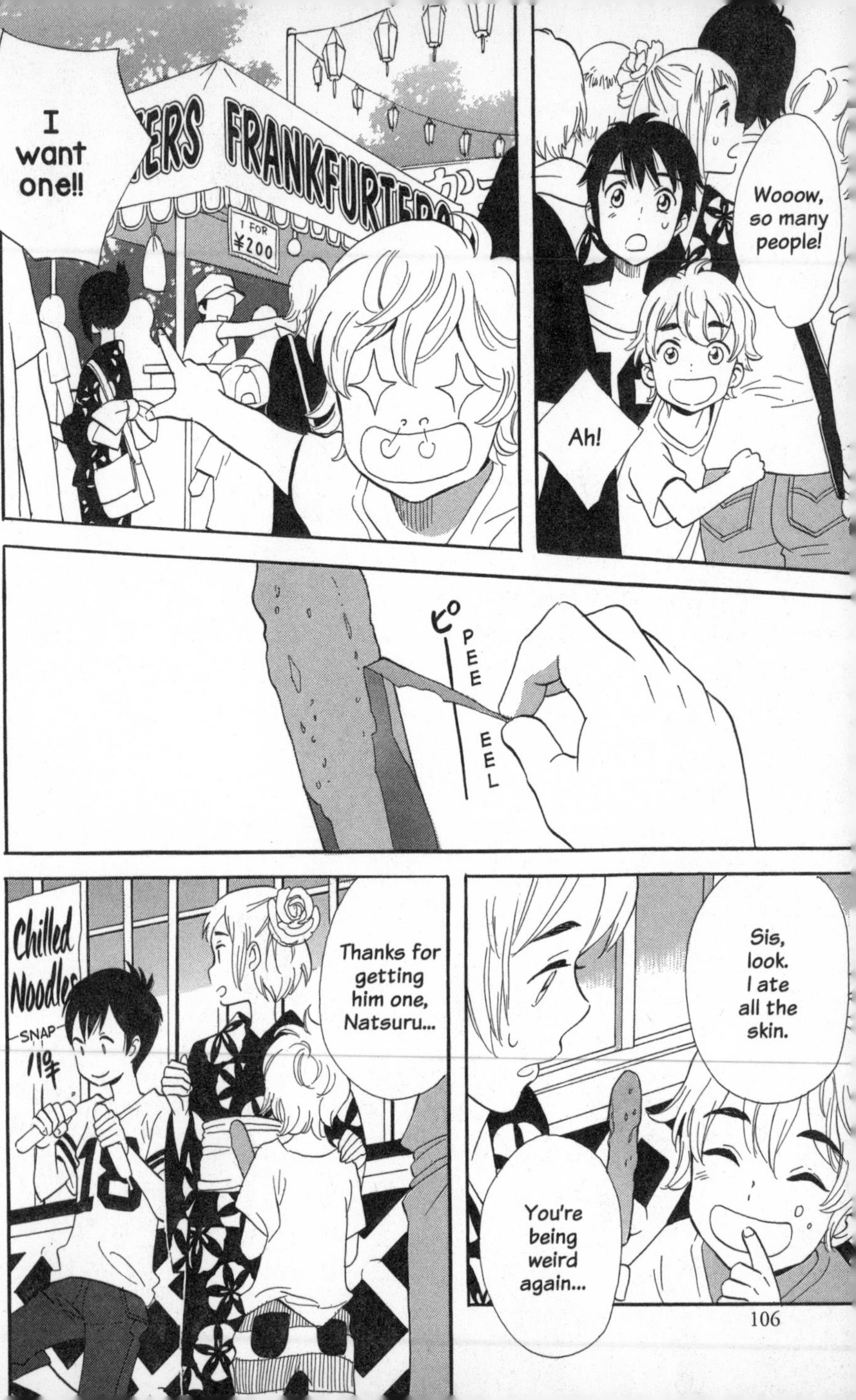
Wooow, so many people!
Ah!
I want one!!
1 FOR ¥200
ピ
PEE EEL
Sis, look. I ate all the skin.
You're being weird again...
Thanks for getting him one, Natsuru...
Chilled Noodles
SNAP

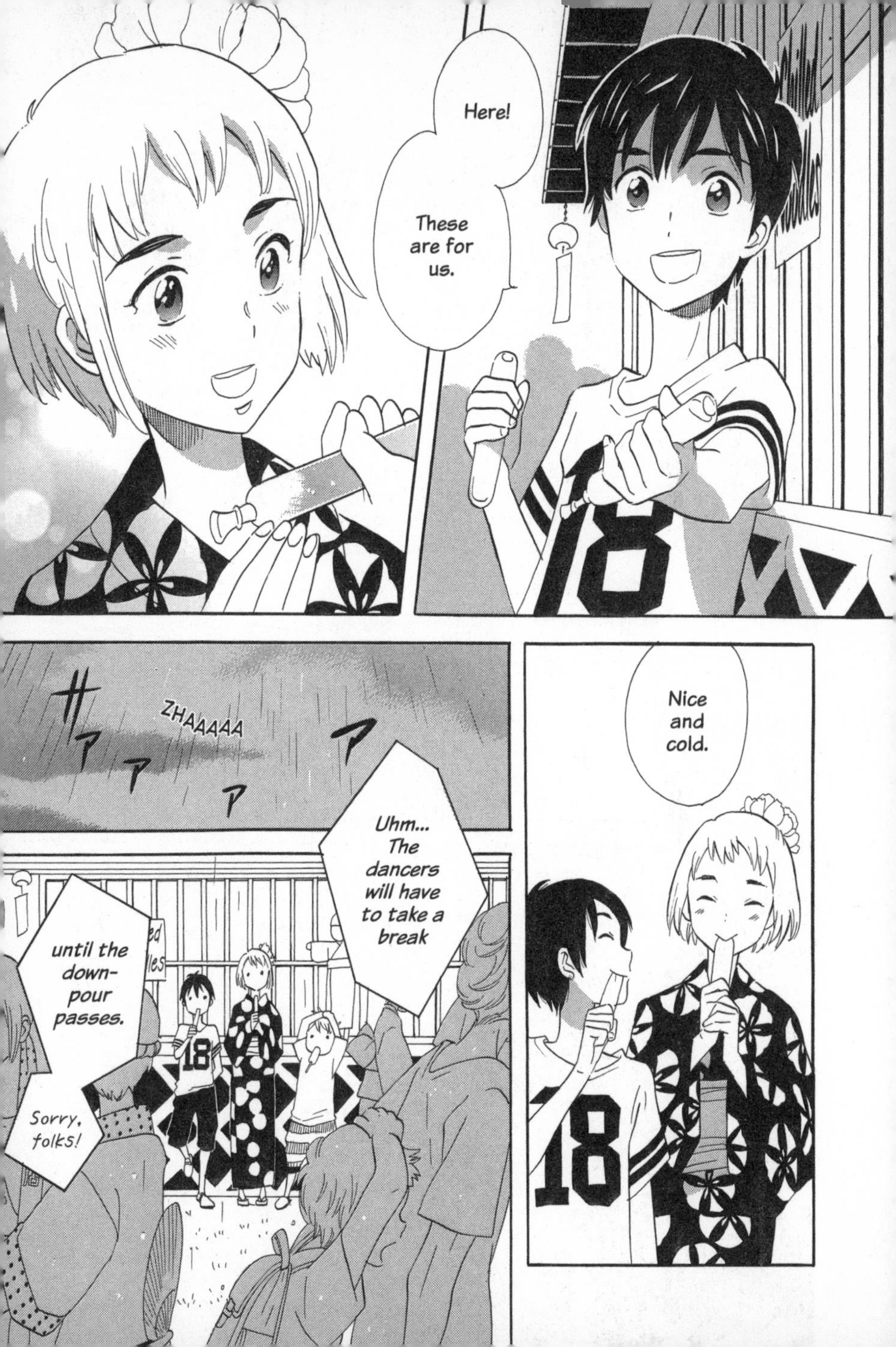
Here!
These are for us.
Nice and cold.
ZHAAAAA
Uhm... The dancers will have to take a break
until the down-pour passes.
Sorry, folks!

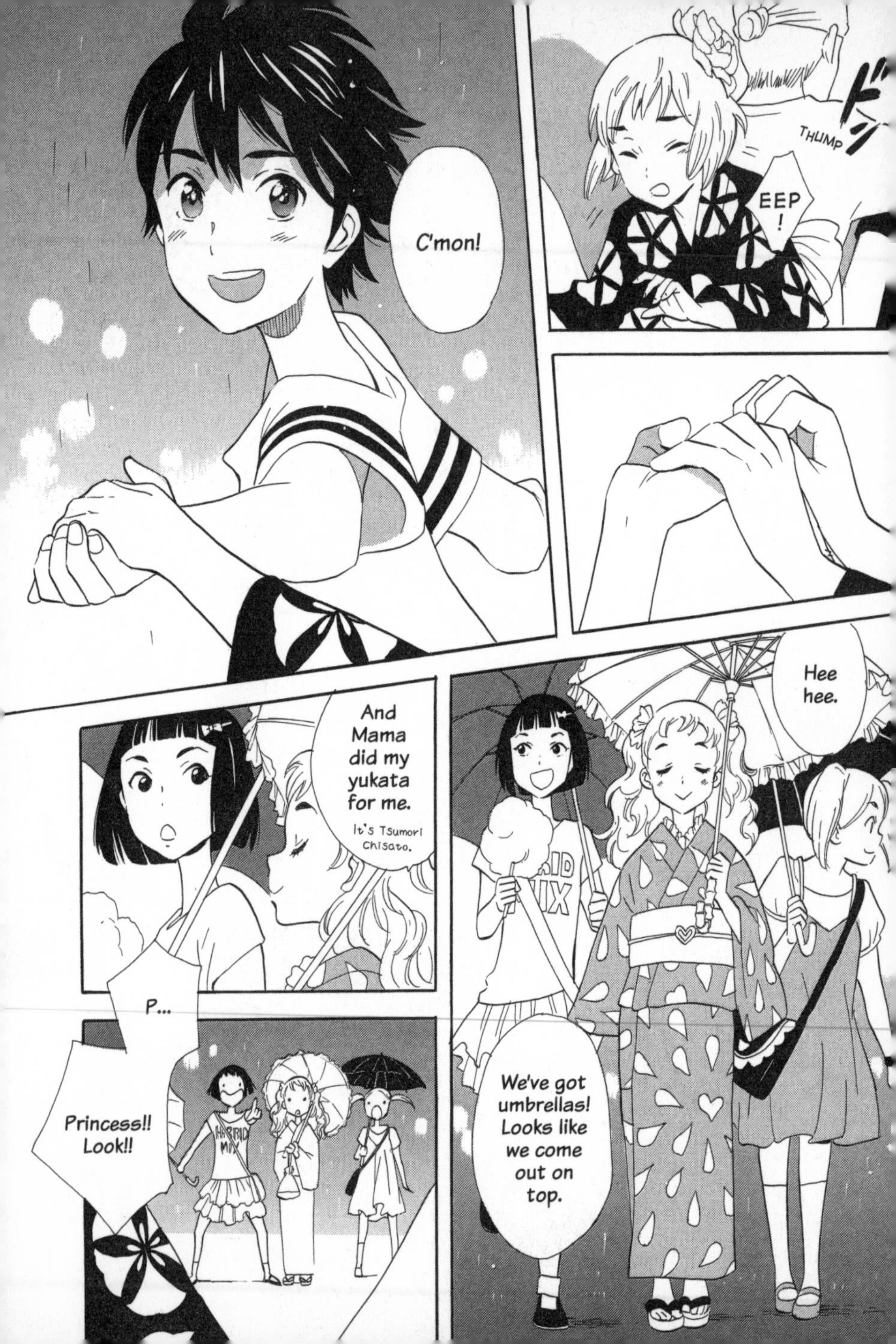
THUMP
EEP!
C'mon!
Hee hee.
We've got umbrellas! Looks like we come out on top.
And Mama did my yukata for me.
It's Tsumori Chisato.
P...
Princess!! Look!!

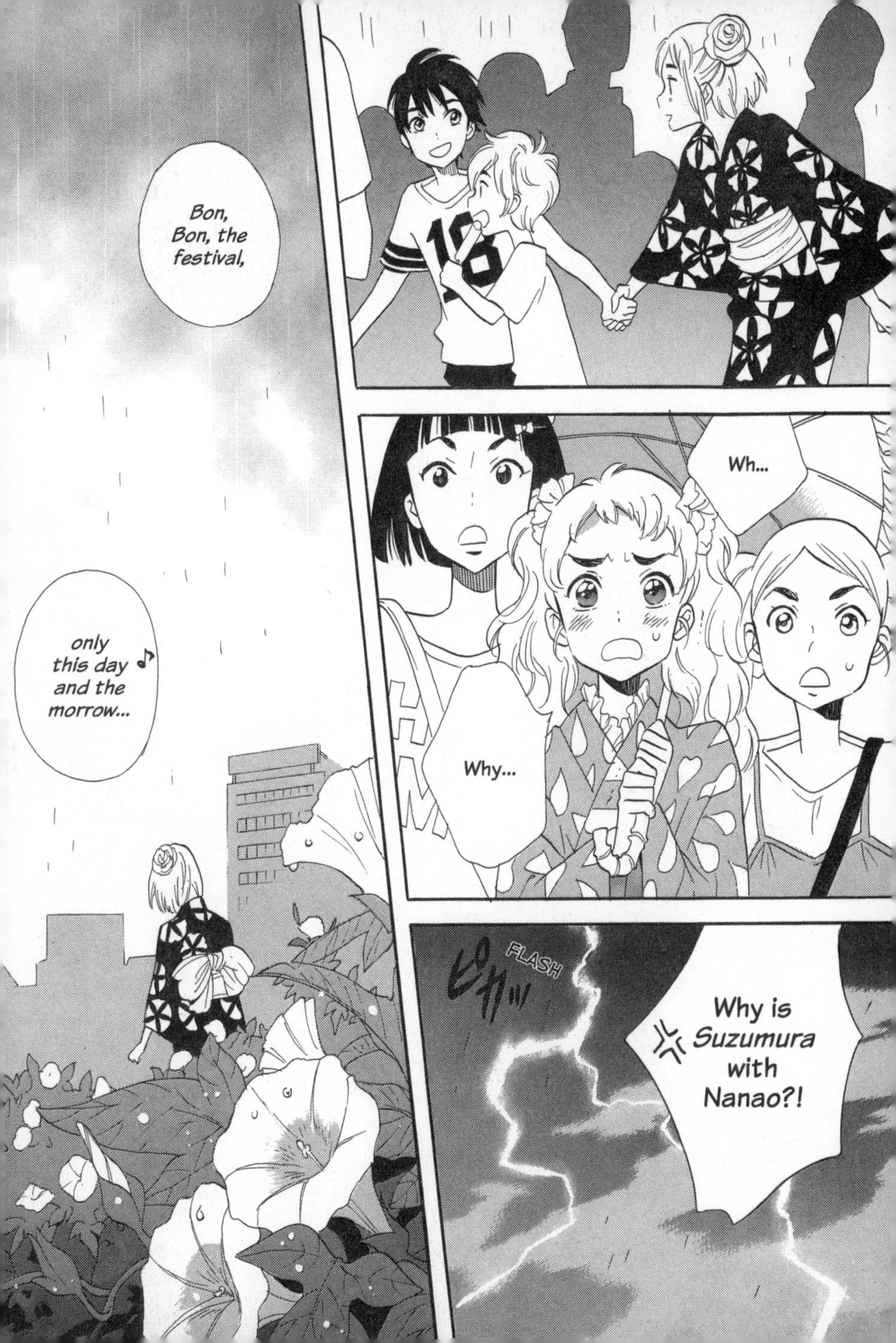
Wh...
Why...
FLASH
Why is Suzumura with Nanao?!
Bon, Bon, the festival,
only this day and the morrow... ♪

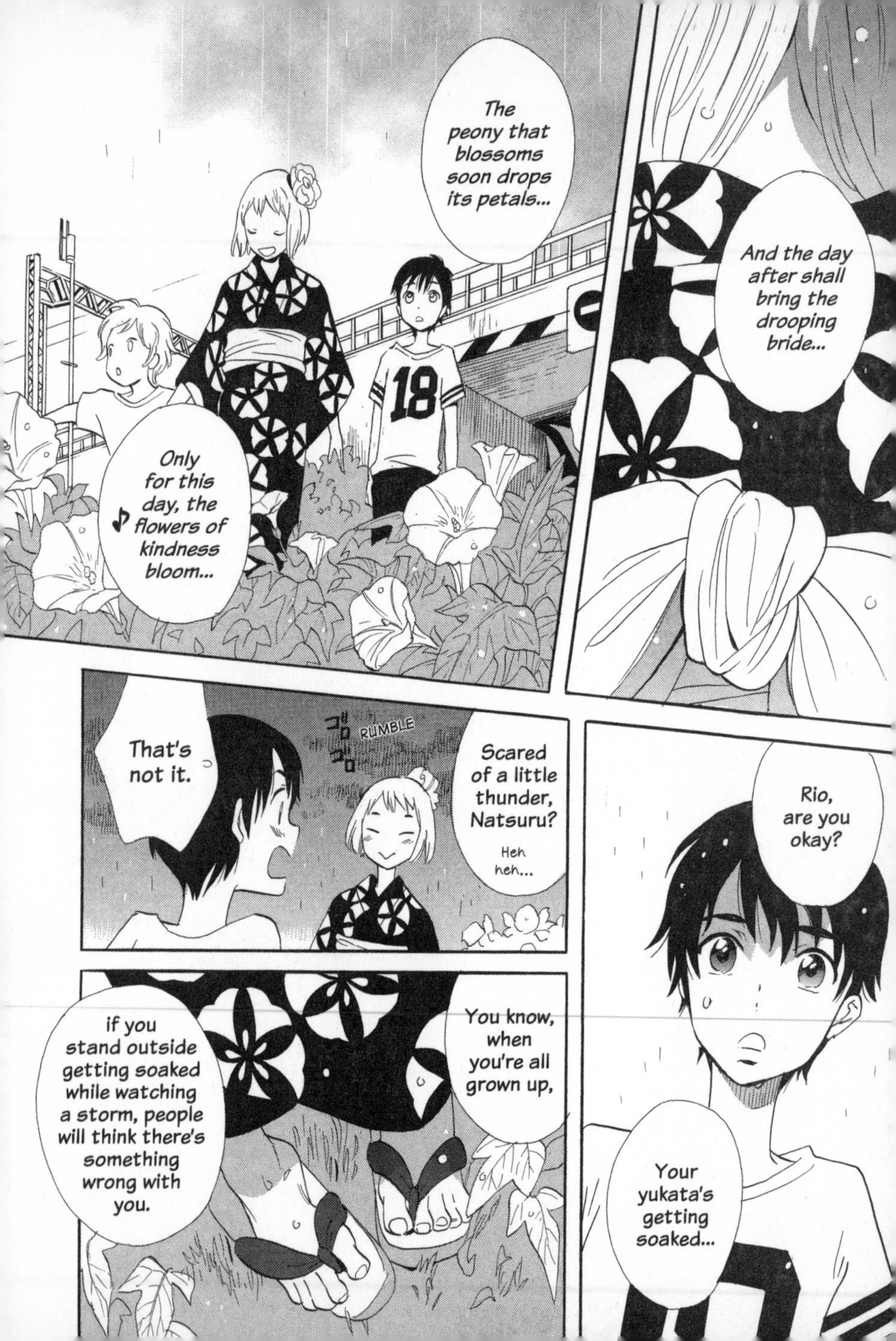
And the day after shall bring the drooping bride...
The peony that blossoms soon drops its petals...
♪ Only for this day, the flowers of kindness bloom...
Rio, are you okay?
Your yukata's getting soaked...
ゴロ ゴロ RUMBLE
Scared of a little thunder, Natsuru?
Heh heh...
That's not it.
You know, when you're all grown up,
if you stand outside getting soaked while watching a storm, people will think there's something wrong with you.

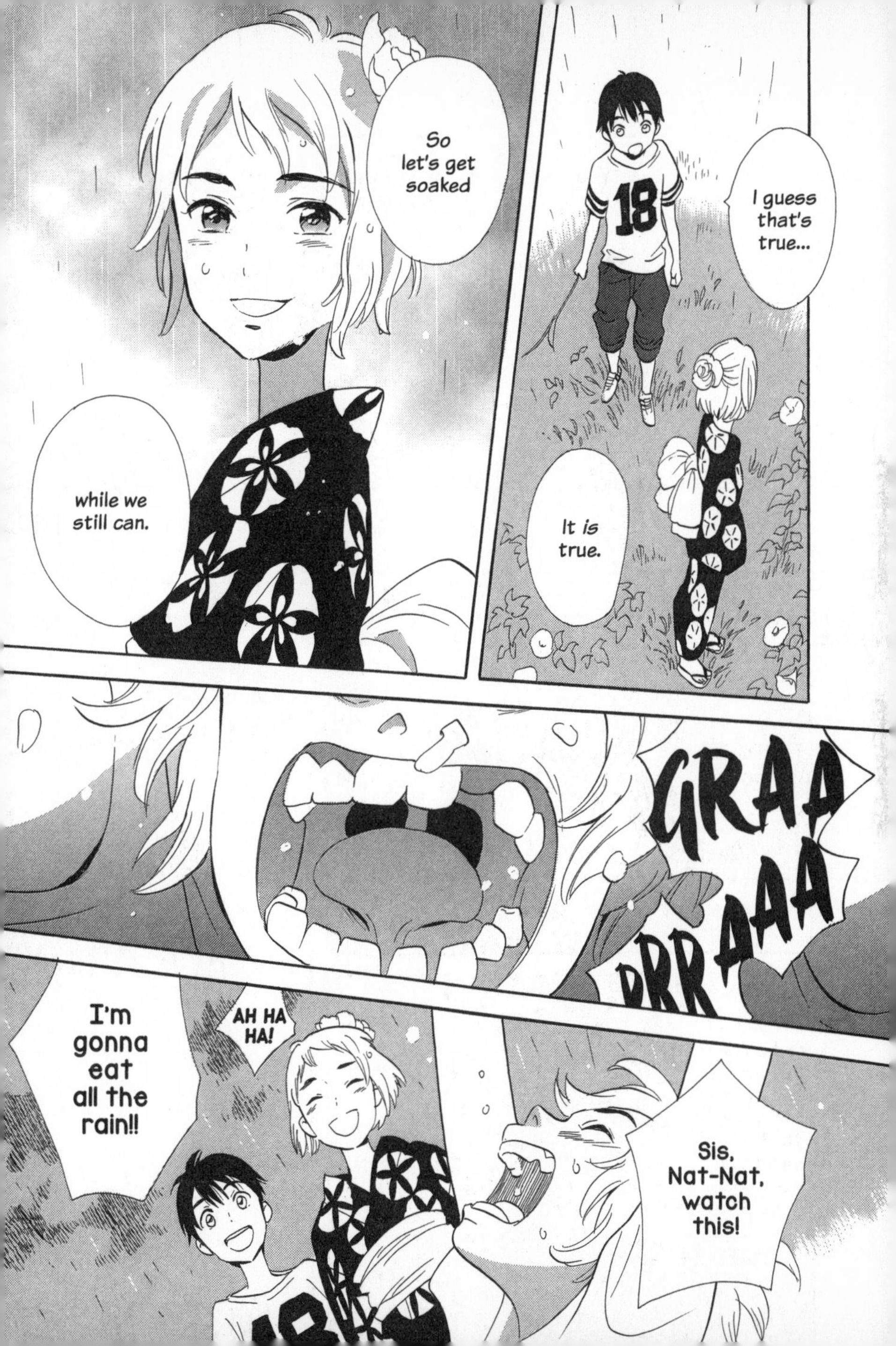
I guess that's true...
It is true.
So let's get soaked
while we still can.
GRAA
AAA
DRR
Sis, Nat-Nat, watch this!
I'm gonna eat all the rain!!
AH HA HA!

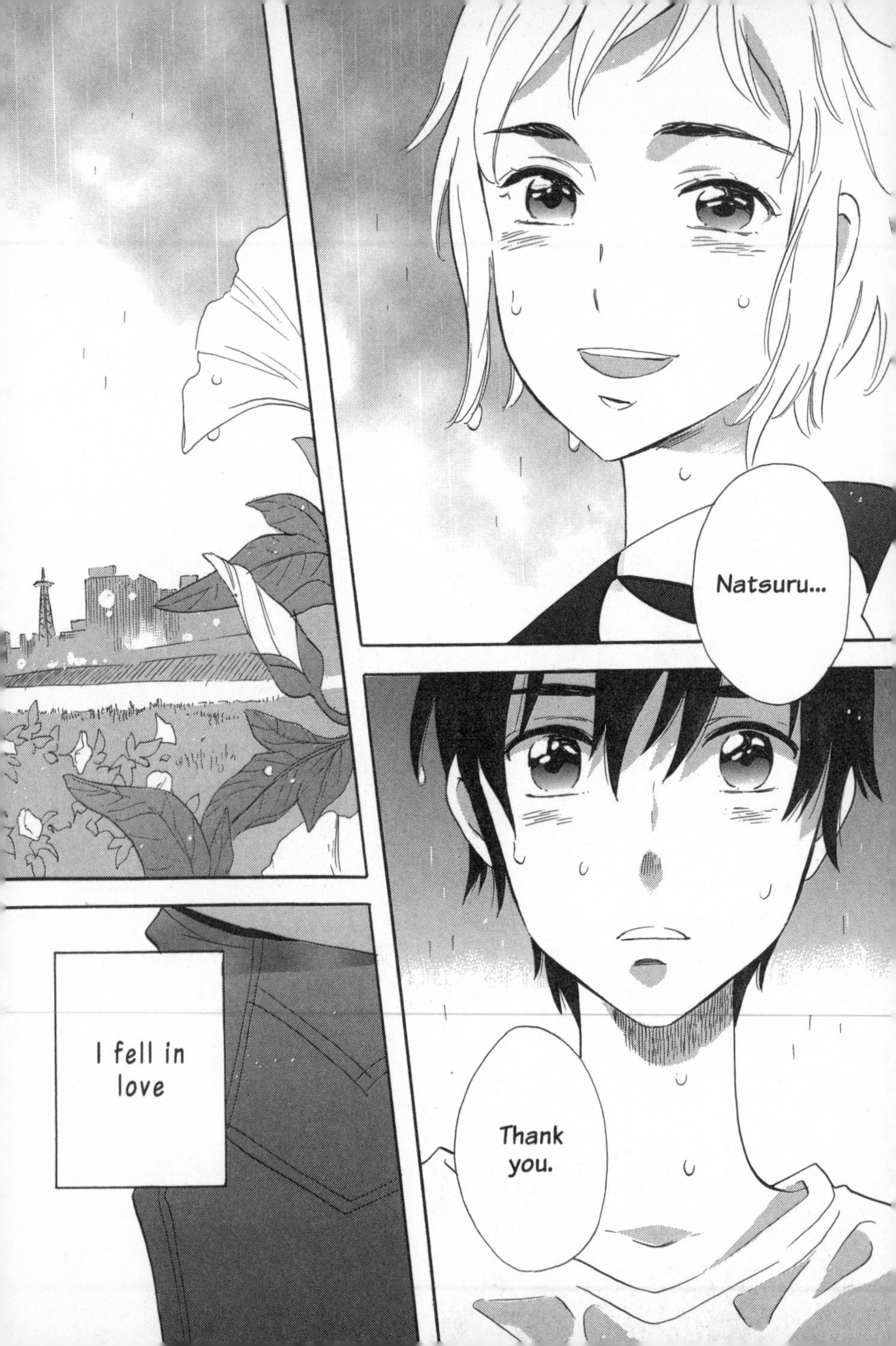
Natsuru...
Thank you.
I fell in love

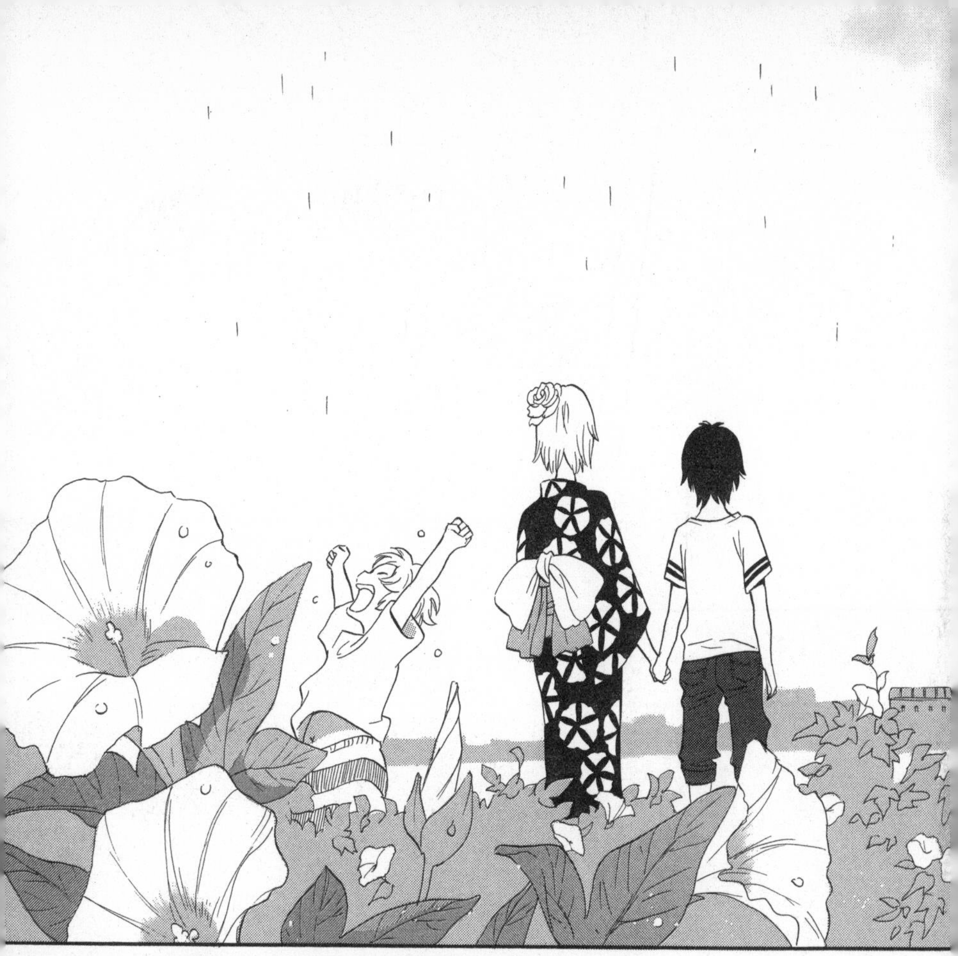

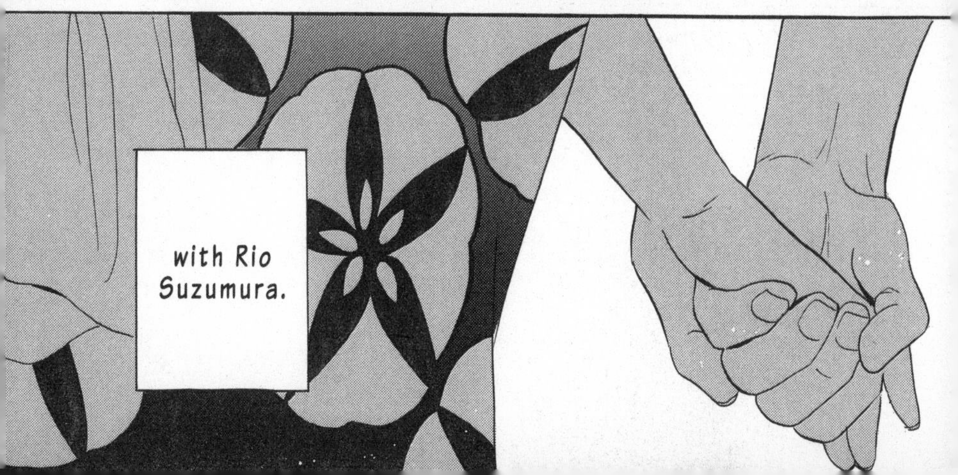
with Rio Suzumura.

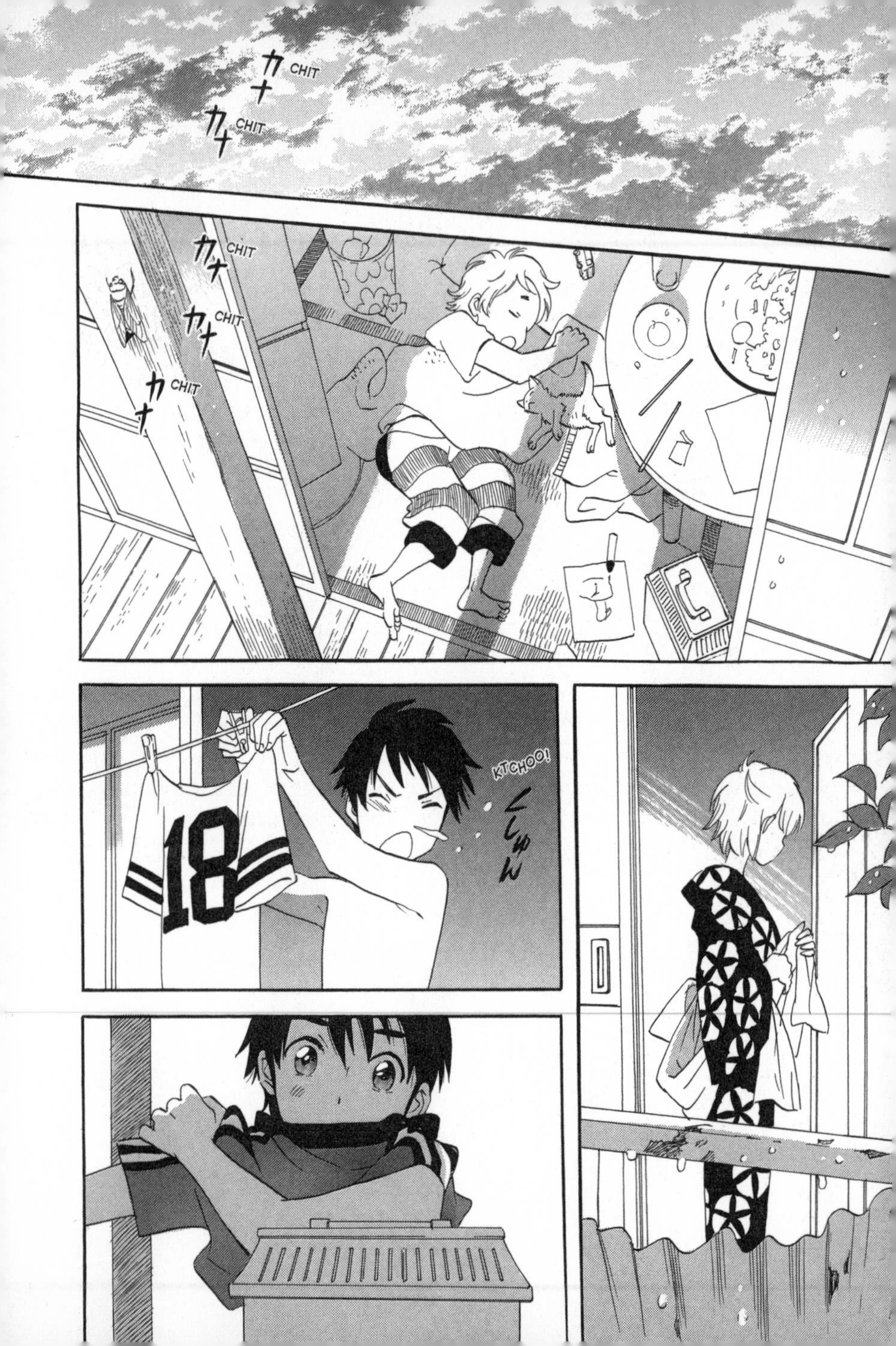
カナ CHIT
カナ CHIT
カナ CHIT
カナ CHIT
カナ CHIT
KTCHOO!
くしゅん

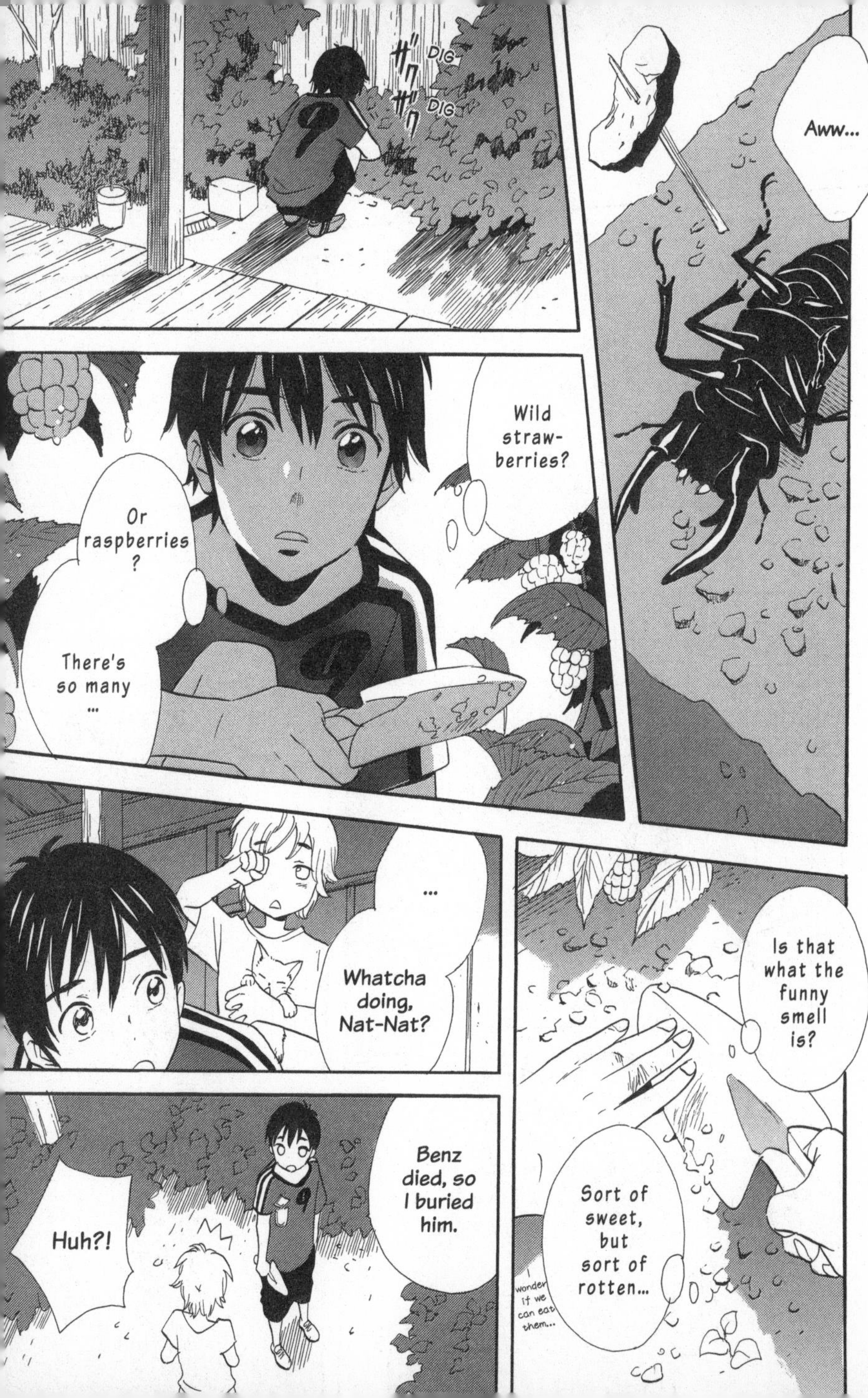
Aww...
ザク DIG
ザク DIG
Wild straw-berries?
Or raspberries?
There's so many ...
Is that what the funny smell is?
Sort of sweet, but sort of rotten...
I wonder if we can eat them...
...
Whatcha doing, Nat-Nat?
Benz died, so I buried him.
Huh?!

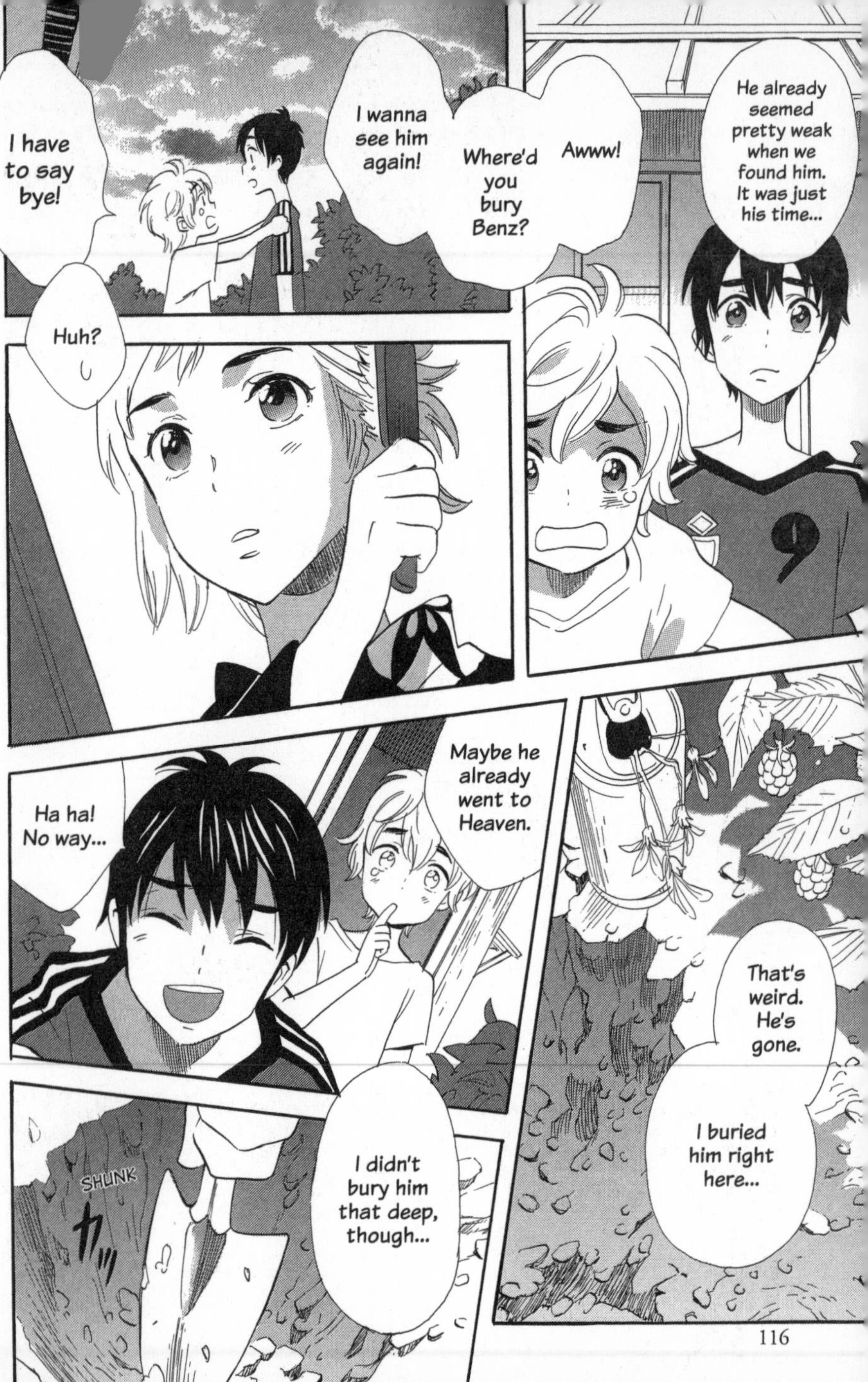
He already seemed pretty weak when we found him. It was just his time...
Awww!
I wanna see him again!
Where'd you bury Benz?
I have to say bye!
Huh?
That's weird. He's gone.
I buried him right here...
Maybe he already went to Heaven.
Ha ha! No way...
I didn't bury him that deep, though...
SHUNK

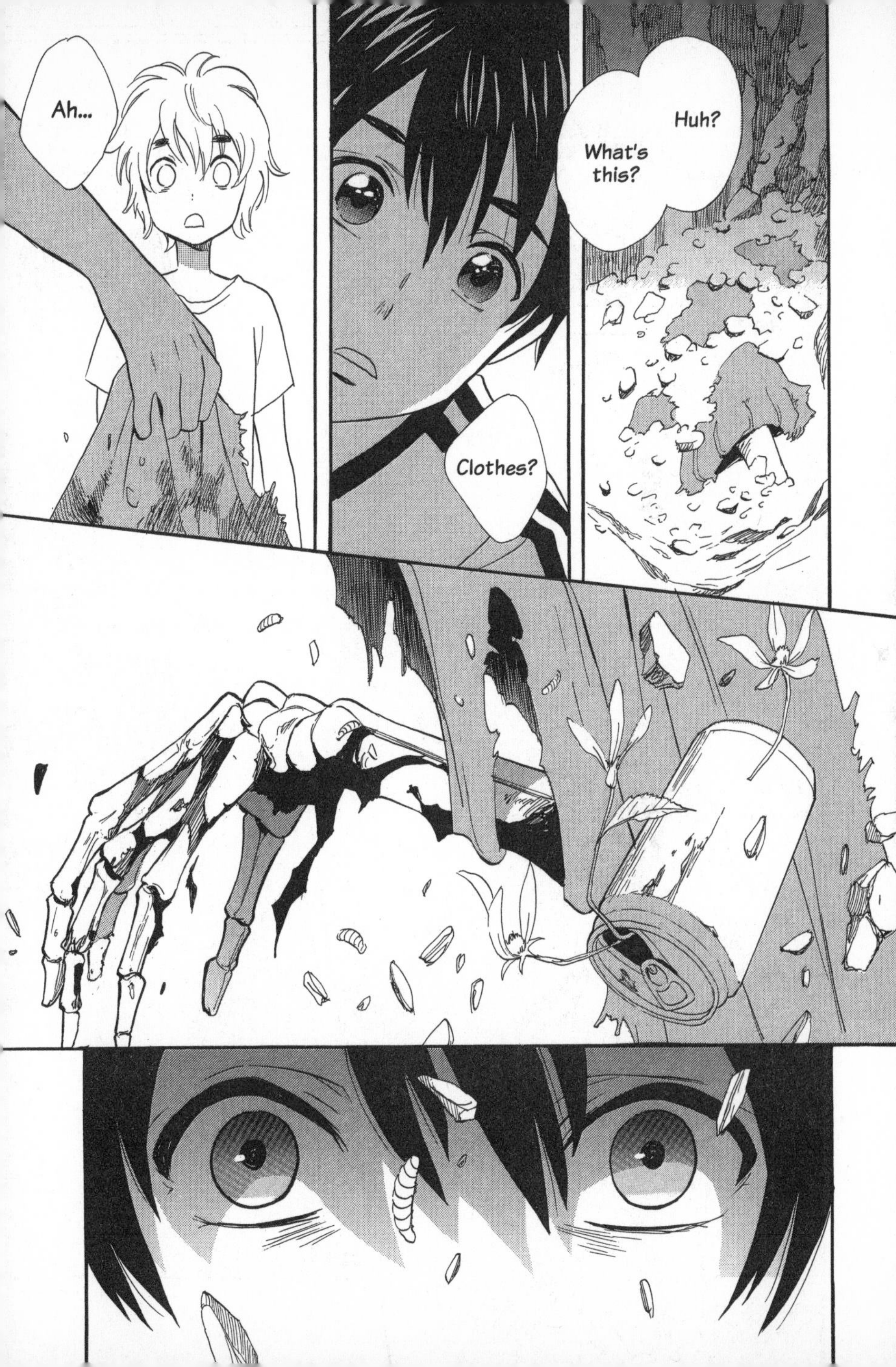
Huh?
What's this?
Clothes?
Ah...

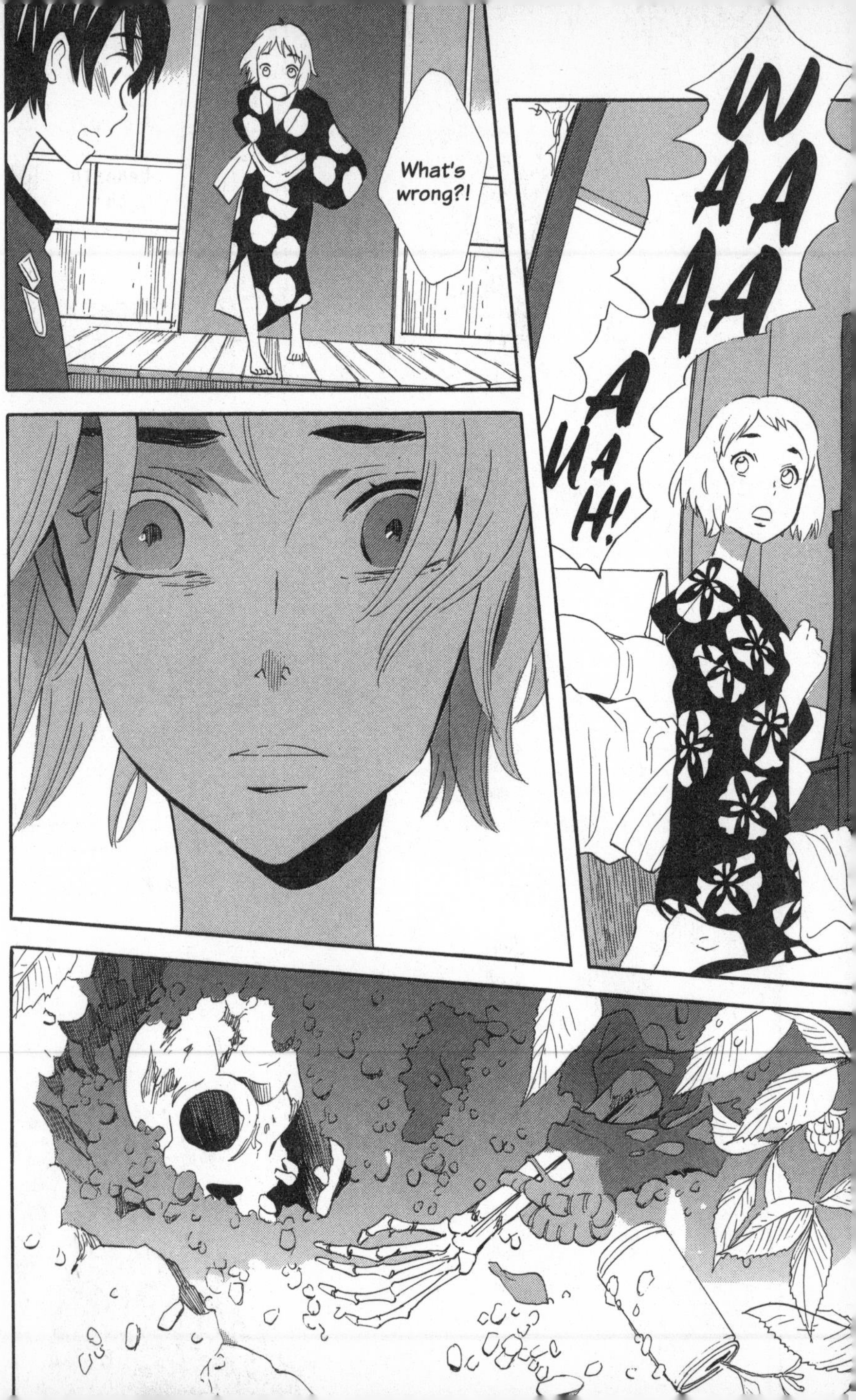
WAAAAAAUAAH!
What's wrong?!

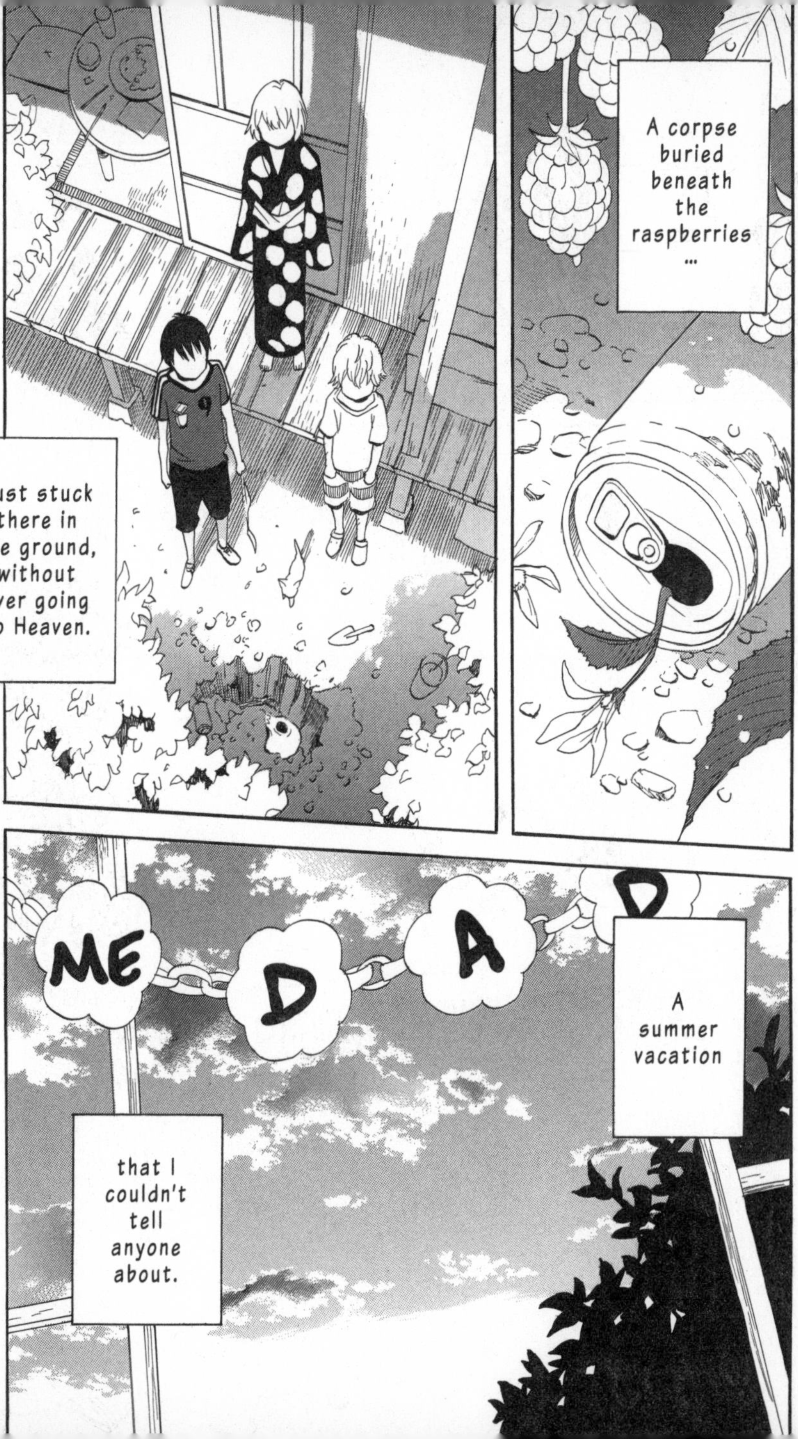
A corpse buried beneath the raspberries ...
Just stuck there in the ground, without ever going to Heaven.
ME D A D
A summer vacation
that I couldn't tell anyone about.

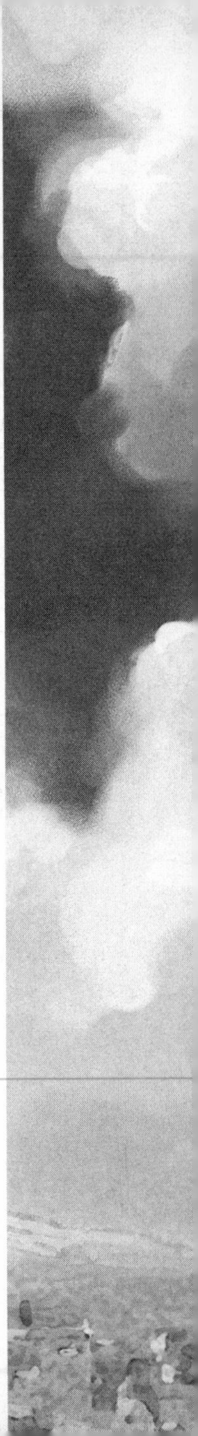

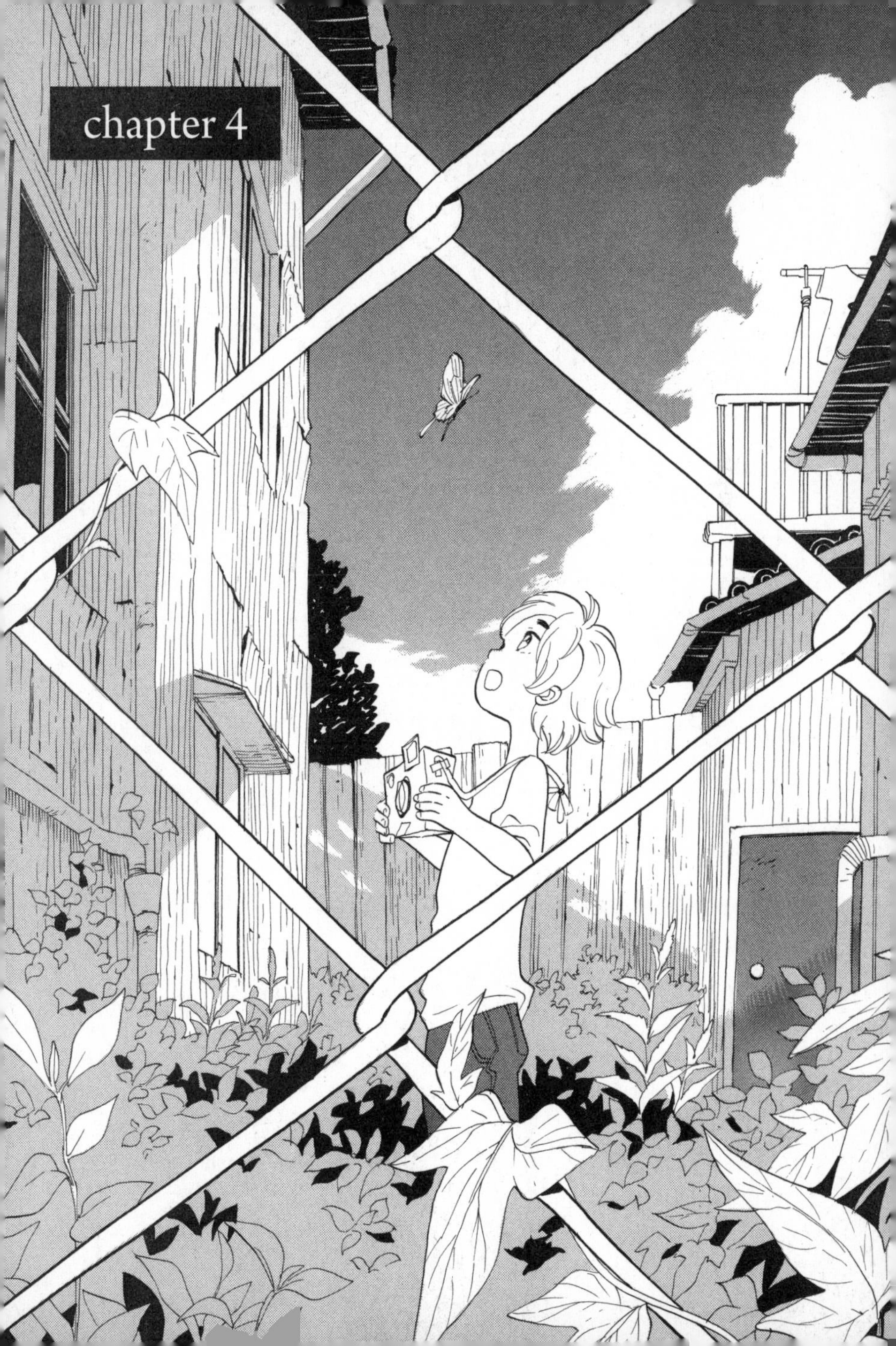
chapter 4

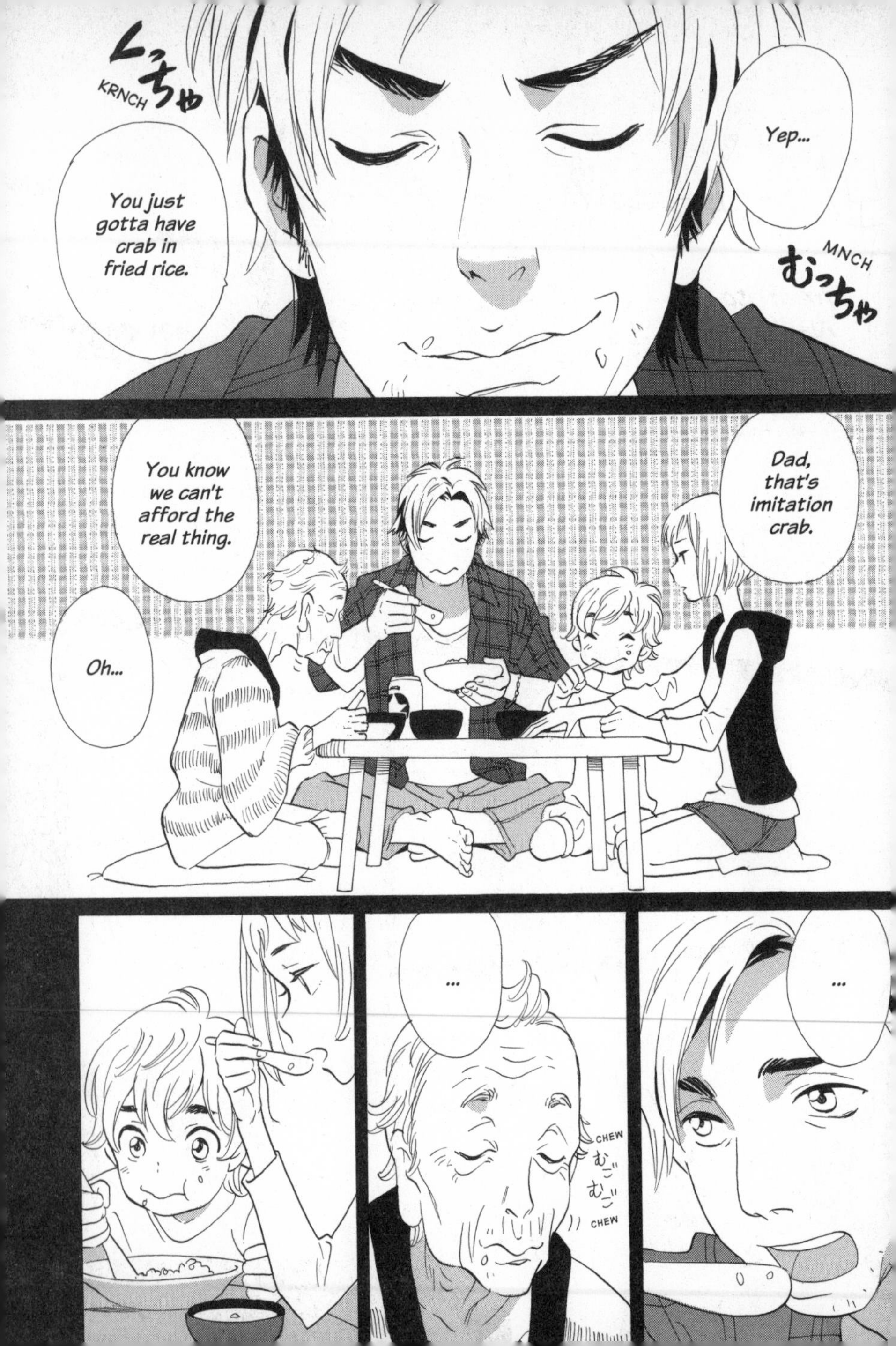

Yep...
MNCH
むっちゃ
KRNCH
くっちゃ
You just gotta have crab in fried rice.
Dad, that's imitation crab.
You know we can't afford the real thing.
Oh...
...
...
CHEW
むごむご
CHEW

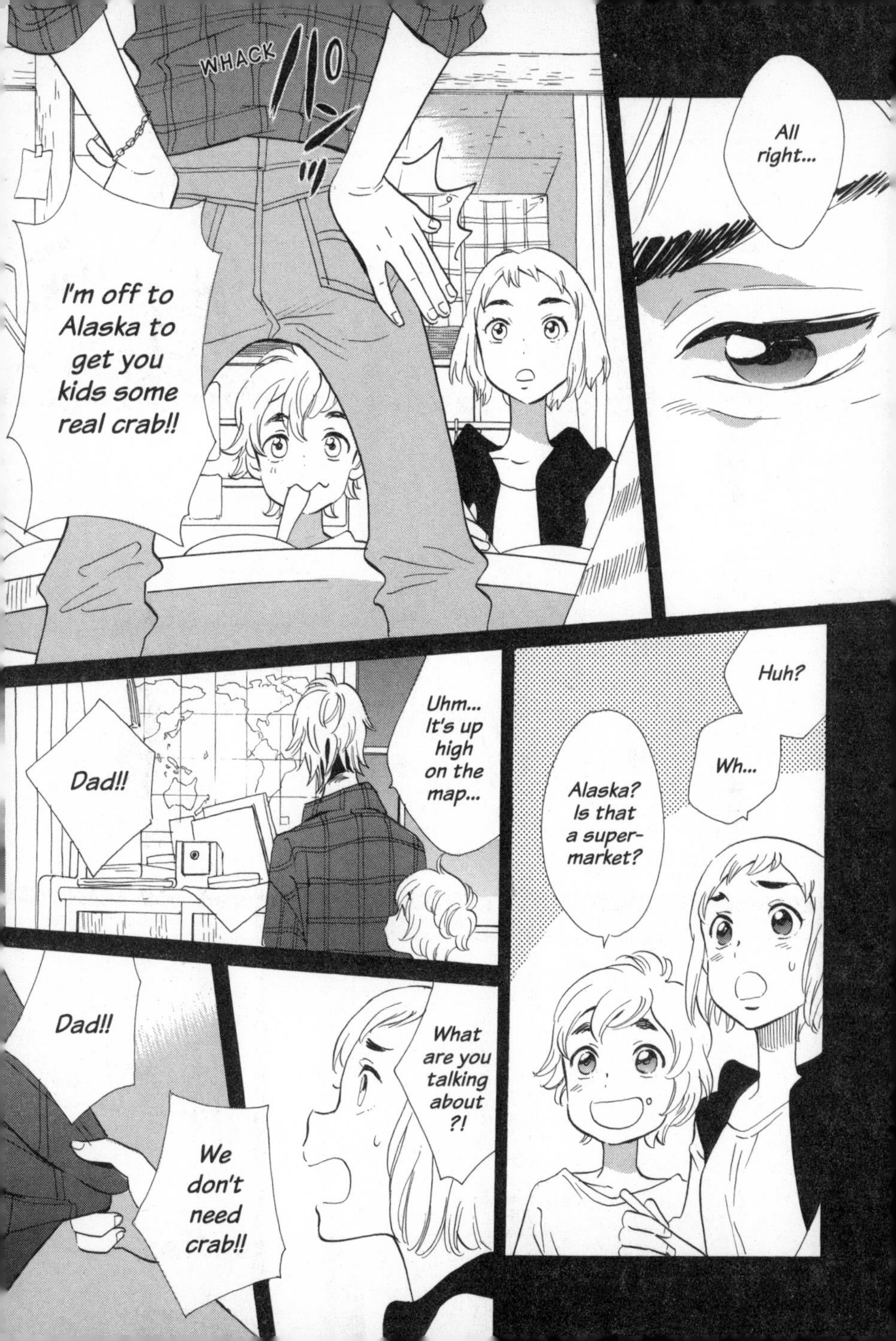
All right...
WHACK
I'm off to Alaska to get you kids some real crab!!
Huh?
Wh...
Alaska? Is that a super-market?
Uhm... It's up high on the map...
Dad!!
What are you talking about ?!
We don't need crab!!
Dad!!

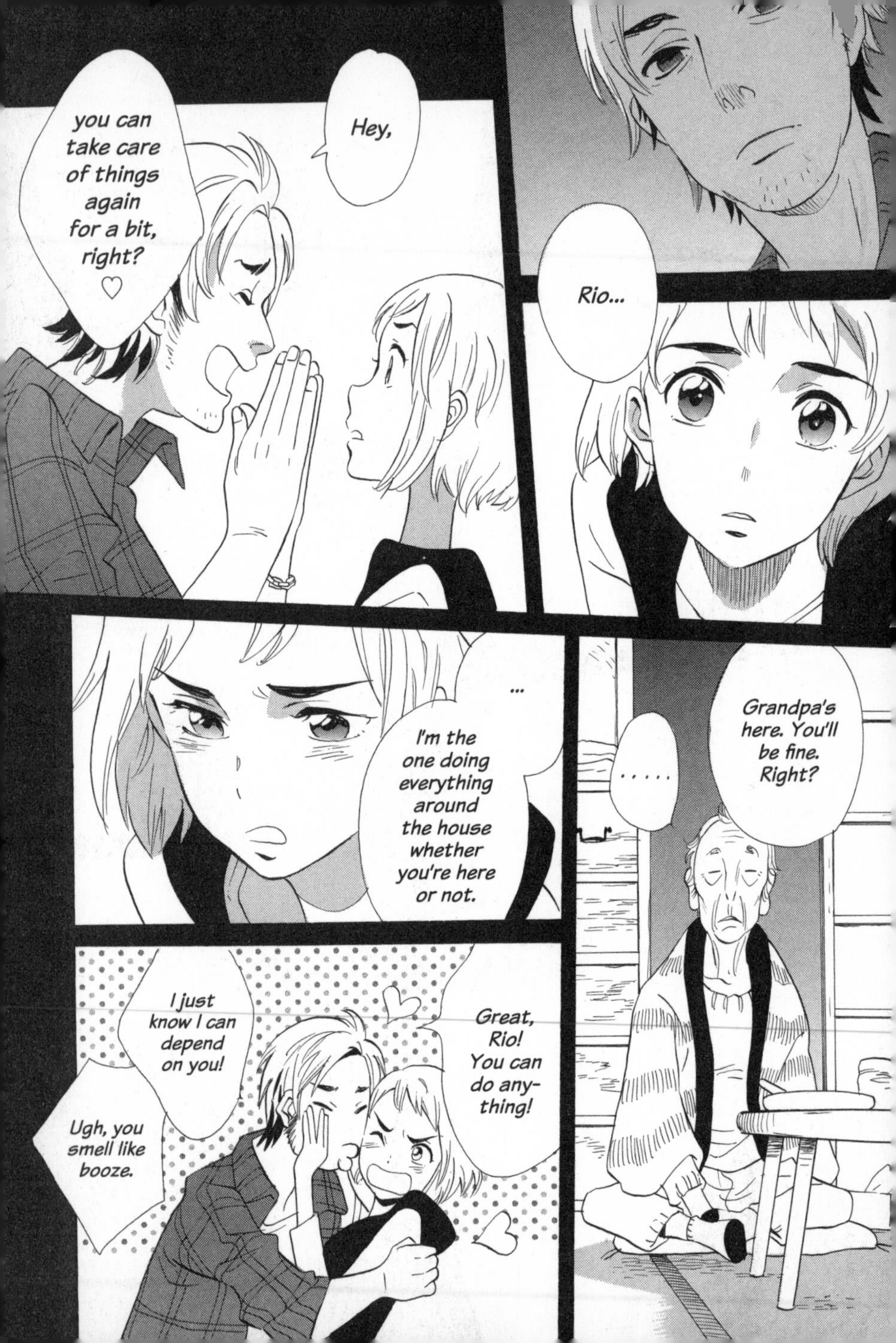
Rio...
Hey,
you can take care of things again for a bit, right? ♡
Grandpa's here. You'll be fine. Right?
.....
...
I'm the one doing everything around the house whether you're here or not.
Great, Rio! You can do anything!
I just know I can depend on you!
Ugh, you smell like booze.

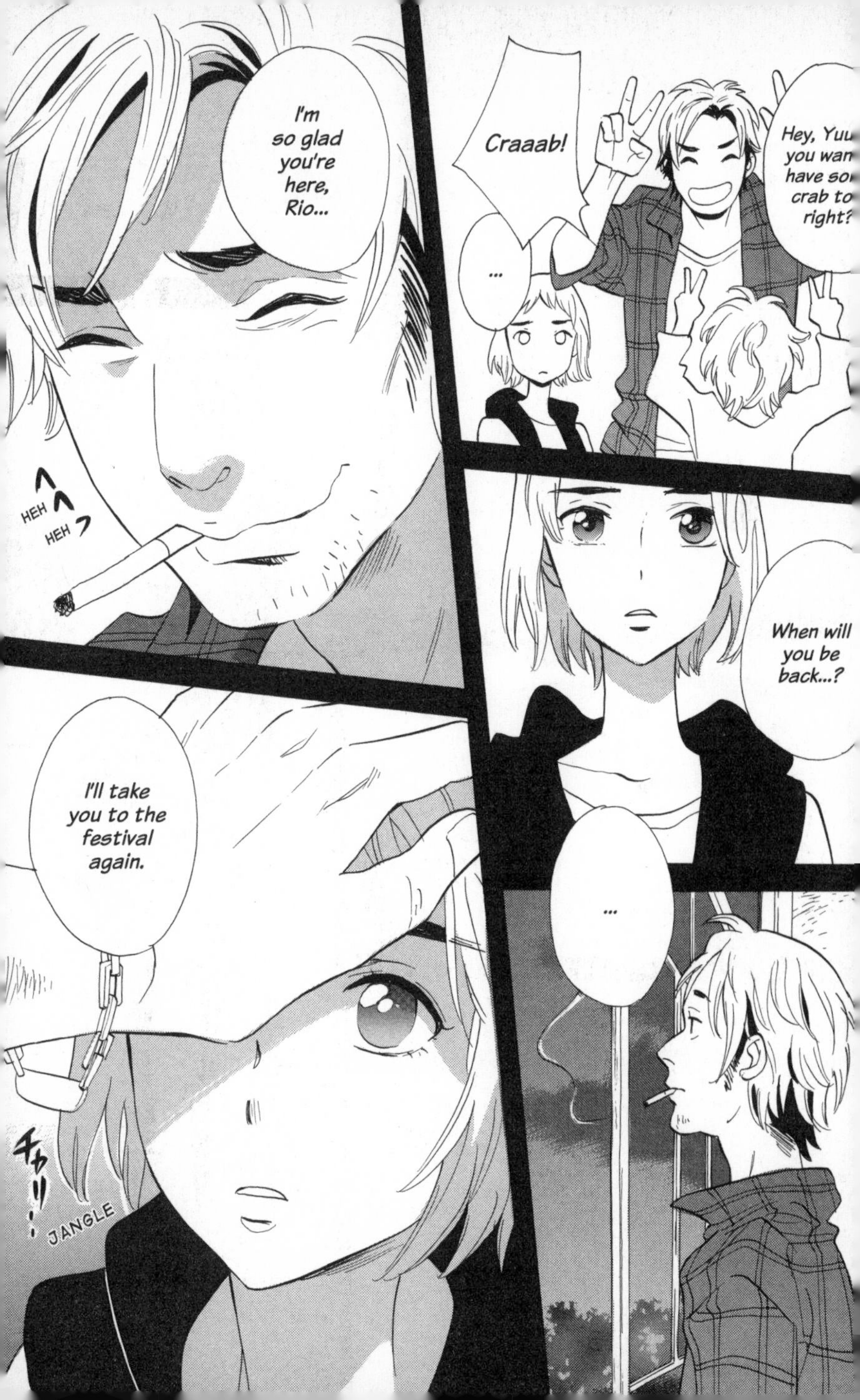
Hey, Yuu you wan have so crab to right?
Craaab!
...
I'm so glad you're here, Rio...
HEH HEH
When will you be back...?
I'll take you to the festival again.
JANGLE
...

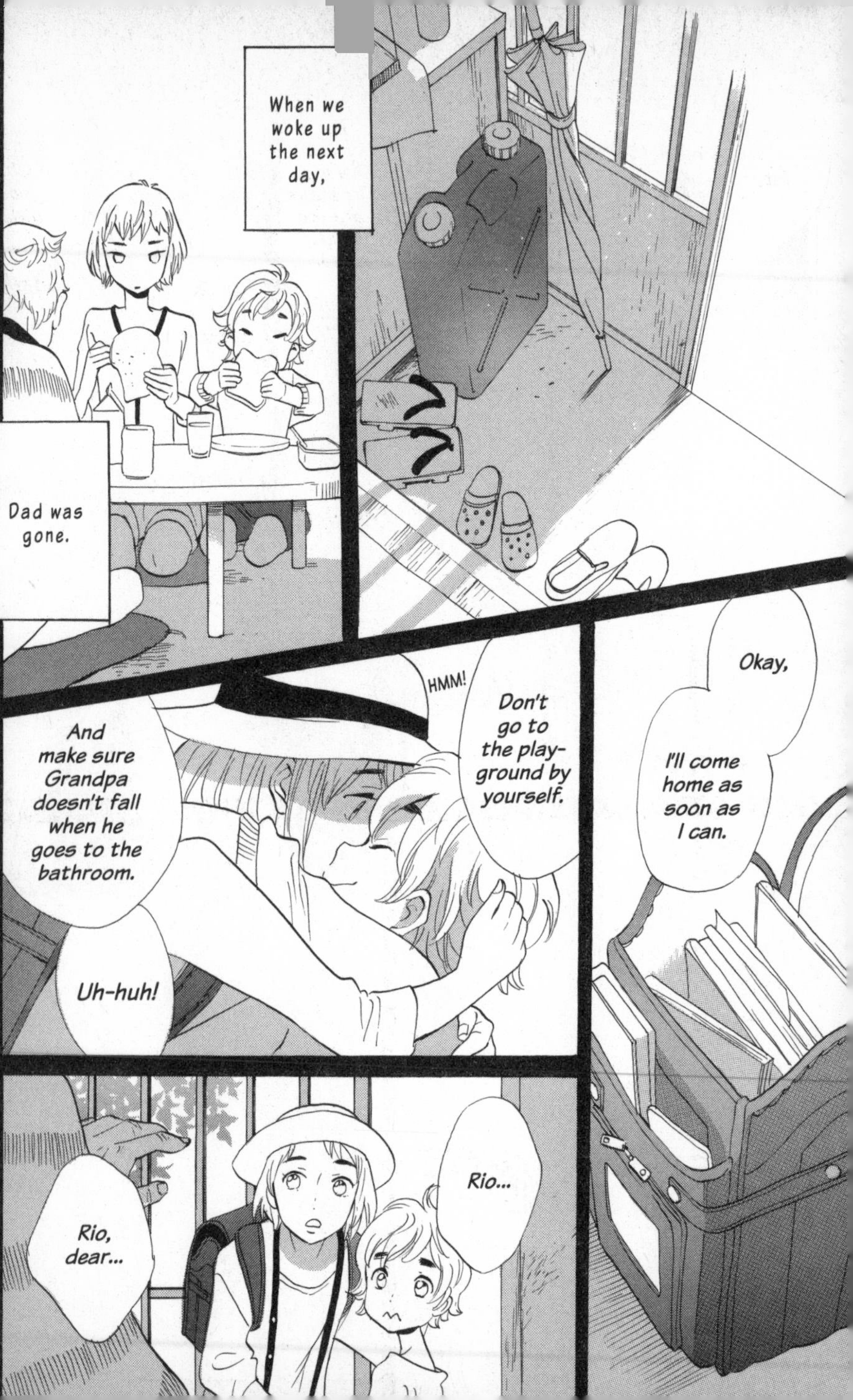
When we woke up the next day,
Dad was gone.
Okay,
I'll come home as soon as I can.
HMM!
Don't go to the play-ground by yourself.
And make sure Grandpa doesn't fall when he goes to the bathroom.
Uh-huh!
Rio...
Rio, dear...

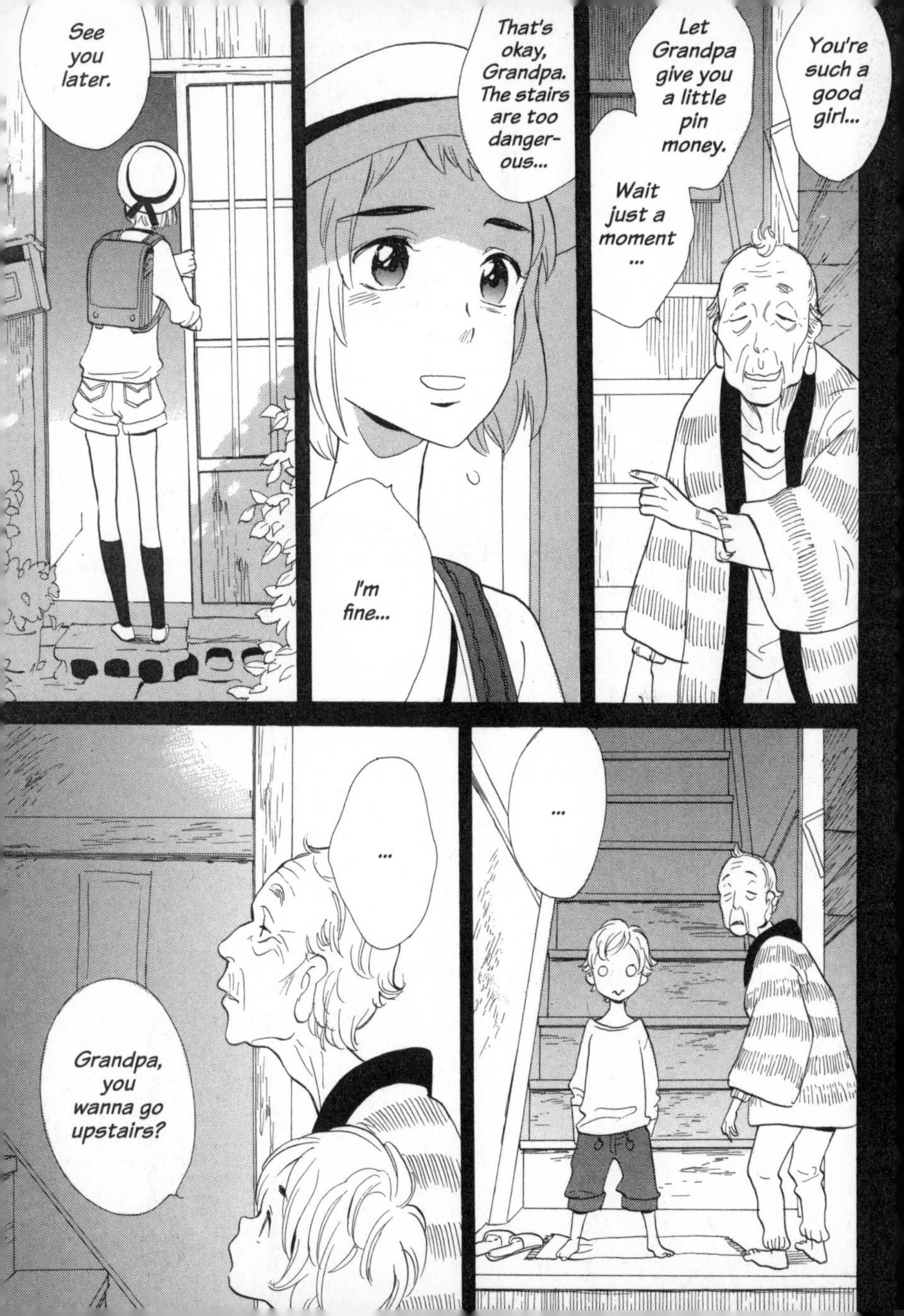
You're such a good girl...
Let Grandpa give you a little pin money.
Wait just a moment...
That's okay, Grandpa. The stairs are too danger-ous...
I'm fine...
See you later.
...
...
Grandpa, you wanna go upstairs?

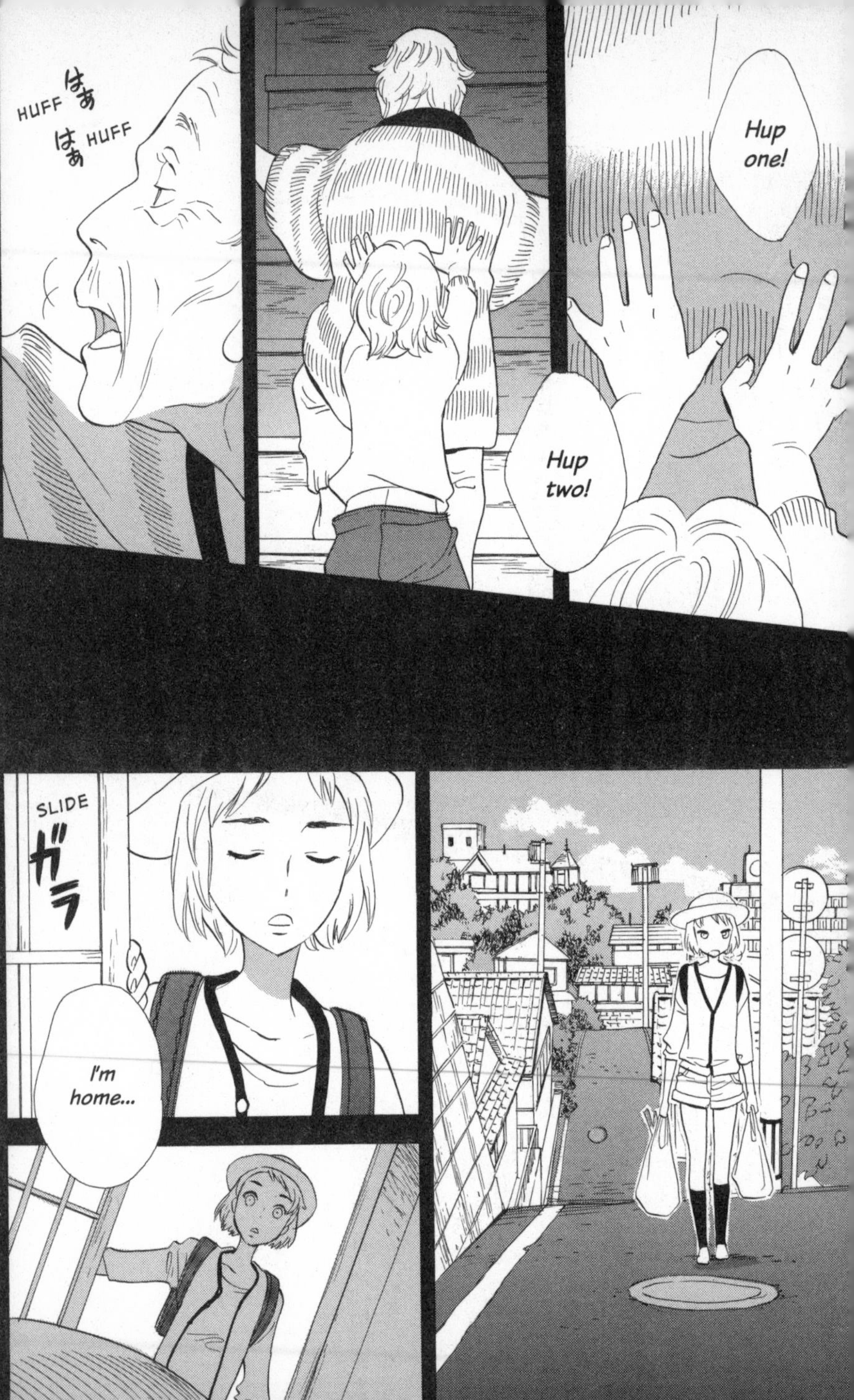
Hup one!
Hup two!
HUFF はぁ
はぁ HUFF
SLIDE ガラ
I'm home...

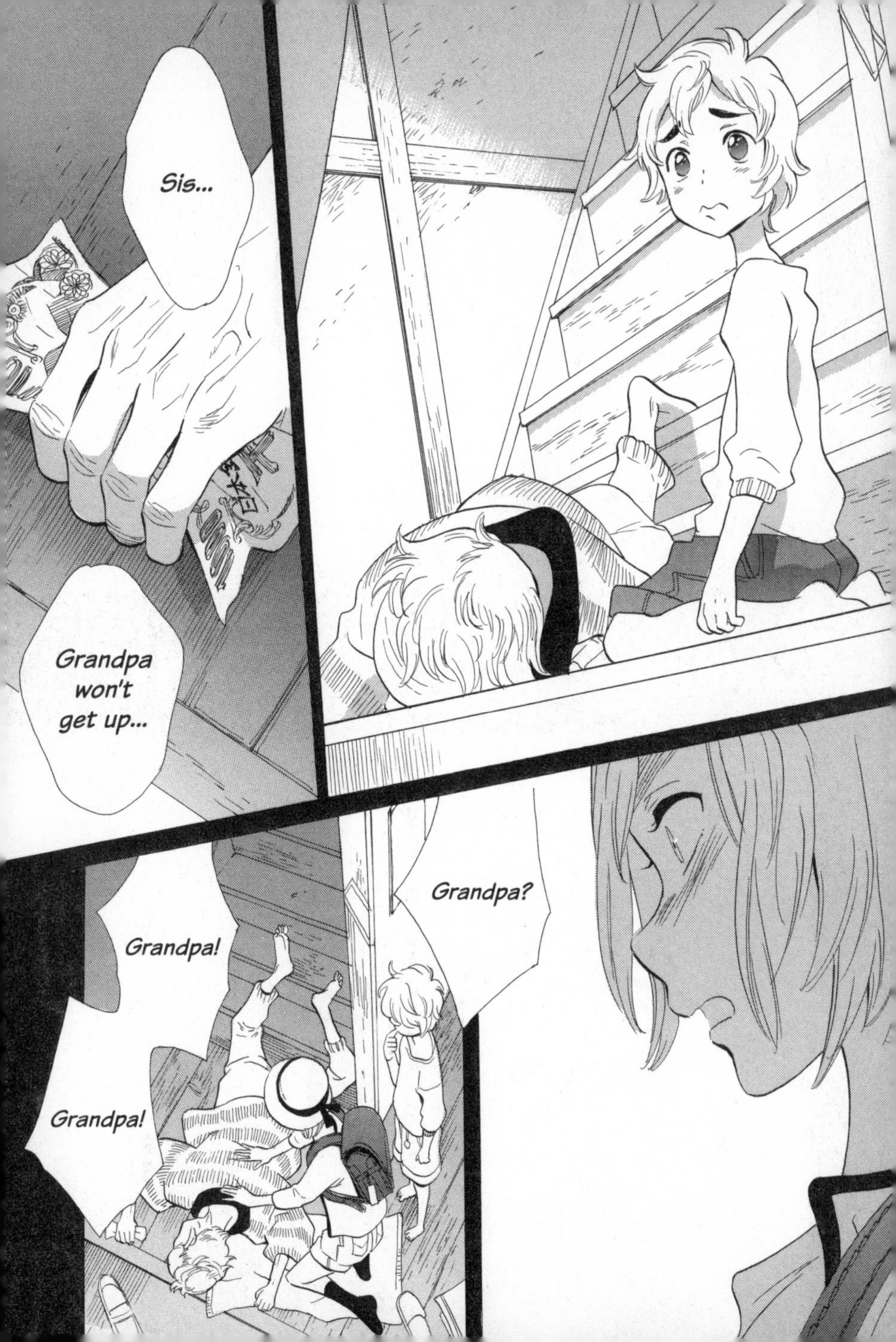
Sis...
Grandpa won't get up...
Grandpa?
Grandpa!
Grandpa!

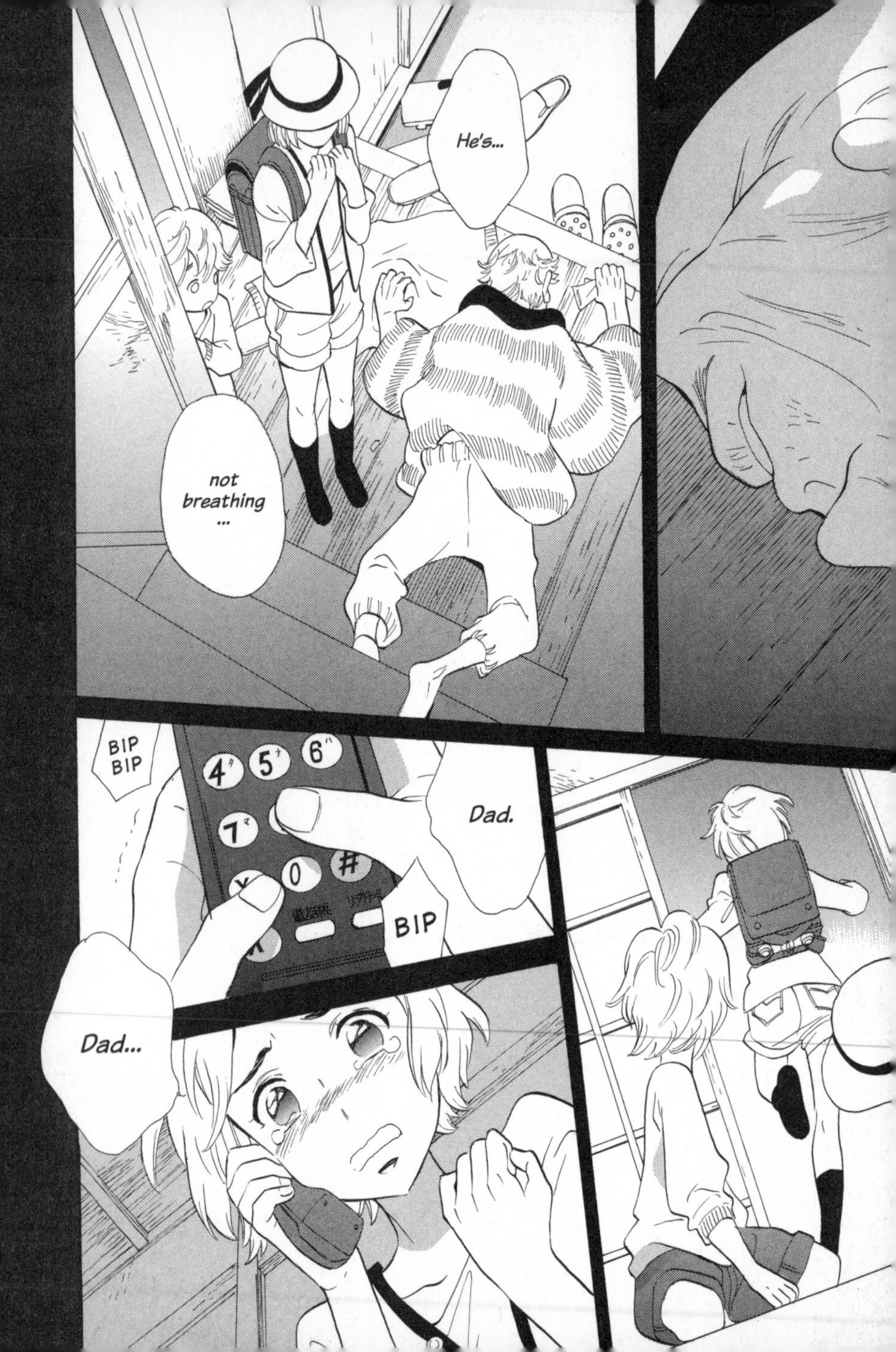
He's...
not breathing ...
BIP BIP
Dad.
BIP
Dad...

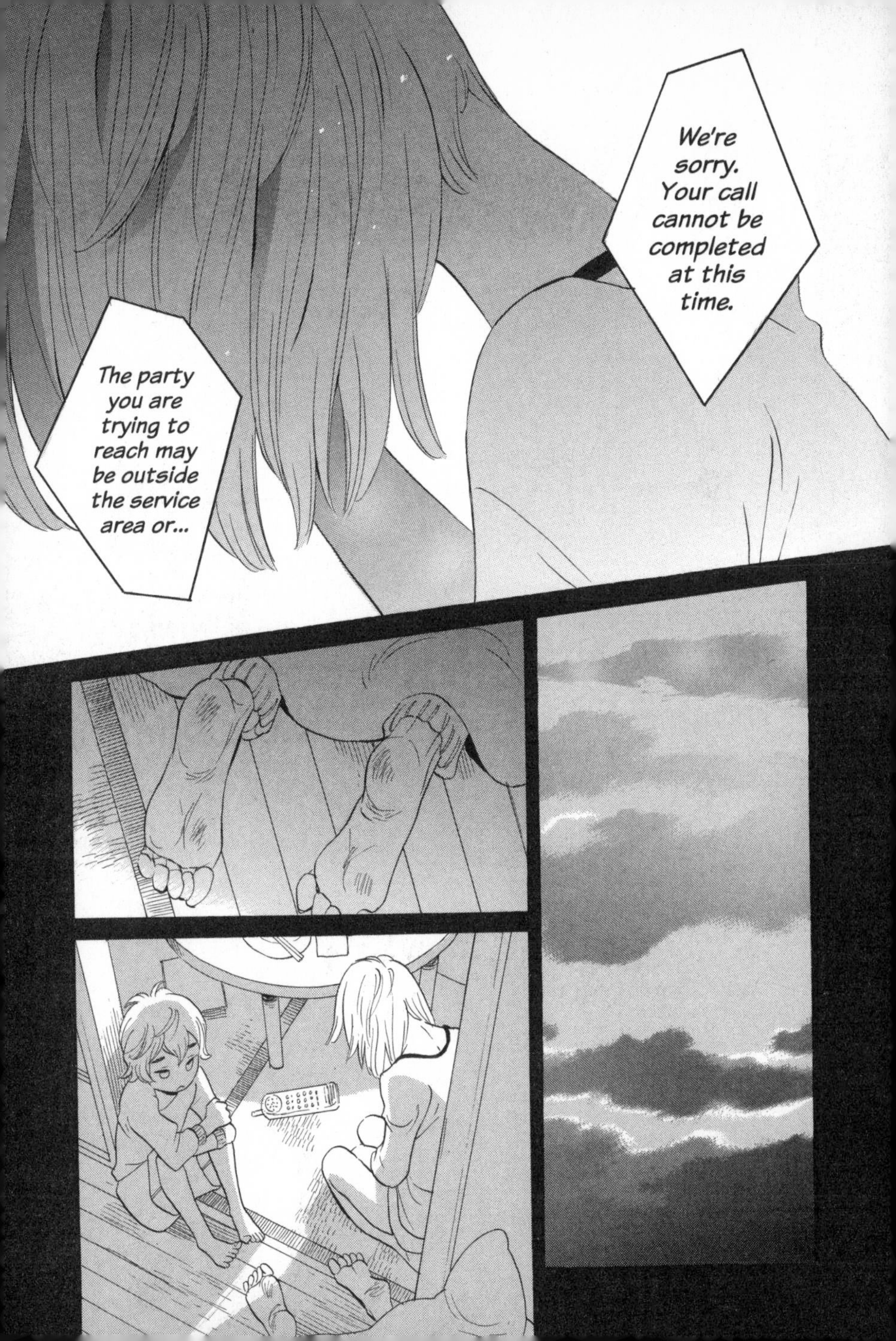
We're sorry. Your call cannot be completed at this time.
The party you are trying to reach may be outside the service area or...

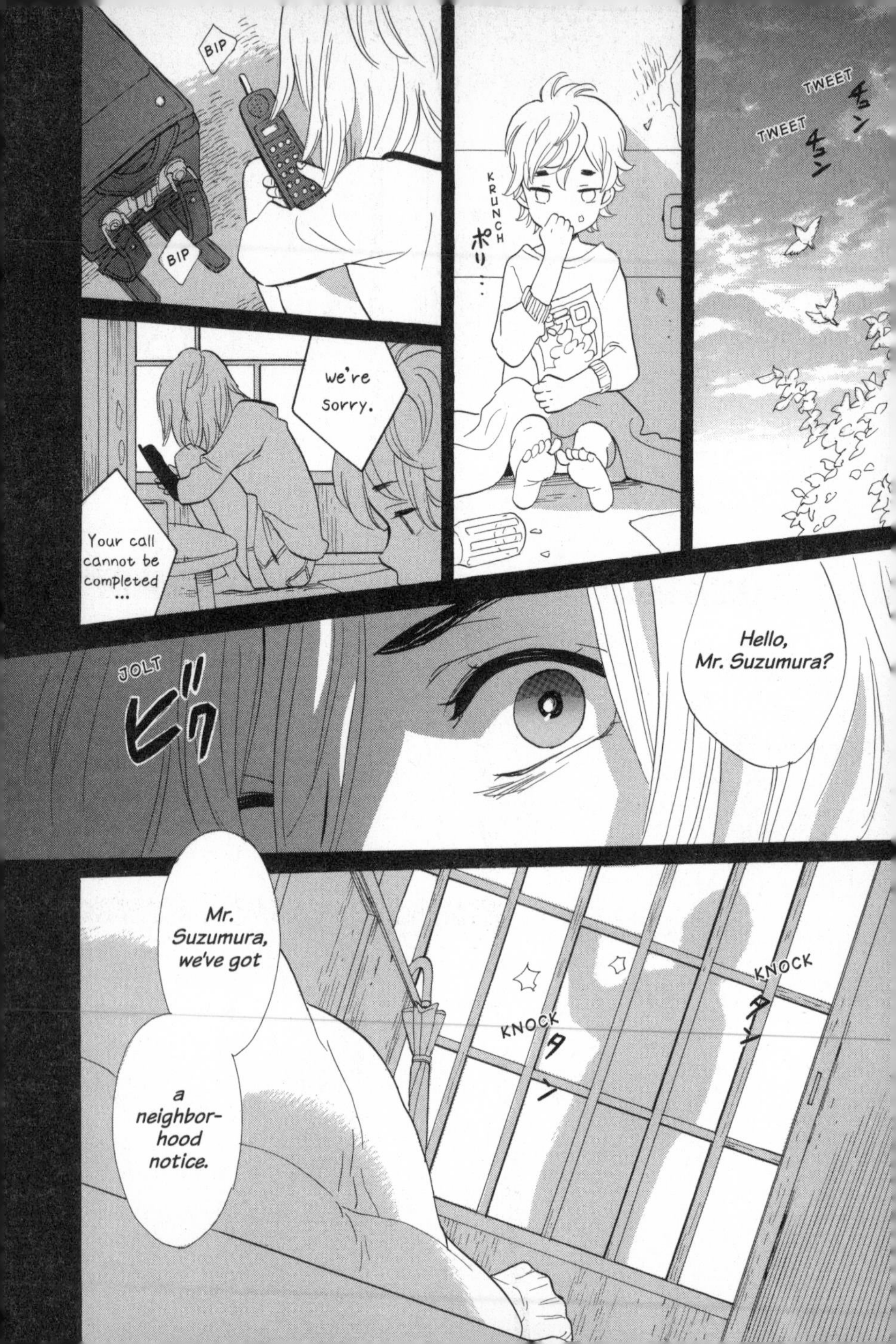
TWEET
チュン
TWEET
チュン
KRUNCH
ポリ…
BIP
BIP
we're sorry.
Your call cannot be completed ...
Hello, Mr. Suzumura?
JOLT
ビク
KNOCK
タン
KNOCK
タン
Mr. Suzumura, we've got
a neighbor-hood notice.

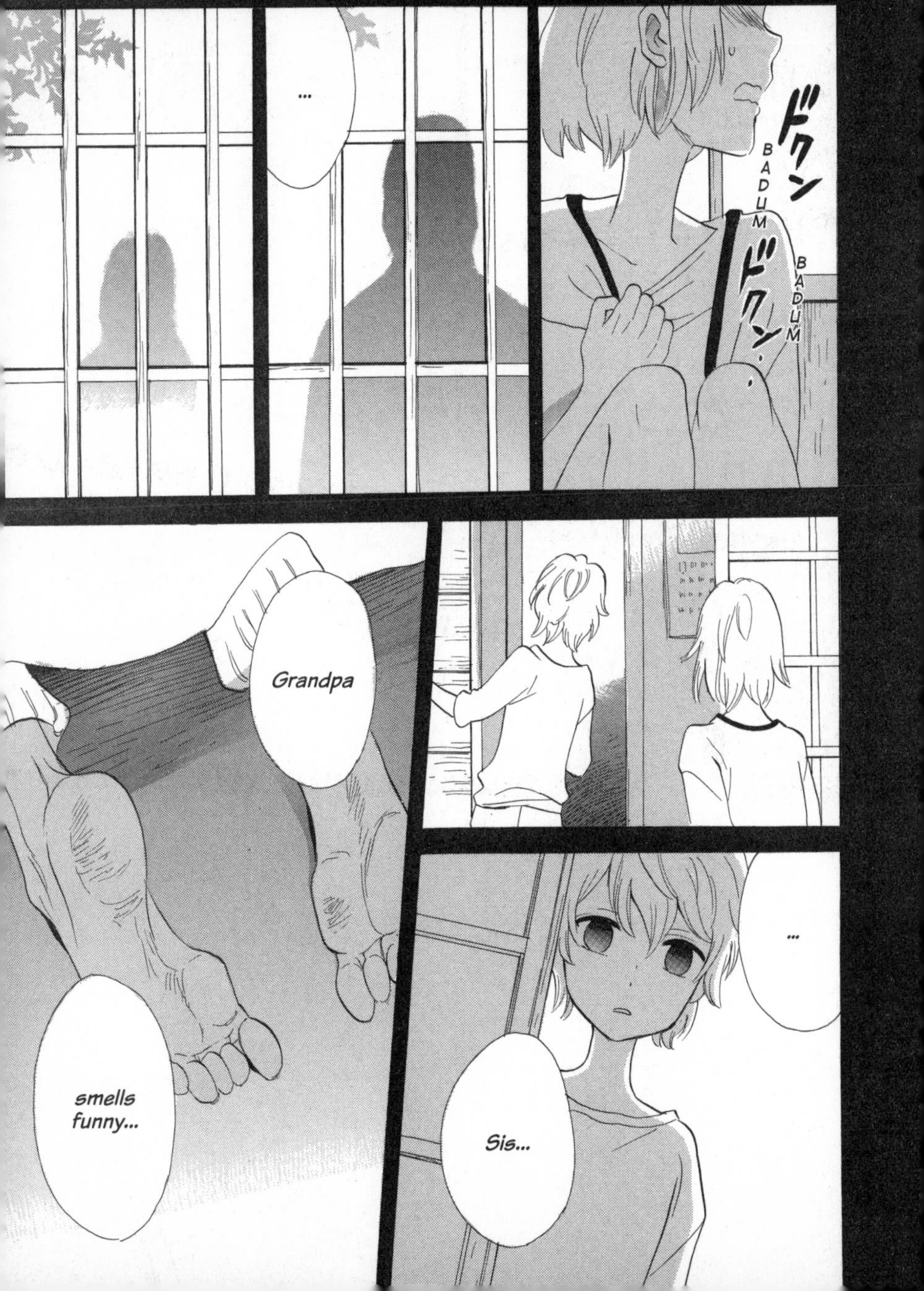
ドクン
BADUM
ドクン
BADUM
...
...
Sis...
Grandpa
smells funny...

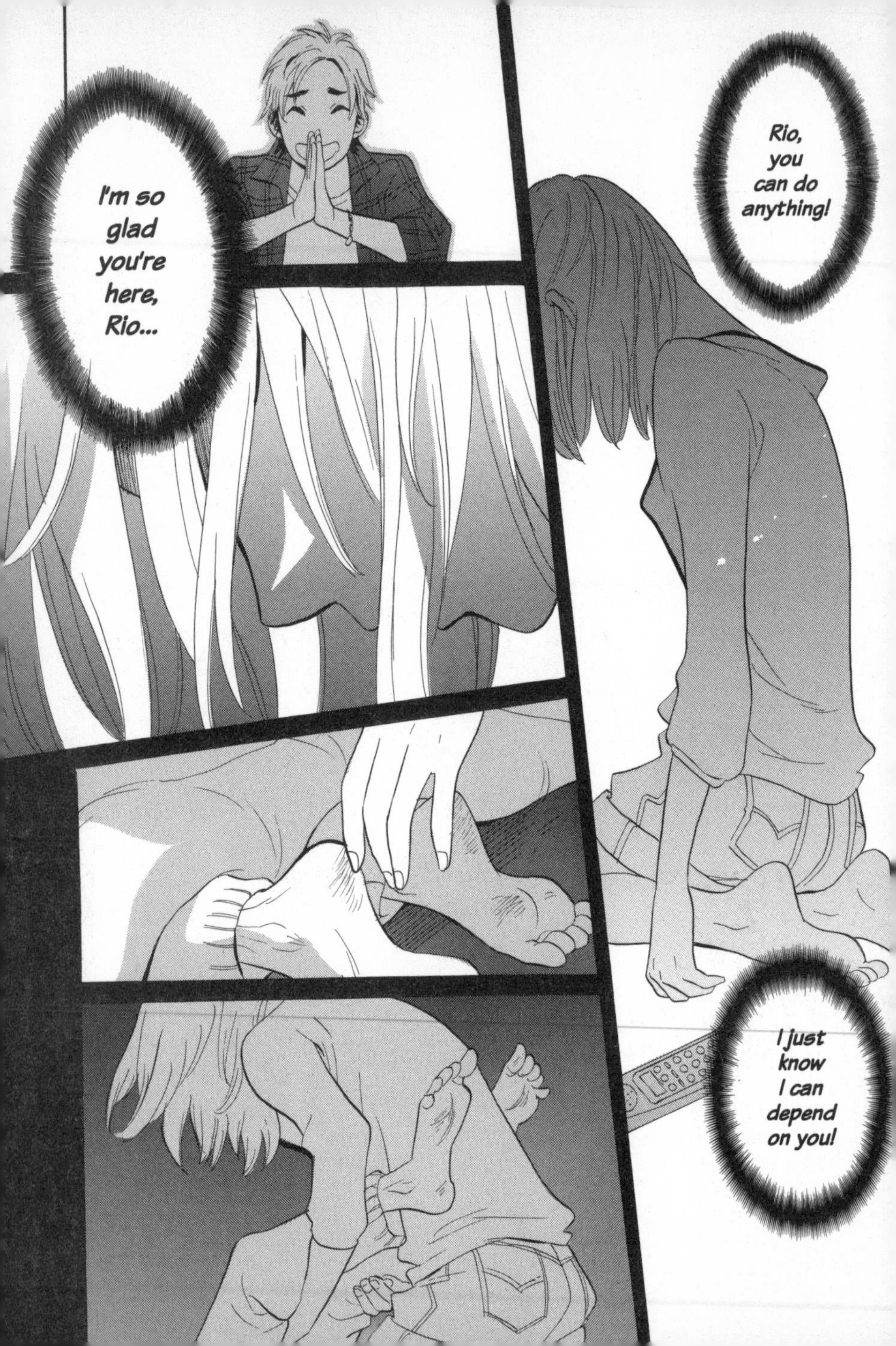
Rio, you can do anything!
I just know I can depend on you!
I'm so glad you're here, Rio...

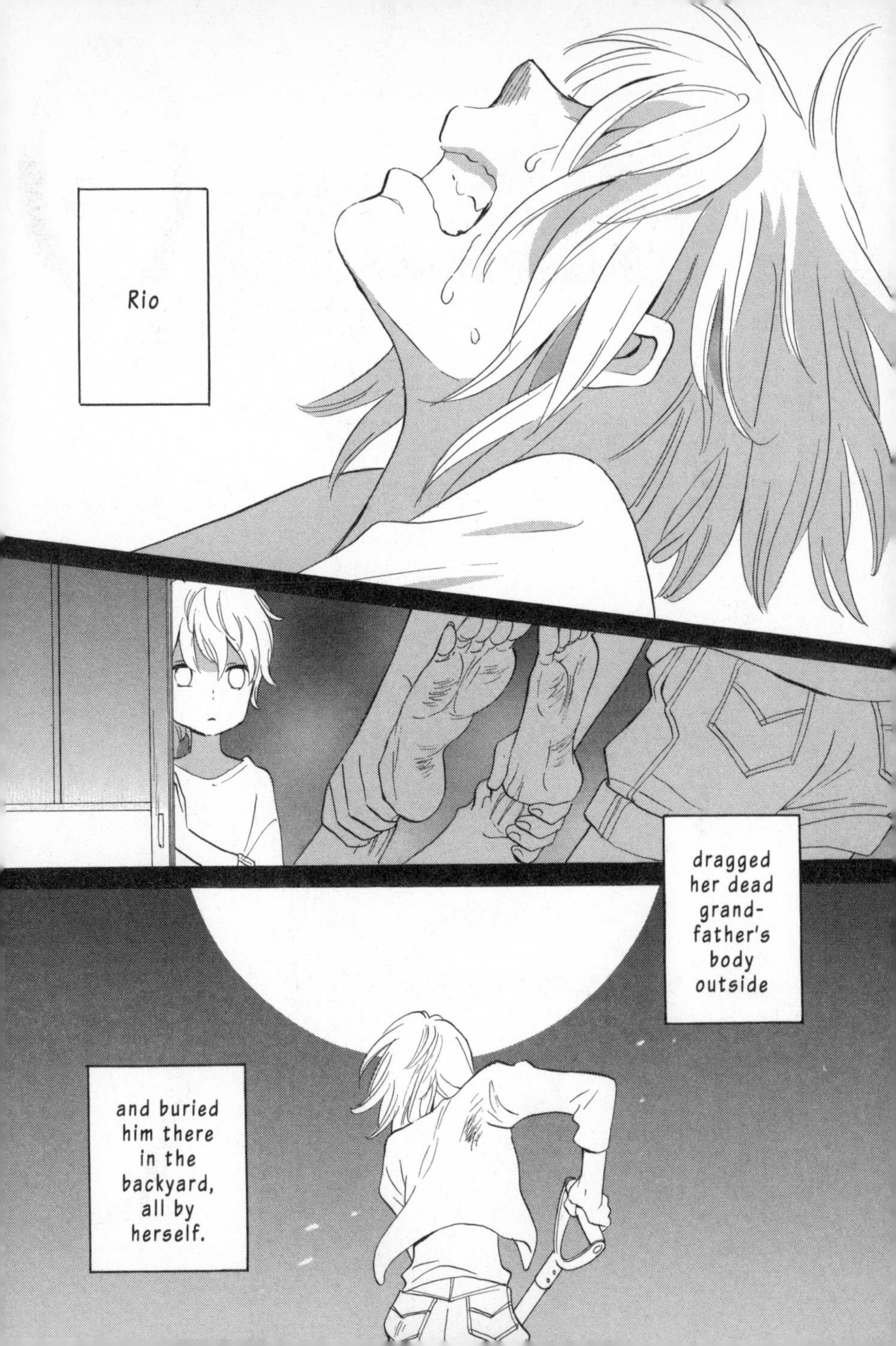
Rio
dragged her dead grand-father's body outside
and buried him there in the backyard, all by herself.

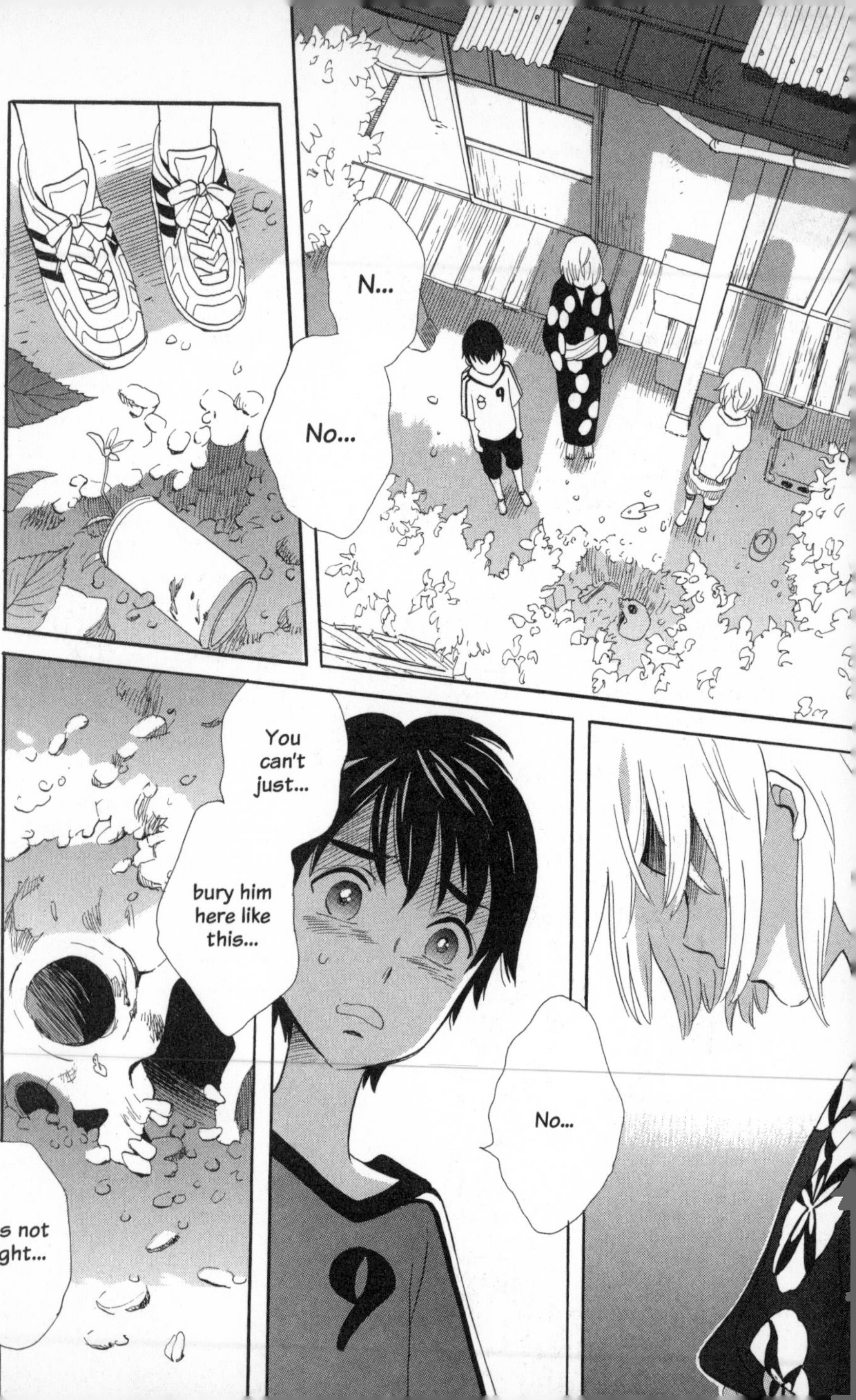
N...
No...
You can't just...
bury him here like this...
No...
It's not right...

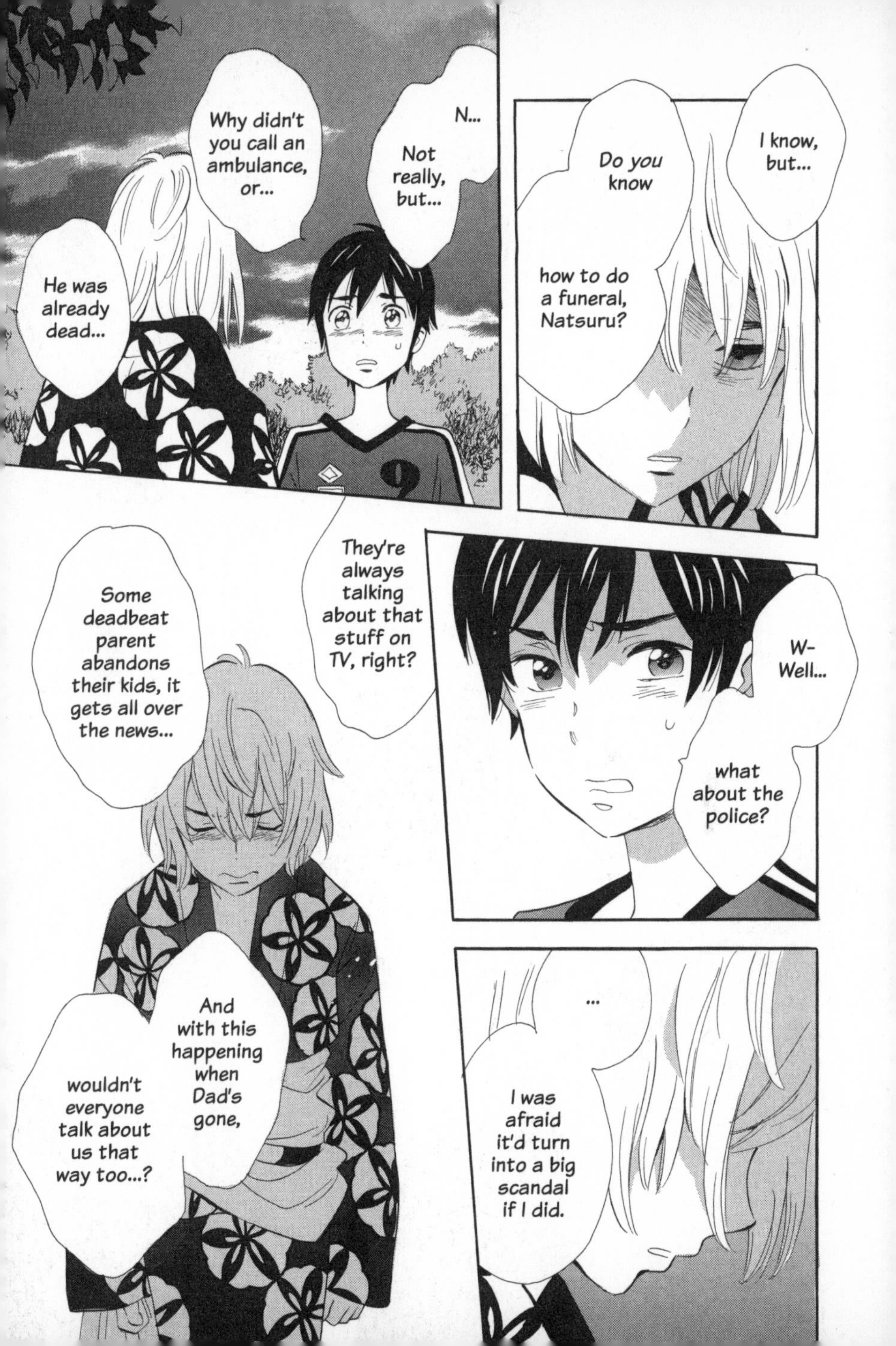

I know, but...
Do you know
how to do a funeral, Natsuru?
N...
Not really, but...
Why didn't you call an ambulance, or...
He was already dead...
W-Well...
what about the police?
...
I was afraid it'd turn into a big scandal if I did.
They're always talking about that stuff on TV, right?
Some deadbeat parent abandons their kids, it gets all over the news...
And with this happening when Dad's gone,
wouldn't everyone talk about us that way too...?

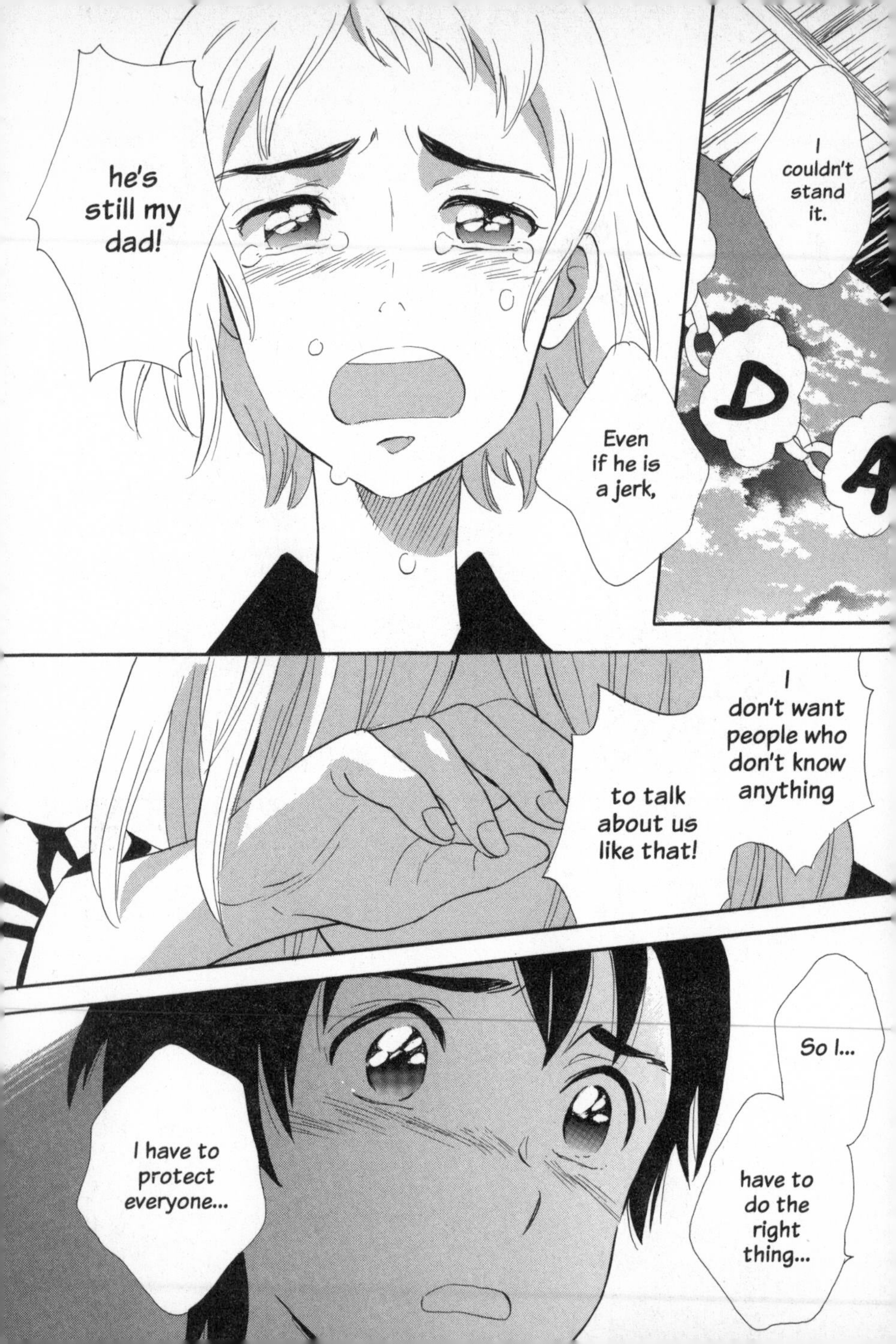
I couldn't stand it.
D
A
Even if he is a jerk,
he's still my dad!
I don't want people who don't know anything
to talk about us like that!
So I...
have to do the right thing...
I have to protect everyone...

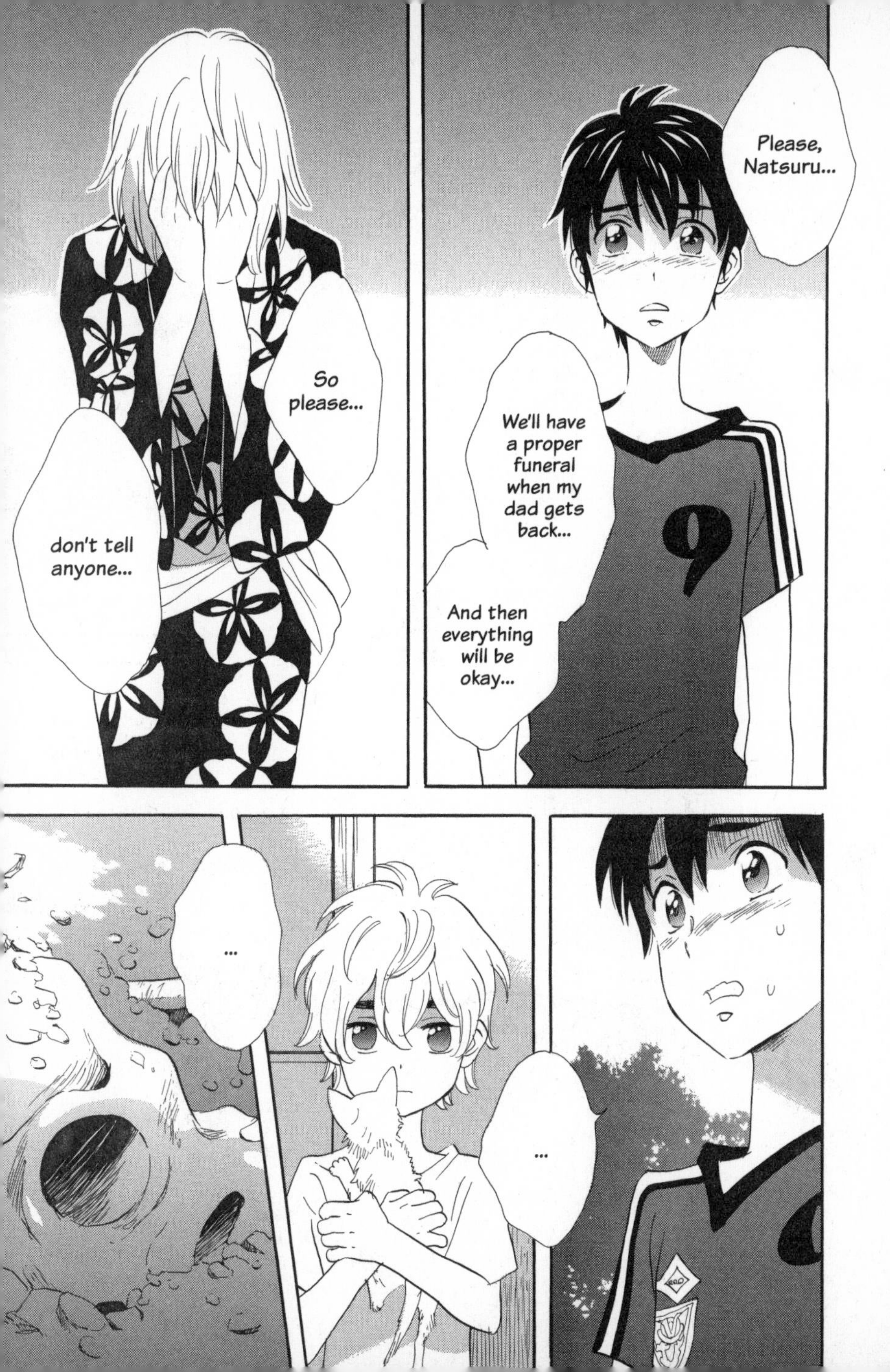
Please, Natsuru...
We'll have a proper funeral when my dad gets back...
And then everything will be okay...
So please...
don't tell anyone...
...
...

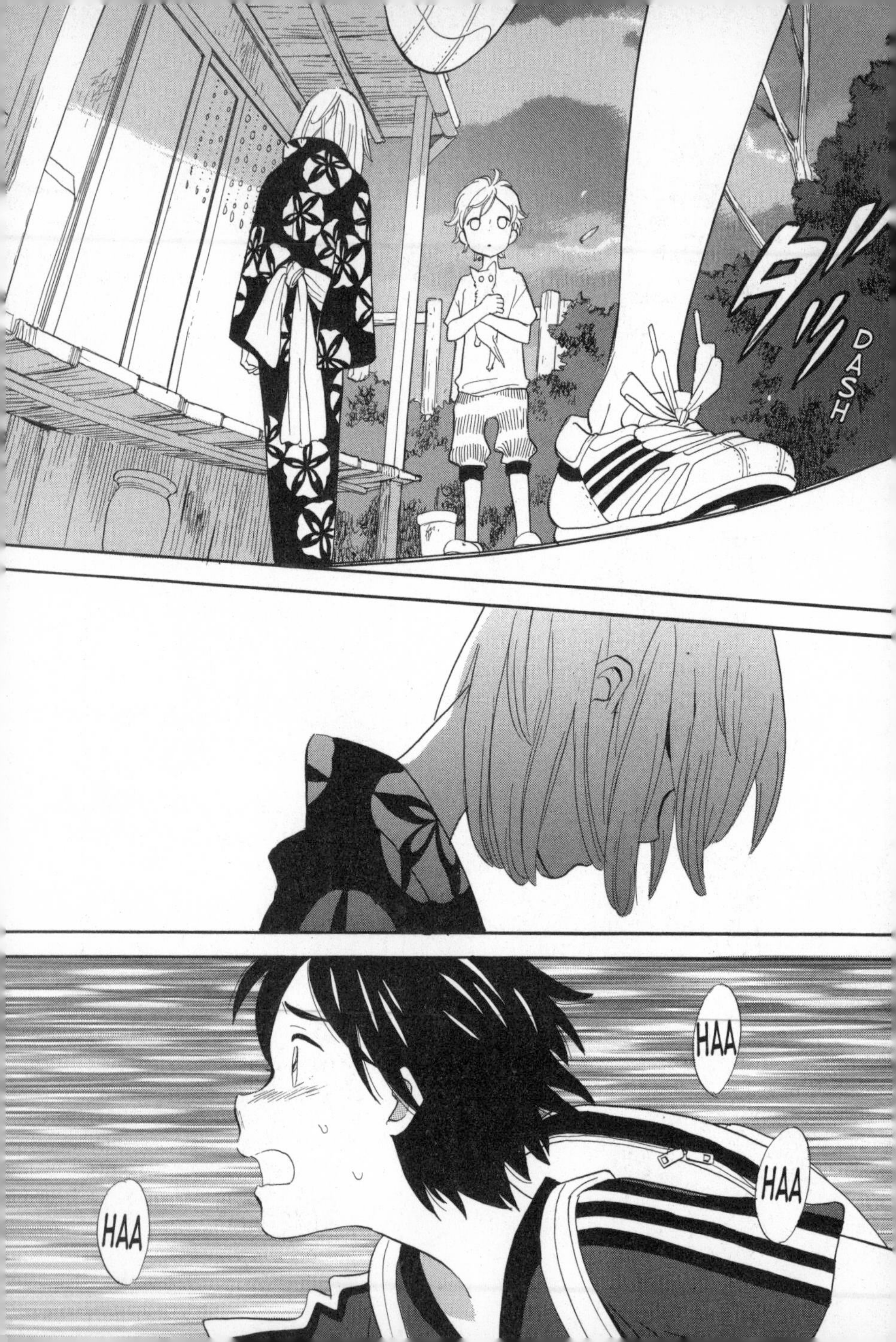
タッ
DASH
HAA
HAA
HAA

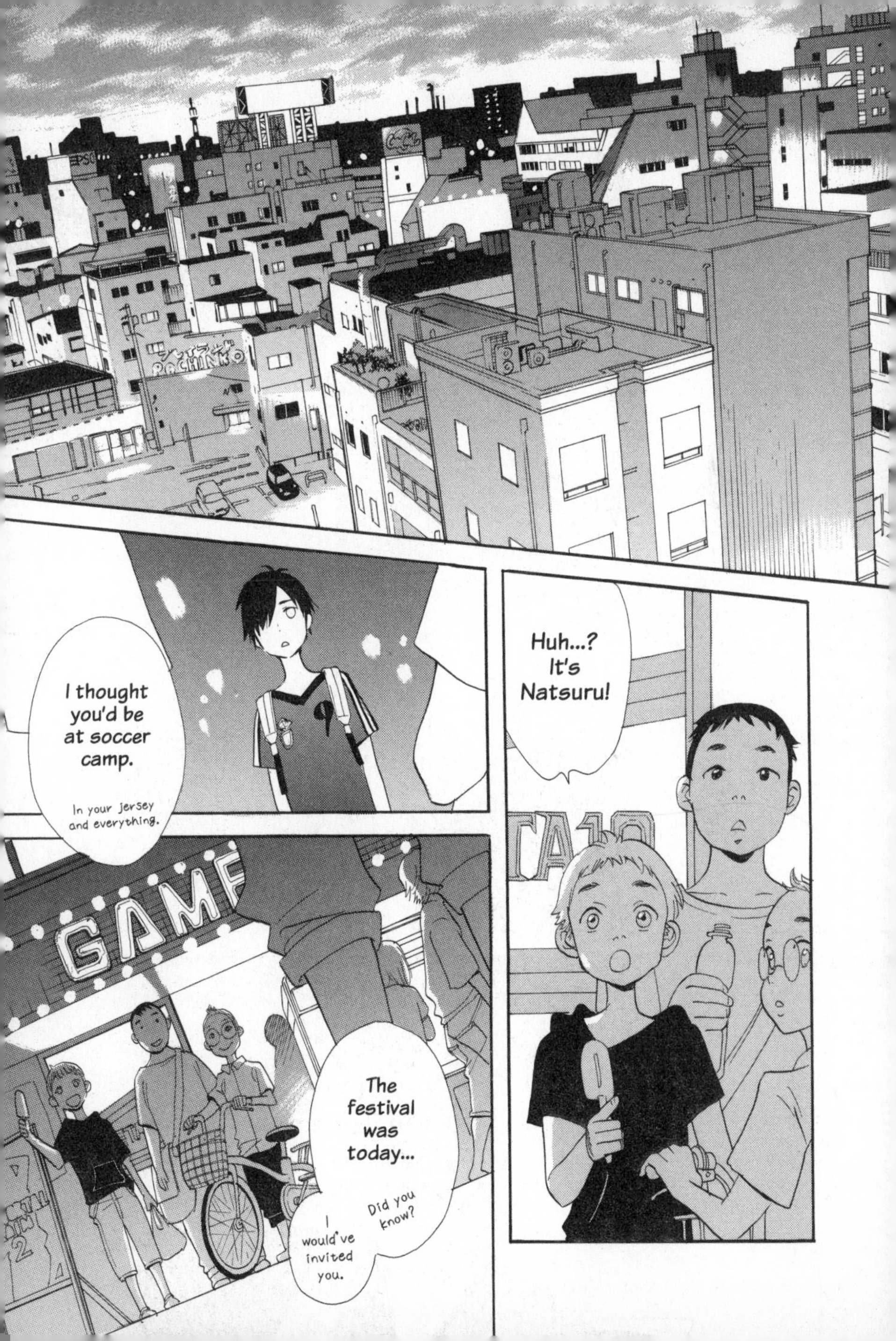
PACHINKO
Huh...? It's Natsuru!
I thought you'd be at soccer camp.
In your jersey and everything.
The festival was today...
Did you know?
I would've invited you.

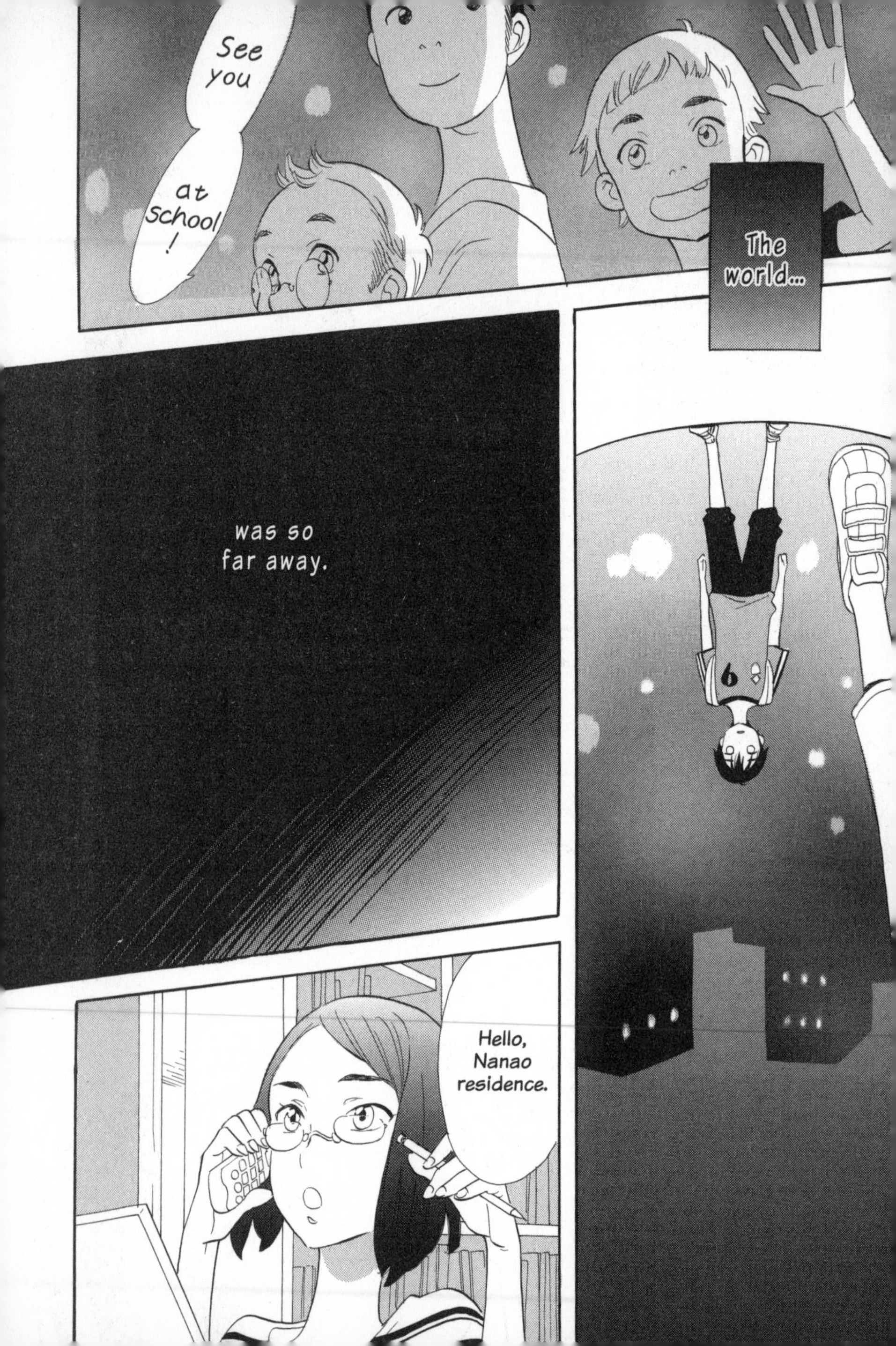
See you at school!
The world...
was so far away.
Hello, Nanao residence.

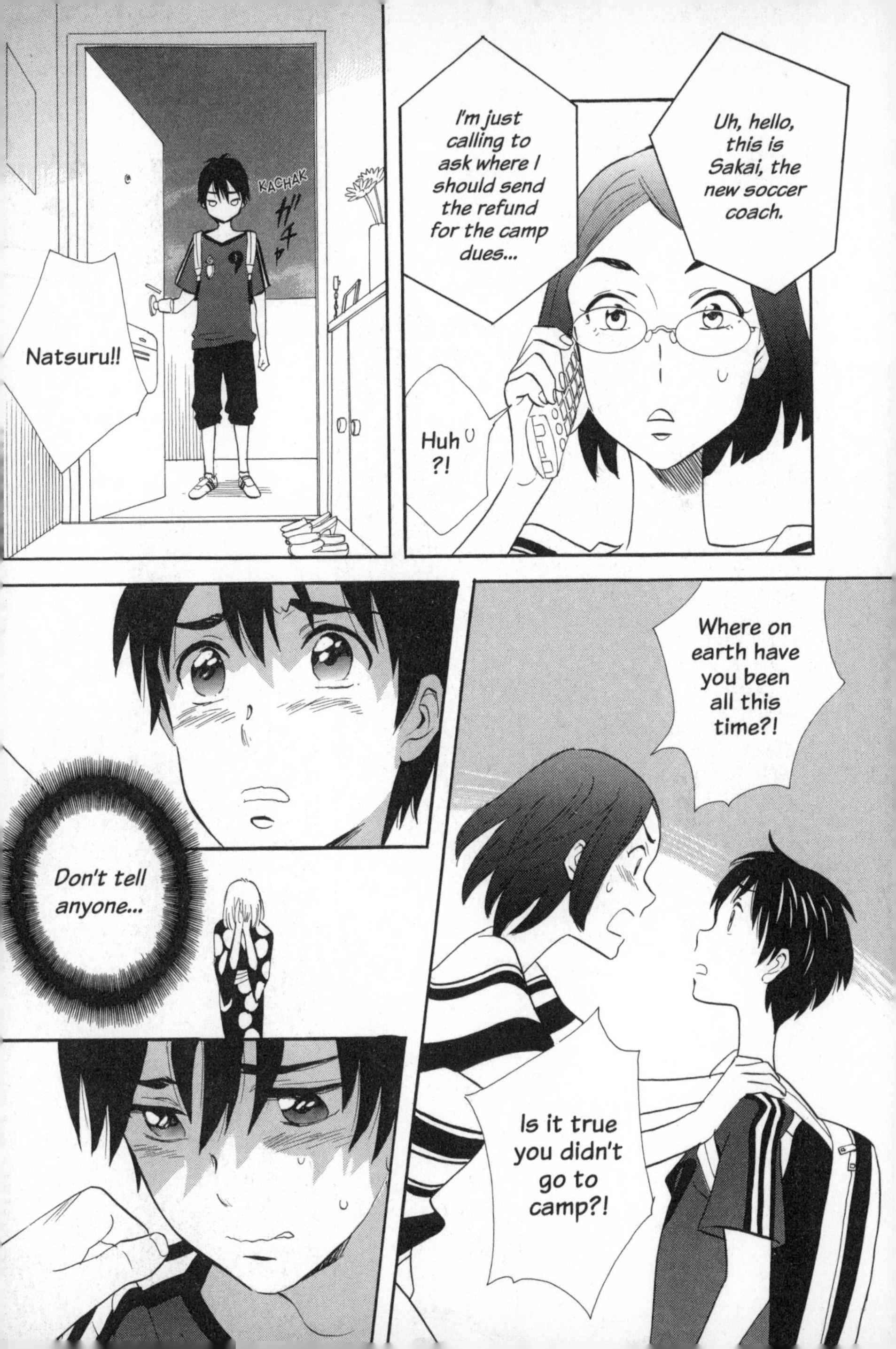
Uh, hello, this is Sakai, the new soccer coach.
I'm just calling to ask where I should send the refund for the camp dues...
Huh?!
KACHAK
ガチャ
Natsuru!!
Where on earth have you been all this time?!
Is it true you didn't go to camp?!
Don't tell anyone...

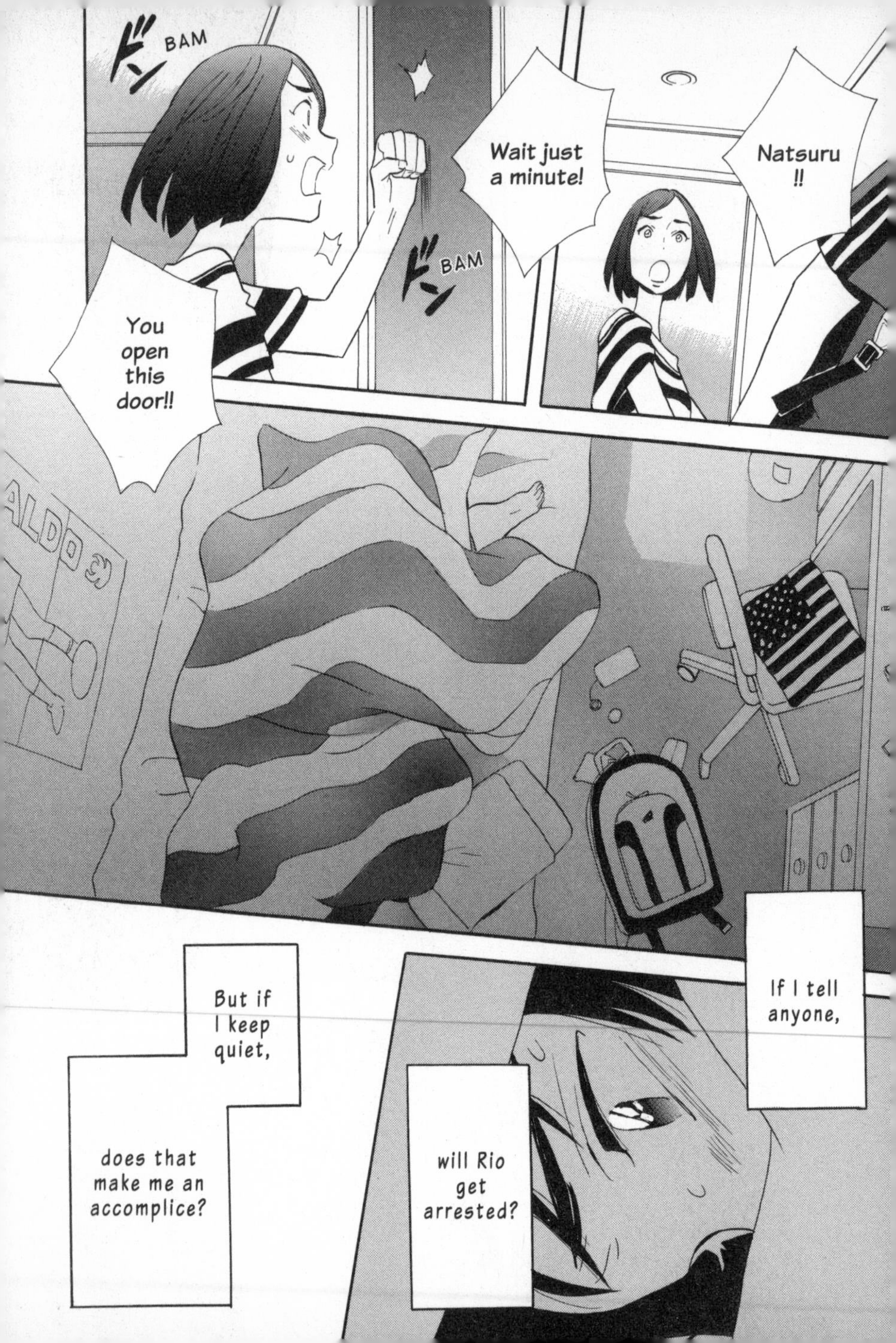
Natsuru !!
Wait just a minute!
ドン BAM
ドン BAM
You open this door!!
If I tell anyone,
will Rio get arrested?
But if I keep quiet,
does that make me an accomplice?

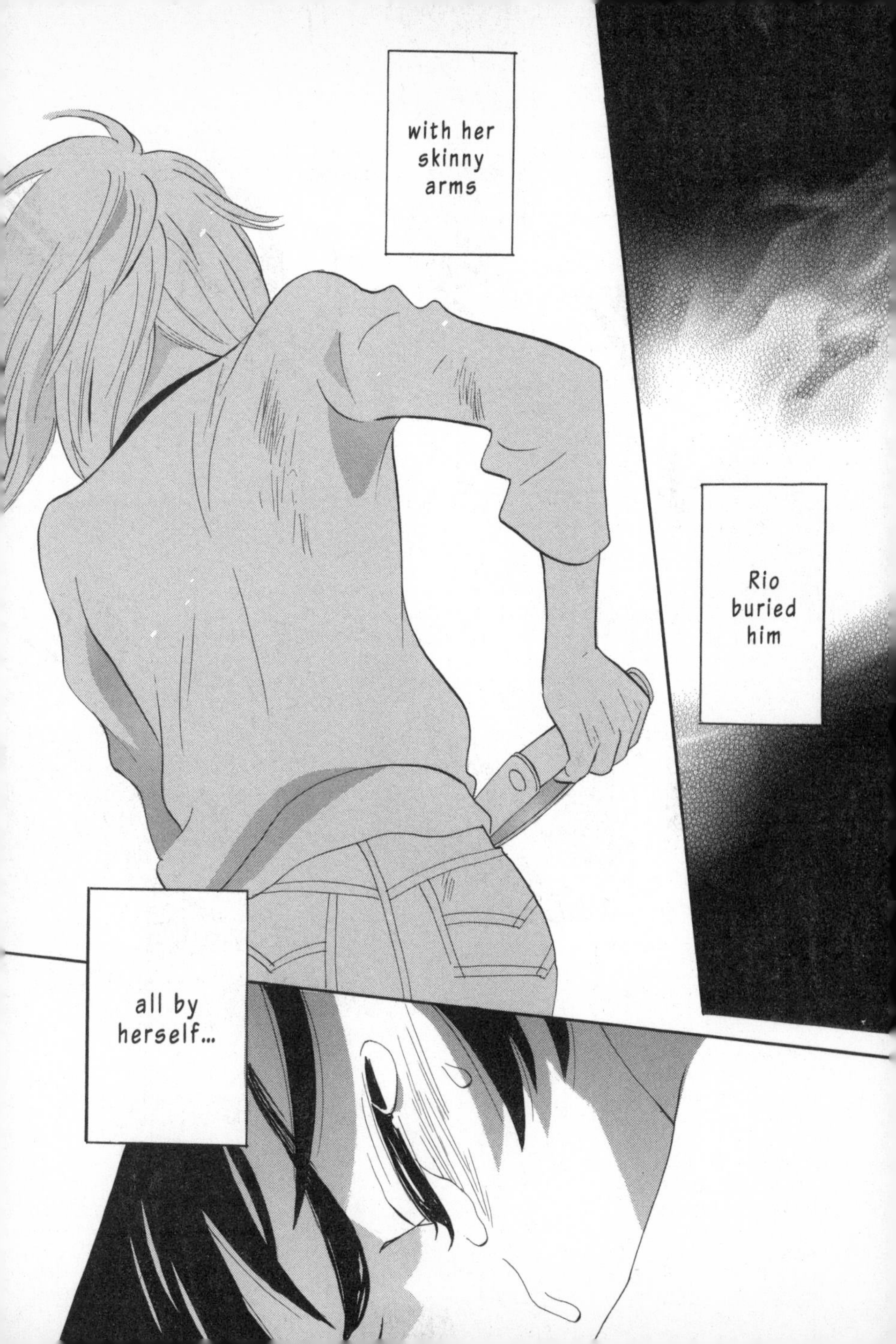
Rio buried him
with her skinny arms
all by herself...

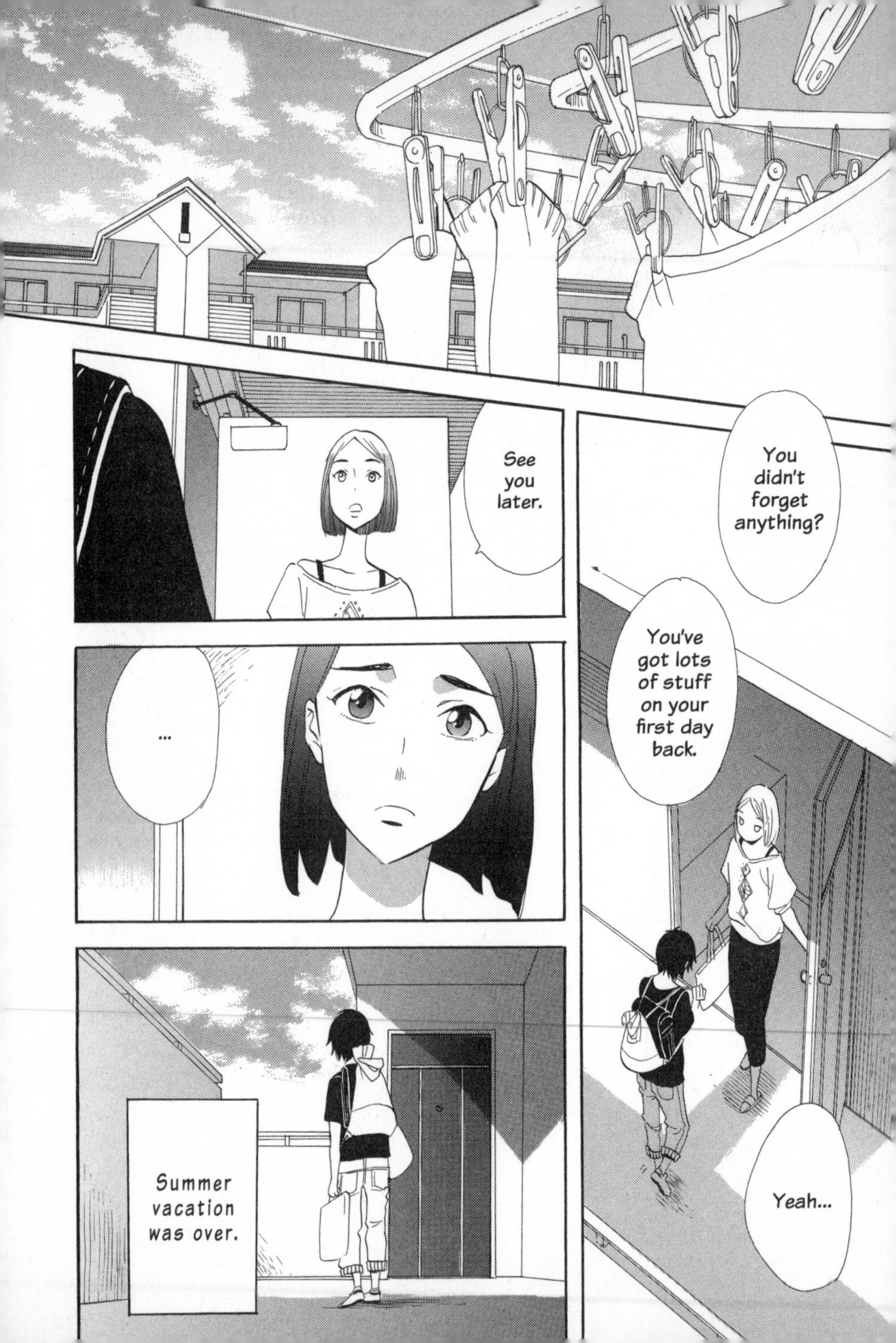
You didn't forget anything?
You've got lots of stuff on your first day back.
Yeah...
See you later.
...
Summer vacation was over.

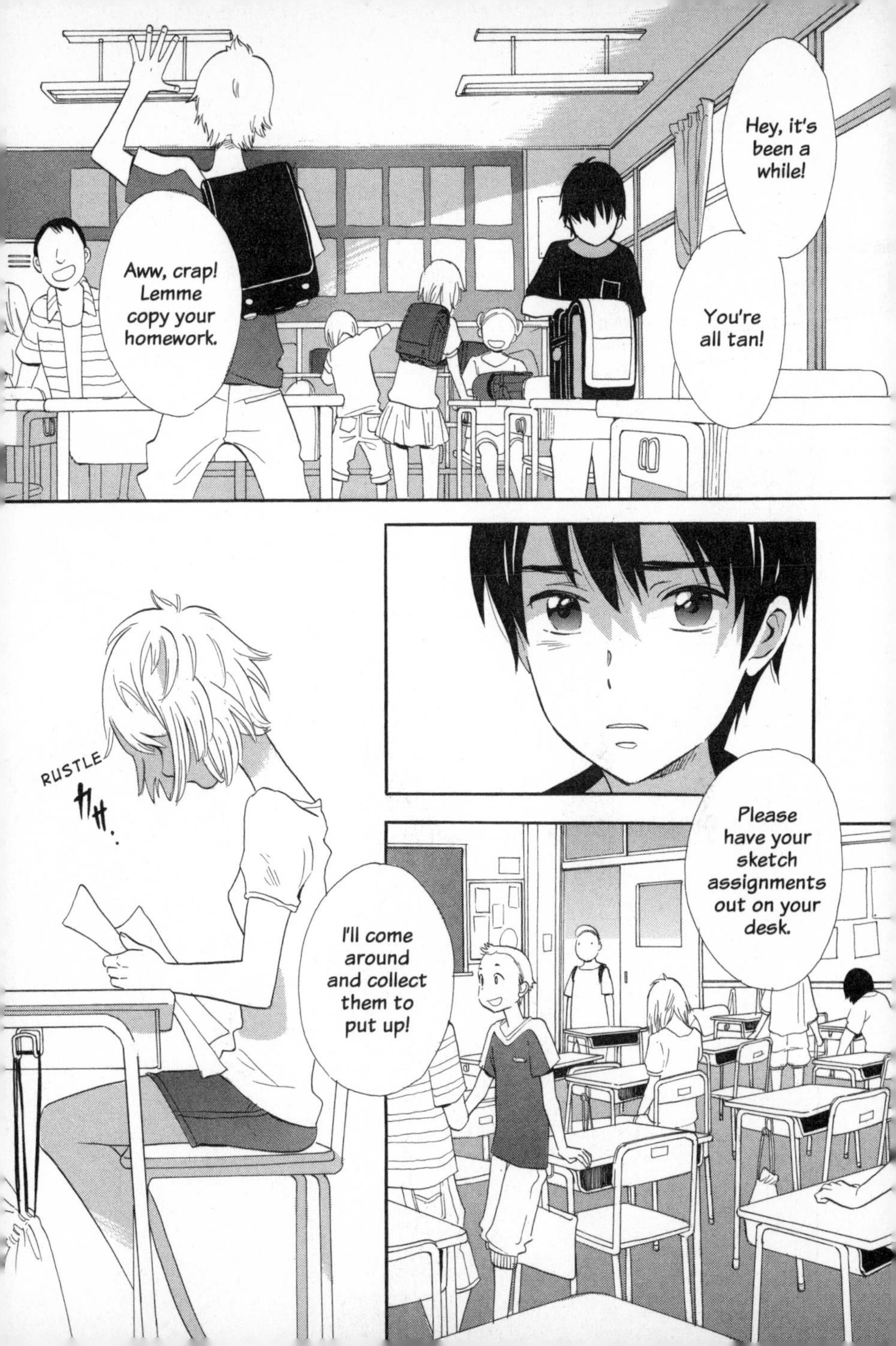
Hey, it's been a while!
You're all tan!
Aww, crap! Lemme copy your homework.
Please have your sketch assignments out on your desk.
I'll come around and collect them to put up!
RUSTLE

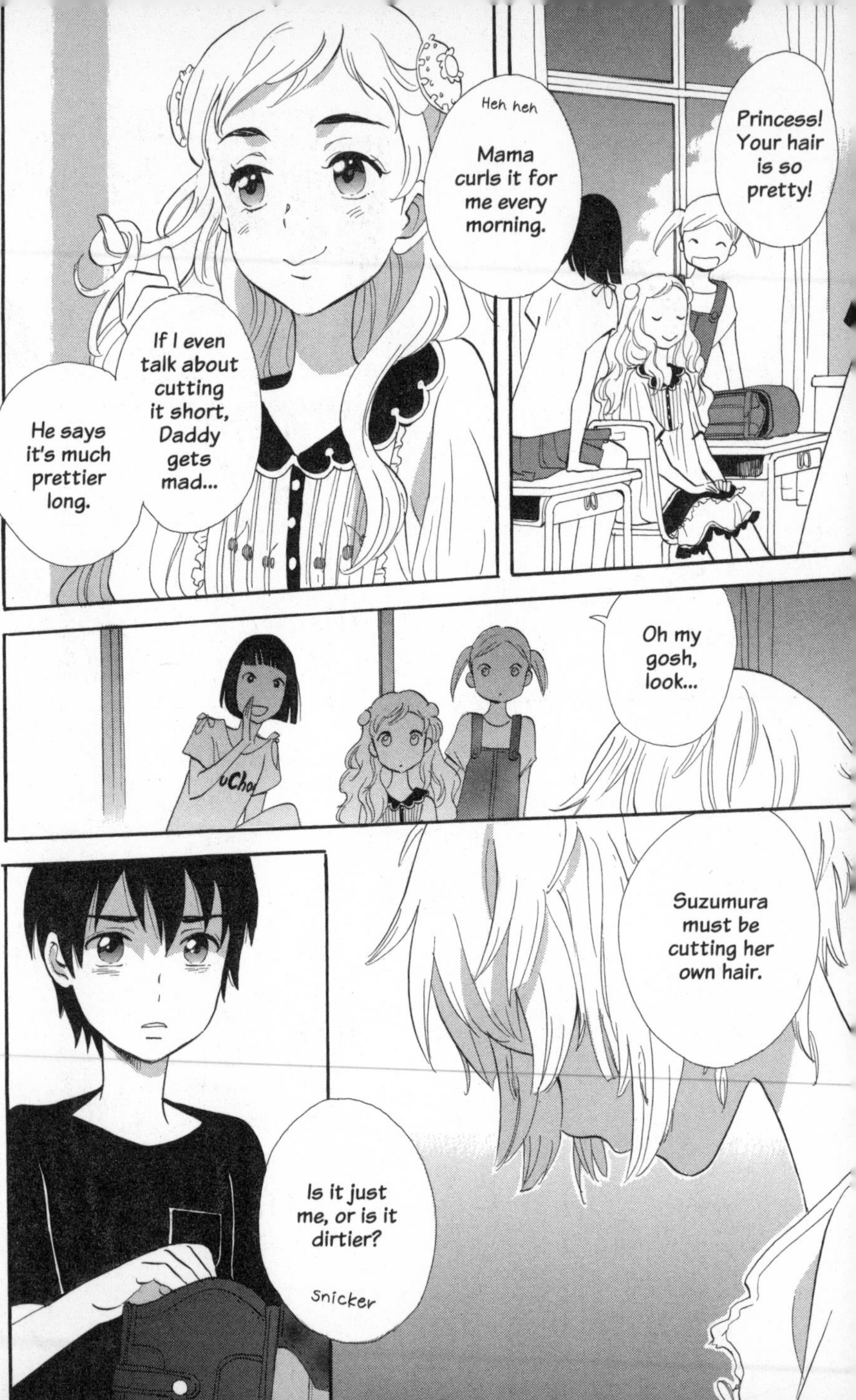

Princess! Your hair is so pretty!
Heh heh
Mama curls it for me every morning.
If I even talk about cutting it short, Daddy gets mad...
He says it's much prettier long.
Oh my gosh, look...
Suzumura must be cutting her own hair.
Is it just me, or is it dirtier?
Snicker

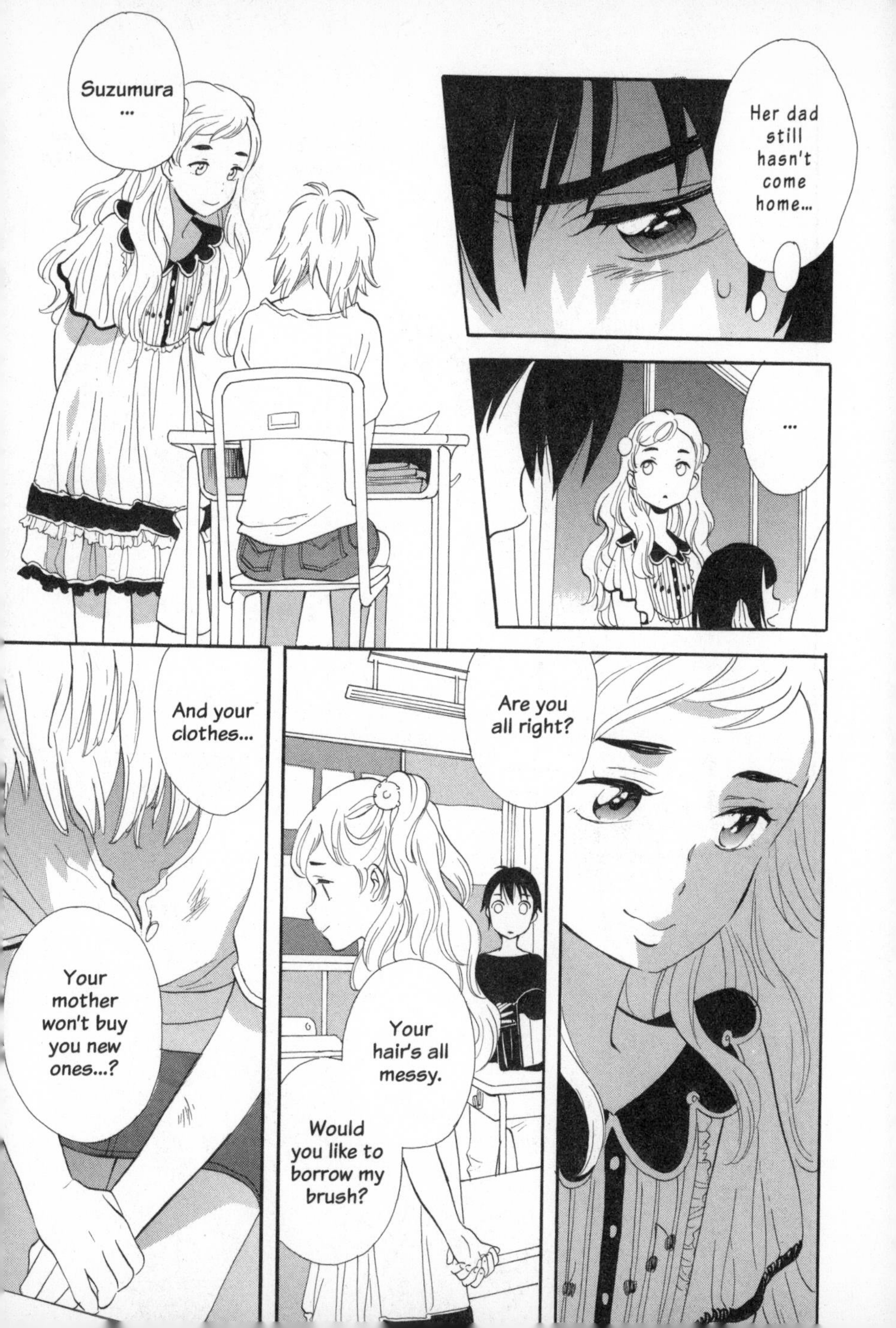
Her dad still hasn't come home...
...
Suzumura ...
Are you all right?
Your hair's all messy.
Would you like to borrow my brush?
And your clothes...
Your mother won't buy you new ones...?

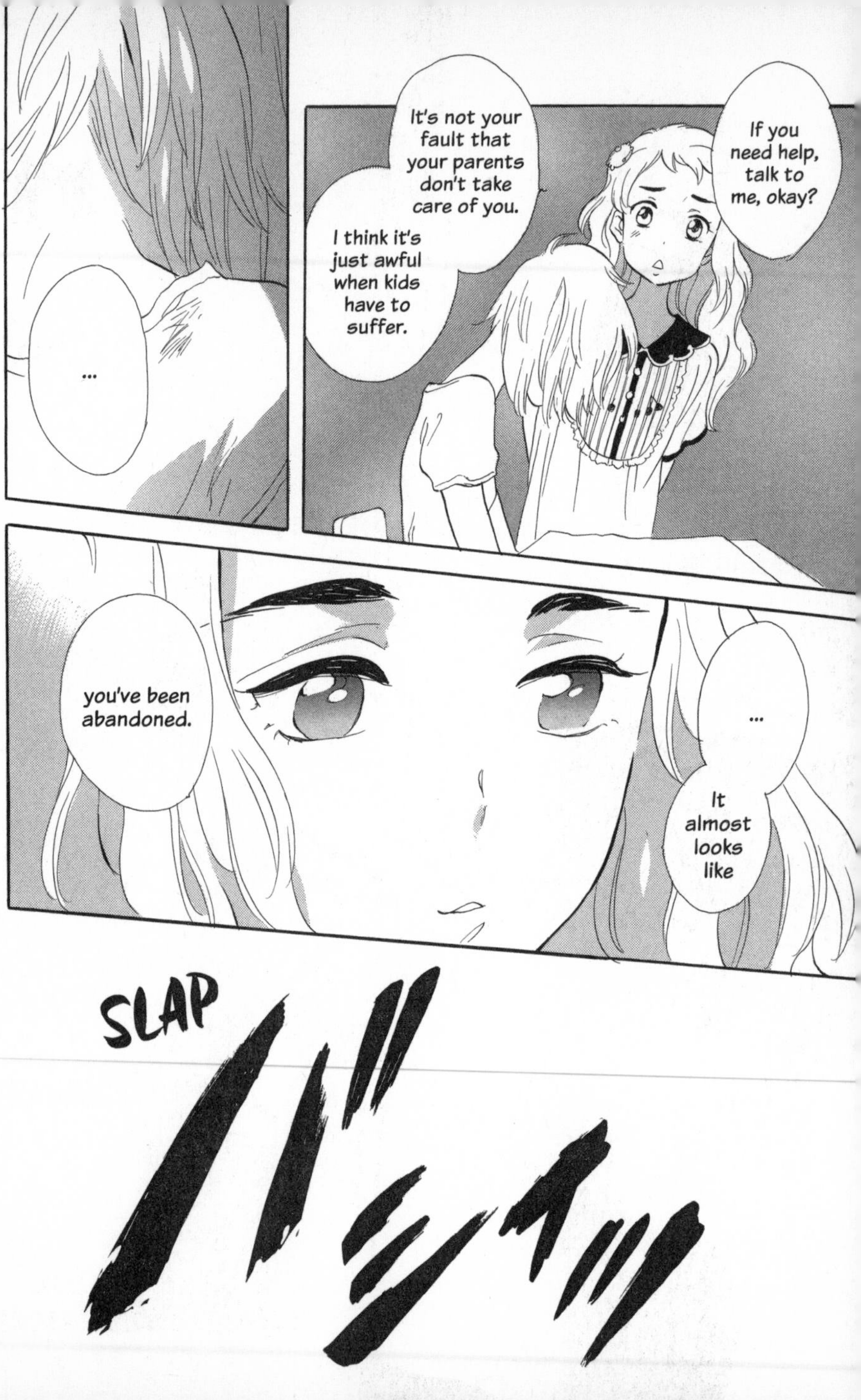
If you need help, talk to me, okay?
It's not your fault that your parents don't take care of you.
I think it's just awful when kids have to suffer.
...
...
It almost looks like
you've been abandoned.
SLAP

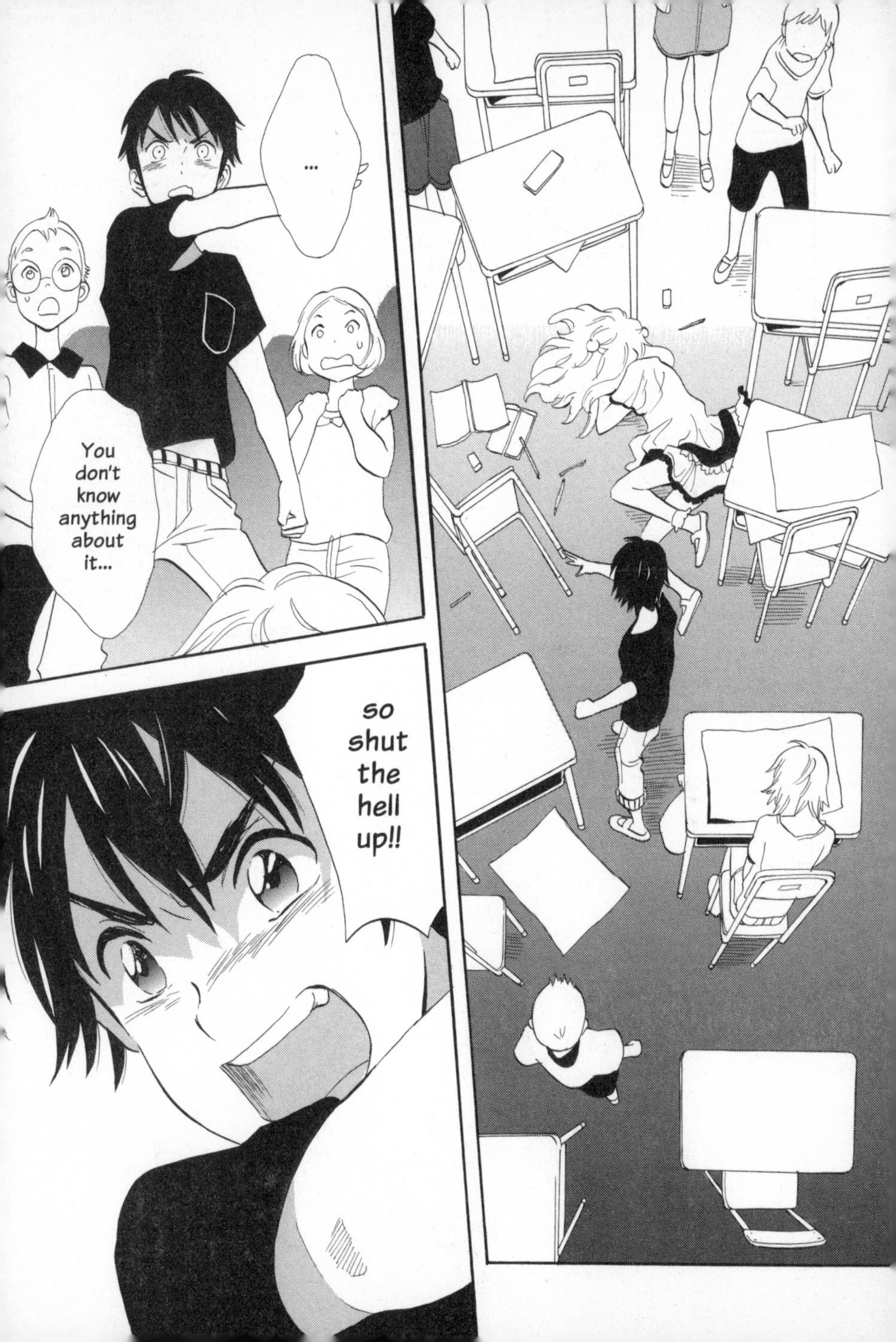
...
You don't know anything about it...
so shut the hell up!!

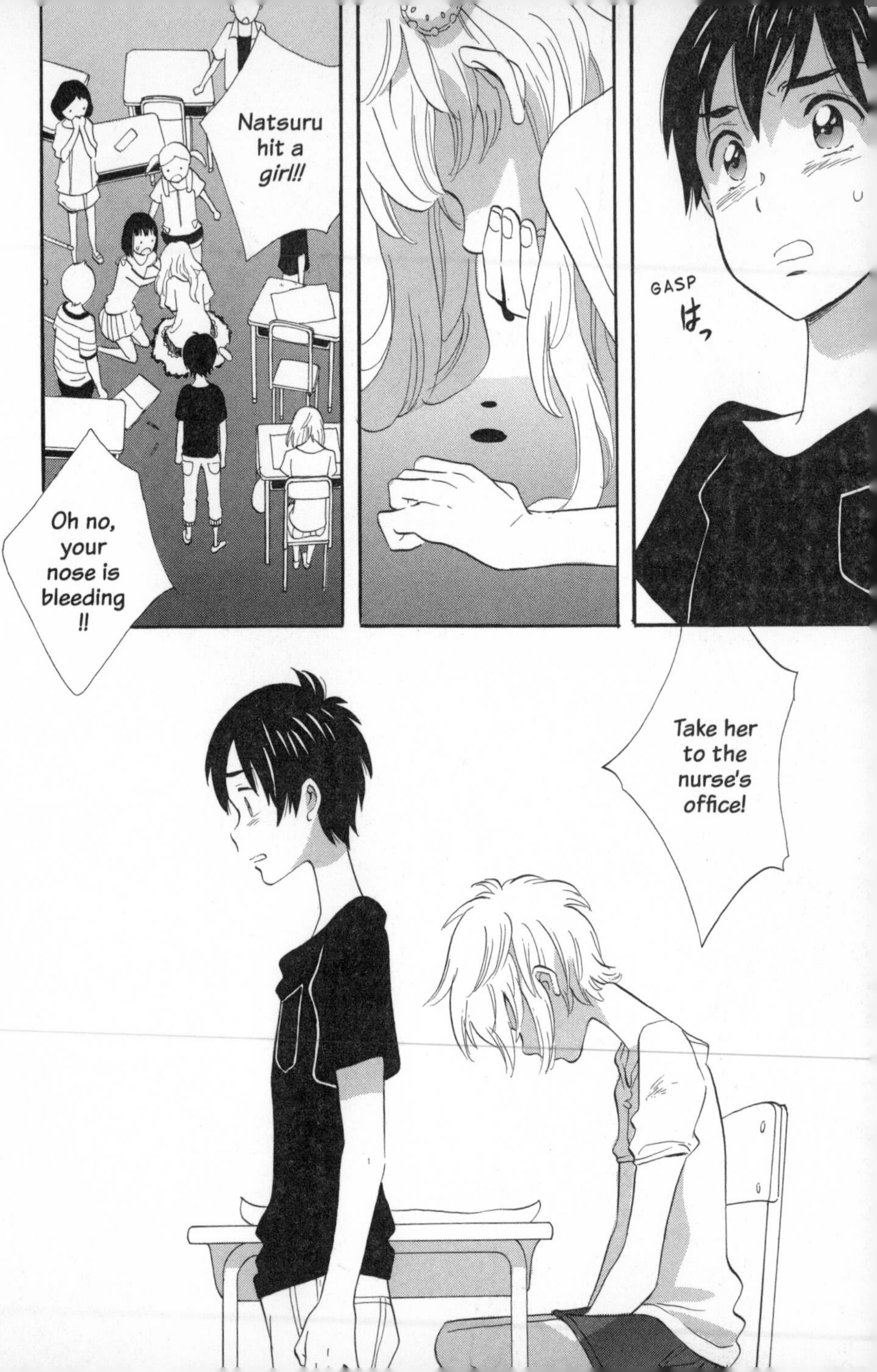
GASP
はっ
Natsuru hit a *girl*!!
Oh no, your nose is bleeding !!
Take her to the nurse's office!

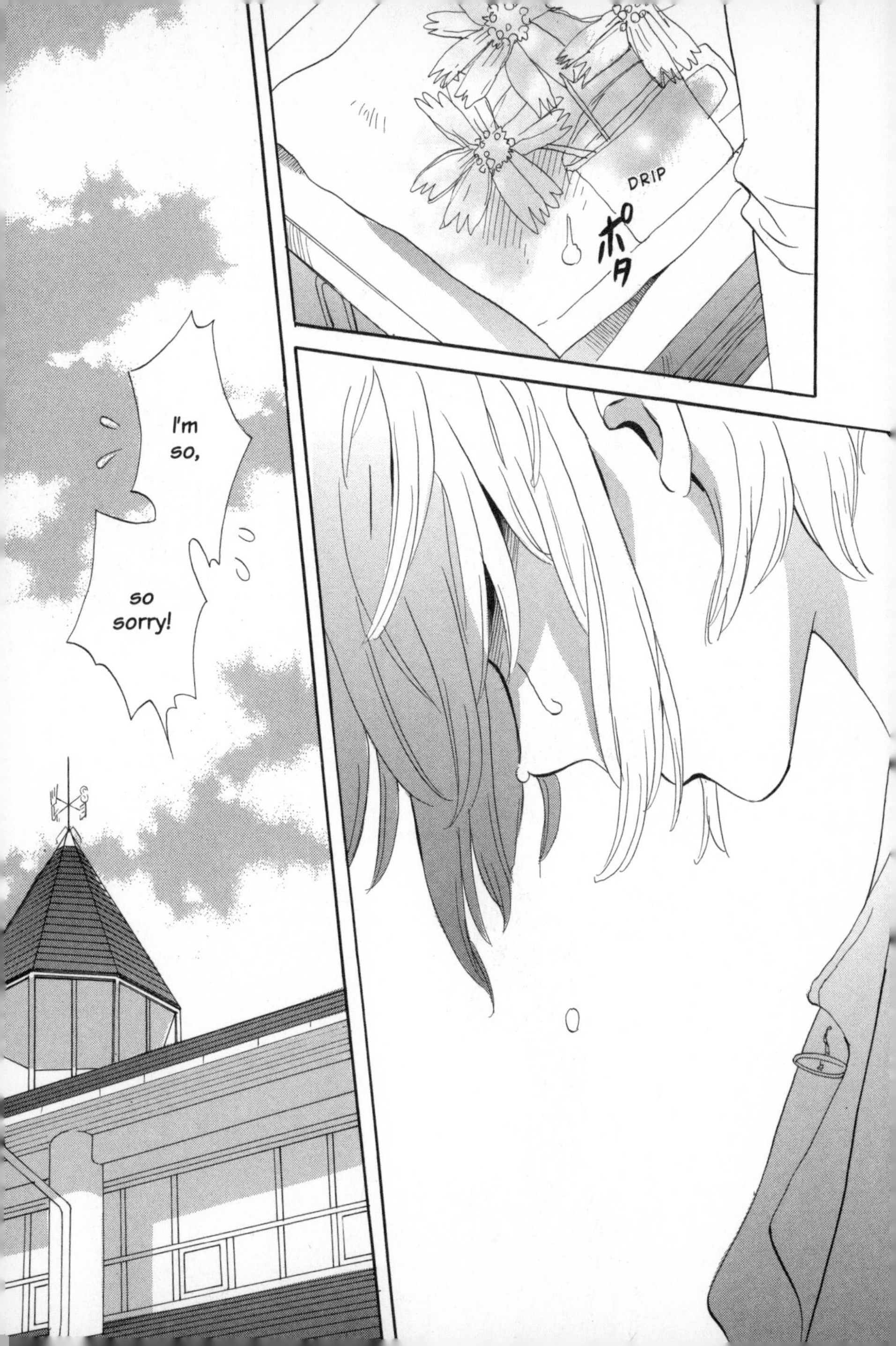
DRIP
ポタ
I'm so, so sorry!

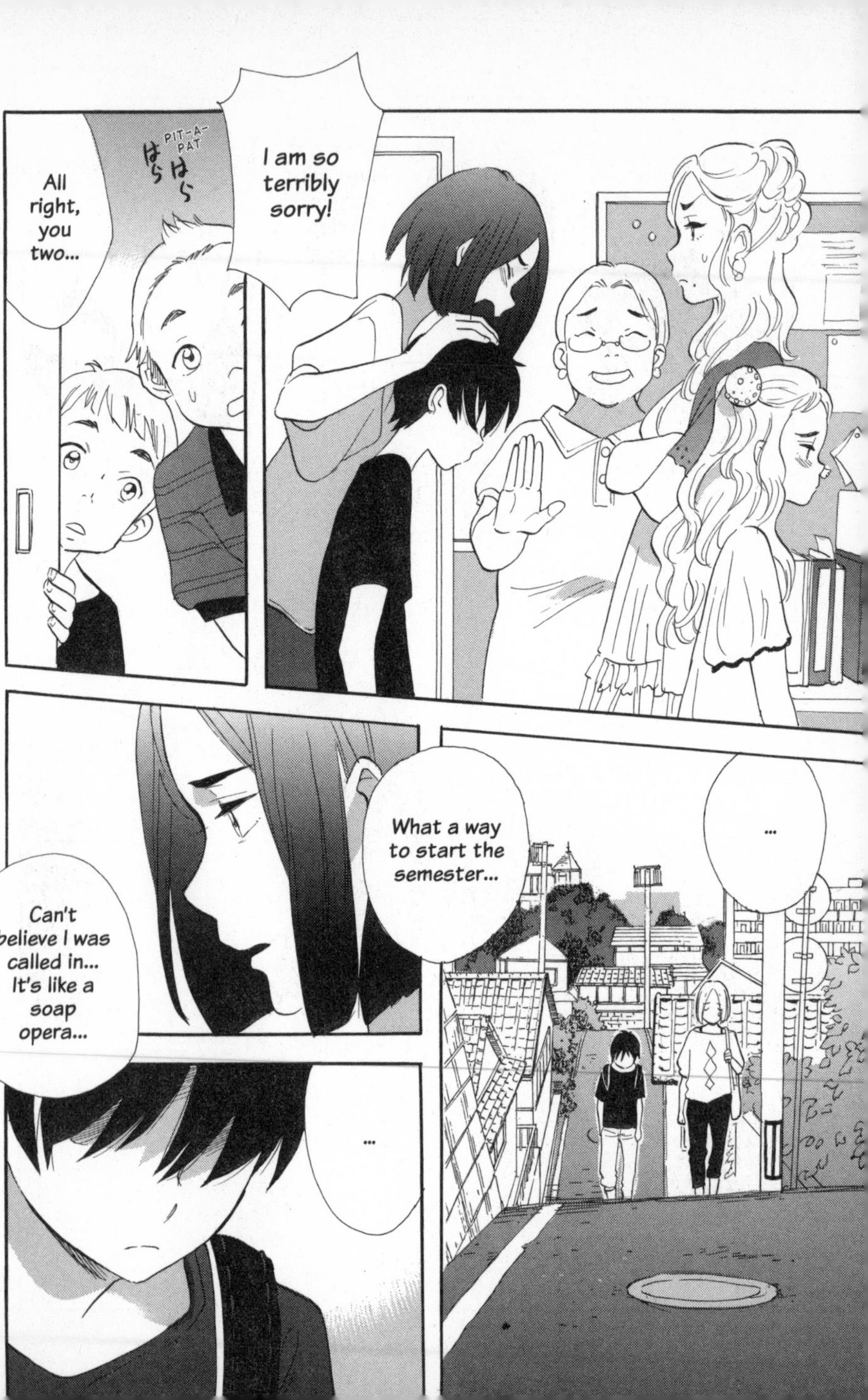
I am so terribly sorry!
PIT-A-PAT
はらはら
All right, you two...
...
What a way to start the semester...
Can't believe I was called in... It's like a soap opera...
...

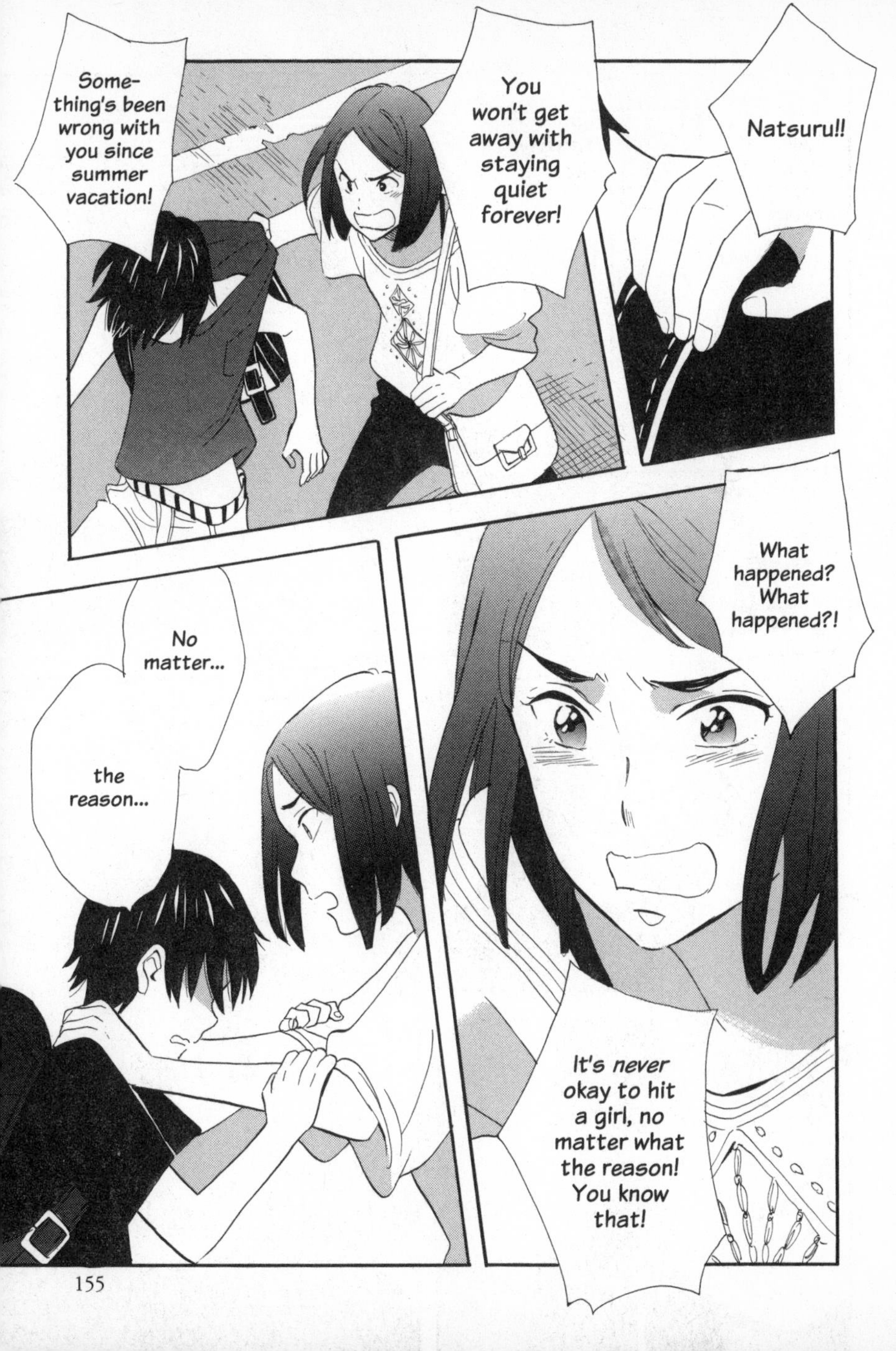
Natsuru!!
You won't get away with staying quiet forever!
Something's been wrong with you since summer vacation!
What happened? What happened?!
It's *never* okay to hit a girl, no matter what the reason! You know that!
No matter...
the reason...

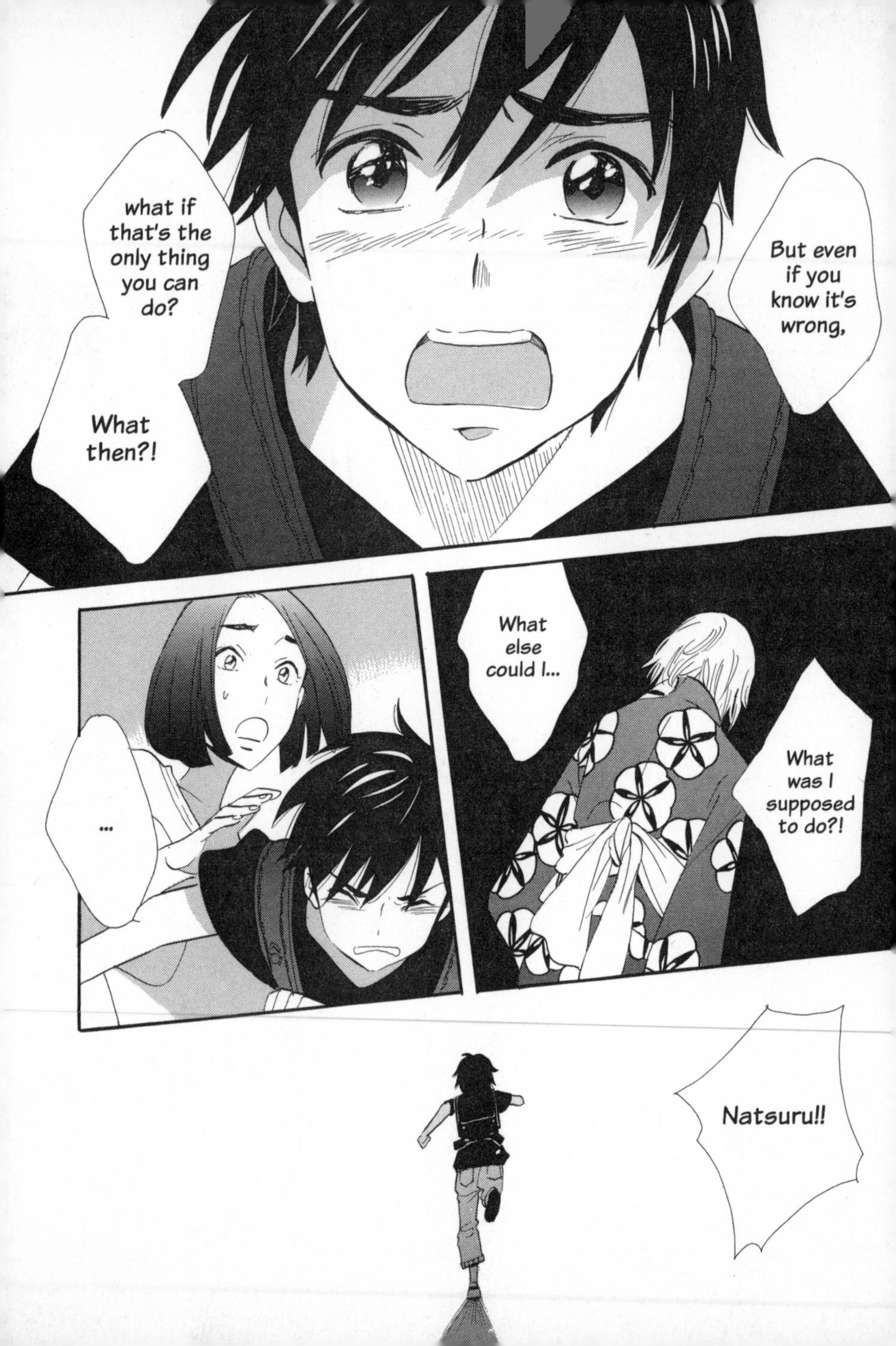
But even if you know it's wrong,
what if that's the only thing you can do?
What then?!
What else could I...
What was I supposed to do?!
...
Natsuru!!

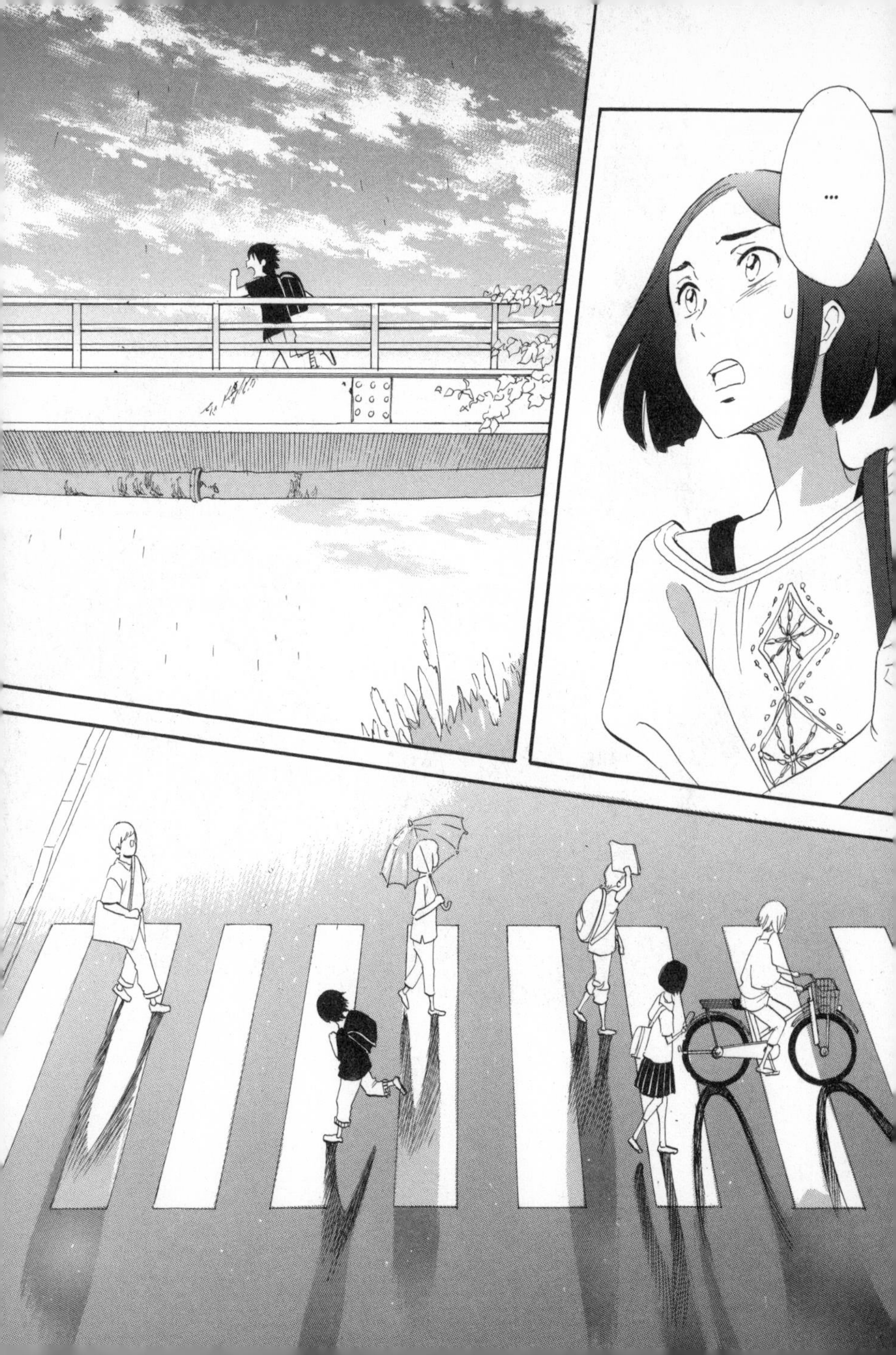
...

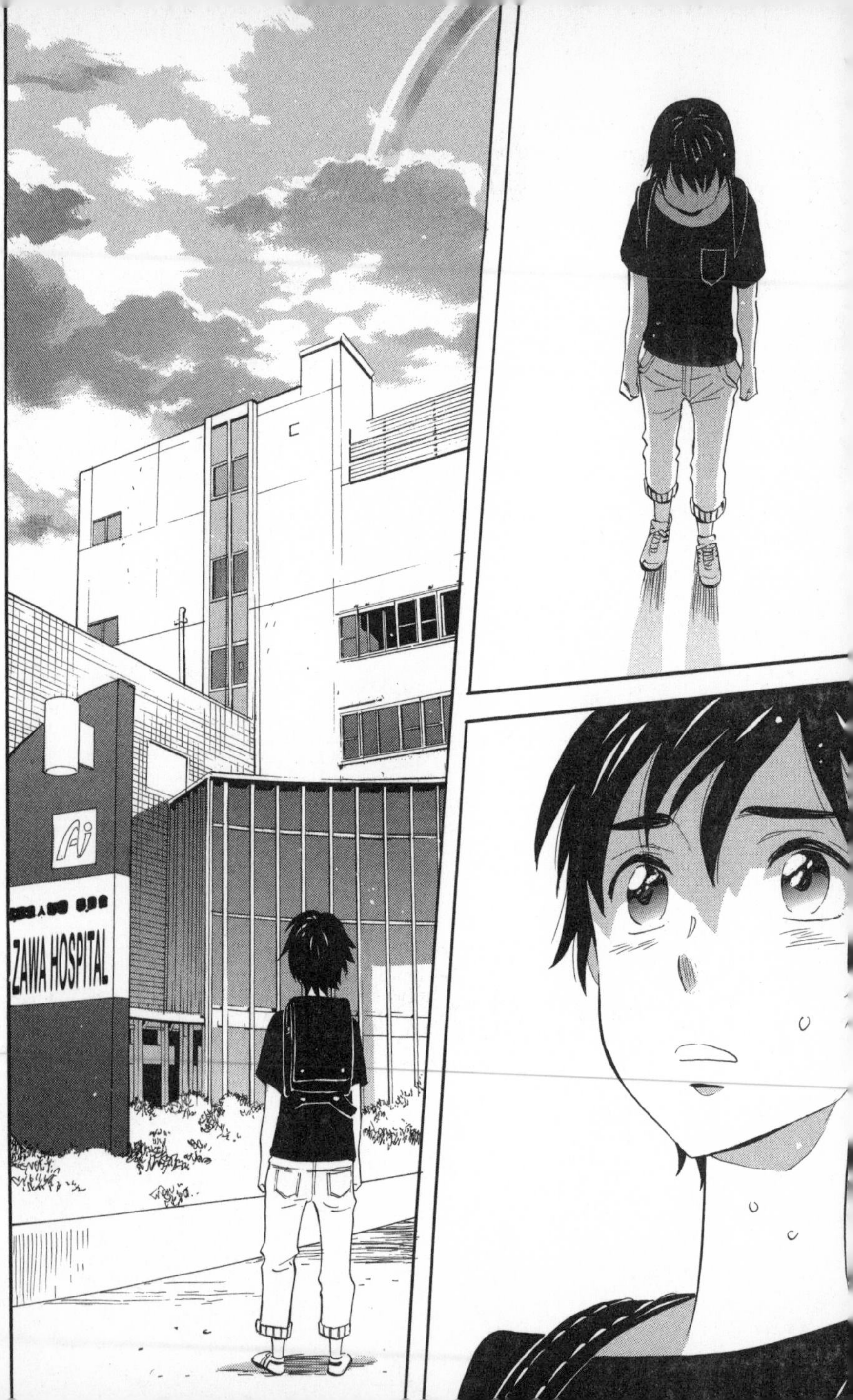
ZAWA HOSPITAL

final chapter

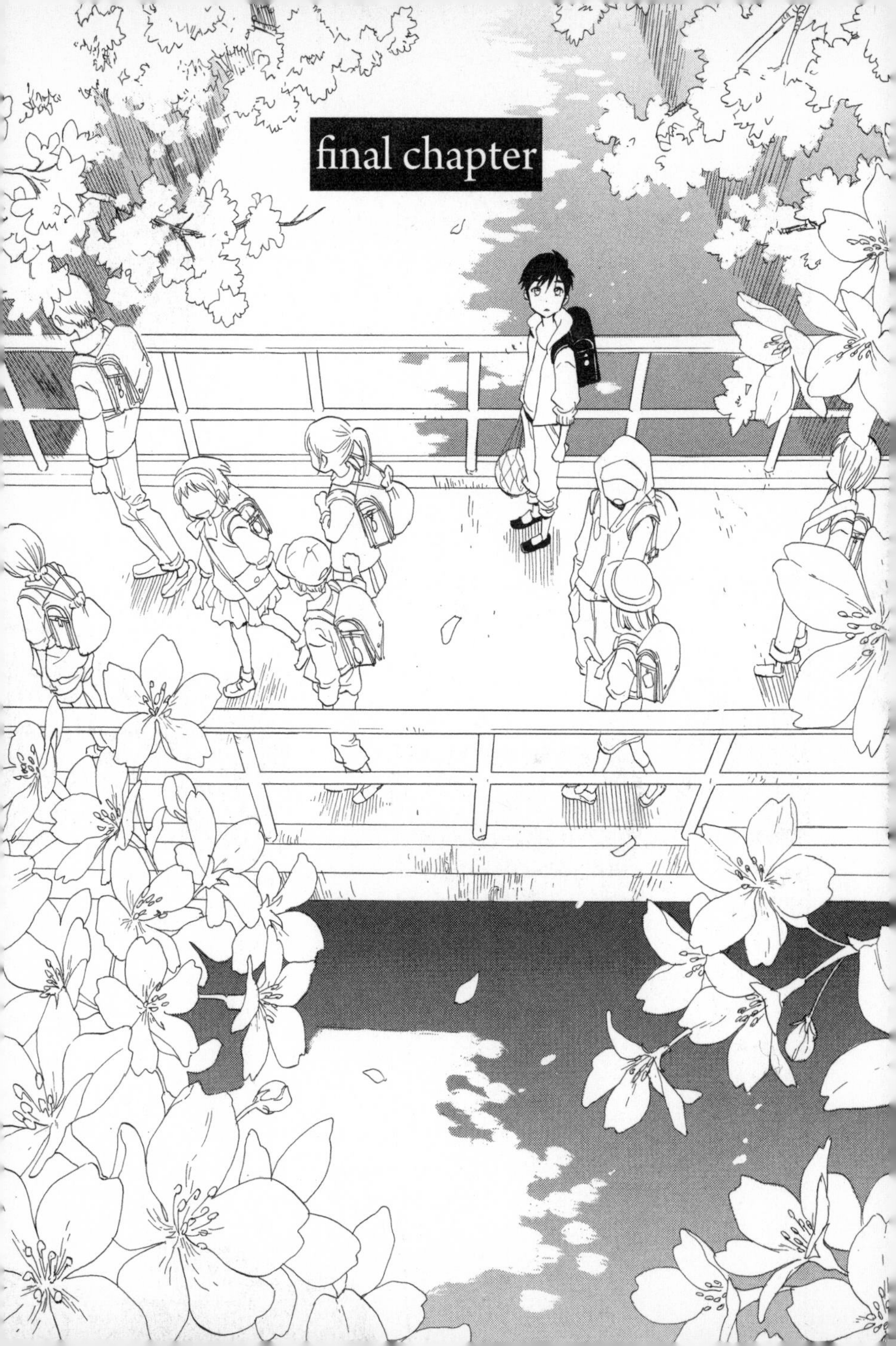

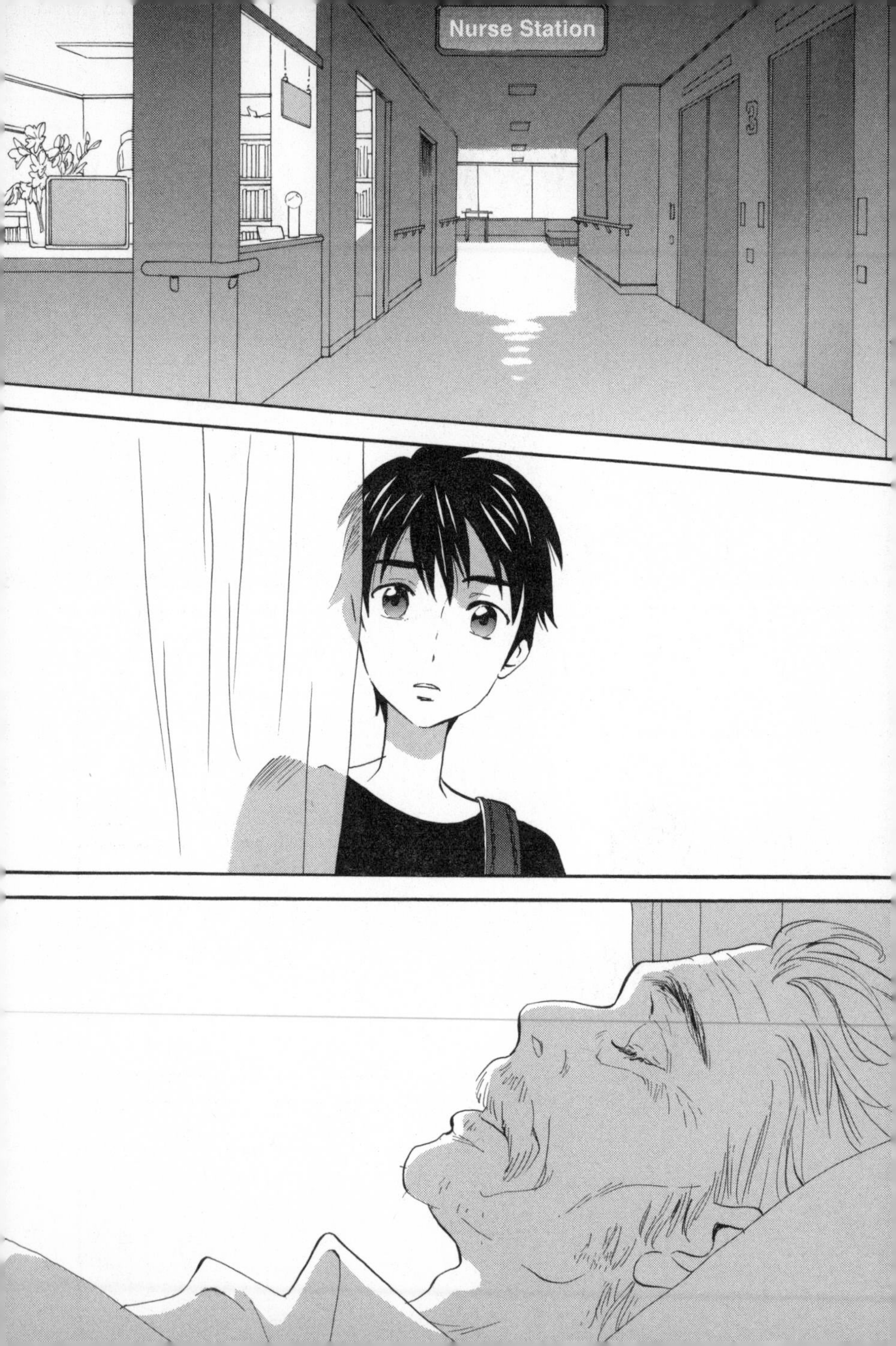
Nurse Station
3

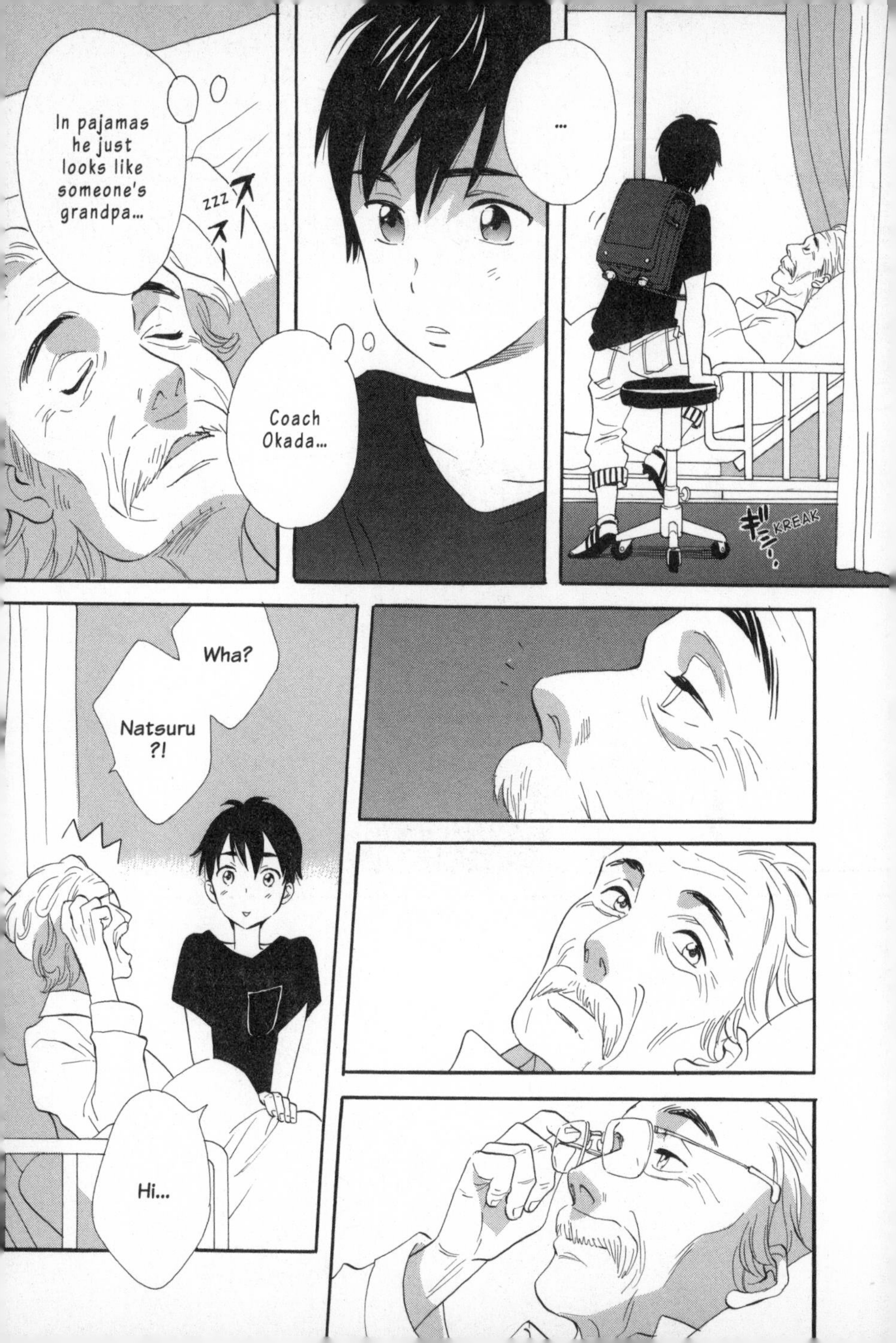
KREAK
...
Coach Okada...
In pajamas he just looks like someone's grandpa...
zzz
Wha?
Natsuru ?!
Hi...

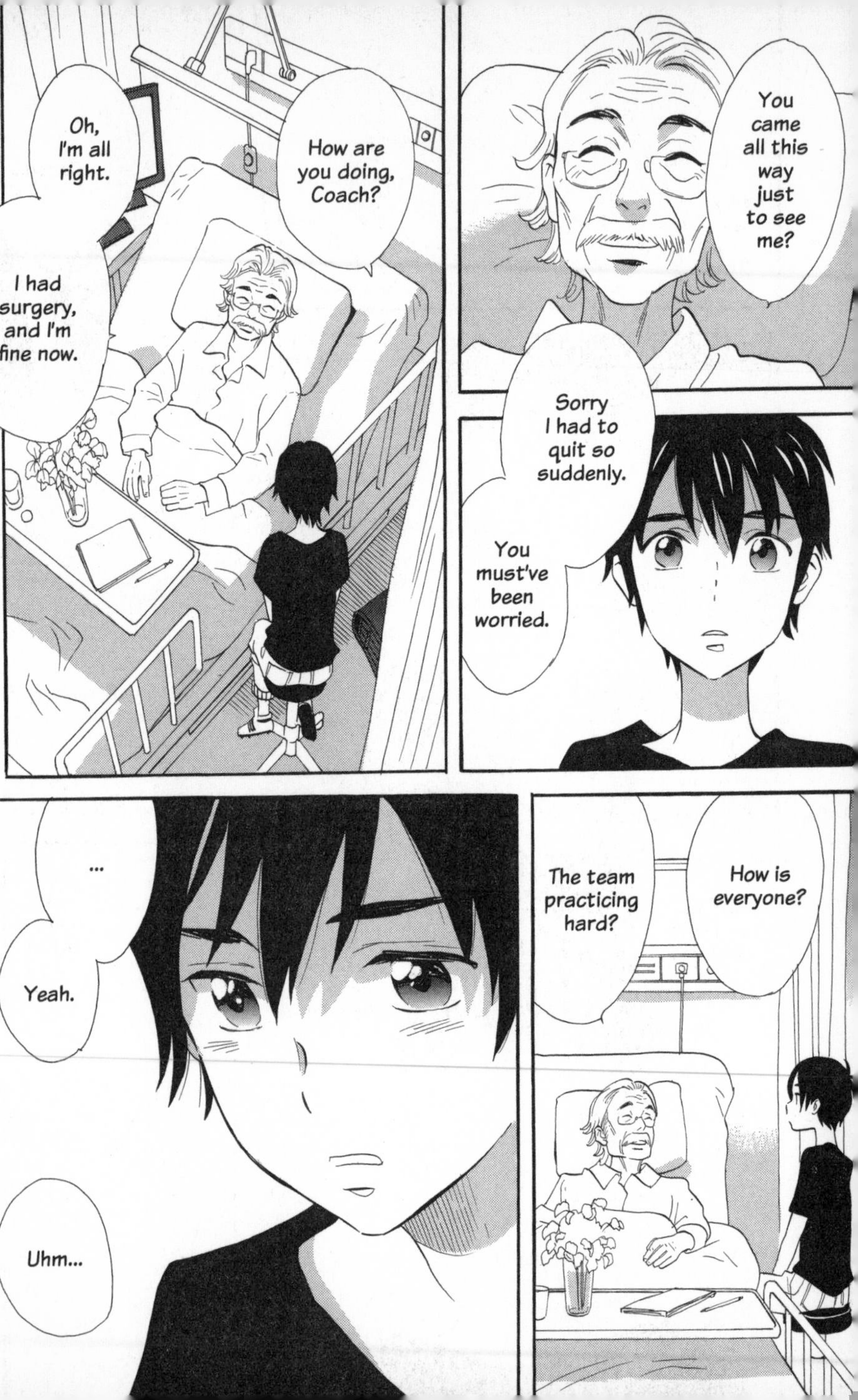
You came all this way just to see me?
Sorry I had to quit so suddenly.
You must've been worried.
How are you doing, Coach?
Oh, I'm all right.
I had surgery, and I'm fine now.
How is everyone?
The team practicing hard?
...
Yeah.
Uhm...

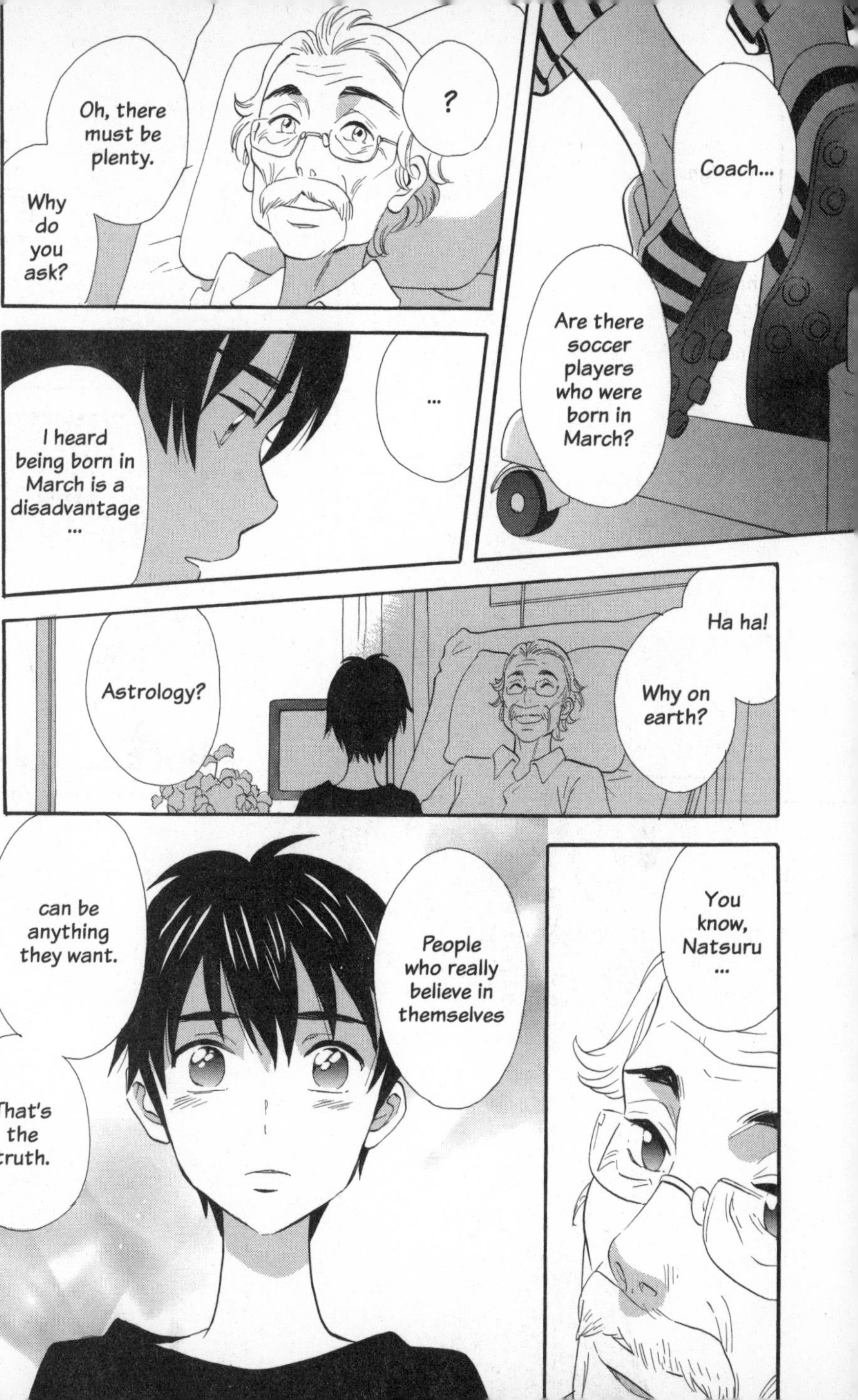
Coach...
Are there soccer players who were born in March?
?
Oh, there must be plenty.
Why do you ask?
...
I heard being born in March is a disadvantage ...
Ha ha!
Why on earth?
Astrology?
You know, Natsuru ...
People who really believe in themselves
can be anything they want.
That's the truth.

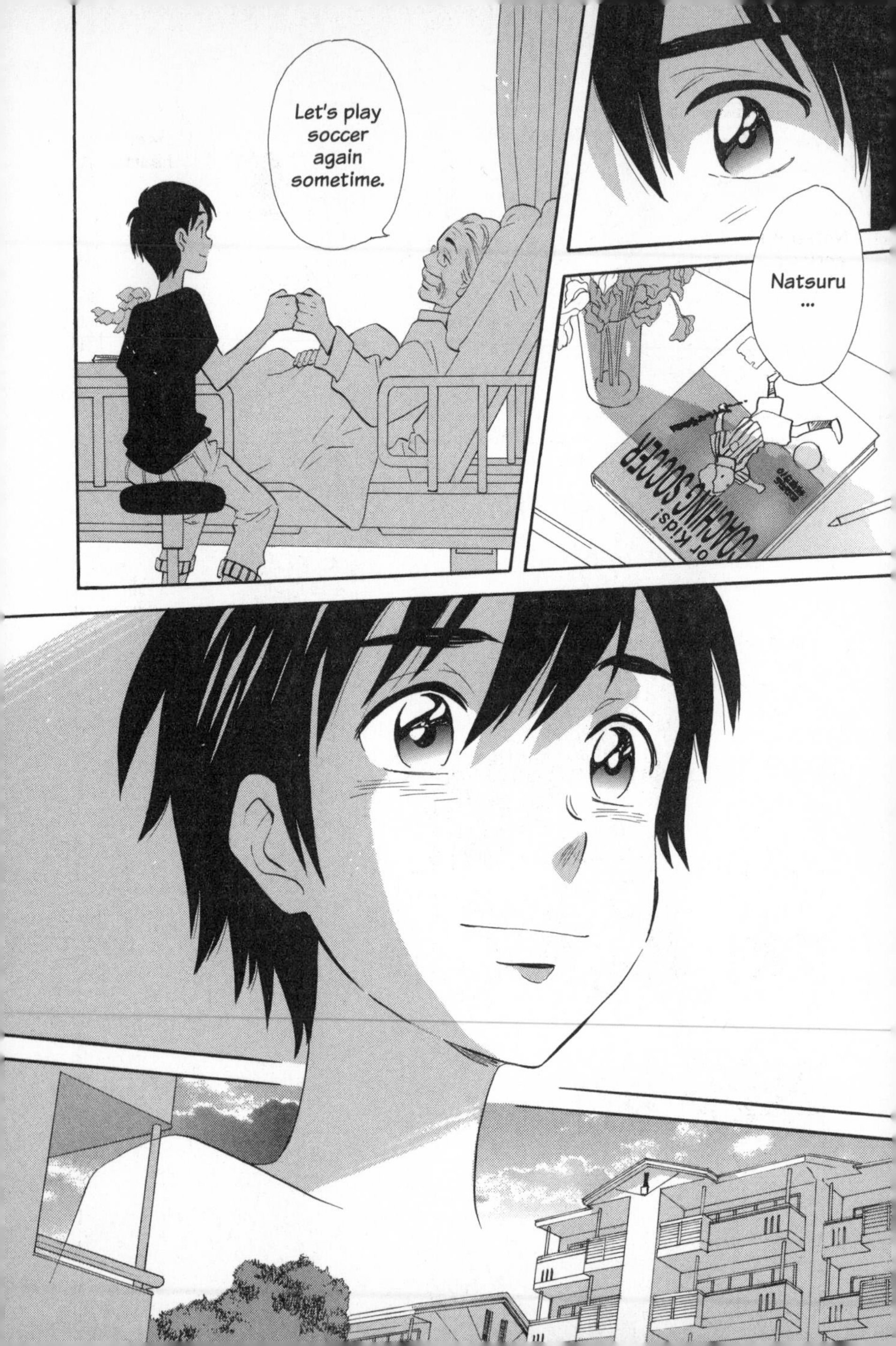
Natsuru ...
Let's play soccer again sometime.

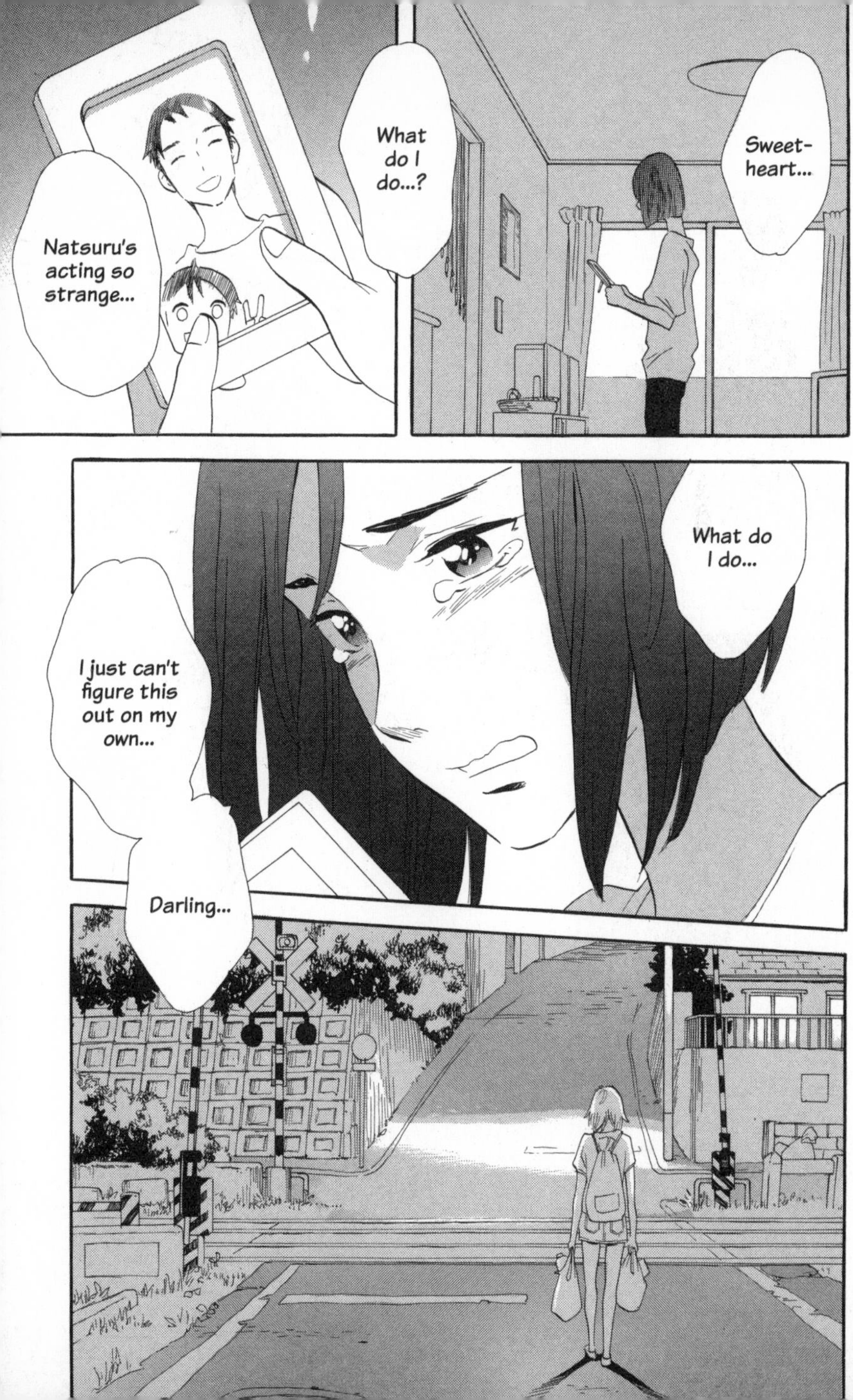
Sweet-heart...
What do I do...?
Natsuru's acting so strange...
What do I do...
I just can't figure this out on my own...
Darling...

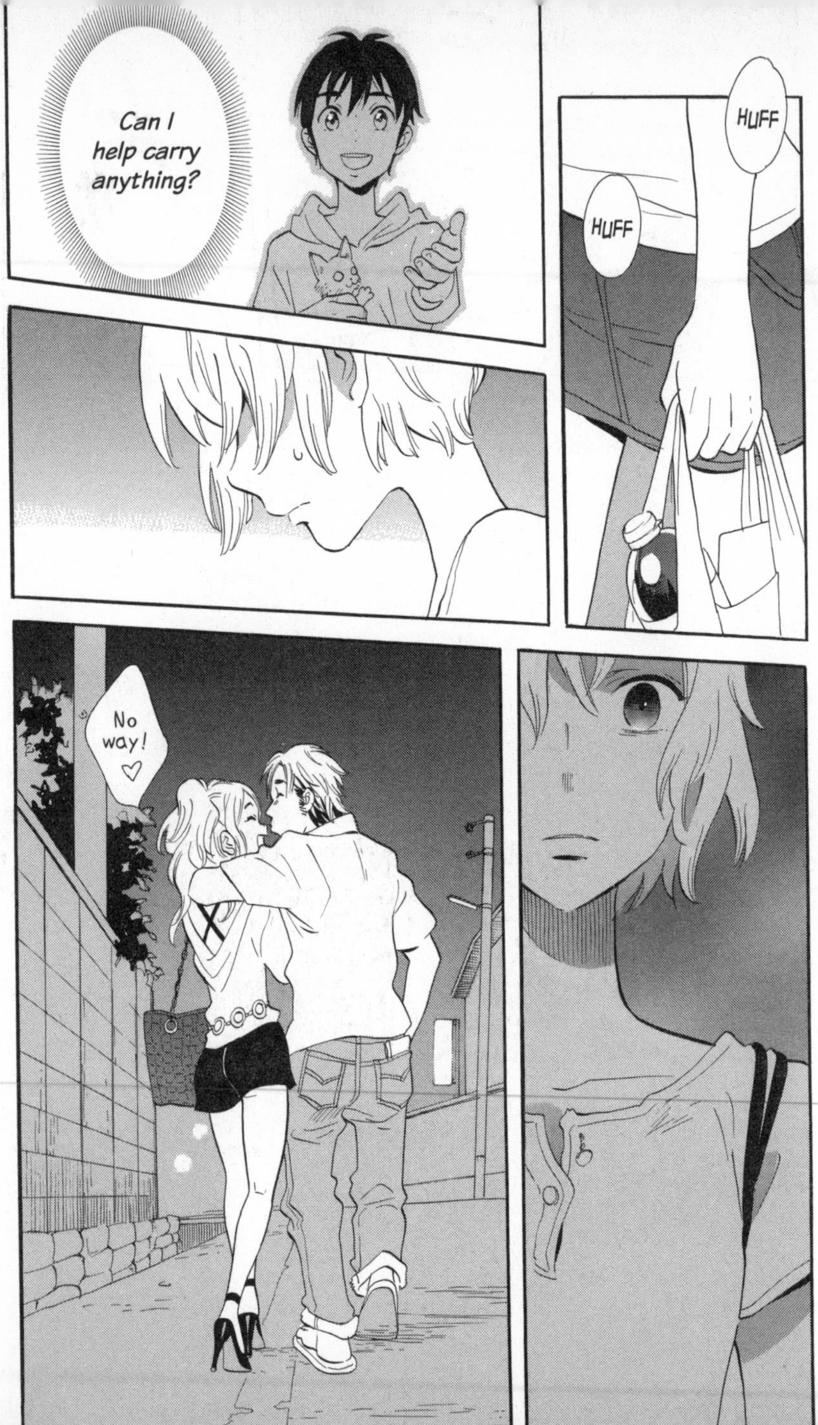
HUFF
HUFF
Can I help carry anything?
No way! ♡

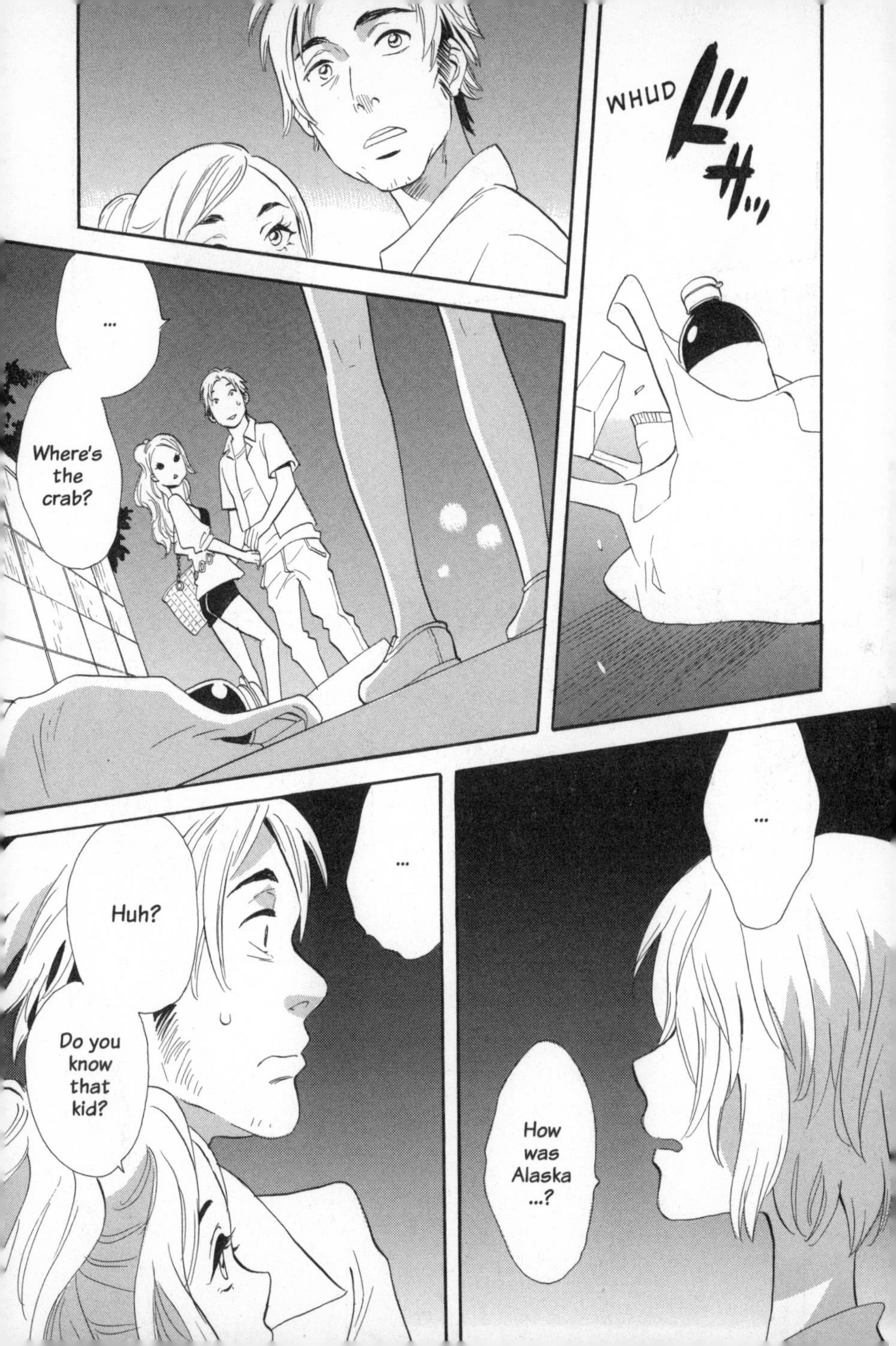

WHUD
ドサッ
...
Where's the crab?
...
How was Alaska ...?
...
Huh?
Do you know that kid?

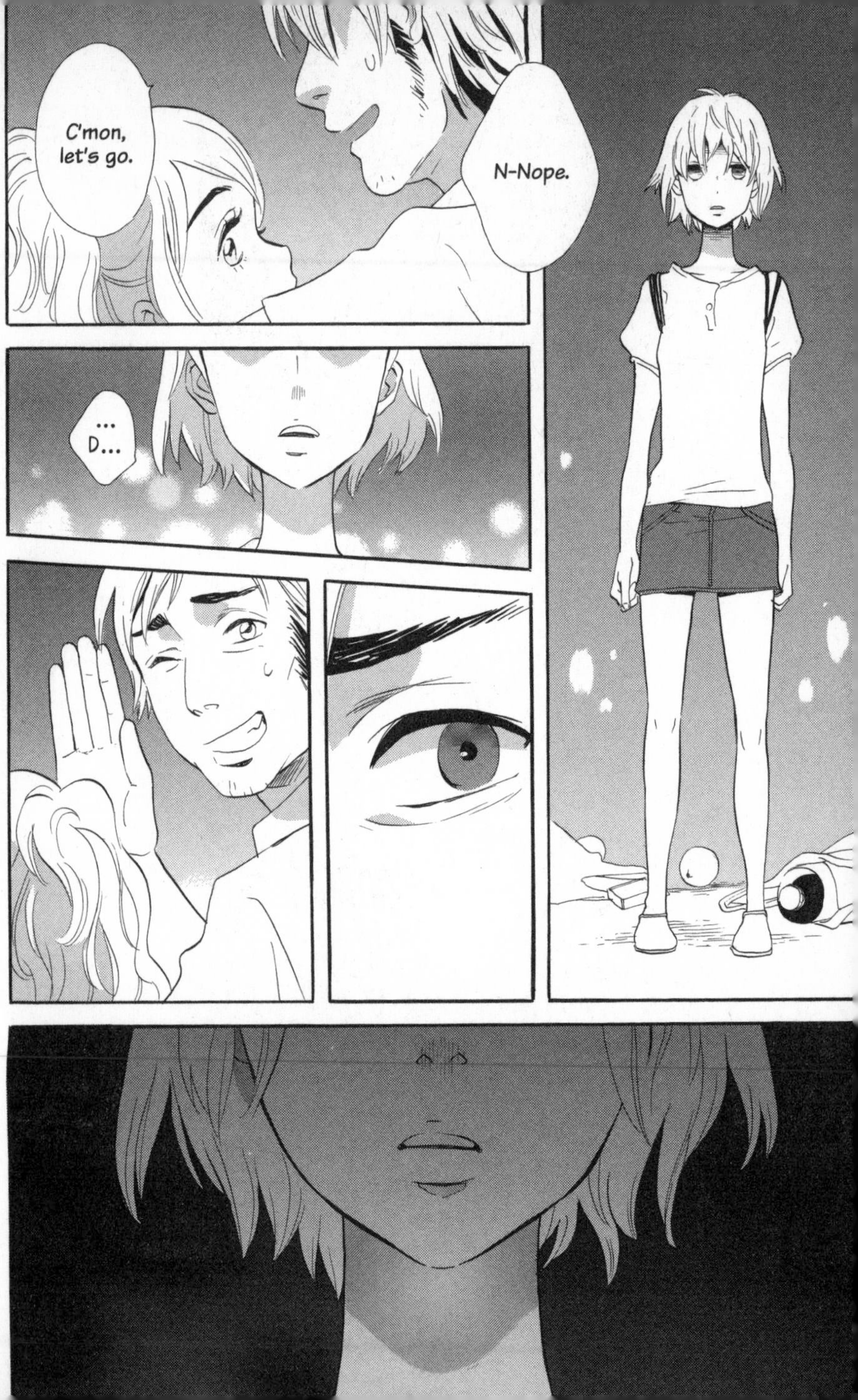
N-Nope.
C'mon, let's go.
...
D...

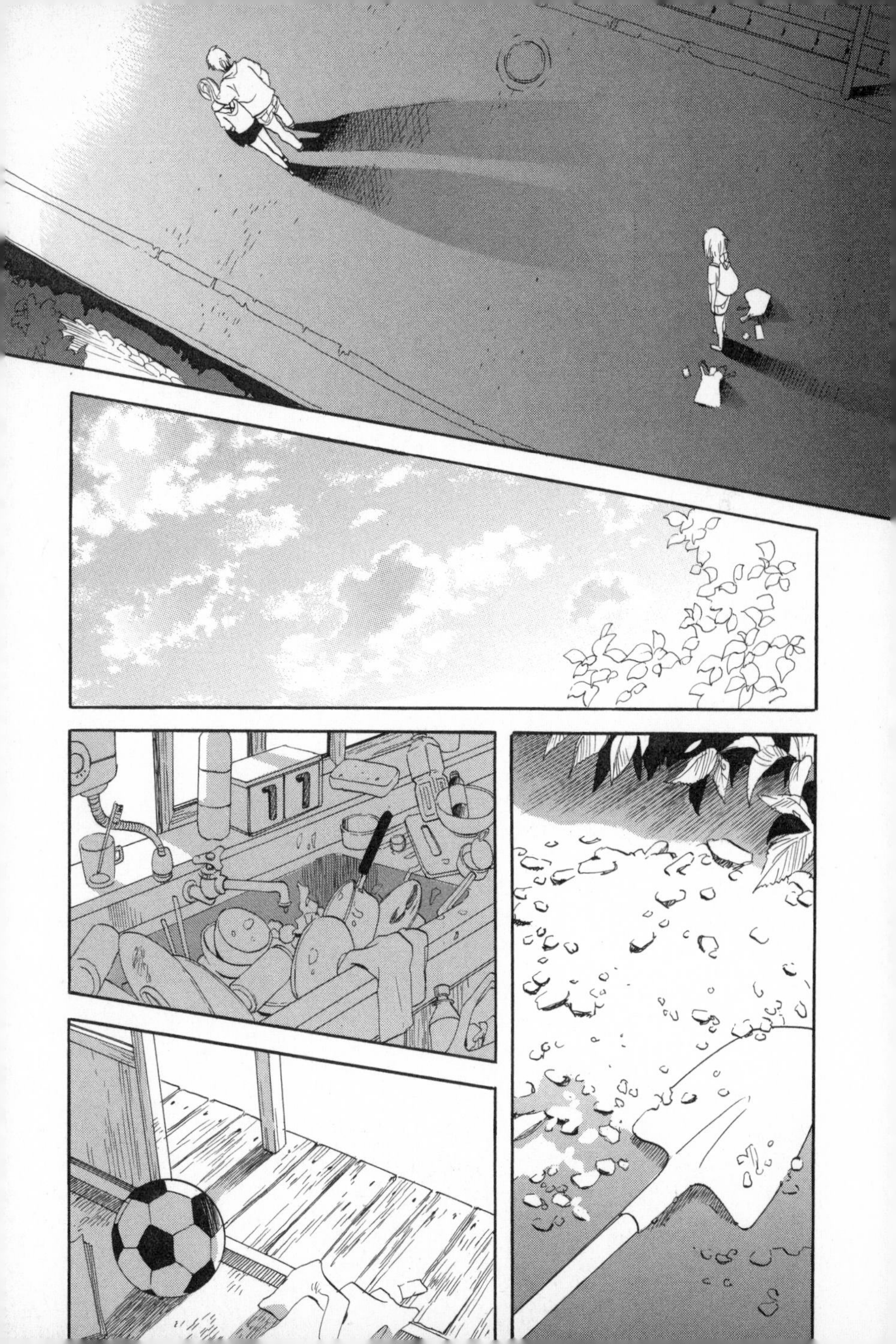
11

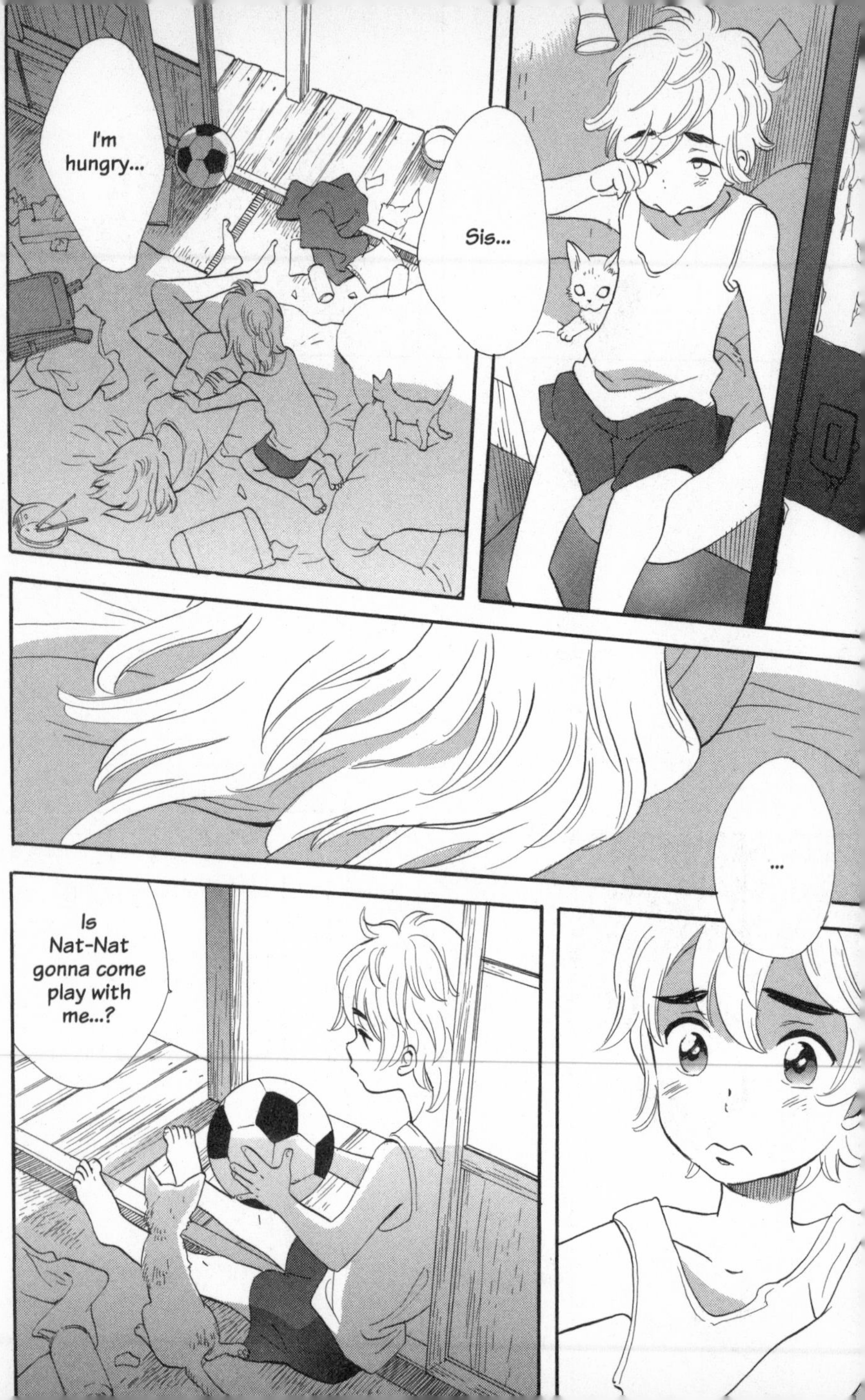
Sis...
I'm hungry...
...
Is Nat-Nat gonna come play with me...?

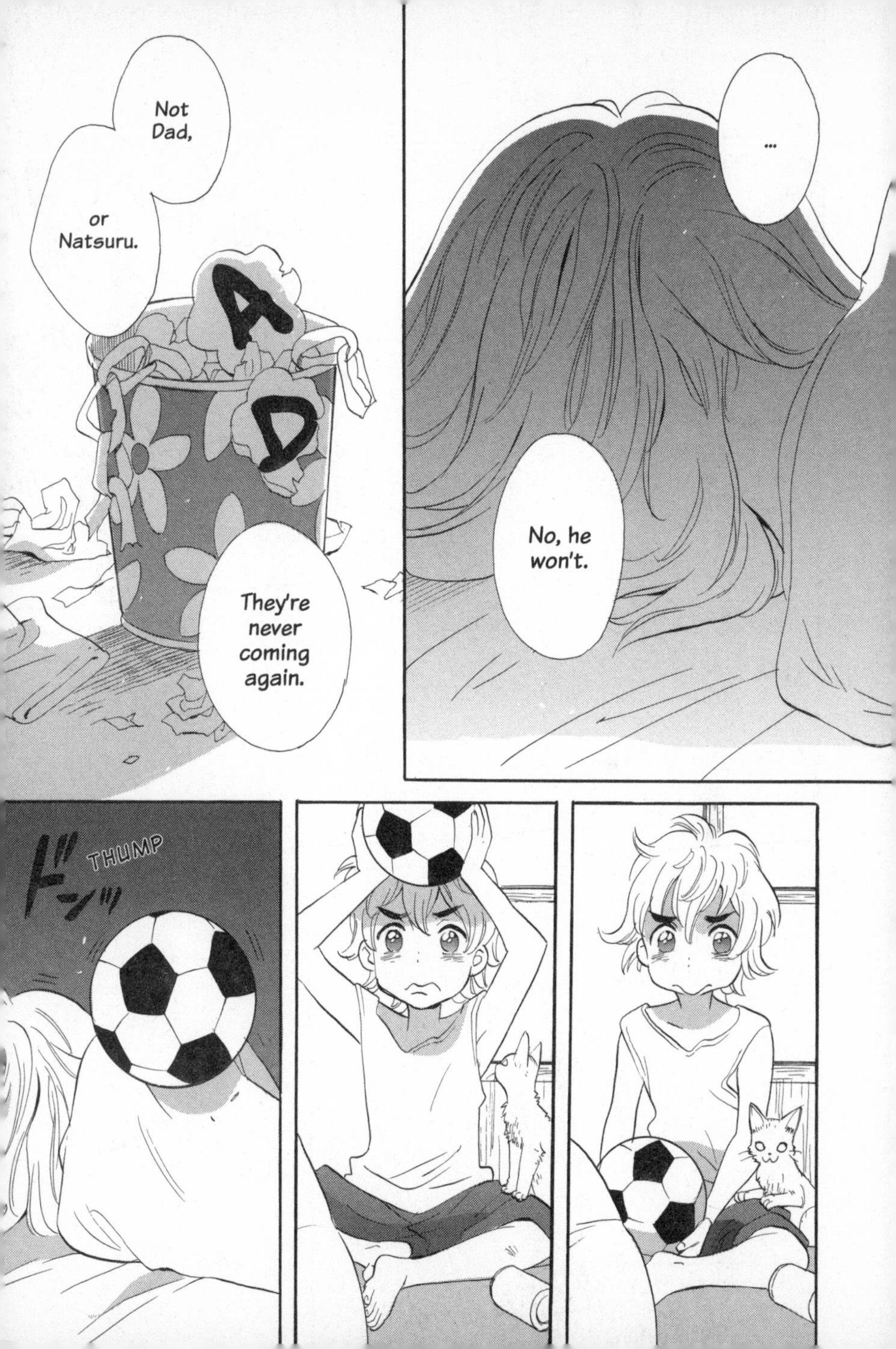
...
No, he won't.
Not Dad,
or Natsuru.
They're never coming again.
ドッッ
THUMP

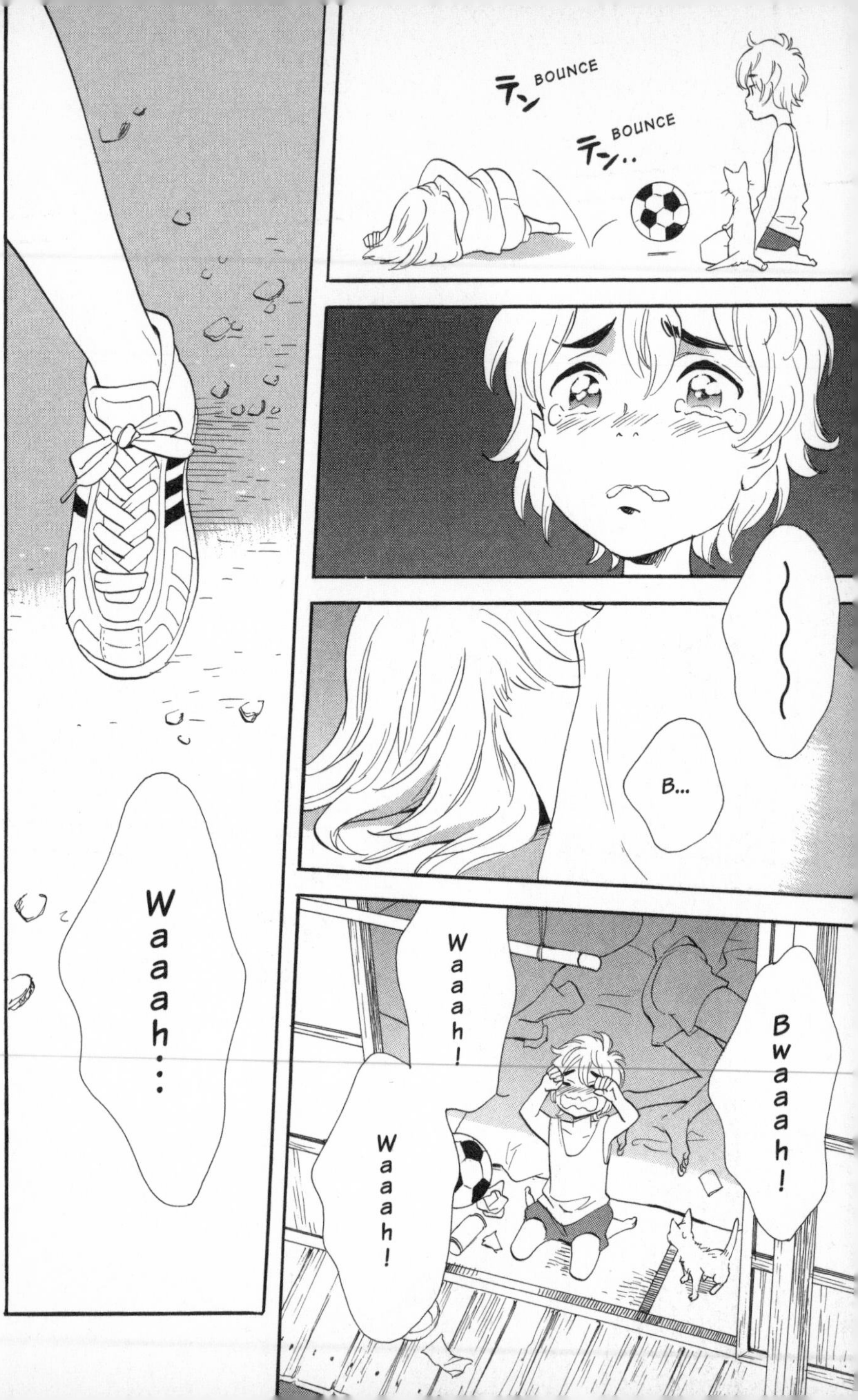

テン BOUNCE
テン.. BOUNCE
B...
Bwaaaah!
Waaah!
Waaah!
Waaah...

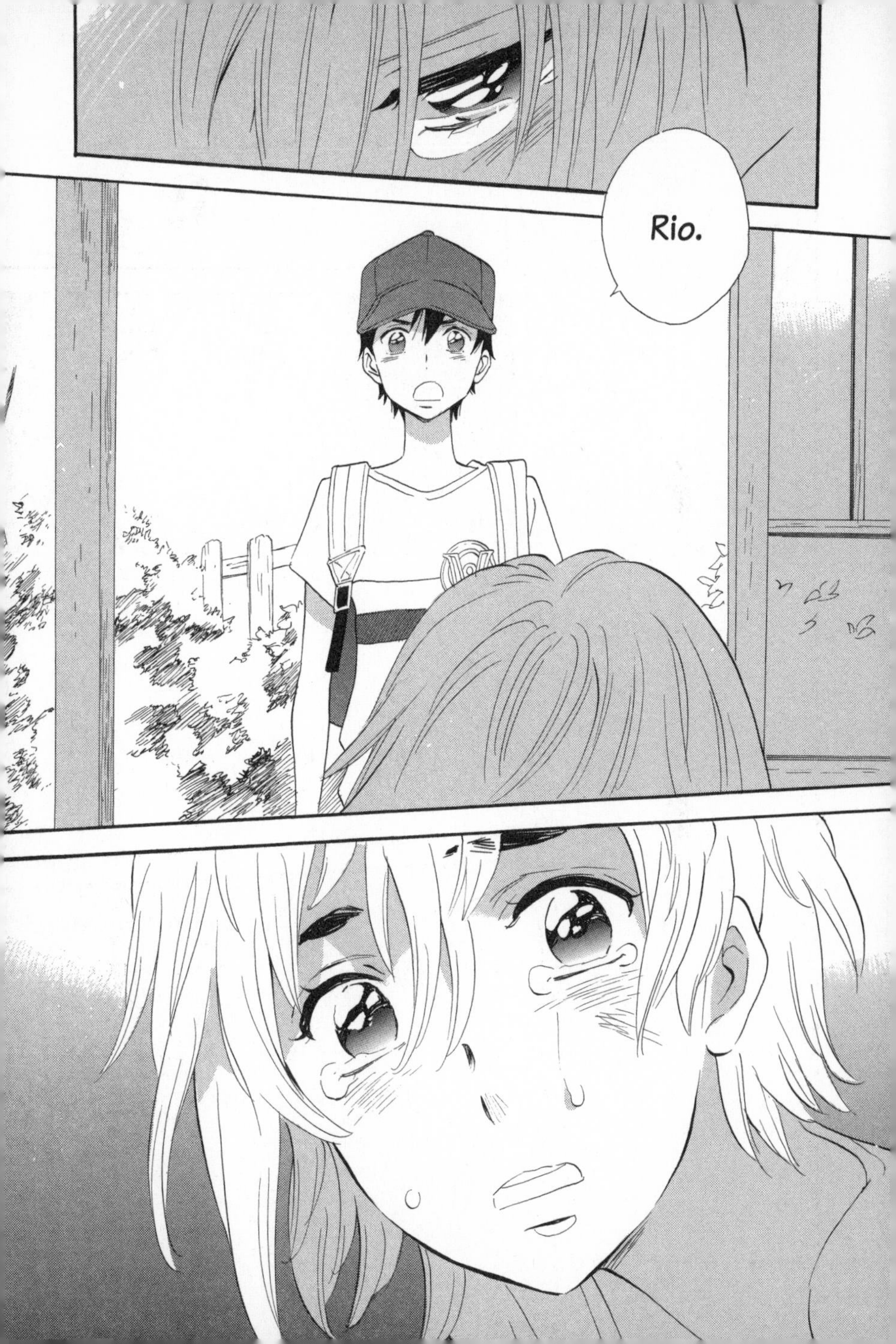
Rio.

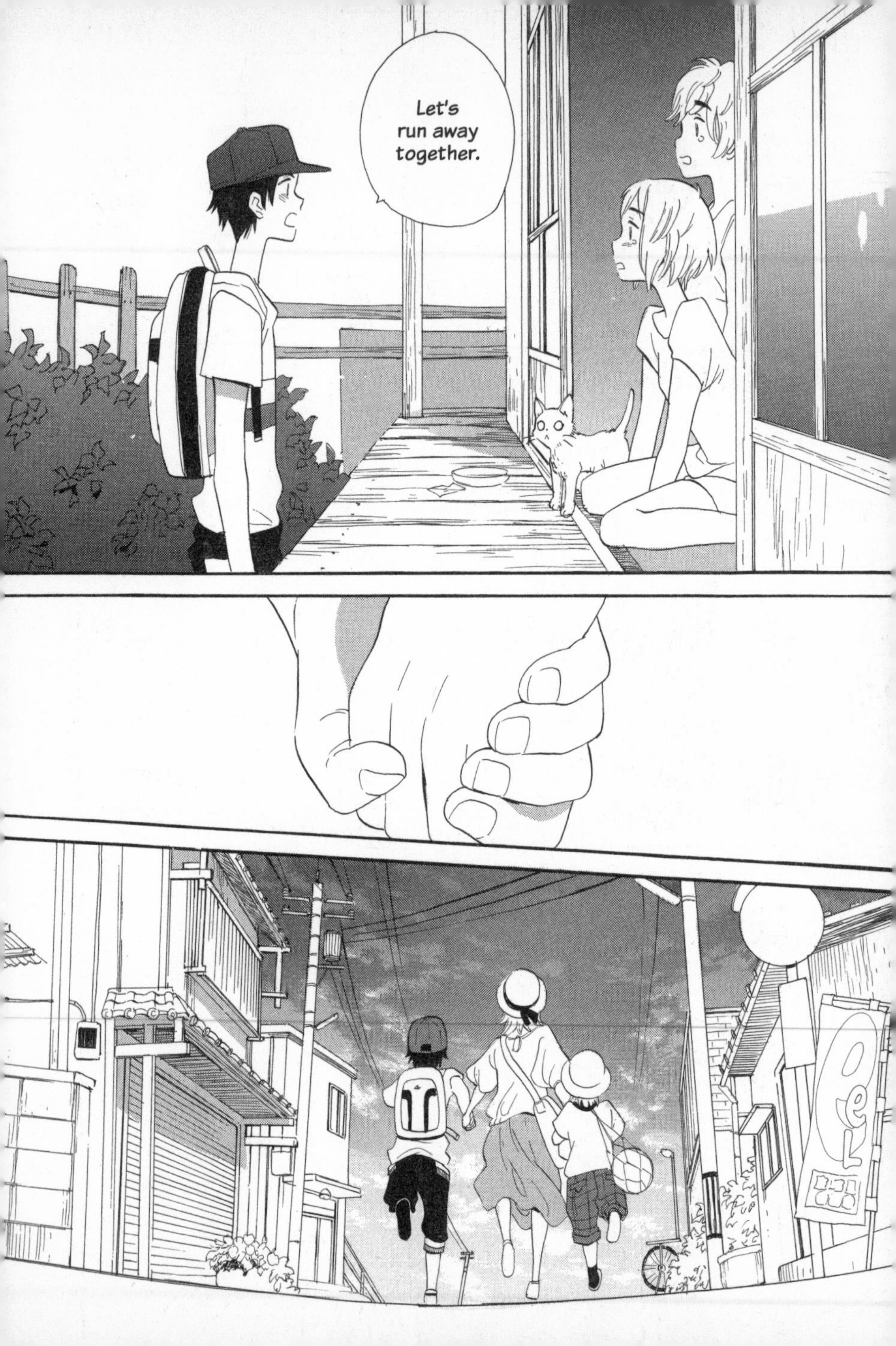
Let's run away together.

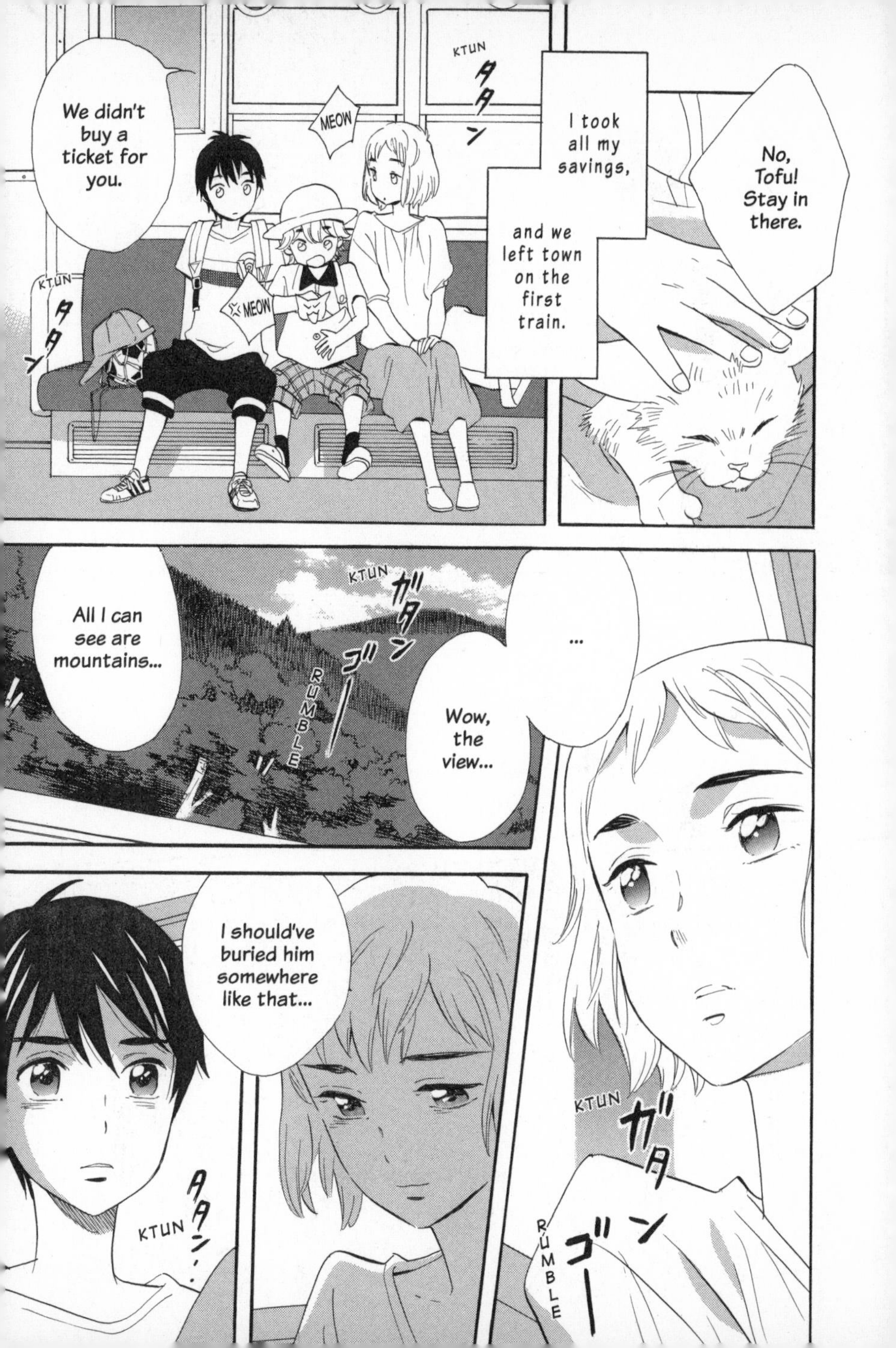
No, Tofu! Stay in there.
I took all my savings,
and we left town on the first train.
KTUN
MEOW
We didn't buy a ticket for you.
MEOW
KTUN
...
Wow, the view...
KTUN
RUMBLE
KTUN
RUMBLE
All I can see are mountains...
I should've buried him somewhere like that...
KTUN

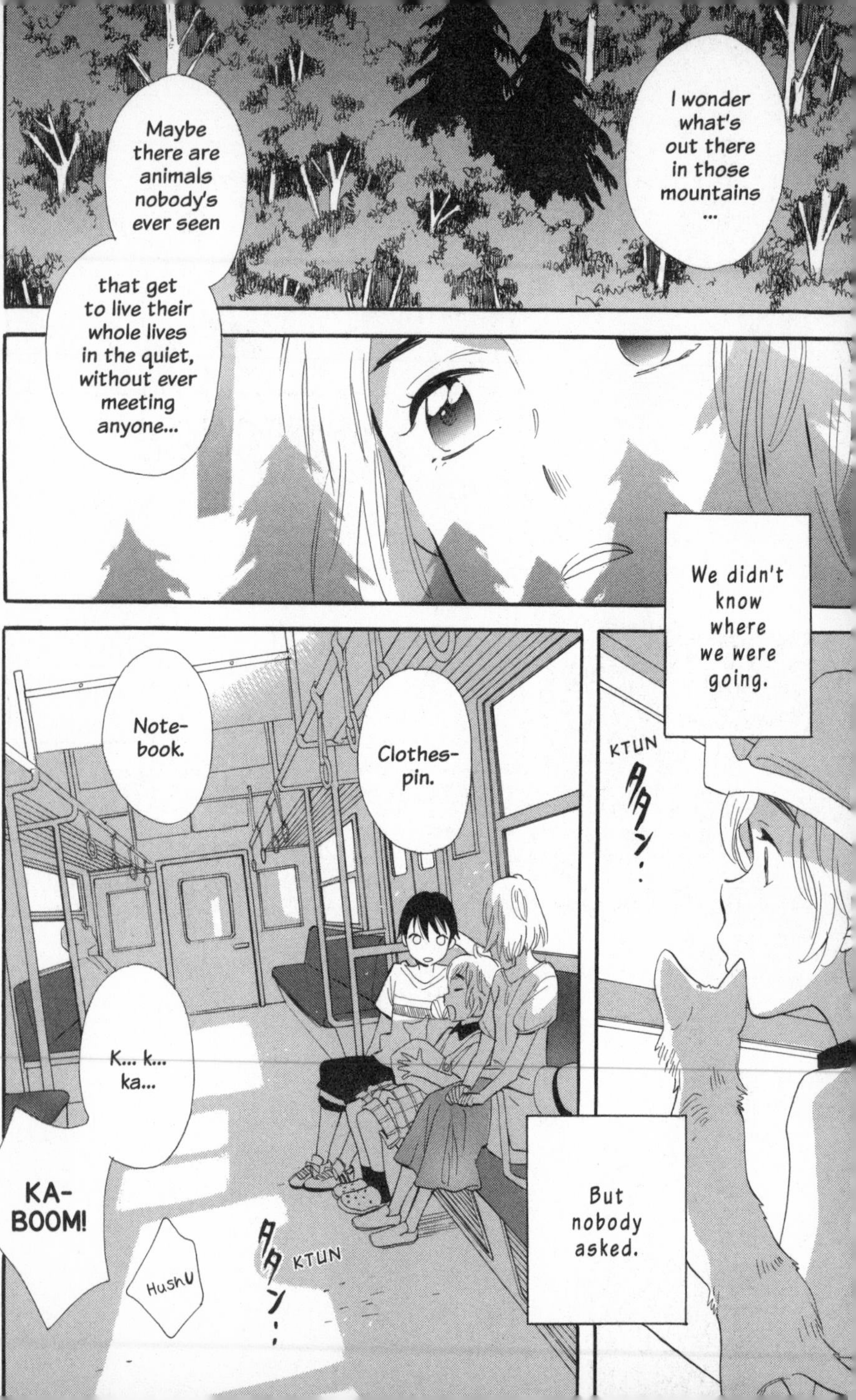
I wonder what's out there in those mountains ...
Maybe there are animals nobody's ever seen
that get to live their whole lives in the quiet, without ever meeting anyone...
We didn't know where we were going.
KTUN
But nobody asked.
Clothes-pin.
Note-book.
K... k... ka...
KA-BOOM!
Hush
KTUN

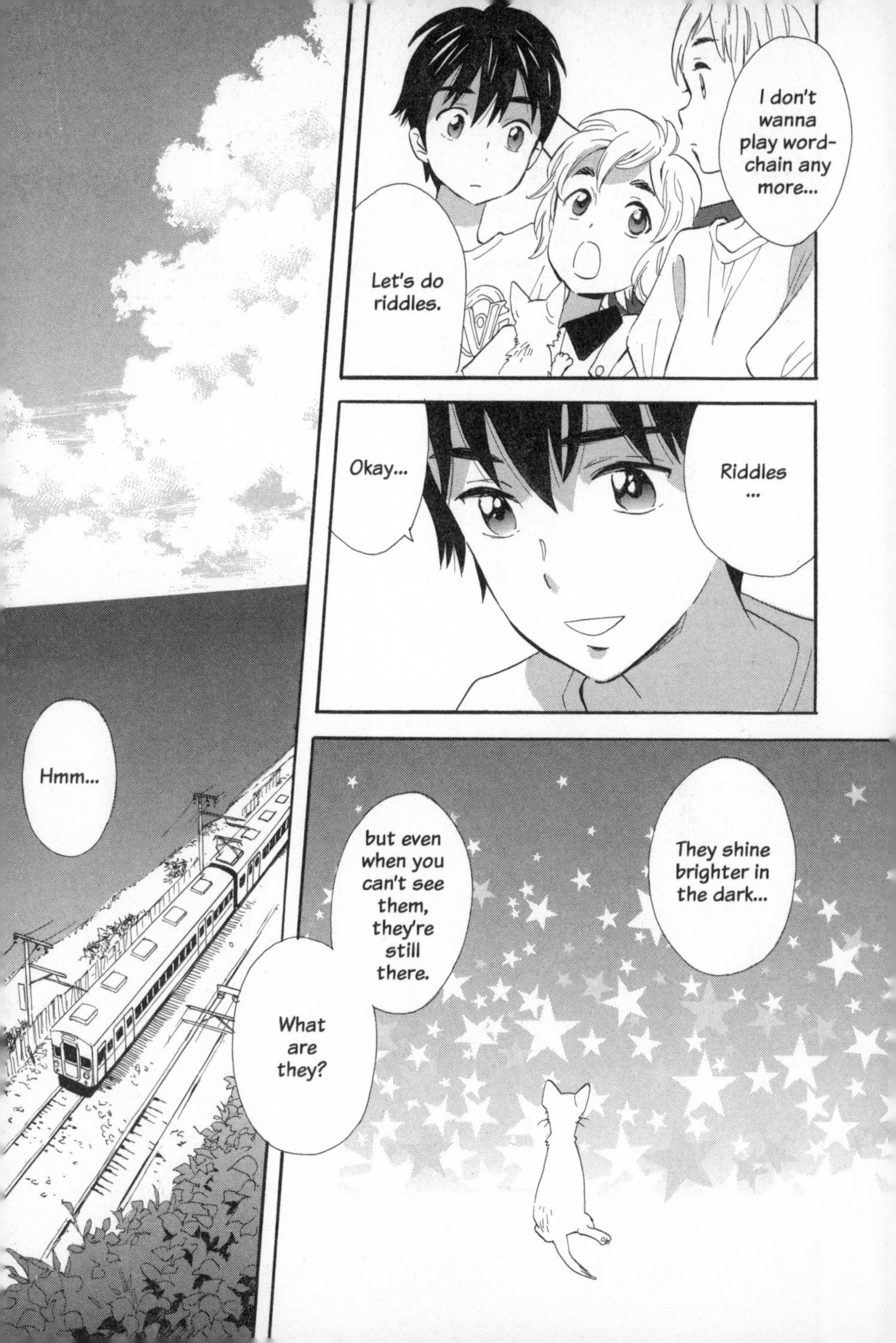
I don't wanna play word-chain any more...
Let's do riddles.
Riddles ...
Okay...
They shine brighter in the dark...
but even when you can't see them, they're still there.
What are they?
Hmm...

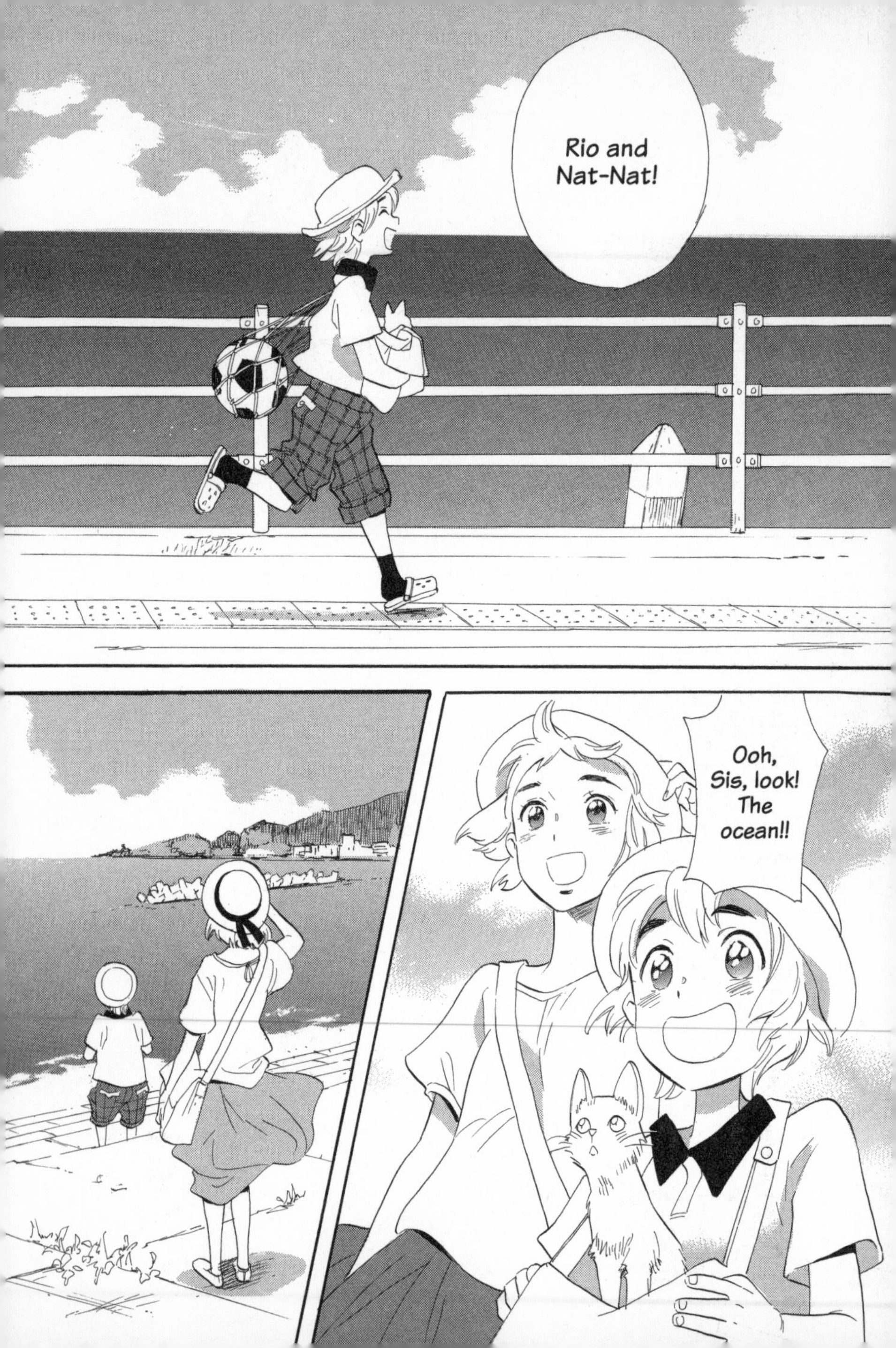
Rio and Nat-Nat!
Ooh, Sis, look! The ocean!!

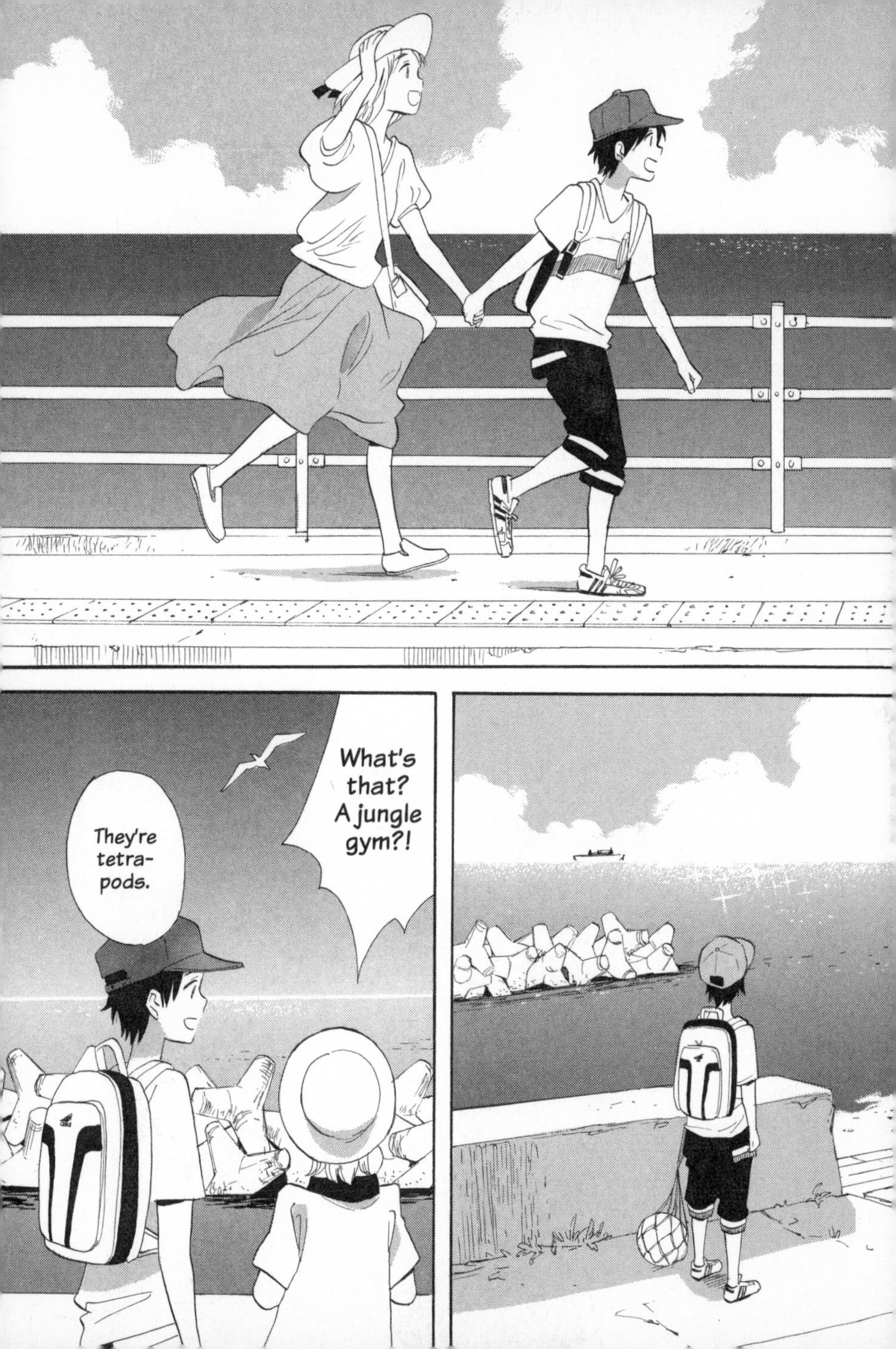
What's that? A jungle gym?!
They're tetra-pods.

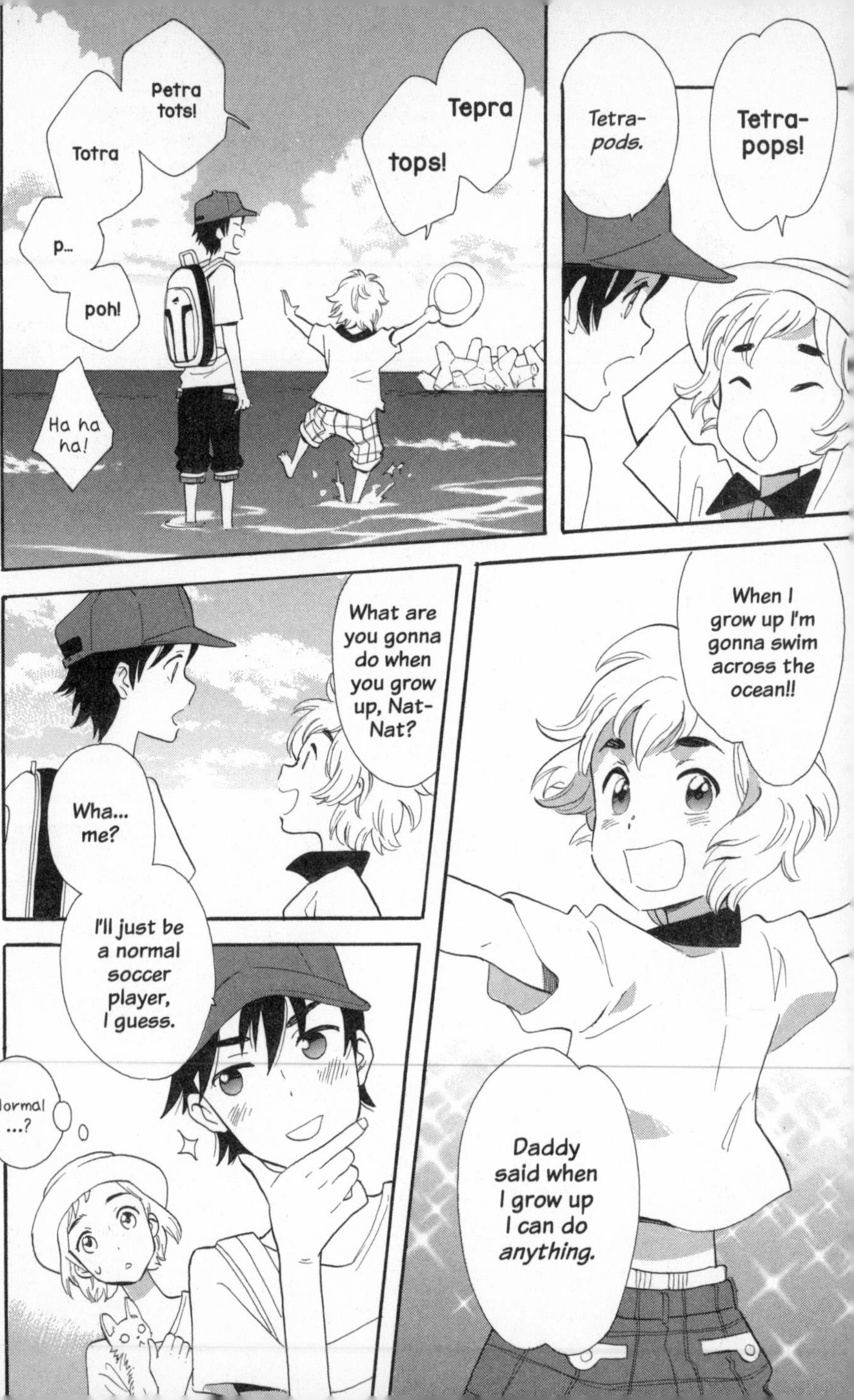
Tetra-pops!
Tetra-pods.
Tepra tops!
Petra tots!
Totra
p...
poh!
Ha ha ha!
When I grow up I'm gonna swim across the ocean!!
Daddy said when I grow up I can do *anything.*
What are you gonna do when you grow up, Nat-Nat?
Wha... me?
I'll just be a normal soccer player, I guess.
Normal ...?

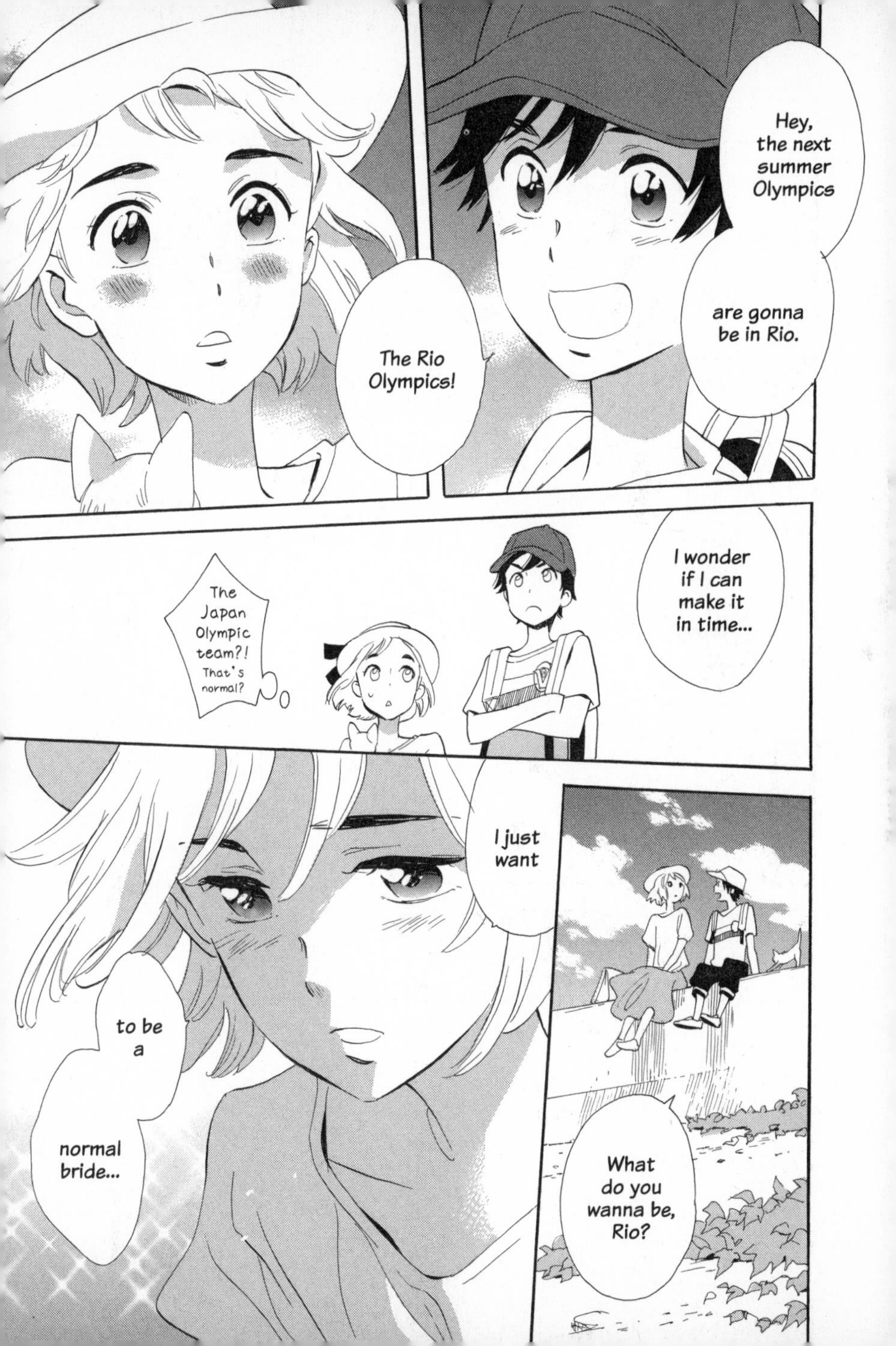

Hey, the next summer Olympics
are gonna be in Rio.
The Rio Olympics!
I wonder if I can make it in time...
The Japan Olympic team?! That's normal?
What do you wanna be, Rio?
I just want
to be a
normal bride...

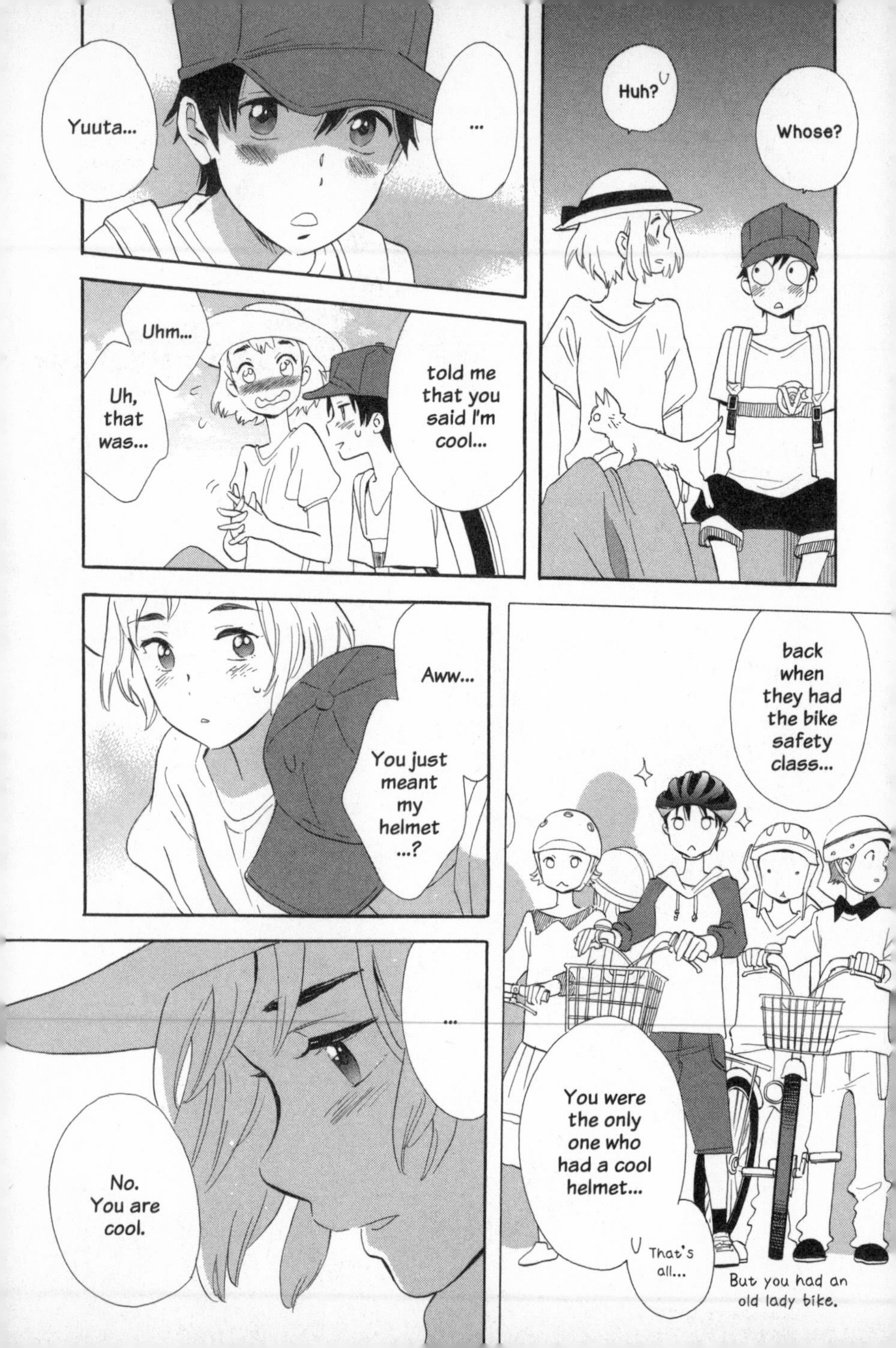
Huh?
Whose?
...
Yuuta...
told me that you said I'm cool...
Uh, that was...
Uhm...
back when they had the bike safety class...
You were the only one who had a cool helmet...
That's all...
But you had an old lady bike.
Aww...
You just meant my helmet ...?
...
No. You are cool.

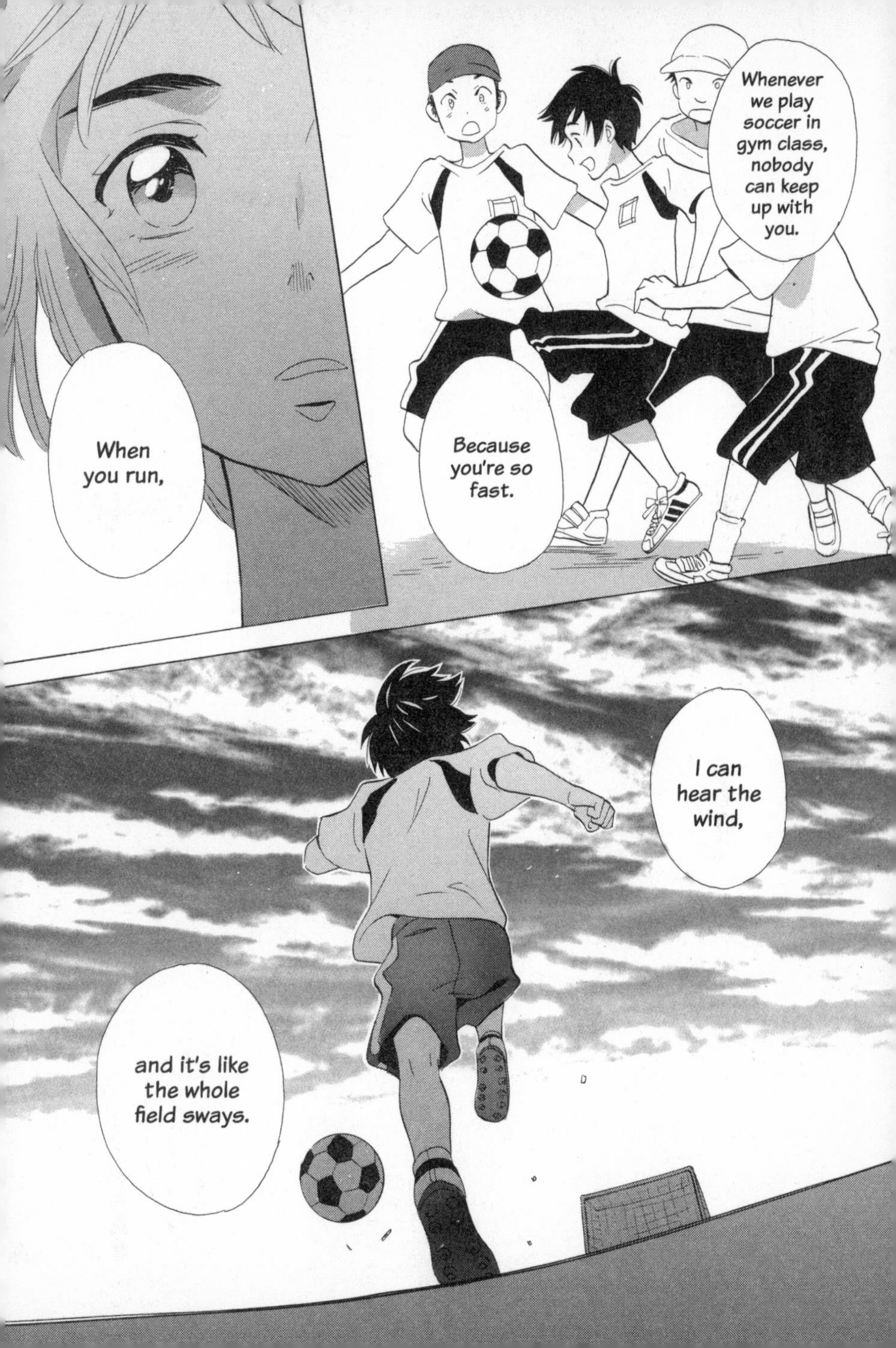
Whenever we play soccer in gym class, nobody can keep up with you.
Because you're so fast.
When you run,
I can hear the wind,
and it's like the whole field sways.

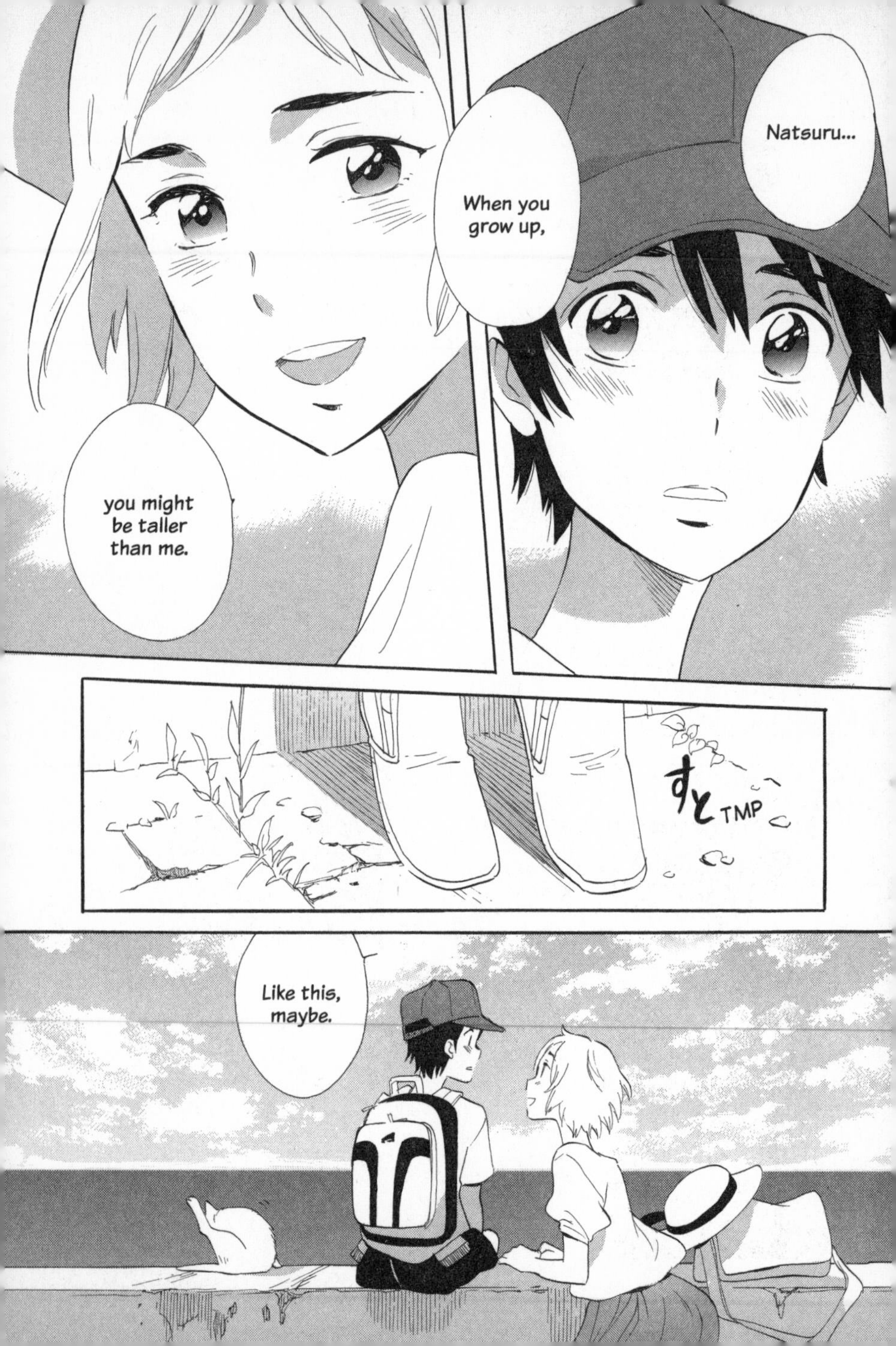
Natsuru...
When you grow up,
you might be taller than me.
すと TMP
Like this, maybe.

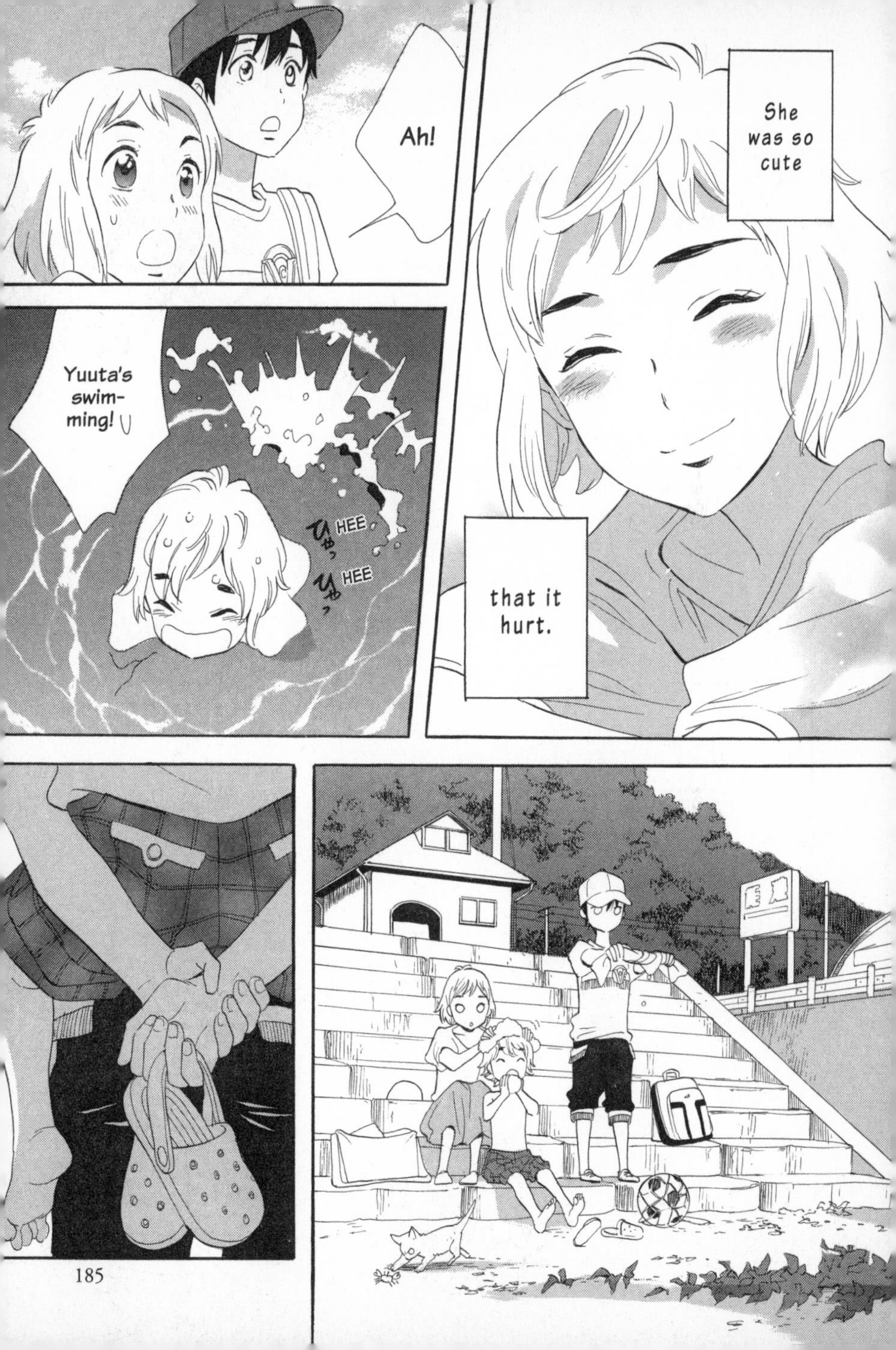
She was so cute
that it hurt.
Ah!
Yuuta's swimming!
HEE
HEE

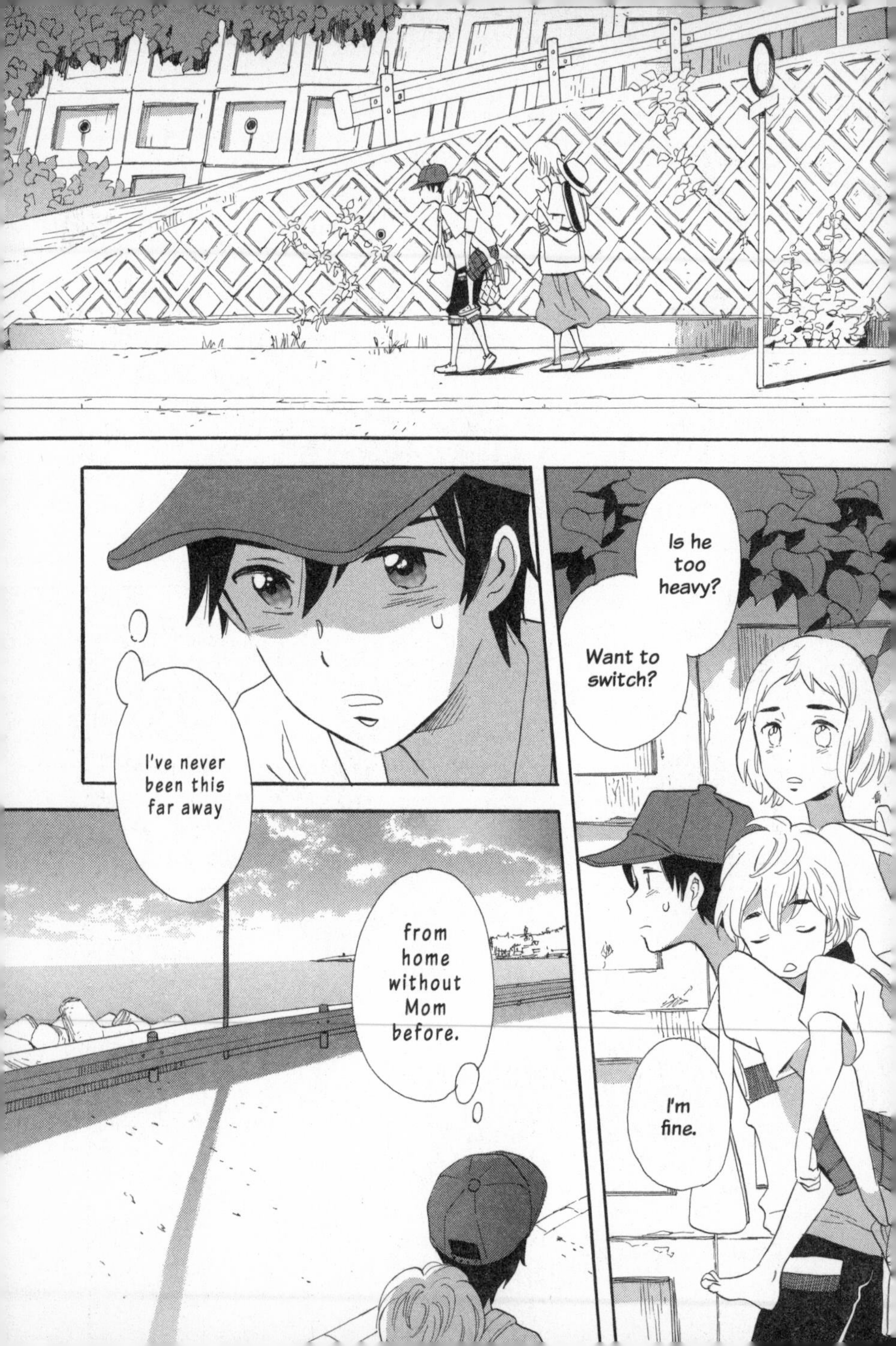
Is he too heavy?
Want to switch?
I'm fine.
I've never been this far away
from home without Mom before.

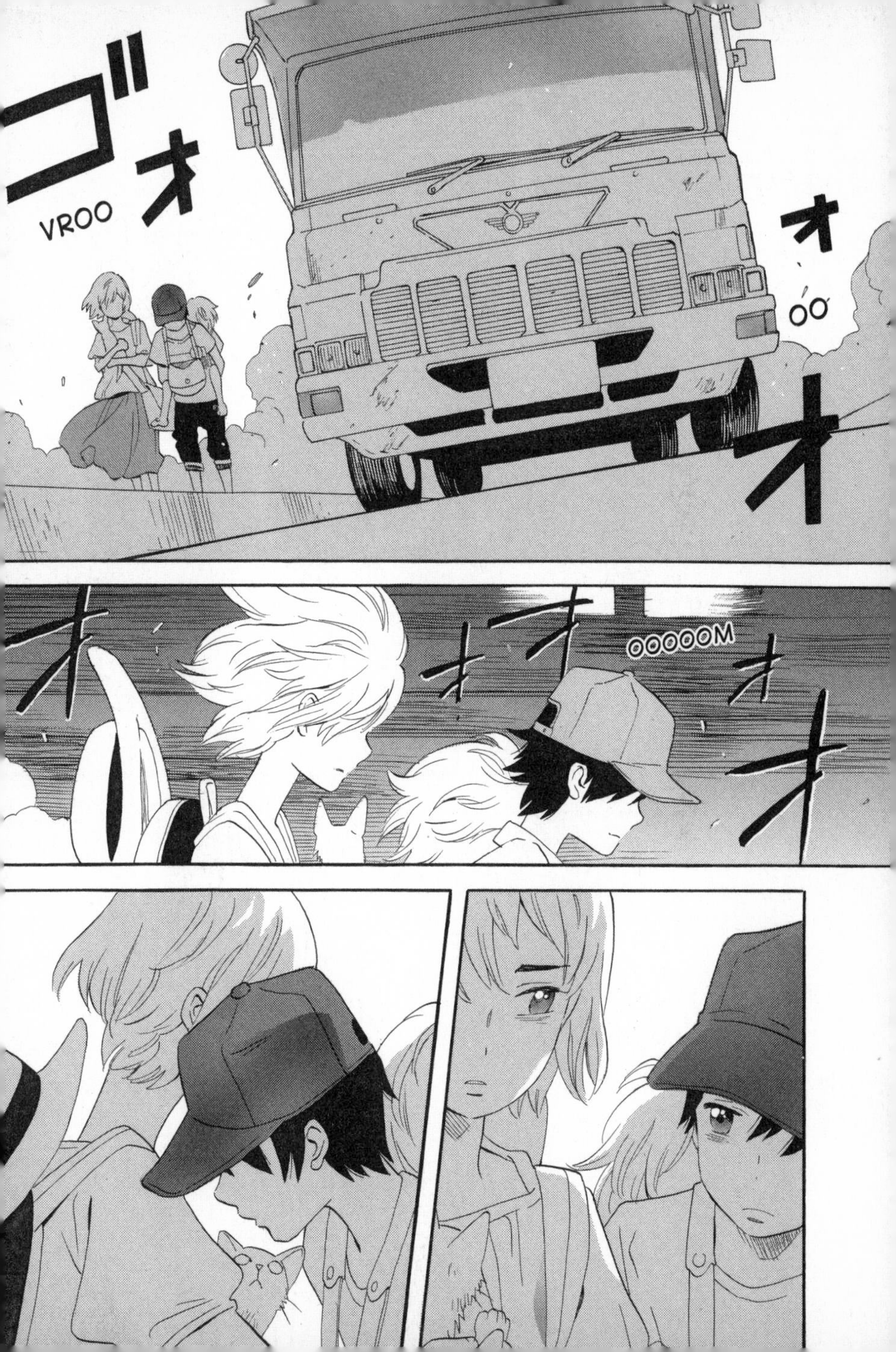
ゴォ
VROO
ォ
OO
オ
オオ
OOOOOM
オオ

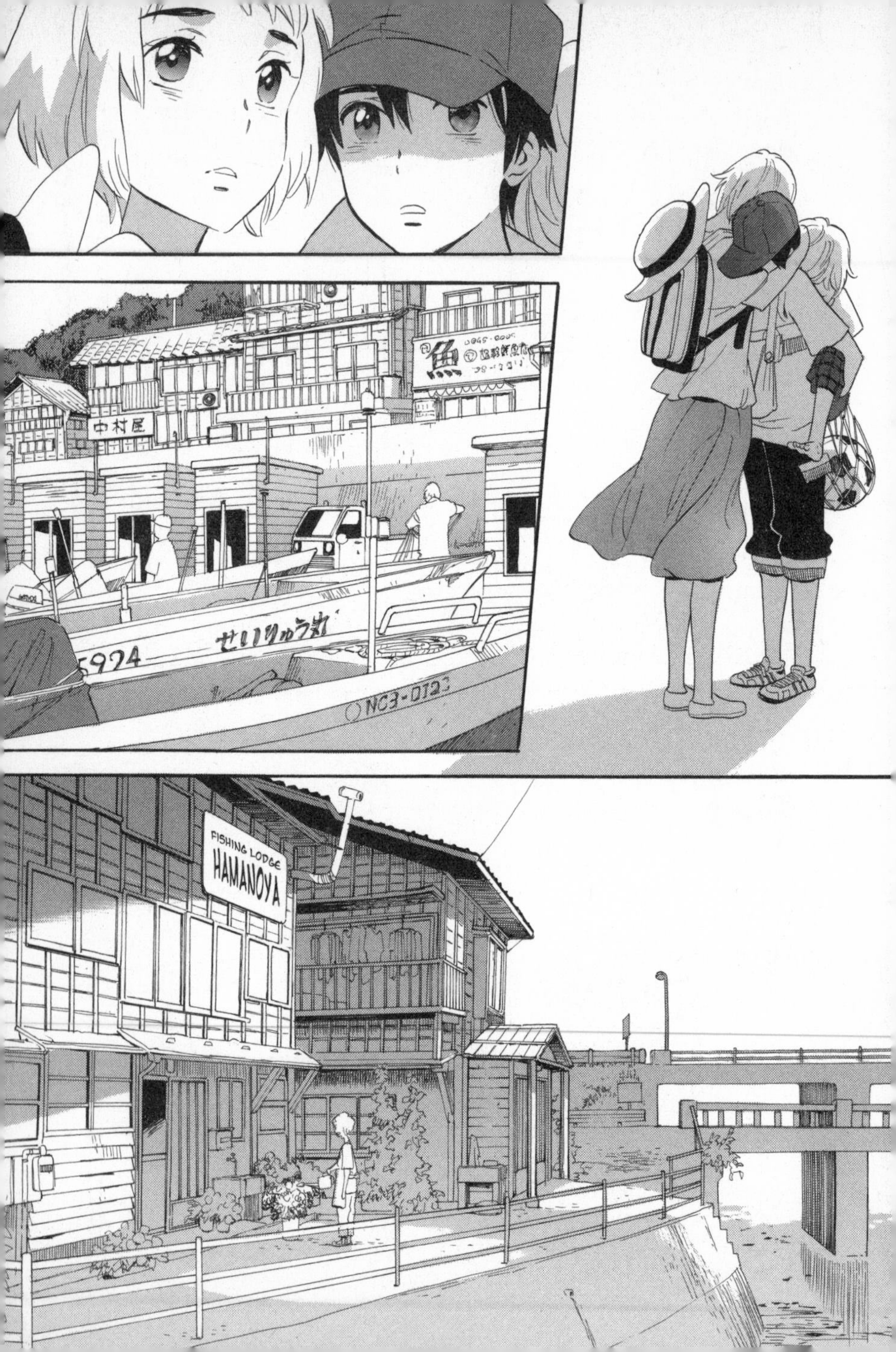
中村屋
せいりゅう丸
5924
FISHING LODGE
HAMANOYA

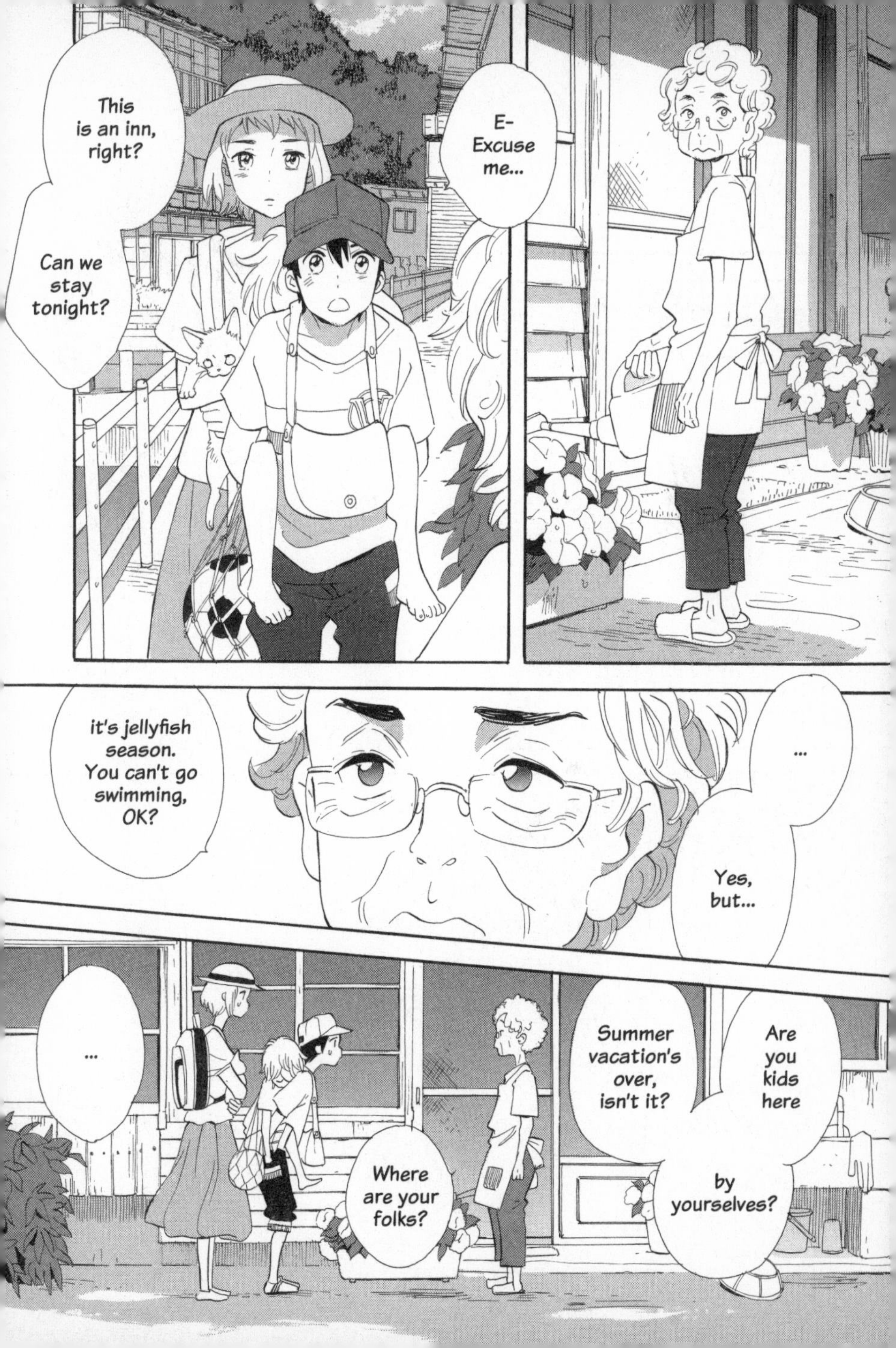
E- Excuse me...
This is an inn, right?
Can we stay tonight?
...
Yes, but...
it's jellyfish season. You can't go swimming, OK?
Are you kids here
by yourselves?
Summer vacation's over, isn't it?
Where are your folks?
...

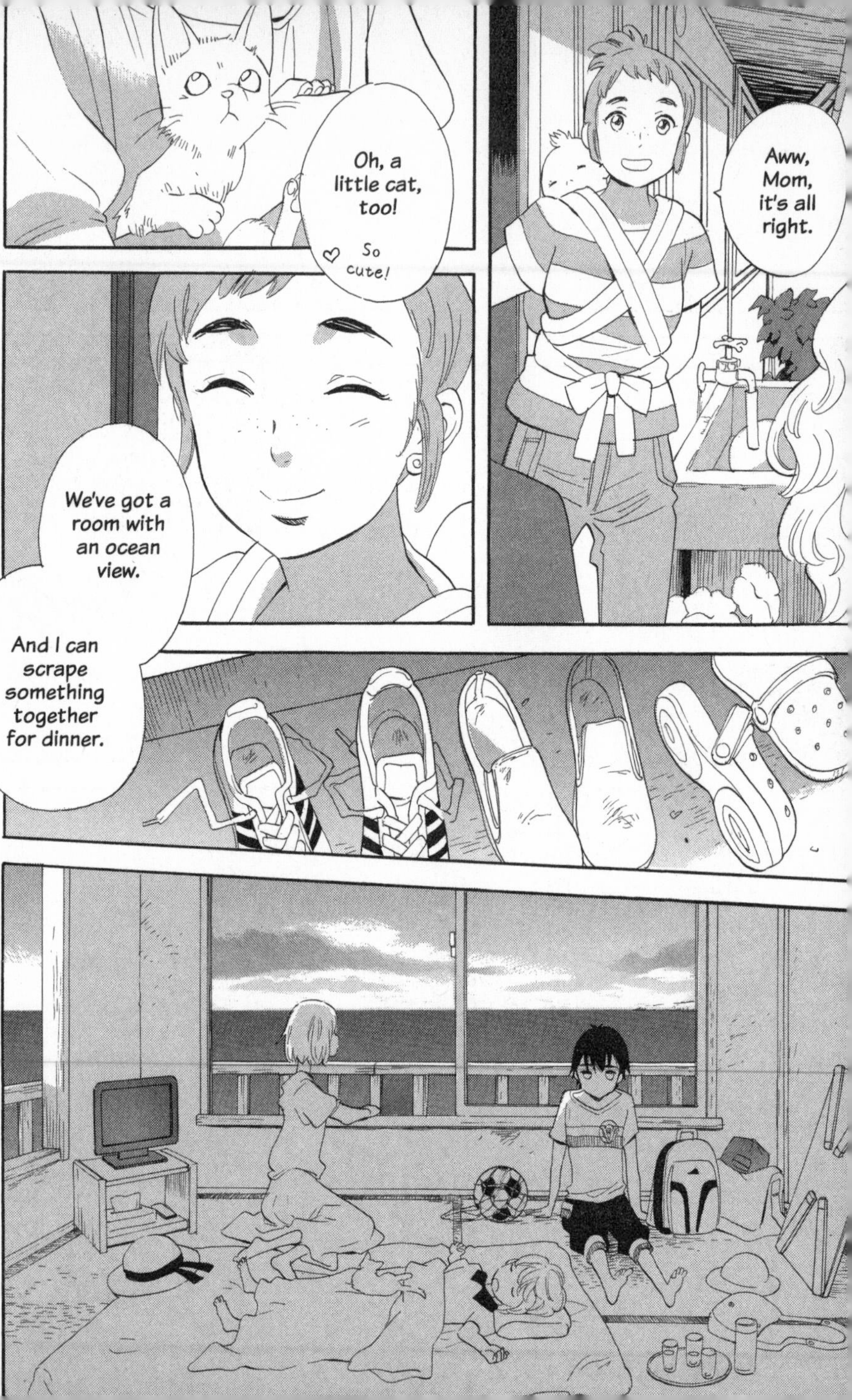
Aww, Mom, it's all right.
Oh, a little cat, too!
So cute!
We've got a room with an ocean view.
And I can scrape something together for dinner.

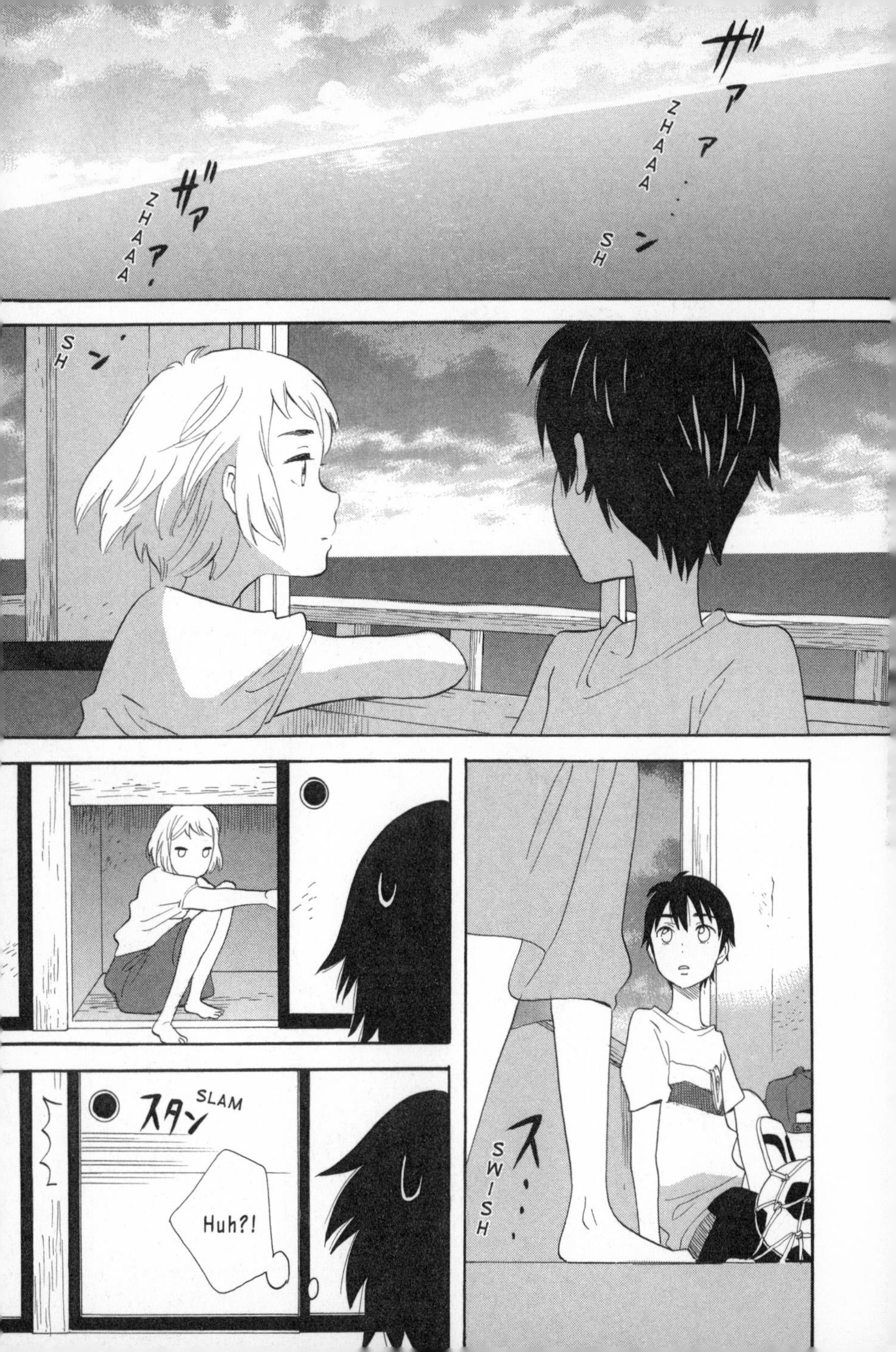
ザァァ・・・ン
ZHAAAA SH
ザァァ
ZHAAA
ン
SH
ス
SWISH
スタン
SLAM
Huh?!

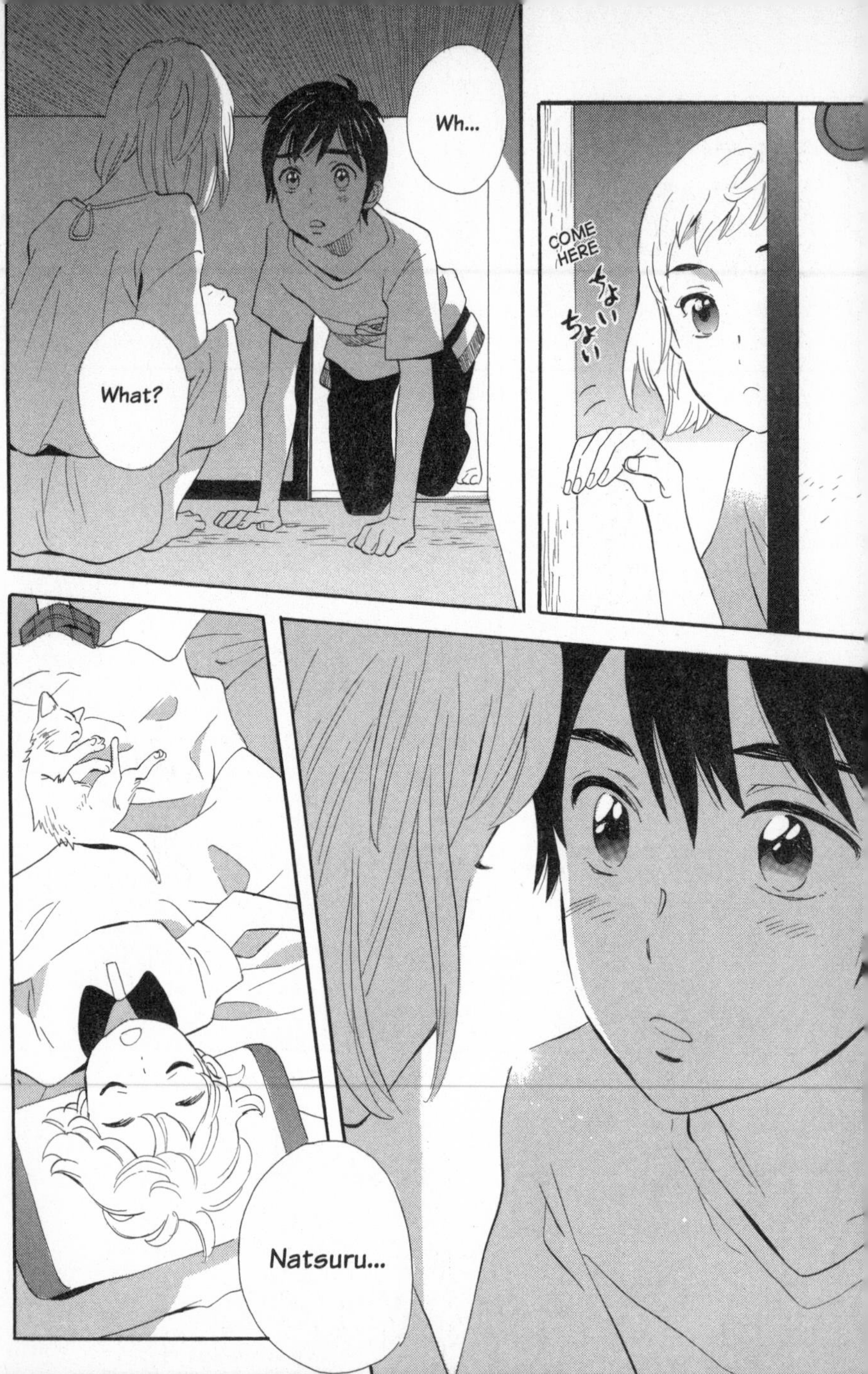
COME HERE
ちょい ちょい
Wh...
What?
Natsuru...

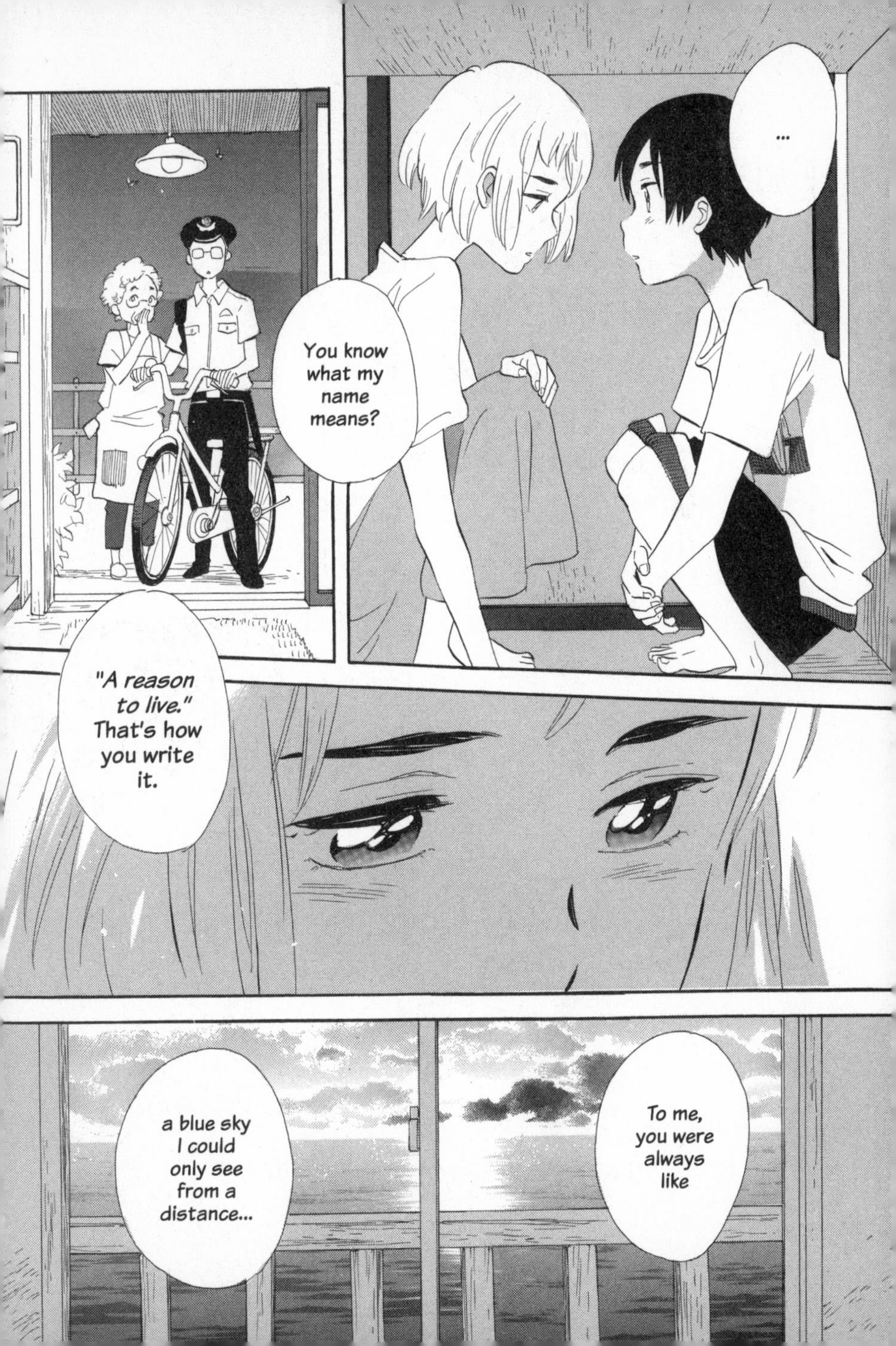
...
You know what my name means?
"A reason to live." That's how you write it.
To me, you were always like
a blue sky I could only see from a distance...

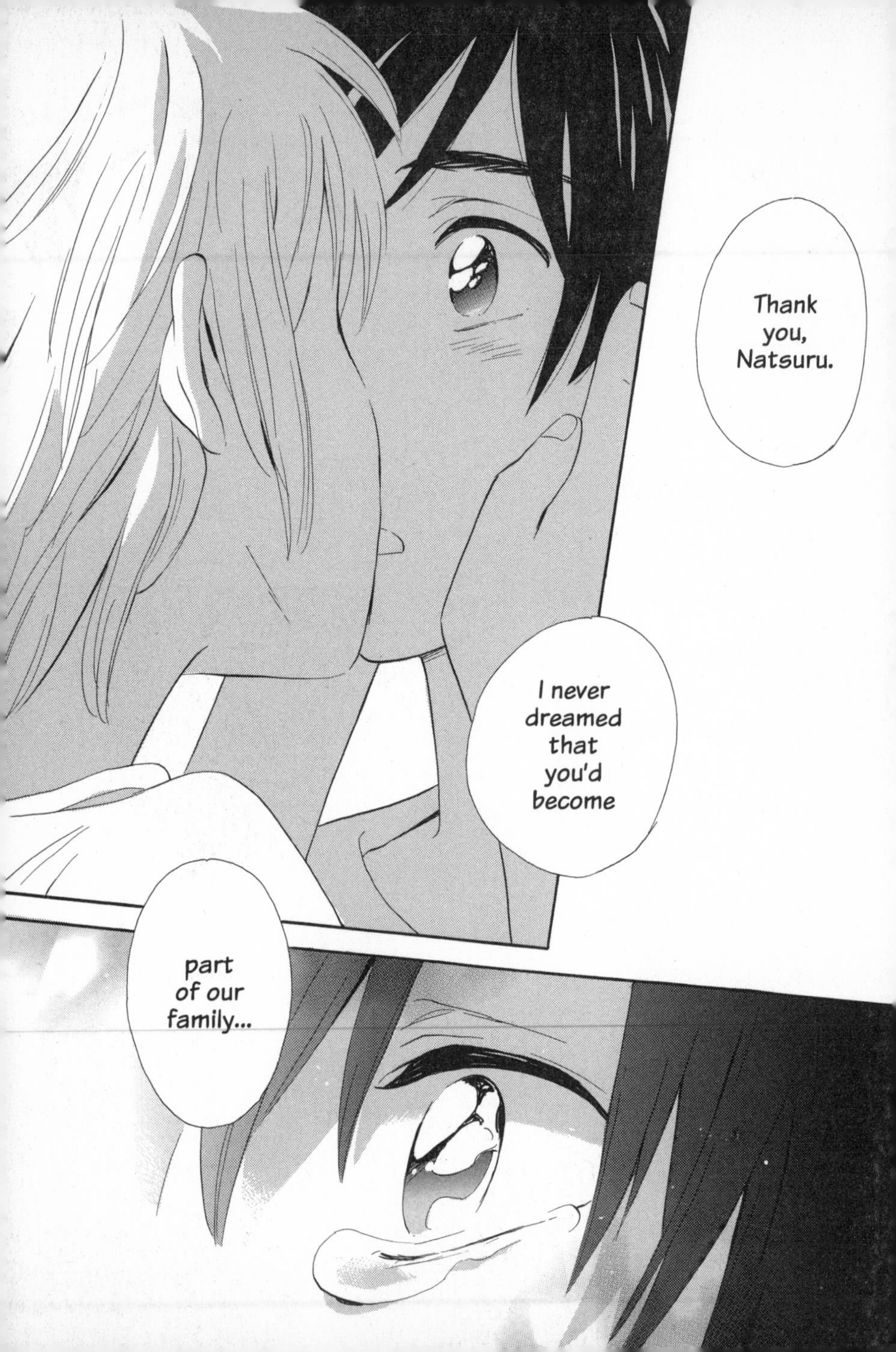
Thank you, Natsuru.
I never dreamed that you'd become
part of our family...

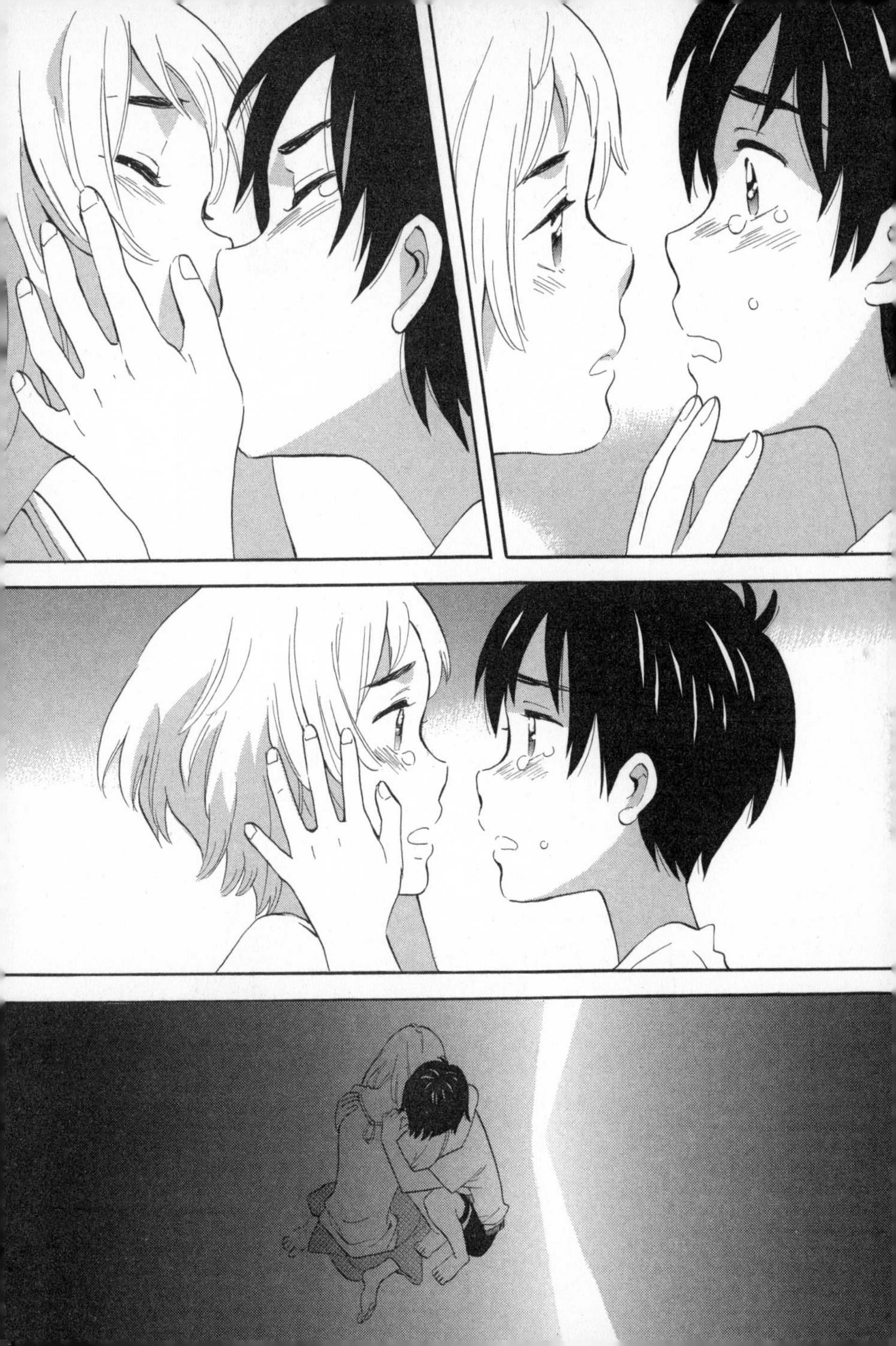

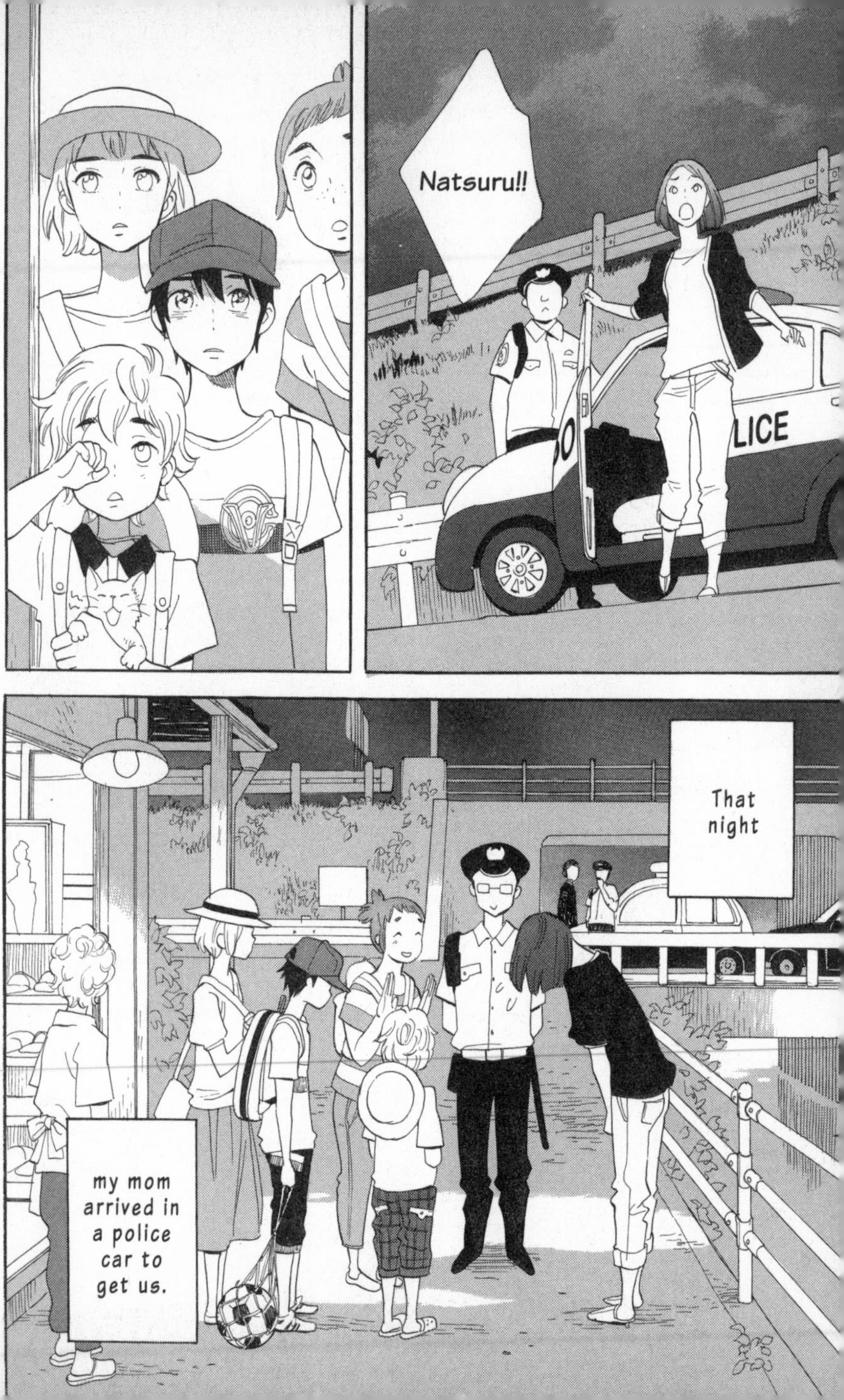
Natsuru!!
LICE
That night
my mom arrived in a police car to get us.

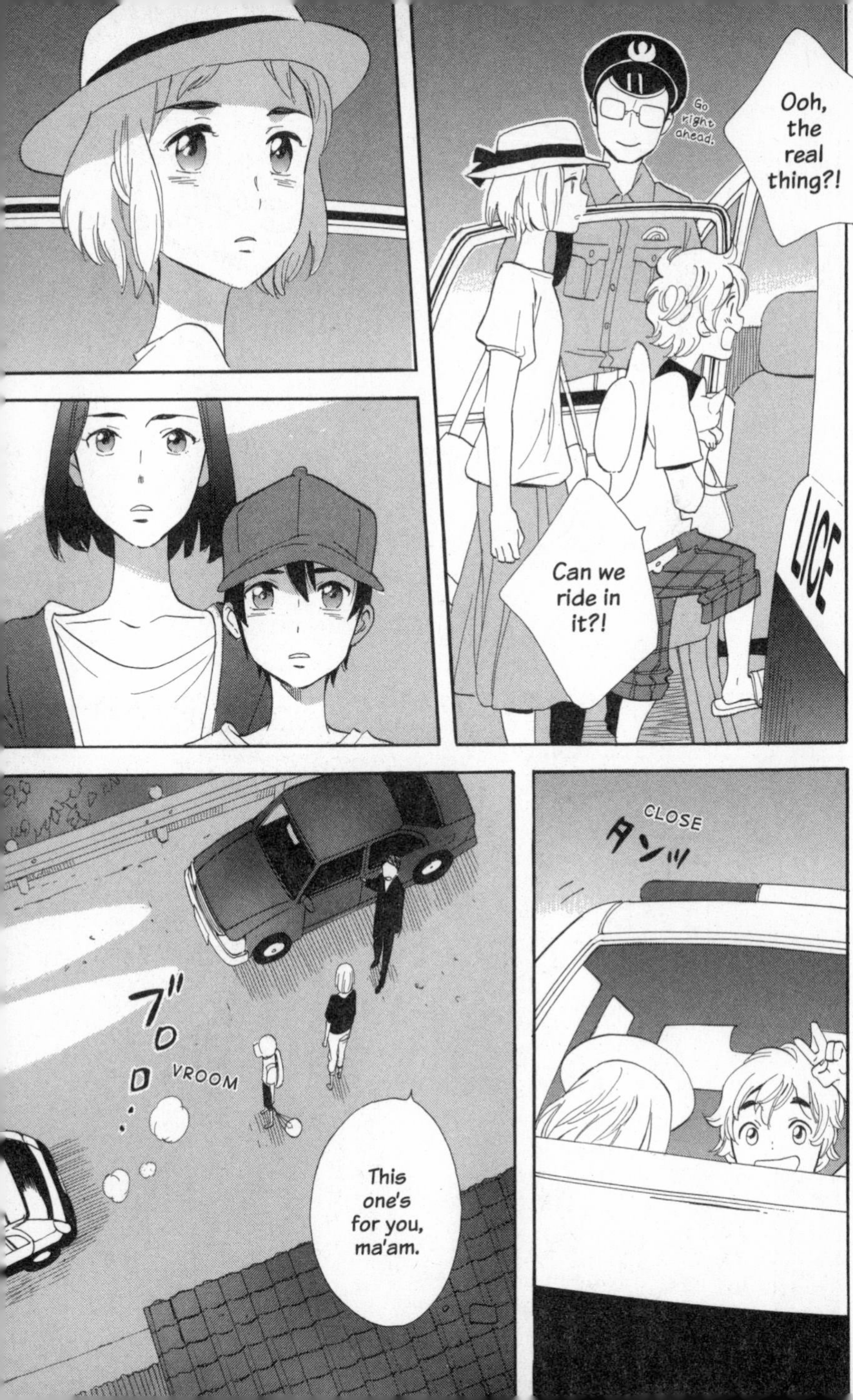
Ooh, the real thing?!
Go right ahead.
LICE
Can we ride in it?!
タンッ
CLOSE
ブロロ
VROOM
This one's for you, ma'am.

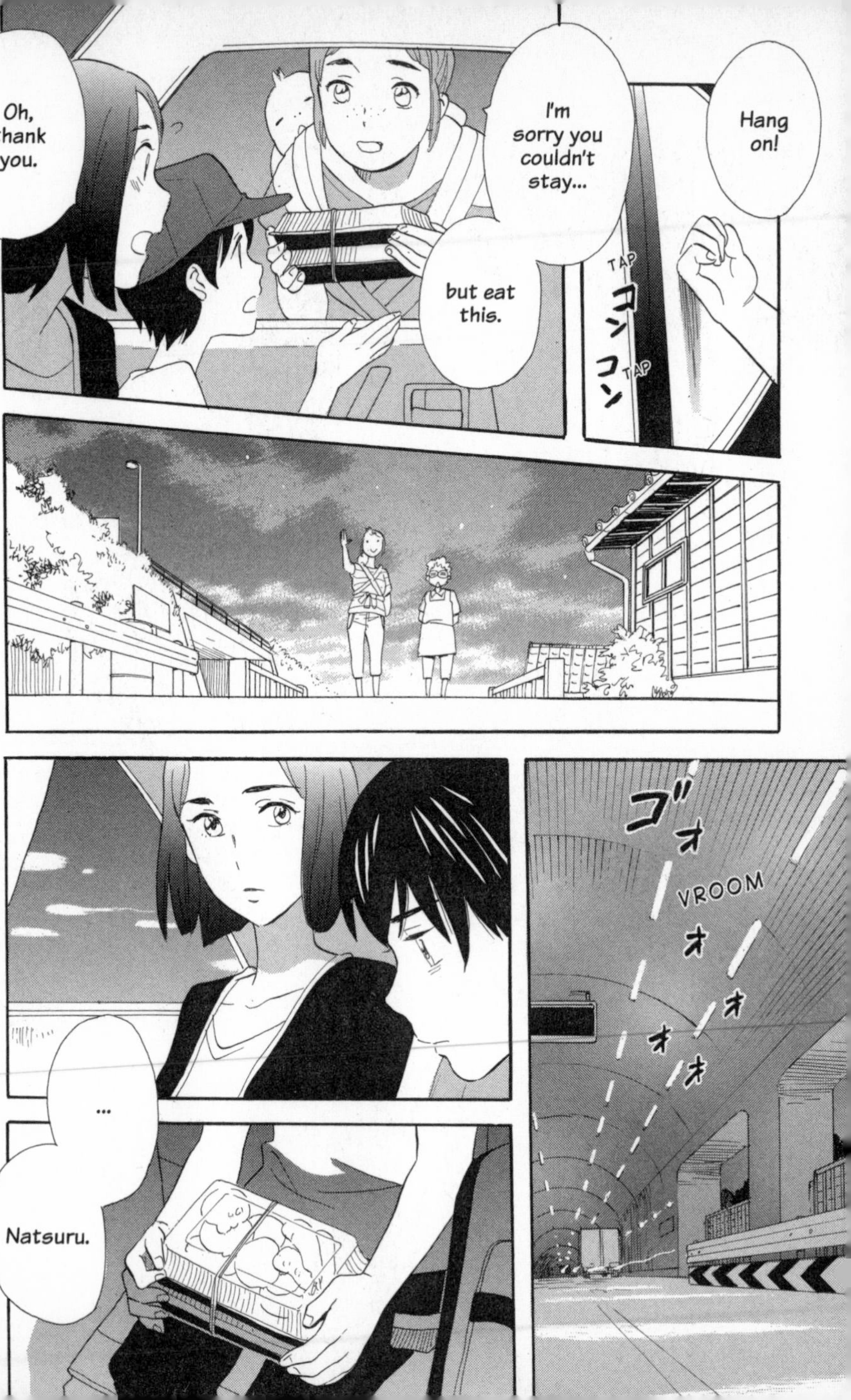
Hang on!
コンコン
TAP TAP
I'm sorry you couldn't stay...
but eat this.
Oh, thank you.
ゴォォォォ
VROOM
...
Natsuru.

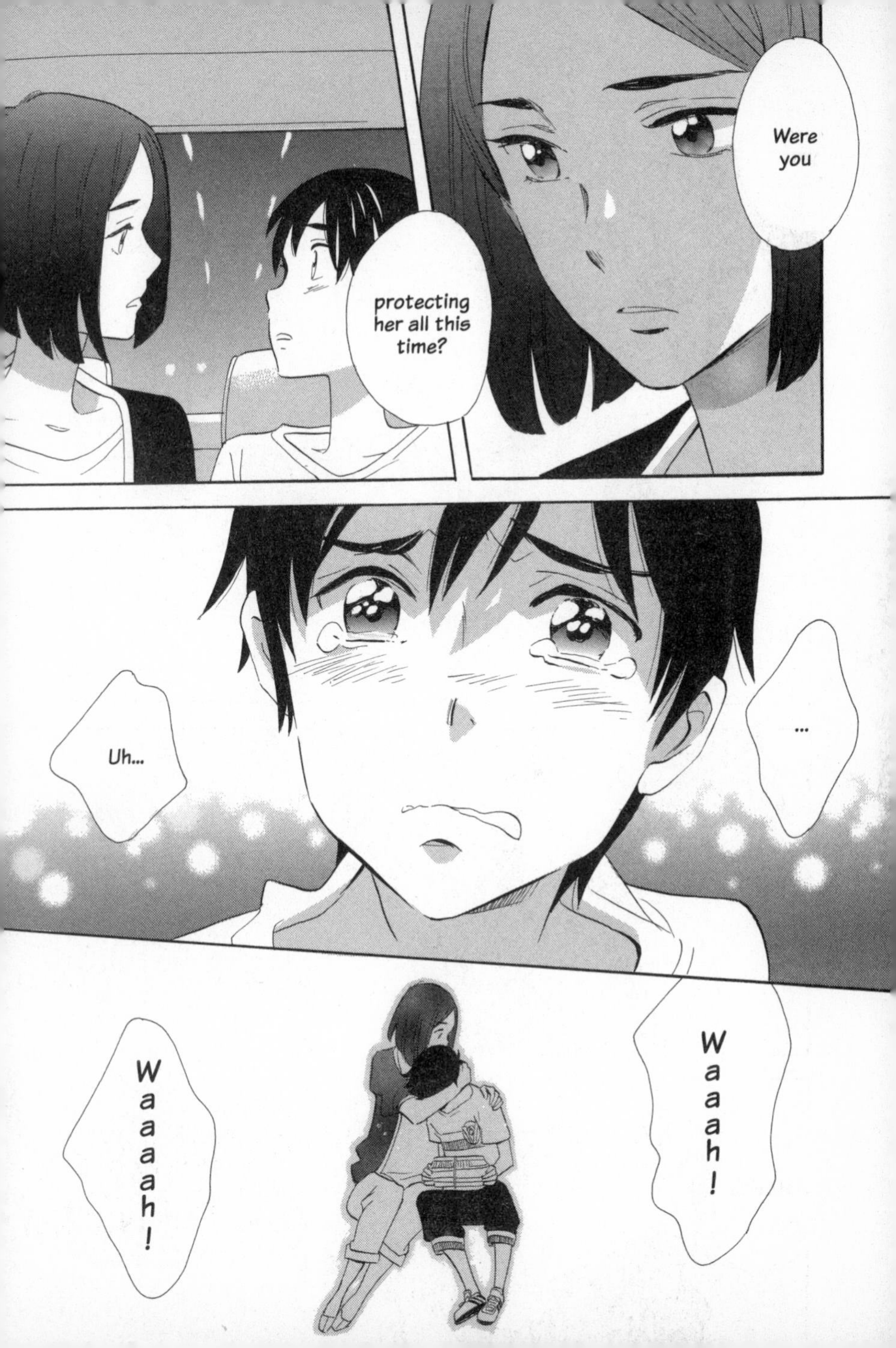
Were you
protecting her all this time?
...
Uh...
Waaah!
Waaaah!

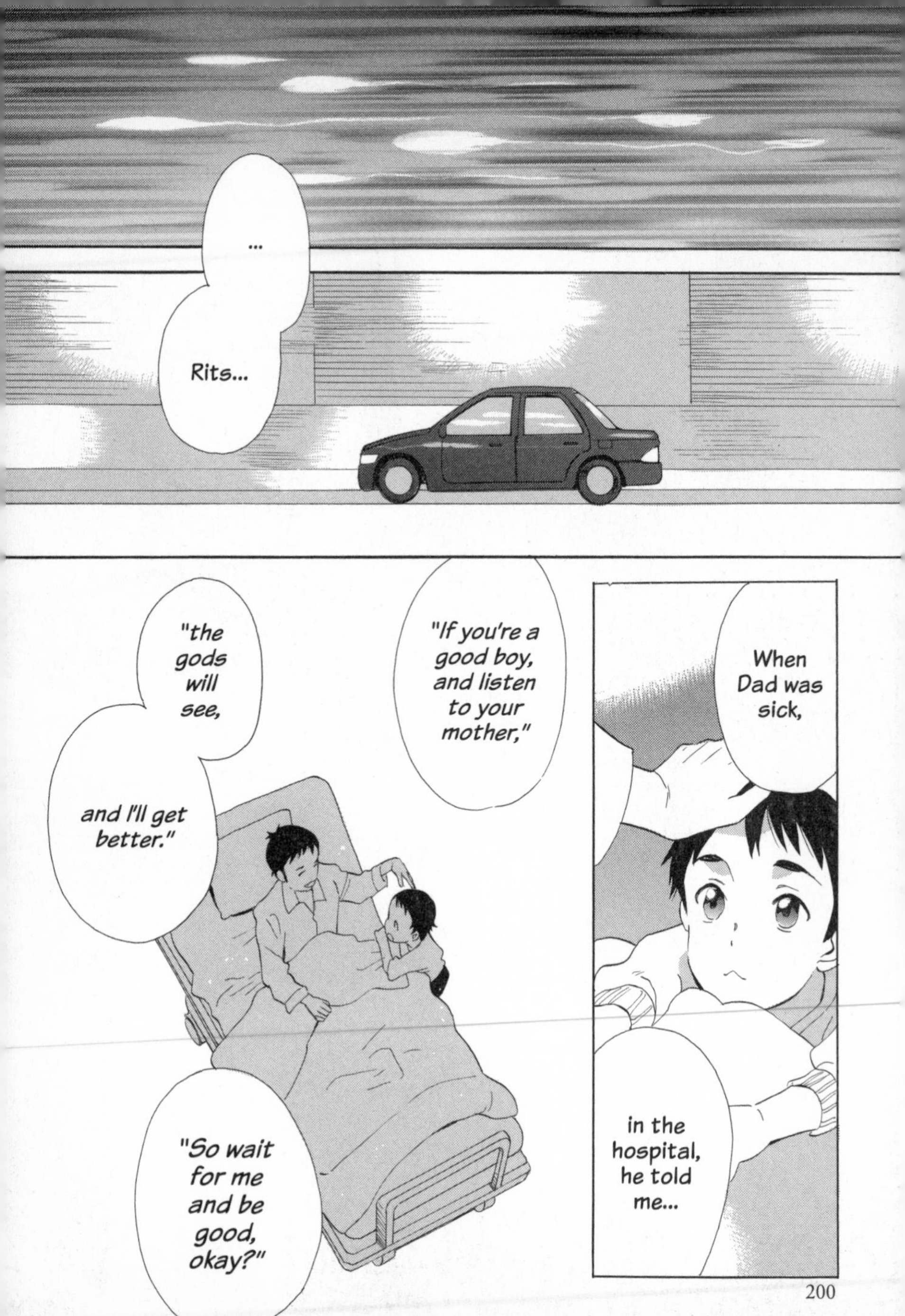
...
Rits...
When Dad was sick,
in the hospital, he told me...
"If you're a good boy, and listen to your mother,"
"the gods will see,
and I'll get better."
"So wait for me and be good, okay?"

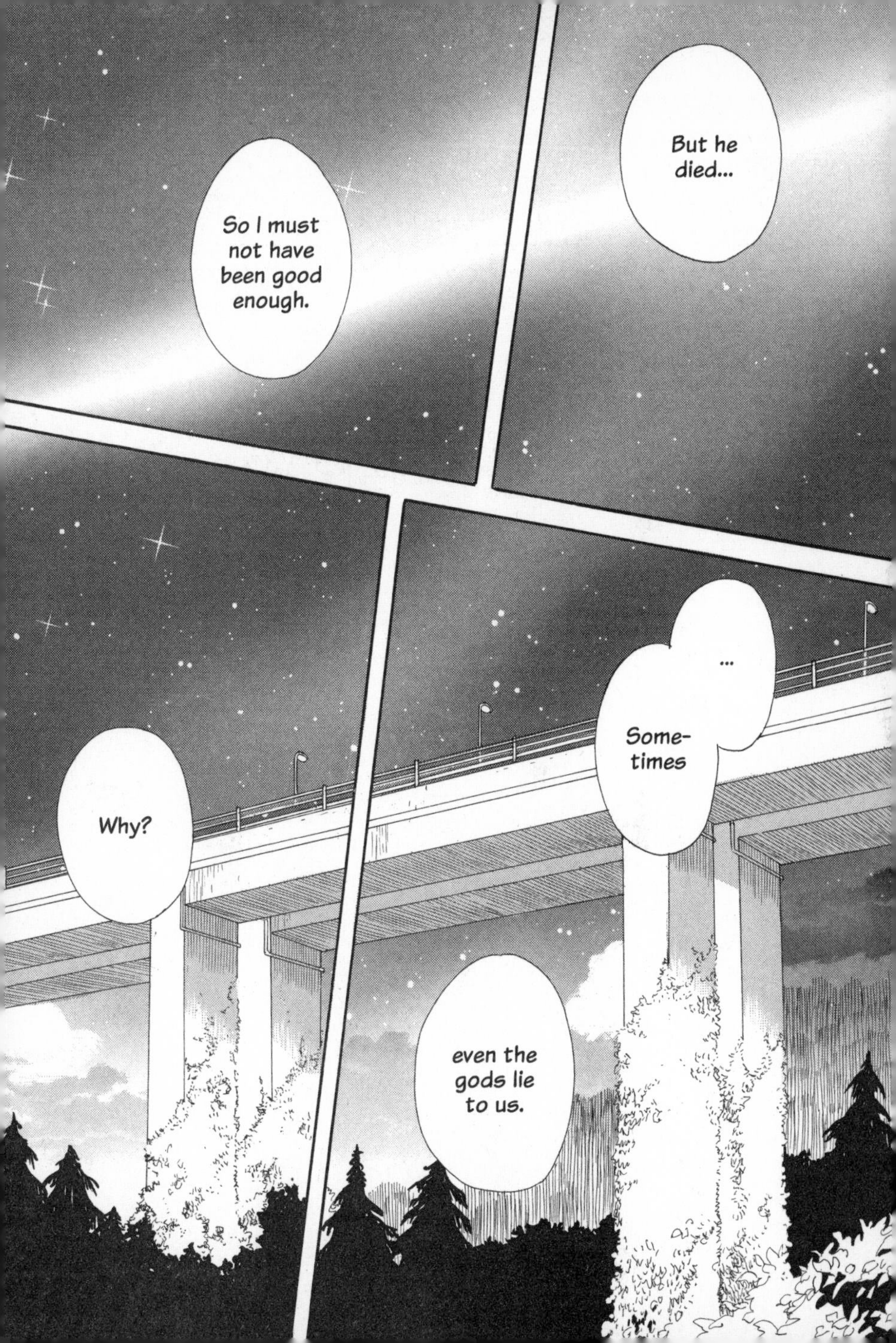
But he died...
So I must not have been good enough.
...
Some-times
even the gods lie to us.
Why?

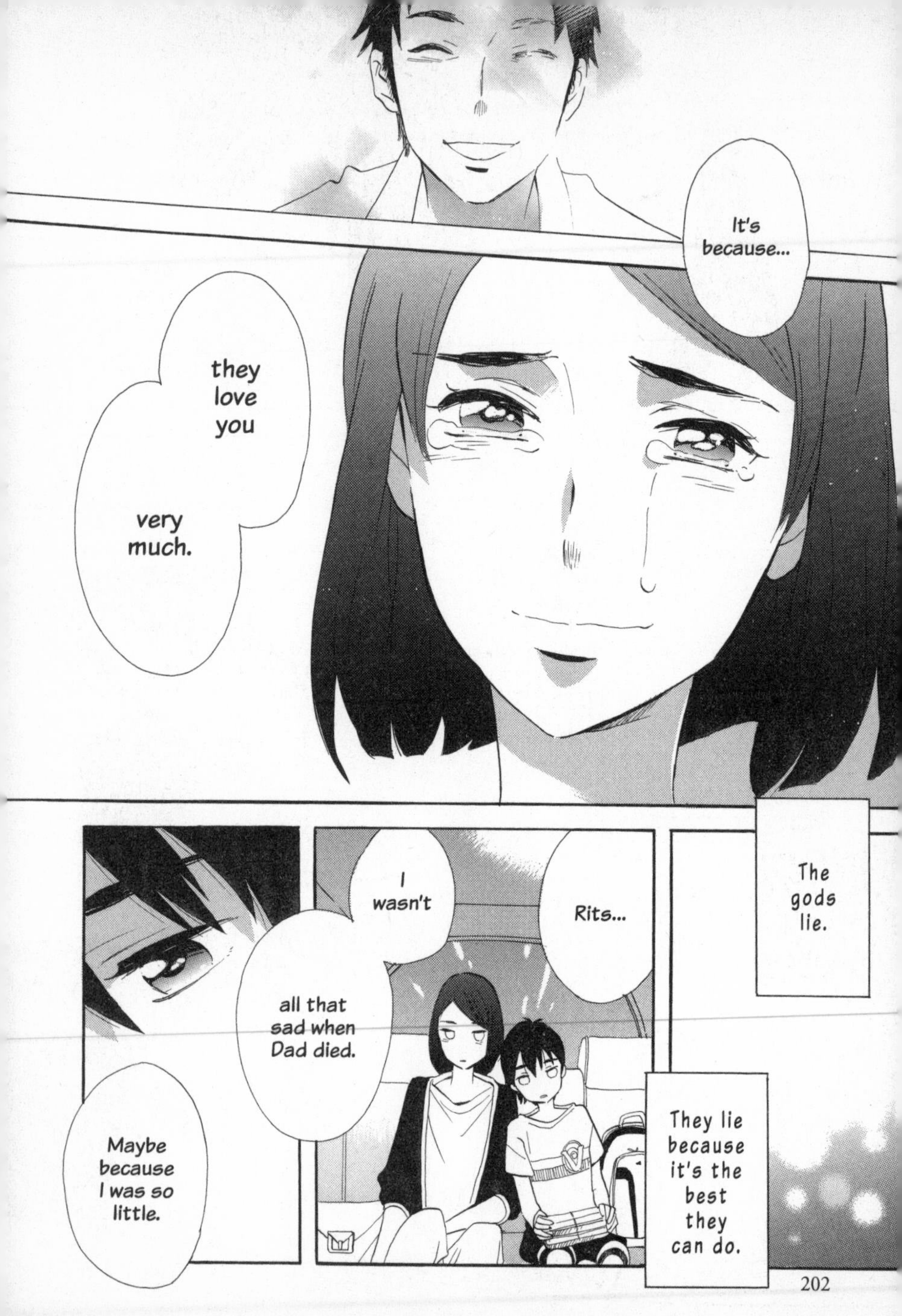
It's because...
they love you very much.
The gods lie.
Rits...
I wasn't all that sad when Dad died.
Maybe because I was so little.
They lie because it's the best they can do.

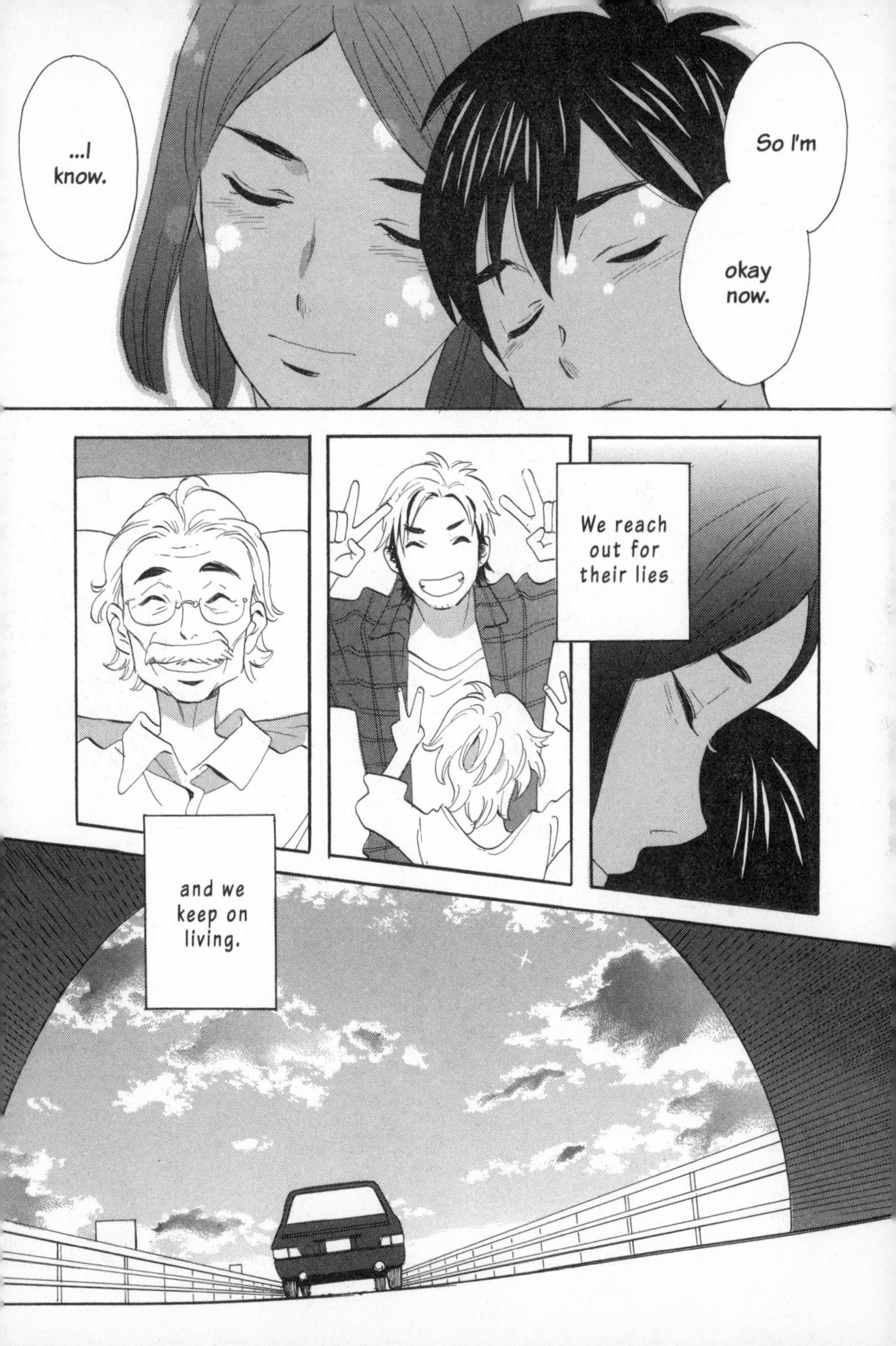
So I'm okay now.
...I know.
We reach out for their lies
and we keep on living.

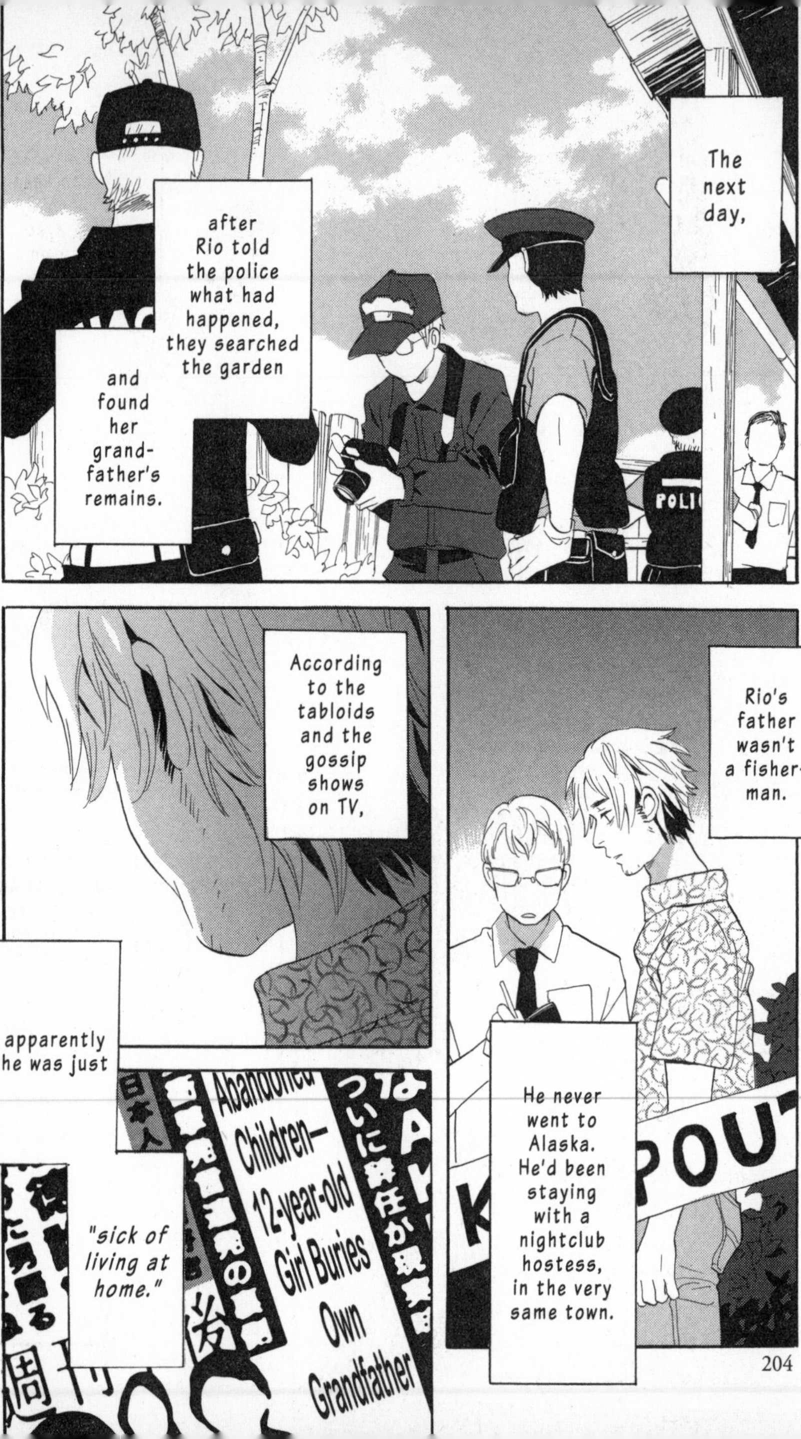
The next day,
after Rio told the police what had happened, they searched the garden
and found her grandfather's remains.
POLIC
Rio's father wasn't a fisherman.
He never went to Alaska. He'd been staying with a nightclub hostess, in the very same town.
According to the tabloids and the gossip shows on TV,
apparently he was just
"sick of living at home."
Abandoned Children— 12-year-old Girl Buries Own Grandfather

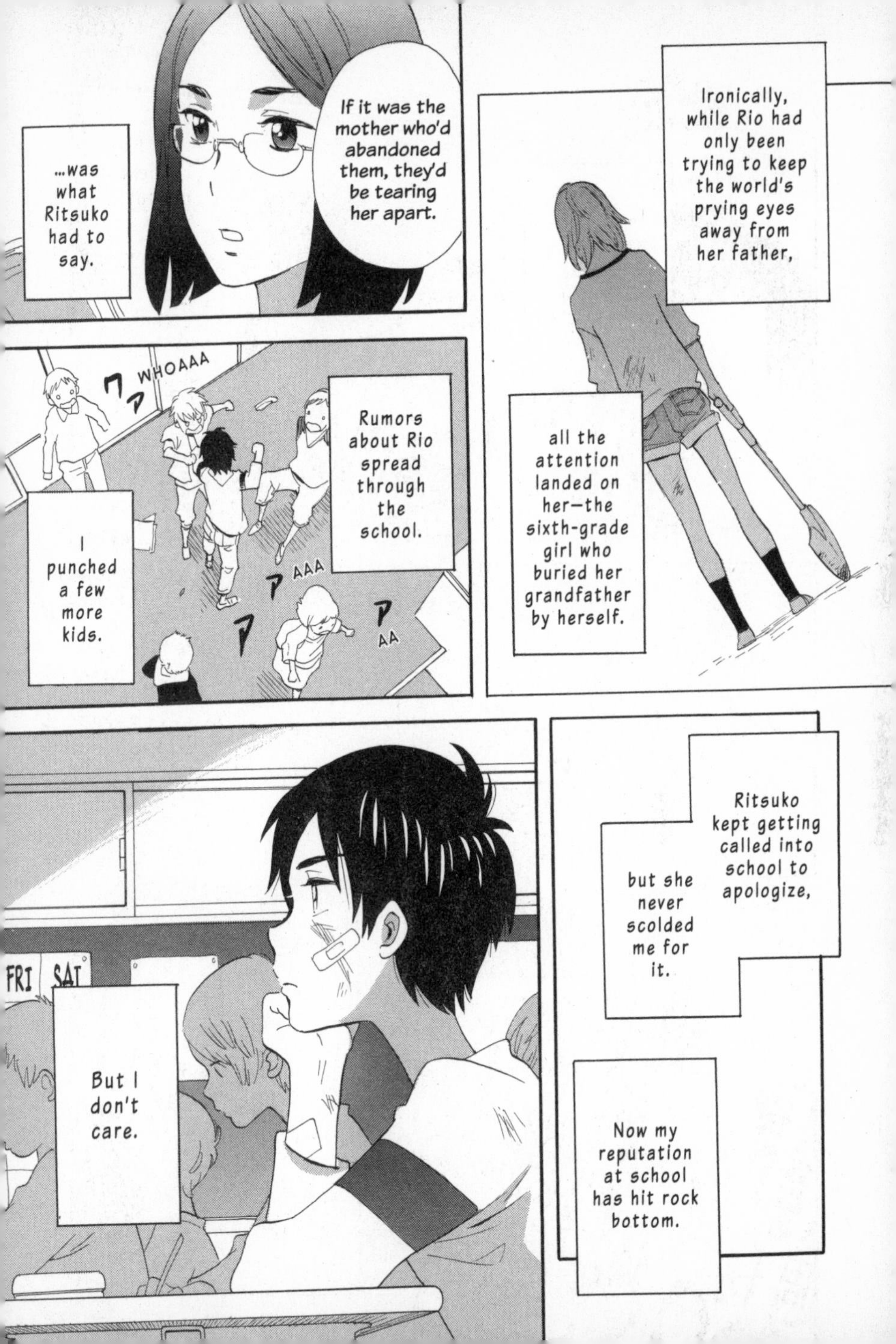
If it was the mother who'd abandoned them, they'd be tearing her apart.
...was what Ritsuko had to say.
Ironically, while Rio had only been trying to keep the world's prying eyes away from her father,
all the attention landed on her—the sixth-grade girl who buried her grandfather by herself.
Rumors about Rio spread through the school.
WHOAAA
AAA
AA
I punched a few more kids.
Ritsuko kept getting called into school to apologize,
but she never scolded me for it.
Now my reputation at school has hit rock bottom.
FRI
SAT
But I don't care.

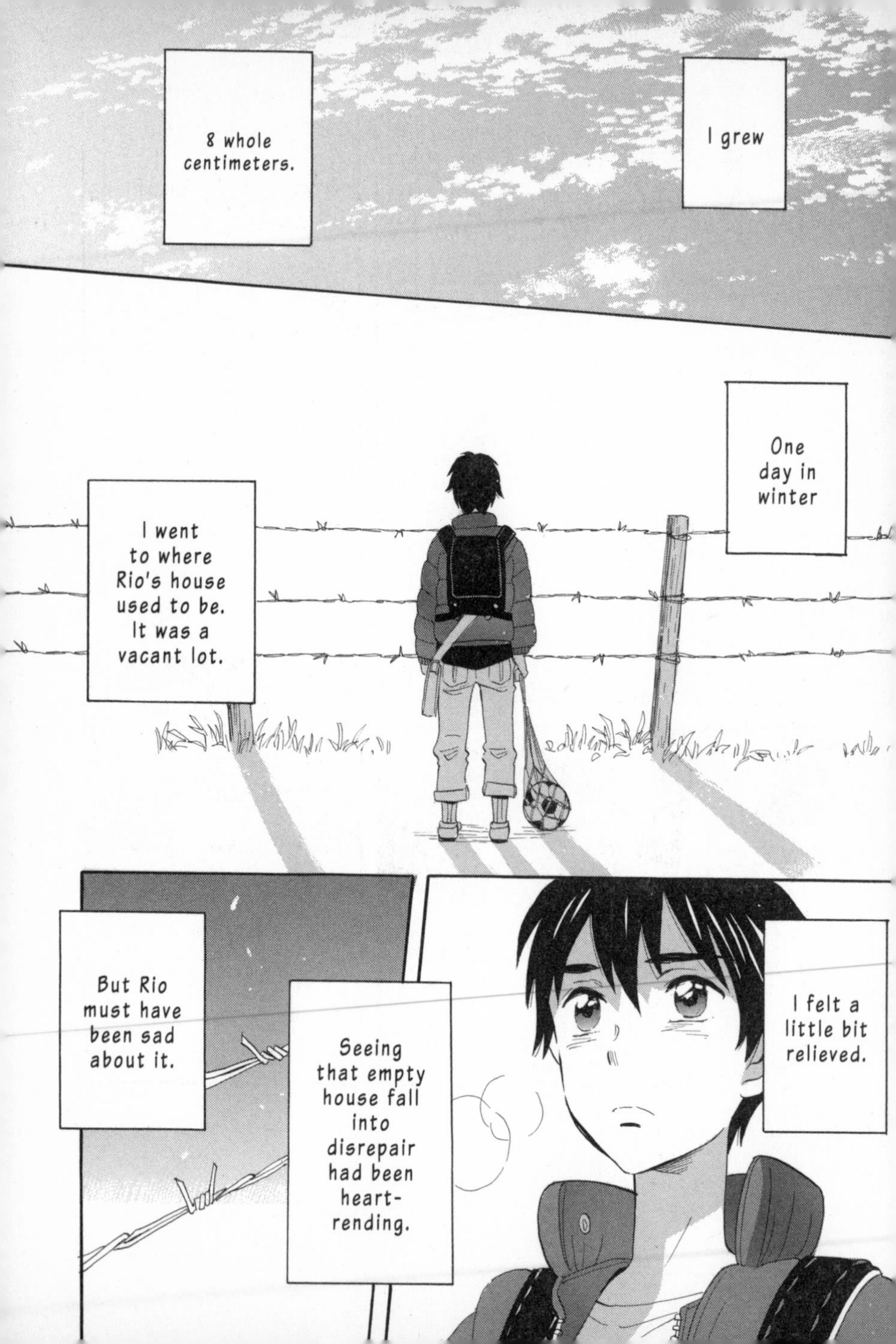

I grew
8 whole centimeters.
One day in winter
I went to where Rio's house used to be. It was a vacant lot.
I felt a little bit relieved.
Seeing that empty house fall into disrepair had been heart-rending.
But Rio must have been sad about it.

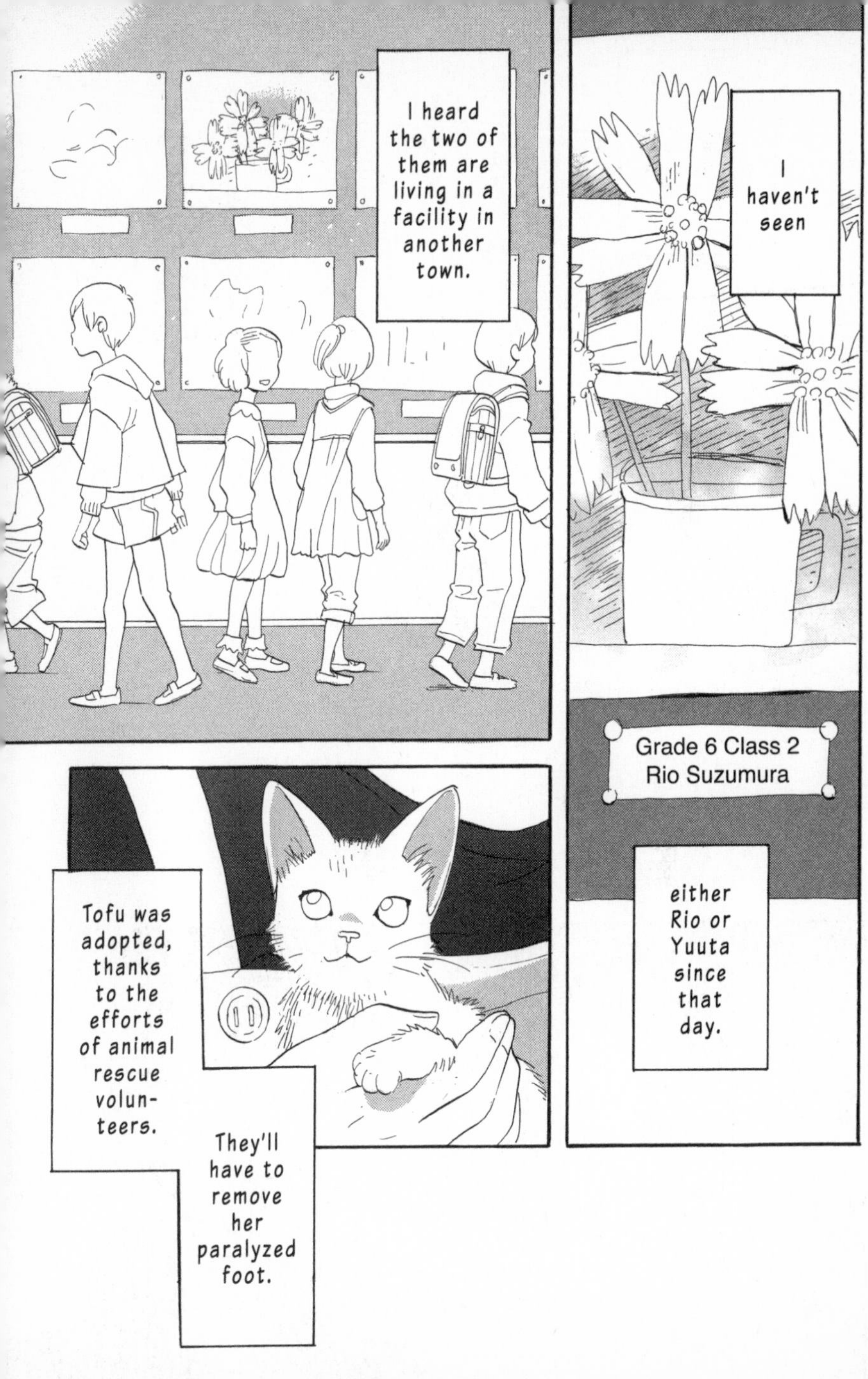
I haven't seen
Grade 6 Class 2
Rio Suzumura
either Rio or Yuuta since that day.
I heard the two of them are living in a facility in another town.
Tofu was adopted, thanks to the efforts of animal rescue volun-teers.
They'll have to remove her paralyzed foot.

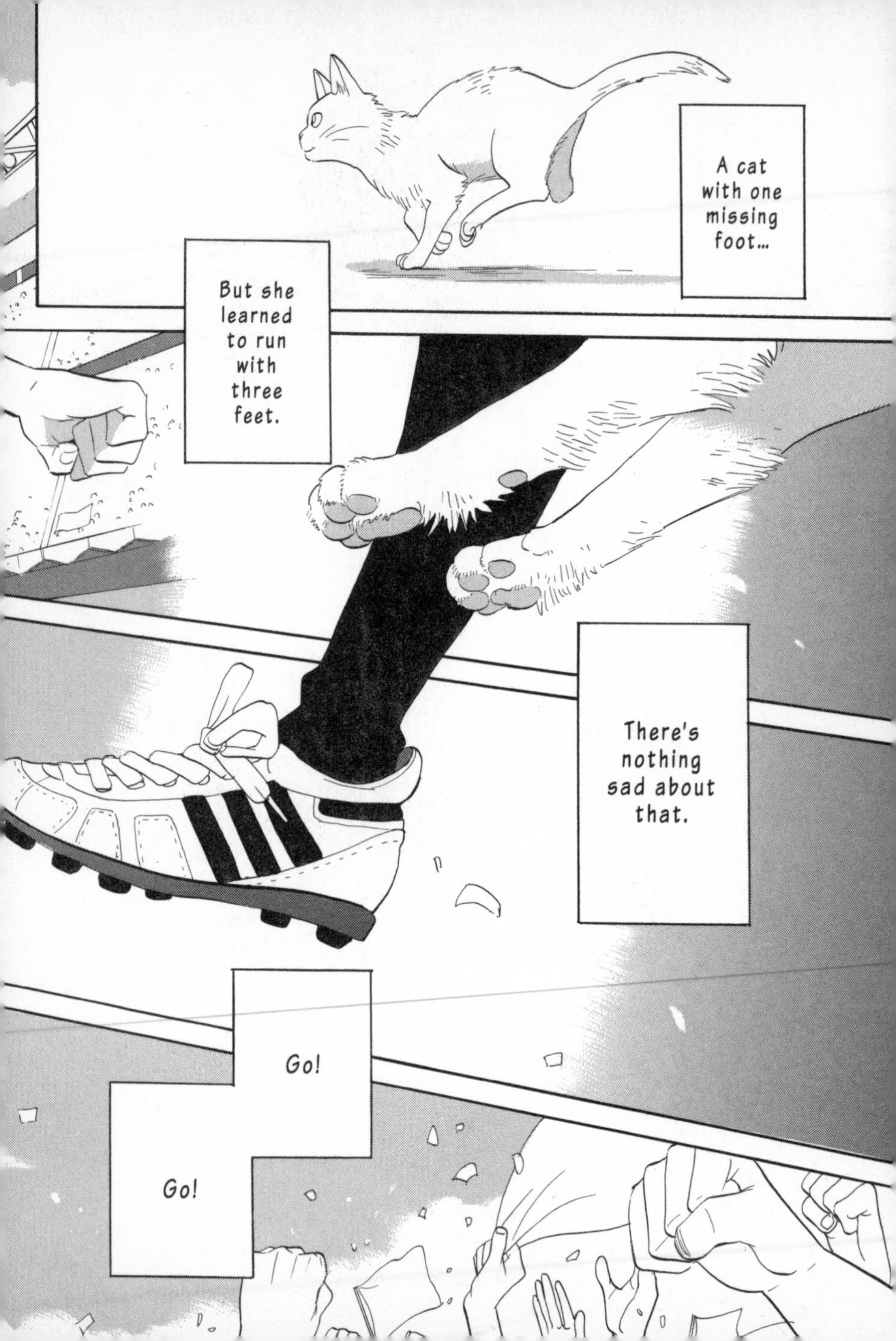
A cat with one missing foot...
But she learned to run with three feet.
There's nothing sad about that.
Go!
Go!

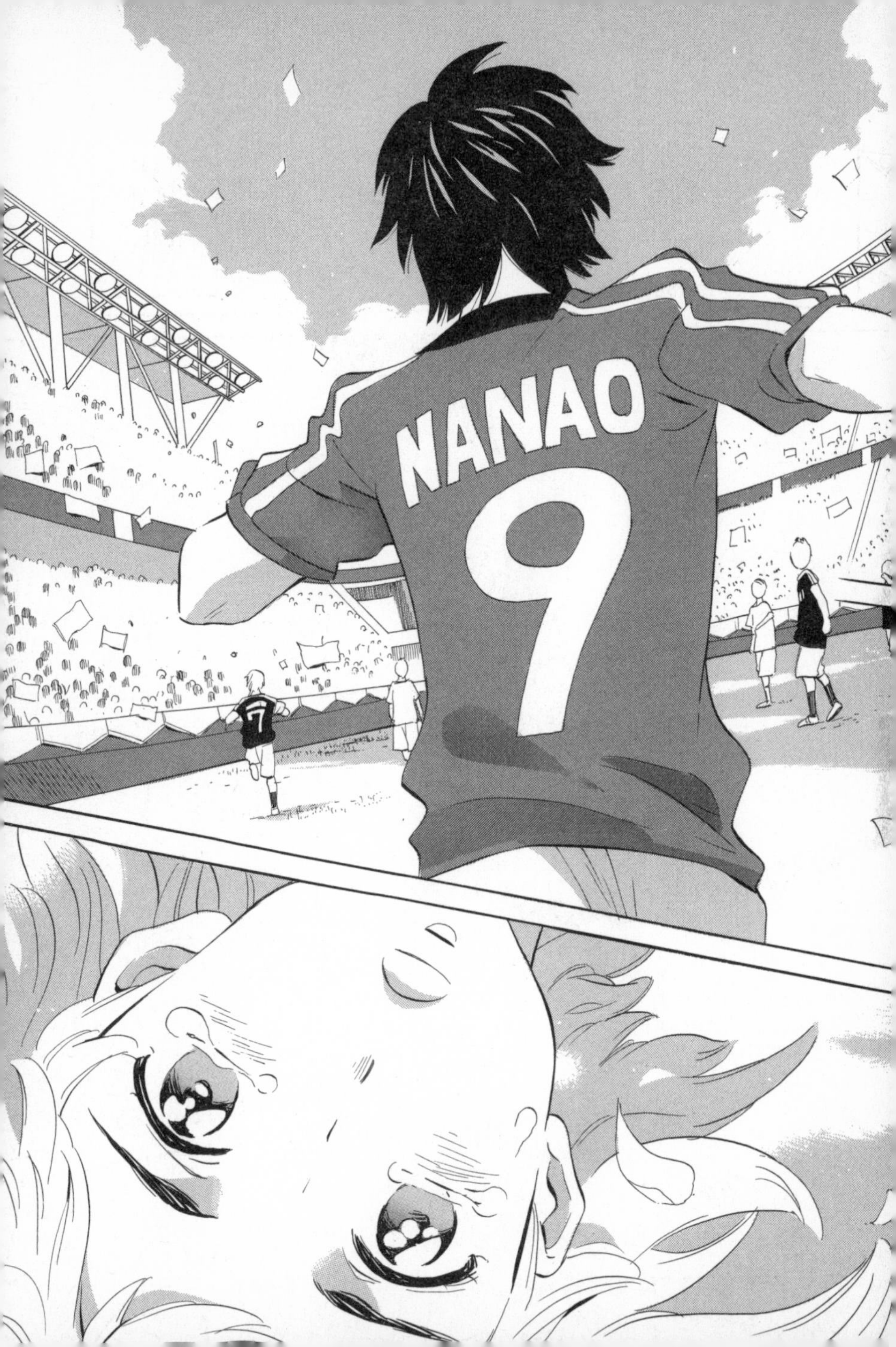
NANAO
9
7

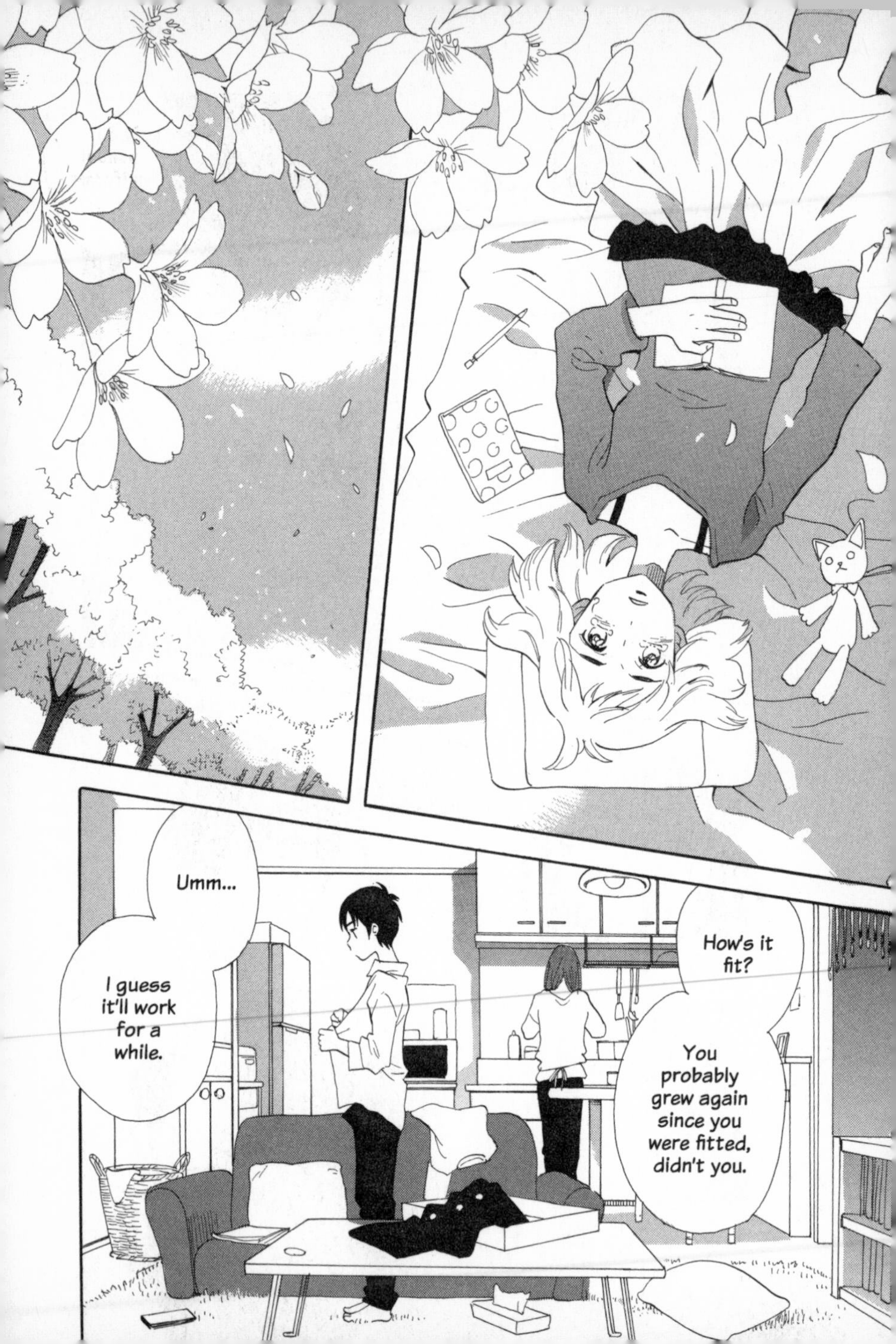
How's it fit?
You probably grew again since you were fitted, didn't you.
Umm...
I guess it'll work for a while.

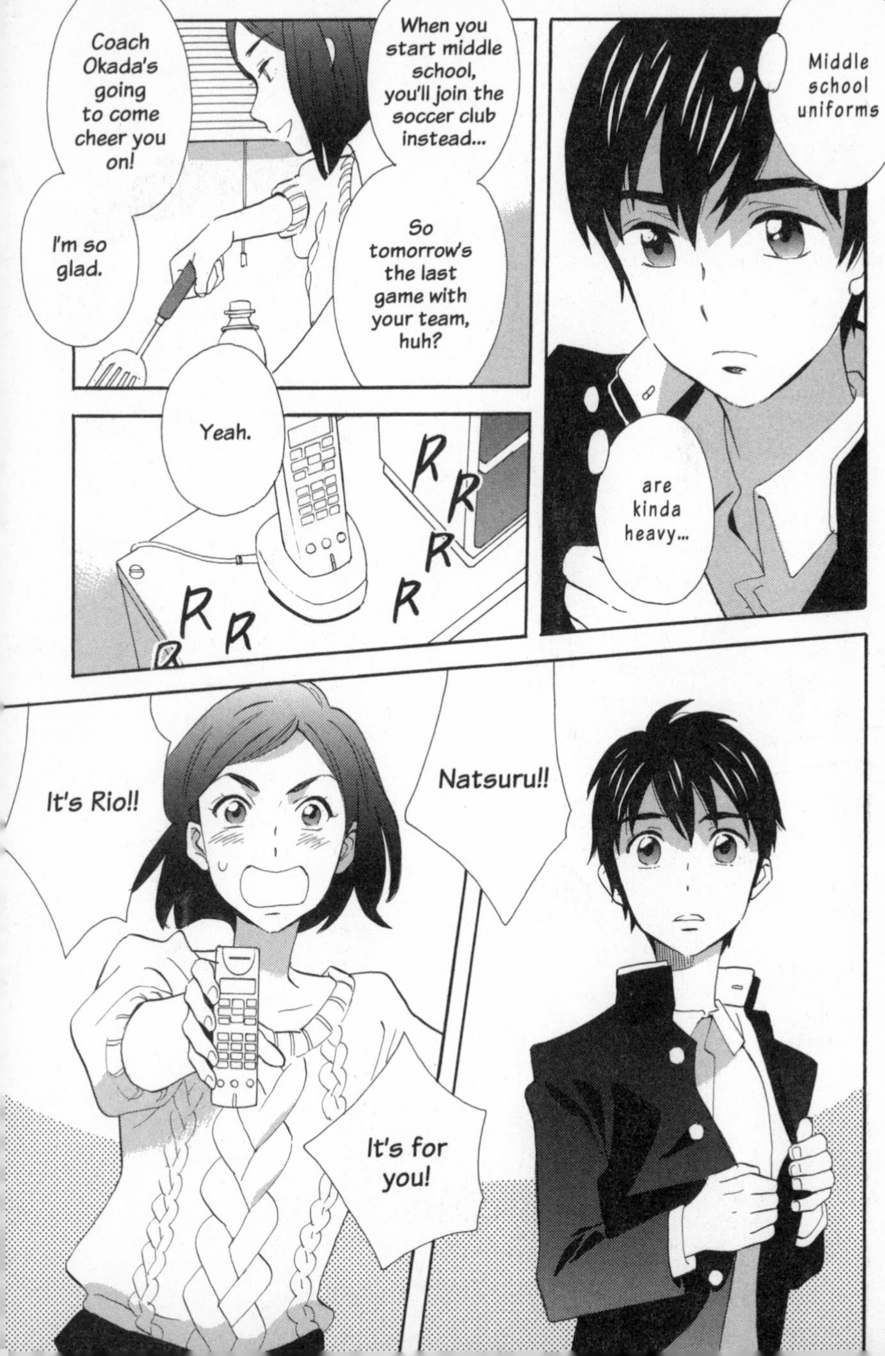
Middle school uniforms
are kinda heavy...
When you start middle school, you'll join the soccer club instead...
So tomorrow's the last game with your team, huh?
Coach Okada's going to come cheer you on!
I'm so glad.
Yeah.
R R R R R R
Natsuru!!
It's Rio!!
It's for you!

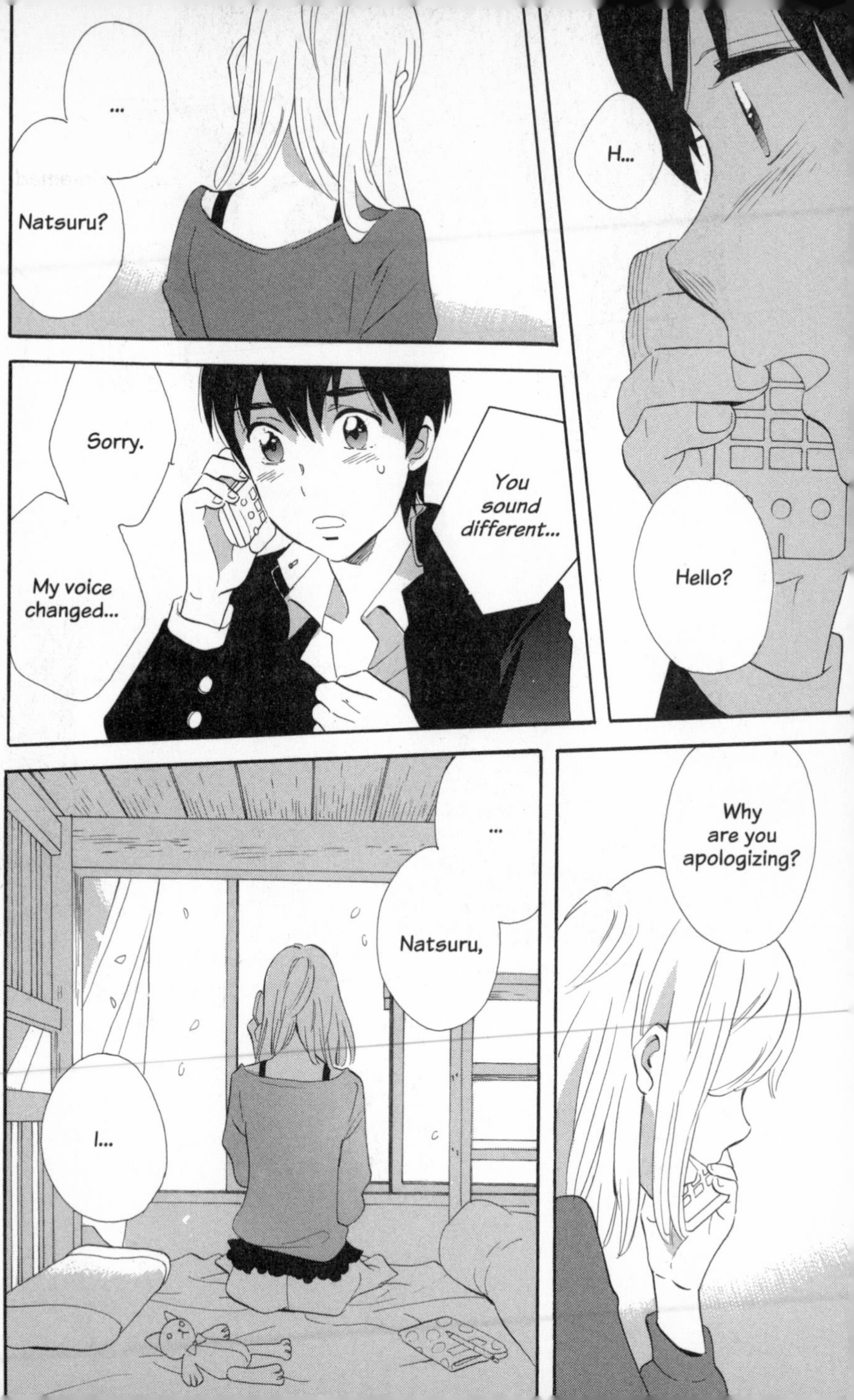
H...
Hello?
...
Natsuru?
You sound different...
Sorry.
My voice changed...
Why are you apologizing?
...
Natsuru,
I...

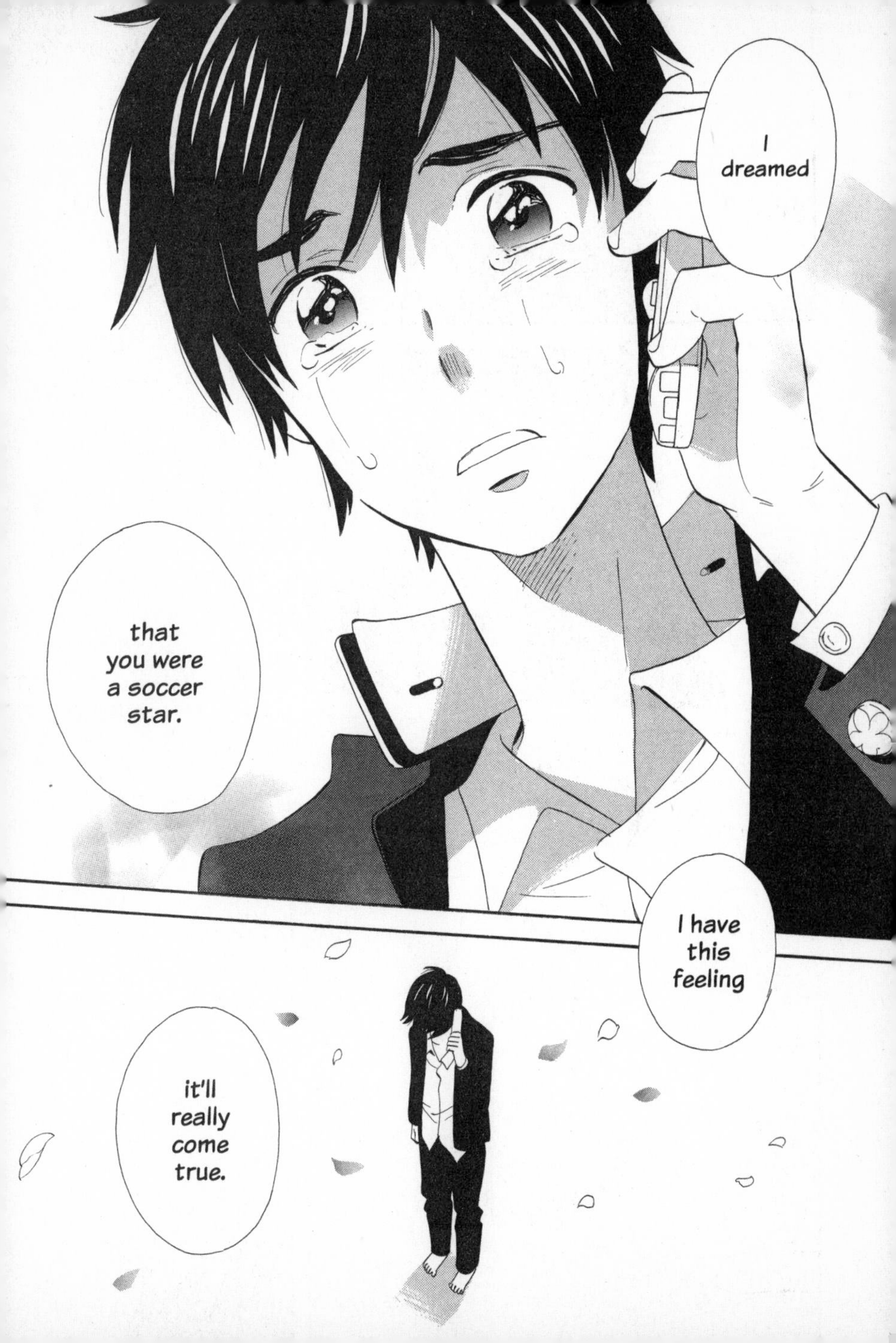
I dreamed
that you were a soccer star.
I have this feeling
it'll really come true.

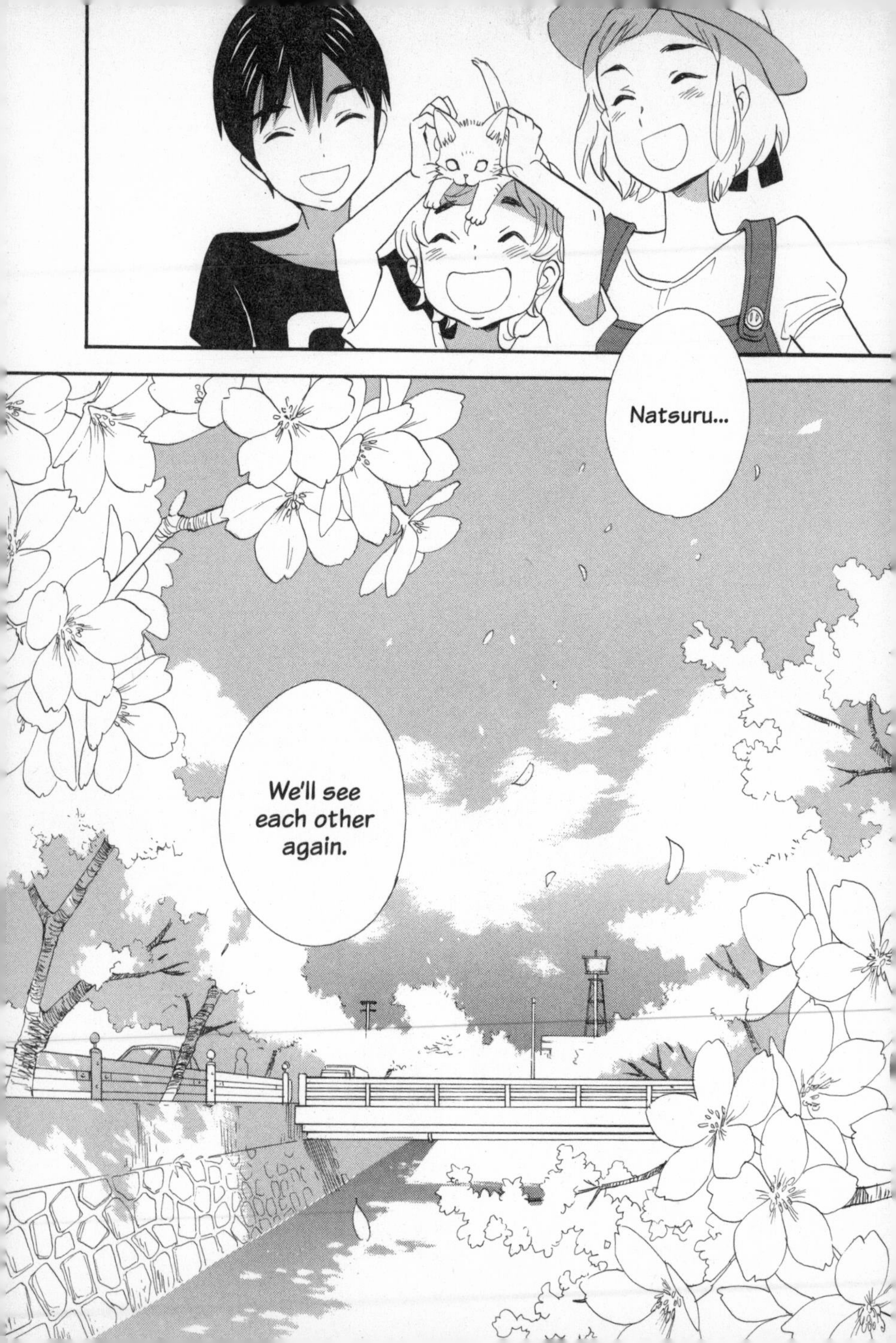
Natsuru...
We'll see each other again.